Dialogues on the Philosophy of Marxism

CONTRIBUTIONS IN PHILOSOPHY

Dialogues on the Philosophy of Marxism

From the Proceedings of
the Society for the Philosophical Study
of Dialectical Materialism

Edited by
John Somerville *and* **Howard L. Parsons**

Contributions in Philosophy, Number 6

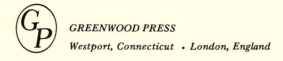

GREENWOOD PRESS
Westport, Connecticut • *London, England*

Library of Congress Cataloging in Publication Data

Society for the Philosophical Study of Dialectical
    Materialism.
    Dialogues on the philosophy of Marxism.

    (Contributions in philosophy, no. 6)
    Includes bibliographical references.
    1. Dialectical materialism—Addresses, essays,
lectures. I. Somerville, John, 1905-   ed.
II. Title.
B809.8.S557   1974   335.4'11   77-149963
ISBN 0-8371-6062-6

Library of Congress Catalog Card Number: 77-149963

ISBN: 0-8371-6062-6

First published in 1974

Greenwood Press, a division of Williamhouse-Regency Inc.

51 Riverside Avenue, Westport, Connecticut 06880

Manufactured in the United States of America

Contents

Preface

On 3 May 1962, at Detroit, Michigan, the setting of the annual meeting of the Western Division of the American Philosophical Association, a group of philosophers met and organized the Society for the Philosophical Study of Dialectical Materialism. The constitution adopted by the society stated that membership would be open "to all members and associate members of the American Philosophical Association irrespective of their philosophical positions."

Since that time, the society has sponsored two symposia nearly every year in conjunction with the annual meetings of the Eastern and Western Divisions of the American Philosophical Association, and since 1969 with meetings of the Pacific Division. It has also conducted dialogue discussions at the meetings of the XIIIth International Congress of Philosophy (Mexico City, 1963) and the XIVth International Congress of Philosophy (Vienna, 1968). The aim of the society in all these discussions has been to bring philosophers of diverse persuasions into dialogue around the central issues of Marxism.

The present volume comprises the text of most of these discussions, with additions which the time-limits of the original occasions did not allow. In grouping the papers here under various topics, we have departed somewhat from the original groupings of the symposium papers. This departure is justi-

fied, we believe, in the interest of a more compact presentation
of the materials.

   We wish to thank the authors, editors, and publishers
listed below for their kind permission to reprint, sometimes
in revised form, the papers that have appeared in their journals
or books:

R. S. Cohen and M. W. Wartofsky, for permission to print
"Marx's 'Science' of History" by Quentin Lauer, S. J. This
essay is based upon a paper first presented to the Boston
Colloquium for the Philosophy of Science at Boston Univer-
sity. It will appear in a forthcoming volume of *Boston Studies
in the Philosophy of Science,* edited by R. S. Cohen and M. W.
Wartofsky (Dordrecht, Holland: D. Reidel Publishing Co.;
New York: Humanities Press, copyright 1971).

   The editors of *Diogène,* for V. V. Mshvenieradze's "Objective
Foundations of Scientific Method," 63 (juillet-septembre 1968).

   The editors of *Inquiry*, for Mihailo Marković's "Marxist
Humanism and Ethics," 6 (1963), pp. 18-34.

   The editors of *International Philosophical Quarterly,* for
P. V. Kopnin's "Dialectical Materialism and Metaphysics,"
vol. 6, no. 1 (March 1966), pp. 34-44; and for John Somerville's
"Ontology, Logic, and Dialectical Materialism," vol. 8 (March
1968), pp. 113-124.

   The editors of *The Journal of Philosophy,* for Brand
Blanshard's "Reflections on Economic Determinism,"
vol. 63, no. 7 (31 March 1966), pp. 169-178.

   The editors of McGraw-Hill Book Company, for Adam
Schaff's "Marxist Humanism," an essay whose subject is
treated in more detail in Chapter IV of his book *Marxism
and the Individual,* copyright © 1970 by McGraw-Hill.

   Northwestern University Press, for Wilfrid Desan's
"The Significance of Jean-Paul Sartre," portions of which
have been published, in revised form, in *Patterns of the
Life-World: Essays in Honor of John Wild,* edited by James
M. Edie, Francis H. Parker, and Calvin O. Schrag (Evanston:
Northwestern University Press, 1970).

   The editors of *Philosophy and Phenomenological Research,*
for Howard L. Parsons's "Value and Mental Health in the
Thought of Marx," vol. 24, no. 3 (March 1964), pp. 355-365;
for Irving Louis Horowitz's "On Alienation and the Social
Order," vol. 27, no 2 (December 1967), pp. 230-237; for

John Somerville's and Dale Riepe's "The American-Soviet Philosophic Conference in Mexico," vol. 25, no. 1 (September 1964), pp. 122-130; and for John Somerville's "Marxist Ethics, Determinism, and Freedom," vol. 28, no. 1 (September 1967), pp. 17-23.

Progress Books, the publishers of *Horizons,* for Barrows Dunham's "Marxism and Existentialism," 24 (Winter 1968), pp. 26-31.

The editors of *Social Research,* for passages from Loyd D. Easton's "Alienation and Empiricism in Marx's Thought" (Autumn 1970).

The editors of *Soviet Studies in Philosophy,* for M. E. Omel'ianovskii's "The Concept of Dialectical Contradictions in Quantum Physics," vol. 2, no. 3 (Winter 1963-1964), pp. 17-30.

The editors of the *Kansas Journal of Sociology,* for Harry Wells' "Alienation and Dialectical Logic," vol. 8, no. 1 (Spring 1972). Dr. Wells has also given his permission.

In addition, we acknowledge the permission of the following to reprint certain passages:

George Braziller, Inc., for passages from *The Words* by Jean-Paul Sartre, translated from the French by Bernard Frechtman. English translation copyright © by George Braziller, Inc. These passages appear in chapter 29.

Doubleday and Company, Inc., for passages from the "Introduction" to *Writings of the Young Marx on Philosophy and Society,* edited and translated by Loyd D. Easton and Kurt H. Guddat, copyright © 1967 by Loyd D. Easton and Kurt H. Guddat, who have also given their permission. These passages appear in chapter 24.

We would also like to thank our colleagues in the society, the participants in the symposia, and the contributors to this volume for their cooperation in making this volume possible. We are indebted to Mrs. Elsie Havanich for her generous assistance in helping to prepare the manuscript for publication. Finally, we wish to thank Mrs. Jeannette Lindsay, Managing Editor, of Greenwood Press, for her work and counsel in seeing this book through the press, and Mrs. Betty Pessagno, Production Editor, for her interest and care.

HOWARD L. PARSONS

Introduction

The larger dialogue that runs through this volume, made up
of separate, component dialogues, took place over a period
of about five years, mainly in the United States. The participating philosophers, however, included representatives from
the Soviet Union, Poland, Yugoslavia, and Belgium, as well
as American philosophers, and part of the dialogue took place
at the XIIIth International Congress of Philosophy in Mexico.
The dialogue is continuing; indeed, it is increasing, in both
intensity and scope, throughout the world. It has two kinds of
significance, philosophical and sociohistorical, each of which
says something essential concerning the new quality of the
day in which we now live.

These dialogues would not have been possible, either in
terms of their philosophic-theoretical content or their empiri-
cal-historical occurrence, a decade or even a half decade before
they actually began, which was in 1962. I well remember, in
1957 in Moscow, sitting in the office of the director of the
Institute of Philosophy, Professor P. N. Fedoseev (later
vice-president of the U.S.S.R. Academy of Sciences) discussing the possibility of future cultural exchanges between
our two countries; there were none whatsoever at the time.
I myself had no official status, or even encouragement of
any kind from our government agencies. Quite the contrary;
my philosophic researches in Eastern Europe (begun as far

back as 1935) were viewed with suspicion and hostility. This view was shared by President Shuster of Hunter College, where I was teaching, whose frankly expressed attitude was that the fact that I had learned the Russian language and written the first Western book on Soviet philosophy from an examination of original sources (it was published in 1946) had to be counted *against* me as a scholar. These conditions were characteristic of the intellectual climate generated nationally by McCarthyism and internationally by the Cold War. In the face of them, Professor Fedoseev and I agreed that there was not much that could be hoped for at the time in regard to cultural exchanges in general or philosophical dialogues in particular.

This was true not only in regard to the United States, but to the capitalist world at large, and the resultant situation had intellectually deplorable and politically dangerous consequences for all concerned. Great ignorance always breeds great fear, and great fear always breeds hysteria. (Today we are involved in the same pathological cycle relative to China.) The day before speaking with Fedoseev I had given a lecture at the Institute of Philosophy in which I frankly and sadly told the Soviet philosophers my opinion that in their criticisms of contemporary American philosophers, and of Western philosophers in general, their tone was so often abusive and hysterical (counterabusive and counterhysterical though it might be) because, like the Americans and Westerners in general, they communicated only with themselves. Each side was shouting at the other, from which it was separated by a void of thousands of miles, to opponents who were not listening, and who, in the vast majority of cases, could not have understood a single word even if they had been able to hear it.

The American Philosophical Association as a national body was too timid to take the initiative to extend invitations to Soviet philosophers to engage in dialogues and cultural exchanges. I, who had been informed personally by the director of the Soviet Institute of Philosophy that his side was entirely willing to accept such invitations, was assured by "scholarly" officials of the association, who had no communication whatever with the Soviets, that it couldn't be done because the Russians "weren't ready for it." However, a minority of university philosophers active in the American Philosophical Association were not intimidated by McCarthyism in general or Professor Sidney Hook's hysterics in particular. From among this group a number (Howard Parsons, who took the lead, Cecil Miller, Arthur Munk, and others in the Western Division of APA, and Dale Riepe, Paul Crosser, Barrows Dunham, myself, and others in the Eastern Division) organized the Society for the Philosophical Study of Dialectical Materialism, adding it to the specialized groups affiliated with the APA.

This small society extended invitations to Soviet philosophers to engage in dialogue with American philosophers in symposia held in conjunction with annual meetings of the American Philosophical Association. The invitations were accepted, and after a year of arguing with the Department of State that it was indeed "in the national interest" to give American scholars and Soviet scholars a chance to try to learn something about one another *from* one another, the Soviet philosophers were finally allowed into the country. (This was 1963; an invitation extended in 1962 had been accepted by the Soviets, but our authorities had refused to issue a visa.) The ensuing dialogue proved very educational. Even Professor Hook attended, put questions to the Soviet philosophers, and learned something, though he had been for years arguing passionately that no Communist should be allowed to teach anyone in America about anything, especially about communism.

This philosophical symposium opened a door to dialogue, which was not only continued in philosophy, but which spread to other fields. Now it is commonplace to find Soviet scholars invited to and participating in the annual meetings of our national scholarly associations in the social sciences, exact sciences, and humanities, and to find American scholars spending time in the Soviet Union for similar purposes. There is now a regular and officially sponsored program of cultural exchange, involving students, professors, and various kinds of educational and cultural materials, publications, and the like. All this is still on a painfully small scale, relative to the magnitude of the problems and the potential values involved. But a beginning has been made, and progress can be seen. It is necessary to recall some of the details mentioned above to realize how dire was our previous situation.

Of course, to make changes in an intellectual climate, certain individuals must act as individuals, Without this, no social institution can or will move. But it is equally obvious that the major causes of so widespread a change as that which took place concerning attitudes towards Marxism go much deeper and broader than the actions of a few individuals as individuals. In this case, two things stand out: the *relevance* of the basic ideas found in Marxism, as philosophical and social ideas, and the new problematics thrown up by the actual development of political and social conditions, nationally and internationally, in the twentieth century.

To recognize this certainly does not mean to give a blanket endorsement to everything "Marxism" stands for, if only for the reason, as these dialogues so clearly show, that there are contradictory interpretations of Marxism contending with one another. This, too, is something that has been dramatically on the increase since the end of World War II. However, this very fact reinforces in its own way the importance, the drawing power of a certain hard core of basic ideas common to all the varieties of Marxism, somewhat as there is a core of basic ideas common to all Christian sects. In another place, I have tried to state this common core of Marxism at some length, and of course there is disagreement about how to state it. But there can be no disagreement about the fact that Marxism, whatever it really is, has an *un*-commonly influential core.

The strictly philosophic significance of Marxism thus expresses itself in two ways: in the content of certain central ideas which are socially challenging, psychologically disturbing, morally fascinating, and intellectually devastating; and in the way these central ideas, like the gravitational mass of the earth, seem to be exerting a constant attractive power, affecting the movement of everything within range, each in a different way. Hence, there are two quite different kinds of doctrinal threads running through these dialogues. One is concerned, whether positively or negatively, with the relatively permanent positions, the primary factors of Marxism which must be the basis and the necessary starting point from which to work. The other is concerned, positively or negatively, with attempts to relate the primary patterns, the central ideas, in some new way—to fuse them with something previously untried, or to select from among them only some to work with, discarding others. Oversimplified terms in which to express this difference would be orthodox and revisionist—oversimplified because it is usually forgotten (strangely enough even by some who consider themselves strong Marxists) that today's orthodoxy is yesterday's revisionism, and that Marxism is precisely the philosophy that gives this generalized historical fact ontological centrality in the whole concept of dialectics.

Yet, of course, not every revisionism of today becomes the
orthodoxy of tomorrow, and there must remain in relative
stability not only a common core of accepted doctrine but a
common attitude, which means something that always includes
an element of moral evaluation. In this case the attitude is
directed especially at the selection of problems, which is a
part of the overall sense of what philosophy and science are
all about (read "assumption" for "sense" if you wish, remembering
that there is no way of doing philosophy or science without
making some assumption, consciously or unconsciously, concerning what it is all about). Marxism has always stood for a
relationship of theory to practice which is neither unconscious
nor amoral nor nonhistorical. When Marx on one occasion said
"I am not a Marxist," it was not only to disassociate himself
from particular doctrinal positions espoused by some who called
themselves Marxists, but to disassociate himself from a certain
attitude towards philosophy, the attitude that to be a philosopher means to study philosophy.

To be a philosopher means to study *the world* in a certain
way; one reads the books of other philosophers only as a
means, not as an end. This is why it is possible to be a reputable
professor of philosophy without being a significant philosopher.
The former is concerned mainly with what the philosophers
have said; the latter is concerned mainly with what the world
does. The former is usually thinking about philosophy and
worrying about promotion; the latter is usually thinking about
the world and worrying about jail. Of course, it is not impossible
to find a good professor of philosophy who is also a good
philosopher; but it is rare, and it sometimes seems that most
good professors are operating on the implicit assumption that
the only good philosopher is a dead philosopher. To put the
point differently, when one picks up a philosophical journal
or book, one can see the extent to which it is trying to solve
problems about schools of thought as distinguished from
problems about the world. For his part, Marx was not primarily
interested in the question, "what is Marxism?" He was primarily interested in the question, "what is going on in the
world of human society, and what can be done about it?"
He was well trained in the subject of philosophy, took a
doctor's degree, and tried to obtain a post as professor, but
did not succeed. The authorities did not really want philosophers (then or now), but rather professors. In this regard,

Marx's fate is classic. The names of Socrates, Spinoza, Francis Bacon, Comte, Bertrand Russell, and many others will come readily to mind.

It is not only Marx's career-fate, in the narrower sense, that is classic. Actually, his whole attitude toward the relation of theory to practice (or, if you wish, philosophy to politics) is also classic, if philosophers like Socrates, Plato, Aristotle, Aquinas, Bacon, Hobbes, Spinoza, Hegel, and Comte are classic. We are speaking of the *relation* of theory or philosophy to practice or politics, not the *content* of the theory or philosophy, and not the *direction* of the practice or politics. The theories of some of these classic philosophers were obviously idealistic and theistic, and some of the politics conservative and reactionary. But the point is that all these philosophers agreed that there must be a conscious (and moral) relationship of philosophic theory to social and political practice, that a philosopher is not a *whole* philosopher, that he does not fully understand the demands of philosophy, unless he draws out and makes explicit the social and political implications and consequences of his doctrines concerning the universe, reality, knowledge, and man.

This is what has always separated the philosopher from the professor of philosophy, and this is where the philosophic significance of Marxism merges with its sociohistorical significance. It says that philosophy must be a true theory of history, and man must have a true theory of history in order better to humanize his own history. To Marx, as to Socrates, Plato, and Aristotle, this meant that politics must become scientific, and morality must be worked out by reason. But, as the classic Greeks saw it, science and reason implied aristocracy and slavery. As Marx saw it, they implied something quite different. That is what the dialogue is all about.

JOHN SOMERVILLE

Dialogues on the Philosophy of Marxism

PART I

PHILOSOPHIC FOUNDATIONS OF MARXISM

Chapter 1

Dialectical Materialism and Metaphysics

P. V. KOPNIN

Before his untimely death in 1971, P. V. Kopnin was director of
the Institute of Philosophy of the Academy of Sciences of the
U.S.S.R. He was a corresponding member of the academy. A member of the Ukrainian Academy of Sciences, a former director of
the Institute of Philosophy in Kiev, and a specialist in the fields
of dialectics, logic, theory of knowledge, and logic of science, he
was the author of a number of books, including *Dialectics as Logic*
(1961), *Introduction to Marxist Gnosiology* (1966), *The Logical
Foundations of Science* (1968), *Philosophical Ideas of Lenin and
Logic* (1969), and *V. I. Lenin and Materialist Dialectics* (1969).

Prior to discussing the problem of the relationship between
dialectical materialism and metaphysics, let us ascertain
the meaning of the term "metaphysics," since it is used in
philosophical literature in different senses. We shall focus our
attention on the two most important variants. In Marxist
literature, metaphysics means a definite method of cognition
characteristic of the science of the seventeenth and eighteenth
centuries. The distinctive feature of this method is the absolutizing of individual aspects of the objective world. The
application of this method yielded beneficial results in the
period when science was mainly engaged in collecting, describing,
and classifying facts, when it had not yet turned to the deeper
study and interpretation of the complex processes of nature
and social life. This conception of metaphysics was presented
also by Hegel.

5

As early as the middle of the nineteenth century, it was found that the metaphysical approach hindered the development of science, whose findings could be understood only on the basis of a more adequate philosophical theory, i.e., materialist dialectics. The relationship between dialectical materialism and metaphysics as methods of cognition has been quite thoroughly and comprehensively worked out in our literature; that is, dialectics overcomes the limitations of the metaphysical method, whose individual rational elements are utilized after undergoing the necessary modifications. The movement of philosophy from the metaphysical to the dialectical method occurs within the general framework of the movement of scientific knowledge from a level of theory with a comparatively limited sphere of application to a more comprehensive construction in which the former level of theory appears only as the expression of particular, restricted cases.

The term metaphysics, however, has also another, more ancient meaning which is still used in philosophical writings, especially non-Marxist ones. Metaphysics according to this variant is understood to be that part of philosophy which elaborates in its own way principles and concepts applicable to being in general. Various schools of modern philosophy have different ideas concerning the subject matter of metaphysics, but as a rule they assert that metaphysics is the study of being, being in general, by which is meant everything that exists in some way or other. Sometimes this study is also referred to as "ontology." This kind of metaphysics is encountered in such philosophical trends as neo-Thomism, which recognizes two metaphysics— general (a code of principles applied to everything that exists, both to God and to the created world) and particular or applied (extending only to the created world)—and existentialism, where metaphysics or fundamental ontology is taken to be the elucidation of the sense and substance of being. Here the principal problem is that of the human being, because the comprehension of the world, of reality, comes only after we have learned what man is and what his fate is.

It is common knowledge that not all schools of modern philosophy recognize the necessity of metaphysics. Positivism in general, and in particular its modern version, logical positivism, rejects metaphysics, considering it to be a vestige of the past, a heritage of undeveloped science. The neopositivist credo in the sphere of philosophy includes the view that all problems associated with the study of being in general are pseudo-problems. Philosophy becomes a logical analysis of the findings of the sciences.

Positivism represents an extreme reaction to a metaphysics divorced from the development of scientific knowledge, engaged in speculative construction of universal principles of being. Positivism cannot, however, overcome such metaphysics, since positivism creates its own metaphysical logical world, detached from the laws of motion of phenomena belonging to objective reality. Sometimes the dilemma is posed: either metaphysics claiming its universal interpretation of the world, drawing its alleged knowledge from sources other than the various branches of modern science, or positivism of different sorts rejecting the problem of being and its universal laws; so formulated, there appears to be no satisfactory way out.

Dialectical materialism, however, is precisely the form of philosophy which equally rejects both the scholasticism of speculative metaphysics and the barrenness of positivism. It is not accidental that since the time of Mach the positivists have been criticizing dialectical materialism for dogmatism and metaphysics, for the alleged recognition of the existence of "things-in-themselves" independent of consciousness, for the presumptuous attempt to express in its concepts and categories the most general laws of development found in the objective world. At the same time, the advocates of metaphysics, in particular those from the camp of neo-Thomism, reproach the founders of dialectical materialism, such as Friedrich Engels and his followers, with a positivist approach to the subject matter and objectives of philosophy. They refer to Engels' words that science does not any longer need philosophy as such, and dialectical materialism

. . . is no longer a philosophy at all, but simply a world outlook which has to establish its validity and be applied not in a science of sciences standing apart, but in the positive sciences. Philosophy is therefore "sublated" here, that is, "both overcome and preserved"; overcome as regards its form, and preserved as regards its real content.[1]

And to many, the following statement by Engels sounds quite positivist:

As soon as each special science is bound to make clear its position in the great totality of things and of our knowledge of things, a special science dealing with this totality is superfluous [or unnecessary]. That which still survives, independently, of all earlier philosophy is the science of thought and its laws—formal logic and dialectics. Everything else is subsumed in the positive science of nature and history.[2]

The question then arises, what is dialectical materialism? If it is the study of the universal laws of being, then it verges on metaphysics. And if it is a universal scientific method of thinking applicable in all branches of scientific knowledge, then it is close to positivism. And the one allegedly excludes the other. In fact, however, the peculiarity of dialectical materialism is that it poses the problem of the subject matter of philosophy in a different way, without detaching the method of thinking from the laws of development of the phenomena of the objective world as this is done by metaphysics and positivism.

The study of phenomena of objective reality and their laws of development has always been and will always remain the objective of philosophy. In this case, dialectical materialism is no exception; it continues the tradition initiated by the ancient philosophers. But then what distinguishes it from metaphysics, its predecessor, and from other schools of modern philosophy? What are the special features of its approach to the study of reality?

First, dialectical materialism considers it impossible to comprehend the laws of objective reality without generalization of the results of the various branches of science. There no longer exists a philosophy which draws its knowledge of the universal principles of being from sources other than the conclusions of natural and social sciences. In the period when philosophy embraced the entire totality of knowledge of the world, and when the individual sciences remained undeveloped, speculative concepts of the world were essential; they were even beneficial, since they contained brilliant ideas which anticipated scientific discoveries.

But now science has no need for metaphysics in general and natural philosophy in particular; it is capable of reproducing in a systematic form the true picture of the world based on facts and laws of science itself. To revive metaphysics under such conditions is tantamount to moving backwards, defying the trend towards development of scientific knowledge.

It is not accidental that such schools of contemporary philosophy as neo-Thomism and existentialism, which are advocates of metaphysics, stand aloof from science, and that their metaphysics or fundamental ontology is actually directed against it. They feel the need for a metaphysical knowledge, which could exist apart from scientific knowledge, since they treat of various mystic essences that cannot find scientific confirmation.[3]

Dialectical materialism cannot conceive its development without generalization of the conclusions of the natural and social sciences; it does not isolate its knowledge from scientific knowledge, but derives the former from the latter. Therefore, a close connection with the various fields of knowledge is essential for it. At the same time, dialectical materialism retains its subject matter which differs from that of the special fields of knowledge. Its subject consists in the study of the universal laws of development of phenomena in the objective world, which cannot be discovered merely on the basis of the experience and conclusions of a single field of scientific knowledge and which require the totality of the entire experience of cognition and practical activity of man.

Here we are confronted with the second feature of dialectical materialism in its study of objective reality. Metaphysics, in all its versions, asserts that the object of its study is being in general, or all existing things as such. Dialectical materialism asserts that speculation about being in general, about existing things as such, is pointless, and that philosophy begins at the juncture where the question of relationship between being and thought is posed. The first definition of being which contains at least some elements of concreteness and extends beyond the tautalogy "Being is the existing" includes the counterposing of being to thought, that is, that being exists outside and independently of the fact, whether or not we think of it. Attempts of philosophy to build up knowledge of being without raising the question of its relation to thought have never led to any results that would promote the development of science and of practical activities directed at the transformation of reality.

We know from the history of philosophy that some philosophical schools and thinkers of the past undertook to solve many problems of being without clearly posing the question of its relation to thought. Philosophy sprang up as the science of the origin of being, but this was in the period when it was the only existing form of scientific knowledge. Many changes have occurred since then. Special fields of science have branched off from this inclusive field, which was called philosophy. Part of its content consisted of metaphysics, speculative meditations on being in general, which had found no confirmation in the development of science. The remaining part, revised and further developed, formed the basis for scientific approaches to being. This process of revision included the scrutiny of being and of all categories expressing it in relation to the basic question of philosophy, the relation of thought to being.

Beginning with the concept of matter, all the other categories of dialectical materialism include in their content the solution of the problem of the relation of thought to being.

Some people, including even certain advocates of dialectical materialism, believe that it is possible to define matter without attempting to solve the problem of its relation to thought—I mean matter as such, as some substance existing independently of consciousness. Yet, matter is objective reality existing by itself, independently of consciousness, and this is its first, essential, defining characteristic, which is indispensable to the further advancement of the science of matter. However, matter, as perceived in dialectical materialism, is not identical with substance in the interpretation of various metaphysical systems. Thus matter is not a metaphysical entity forming the basis of all things; actually, it represents the natural content of all phenomena, things, processes existing outside and independently of man's consciousness. The concept of matter is devoid of sense if detached from the question of the relationship between being and thought.

Hence, dialectical materialism rejects ontology as the study of being outside of its relation to consciousness, and gnosiology as the study of cognition irrespective of its relation to the forms of being. It considers that the relationship between thought and being is the starting point of all philosophical categories of dialectical materialism. Thus it joins and unifies ontology and gnosiology. It does not hold that there exist separate systems of ontological and gnosiological categories; rather it states that all categories of dialectical materialism are at the same time both ontological, in the sense that their content is taken from the objective world, from being, and gnosiological, since they help to solve the problem of the relationship between thought and being, and they themselves serve as a step in the advancement of knowledge.

A simple combination or sum of the science of being and the science of cognition can be encountered now in the works of some authors who accept the idea "of metaphysics in a wide sense including both existence and cognition."[4] Sometimes dialectical materialism is represented as also comprising two parts, ontological and gnosiological. The science of matter, its forms of existence and the laws of its motion, is alleged to be ontology; and the science of cognition and its laws, gnosiology. It is said that there are laws which are common both to being and to cognition; but, in addition, cognition has its own, specific laws.

This conception, however, is wrong; there is no such division into ontology and gnosiology in dialectical materialism. Here we approach another distinctive feature of dialectical materialism in its study of being. Metaphysics proceeded from a sharp division, verging on complete isolation, of the laws and principles of being, established by it, and the laws of cognition, which it does not deal with. In contrast to metaphysics, dialectical materialism does not simply deal with both the laws of being and the laws of thought; it proves their unity, their coincidence in content. Materialist dialectics is a science "of the general laws of motion, both of the external world and of human thought—two sets of laws," writes Engels, "which are identical in substance, but differ in their expression in so far as the human mind can apply them consciously, while in nature and also up to now for the most part in human history, these laws assert themselves unconsciously."[5]

When we approach rationally the laws of being and the laws of cognition, we draw a distinction between them, in particular with regard to the form of existence: the former exist in the external world and the latter in man, in his consciousness. Absolutization of this difference may lead to agnostic detachment of thought and its laws from the forms and laws of being. Thought is considered to move according to its own laws; therefore it is concluded that it cannot coincide with the laws and forms of being. Now, inasmuch as any attempt to cognize being would depend upon the forms of thought, being becomes altogether inaccessible to science and turns into a subject of religious belief or of some other supernatural revelation.

Proceeding from the coincidence of the laws of thought and the laws of being, dialectical materialism overcomes the agnosticism which denies the objective validity of the content of human thought. Thought attains objective truth, it coincides in its content with the object which is outside it only due to the fact that thought itself moves in accordance with the laws of the object.

Let us assume that in the process of cognition thought followed other laws rooted in some mysteries of thought itself possessing a nature absolutely contrary to the laws and forms of being— then thought and being would be completely separated in their activity, and there would be two independent worlds, being and thought. That is how some philosophers have been reasoning both in the past and now.

However, thought, in substance, cannot be anything else but the reflection of the laws and forms of being, and it moves within the framework of objective content. Even when it escapes into the sphere of imagination, to say nothing of its psychotic manifestations, it still follows discoverable laws. Thought, moving in accordance with the laws of the object, arrives at results identical with the object itself. Hence what was considered to be metaphysics (establishment of the laws and principles of being) becomes logic. The laws and forms of being, after man apprehends them, become also laws and forms of thought.

Thus, dialectical materialism simultaneously represents logic in still another sense, besides the fact that it includes some logical laws and categories; namely, all its content, all laws and categories fulfill logical functions. Logic is often interpreted as a science which deals only with the kind of proof whose validity depends on the form of the premises. Such is modern formal logic, branching off into a multitude of calculation systems. Dialectical materialism does not claim to replace this logic, to build up some kind of new formal-logical calculation system. This is not its task or function. But since the time of Aristotle logic has included the study of the general laws and forms of the movement of thought. Aristotle's logical categories were not only forms of thought but also universal concepts of being, essential definitions of being. This tradition was continued by Bacon, Descartes, Spinoza, Kant, who already distinguished between two logics, i.e., the general or formal and the transcendental, and by Hegel. In dialectical materialism, the tradition developed into the proposition affirming the coincidence of dialectics, logic, and theory of knowledge. When critics of Marxist philosophy direct attention to dialectical materialism as the science of the general laws and forms of being, they see it only as metaphysics or ontology. But when they confront the thesis that materialist dialectics is the science of thought, of its laws and forms, they see it only as logic, as something akin to modern positivism. In these circumstances, it would seem that dialectical materialism comprises two different philosophies, metaphysics and logic. In actual fact it cannot be reduced to either or to their sum. What is taken as metaphysics proves to be logic, and the latter becomes the science not only of thought but also of the forms of being itself, which are reflected in the laws and categories of thought.

The positivists' assertion that philosophy is logic is not incorrect per se; all depends on the interpretation of logic. If one reduces it to formal-logical calculation systems, to logical syntax and semantics, as is often the case, then it is, of course, erroneous, and essentially tantamount to the elimination of philosophy, since formal logic, through the contemporary development of knowledge, has become a special scientific subject similar to mathematics, linguistics, psychology, etc.

Being exists objectively, outside and independently of thought. But how is it approached, as a subject of contemplation or an object of material, perceptive, practical activity of man? Metaphysics, as a rule, excludes the practical activity of man from the consideration of being, striving to perceive it in its pure state. Dialectical materialism considers being and its forms proceeding from the needs of the transforming activity of man.

Those who reproach dialectical materialism with being interested in things, not in people, in the structure of lifeless matter, not in the fate of living humanity, have no firm ground to stand on. Man is in the center of the Marxist world outlook; but man and his practical activity require knowledge of the objective world, of the trends in the development of its phenomena.

Dialectical materialism strives to perceive being not only as something that exists, but also as something that must be what it must become as a result of the practical activity of man. Consequently, existence is perceived through necessity, but the latter is itself based on the knowledge of objective reality, of the laws of its motion.

Dialectical materialism does not exclude men's goals from the consideration of being, but it does not separate these ends from objective laws. In his practical activity, man proceeds from and depends upon the objective world as the determining factor. "Men's ends," writes Lenin, "are engendered by the objective world and presuppose it."[6]

Men's goals, if they are based on knowledge of objective laws, do not interfere with the perception of being and its forms in their true light; and they serve as preconditions for such perception. Moreover, men's ends are social, not those of a separate individual; they are conditioned by knowledge of the laws of development of society. Therefore, the objectives of Marxist philosophy include the study of the laws of social development. Sometimes Marxist philosophy is divided into dialectical materialism and historical materialism as two independent parts having each its own separate subject. In actual fact, this is not so; there is no dialectical materialism without historical materialism. Not a single problem of dialectical materialism, beginning with the basic question of philosophy and ending with the theory of truth, can be solved without a materialistic understanding of history. For example, an understanding of the laws of social development is indispensable for substantiating the thesis concerning consciousness as a property of matter and a product of social development, the conception of practice as the basis and criterion of truth, and other such positions. Without knowledge of the laws of social development, it is impossible to create a dialectical conception of evolution.

The opinion is voiced occasionally that the laws of dialectics, in particular the law of unity and struggle of opposites, are anthropomorphic, are borrowed from human society and transferred to the development of natural phenomena, animate and inanimate. But this is not true; dialectical materialism does not transfer the laws of nature to society or, conversely, the laws of society to nature as a whole. For instance, neither the law of conservation of energy, which is valid in nature, nor the law of succession of socio-economic formations, which is valid in society, is turned by dialectical materialism into universal principles of every aspect of being, although they are important for the substantiation of the dialectical-materialist world outlook. We establish, on the basis of generalization of the entire experience of cognition and practice, universal laws of development, but the knowledge of the laws of social development acquires special significance because society is the highest and most mature form of development. A knowledge of the highest is the starting point for the understanding of the lowest. (Marx emphasized that the ape cannot serve as the key to the understanding of man so much as man serves as the key to understanding the ape's place in the development of animate nature.) Thus, social laws are not transferred to nature, becoming universal, but rather the knowledge of social regularities is the necessary condition for the discovery of the universal laws of development valid both in nature and in society.

If it is necessary to consider the highest form, i.e., society, for the understanding of development, of evolution, society must be taken in its most mature form, that is, modern society in the main trends of its development. According to Marxism, such a society is communism. The scientific consideration of this social formation represents a special branch of science distinct from philosophy in general: the theory of scientific communism. However, in a sense communism is included in the teaching of dialectical materialism about the universal laws of development of nature, society, and thought, included in terms of the social needs of the subject with which it practically approaches the object. What is being dealt with is the forms and laws of being as some social but (like everything else) historically transient ideal, through whose prism the world is viewed.

When some people try to convince others that they apprehend reality, being as such, abstracted from society, from its needs, from the subject, they mislead themselves in the first place. If *they* perceive the world, it is obvious that *they* look at it with the eyes of their society, class, and so on. This is the manifestation of the historicism of human cognition in general, and of philosophical cognition in particular.

If the objective of philosophy is not meditation upon the world, but its study for the purpose of practical transformation, such a purpose should be related to a definite, practically attainable social ideal, which, for dialectical materialism, is communism, following from the nature of both. Dialectical materialism as a philosophical system thus differs radically from metaphysics; however, it retains some elements of metaphysics or ontology in the sense that it also pursues the purpose of studying the universal laws and forms of being, of objective reality.

But in contrast to the various systems of metaphysics of the past and present, dialectical materialism: (1) sets before itself the task of discovering these laws and forms, not in some special speculative-metaphysical way, but by means of modern scientific knowledge, by generalizing scientific data; (2) considers being in its relation to thinking, fulfilling the functions both of ontology and gnosiology; (3) proceeds from the identity, the coincidence in content, of the laws of thought and those of being, acting as logic establishing the universal method and forms of the motion of thought towards objective truth; (4) treats being and its forms, not simply contemplatively, but as the object of the perceptual-material, revolutionary-critical practical activity of man, and (5) studies also the laws of social development, in terms of historical materialism, validating communism as an historically generated ideal of society.

All these aspects are logically interconnected in dialectical materialism, forming a complete whole which differs from any other philosophical system, both in the past and at present. Certain schools of modern philosophy concentrate their attention on these separate aspects, which are included in the scientific-philosophical world outlook. For instance, positivism insists on the idea that modern philosophy should necessarily be logic; pragmatism emphasizes the active role of the subject in considering the forms and laws of being; existentialism proceeds from the proposition that without considering man's being it is impossible to comprehend being in general. These aspects are, however, absolutized by them, are isolated from others, are represented in a distorted state, and, consequently, the systems of philosophy created on this basis become one-sided, fragmented.

Dialectical materialism cannot be understood and correctly evaluated if attention is focussed on just one single aspect of it, a component detached from the others, though this is often done by its critics. Only the whole represents truth; only by considering dialectical materialism in the fullness of its content is it possible to understand its place and significance in the system of modern scientific knowledge, in the struggle of ideas which is taking place in society at present.

NOTES

1. Frederick Engels, *Anti-Dühring: Herr Eugen Dühring's Revolution in Science* (Moscow: Foreign Languages Publishing House, 2nd ed., 1959), p. 191.

2. Ibid., p. 40.

3. Attempts to substantiate metaphysics by arguments other than scientific can be found, in particular, in Lewis Hahn's "What Is the Starting Point of Metaphysics?" *Philosophy and Phenomenological Research* (18) (1958): 293-311. The author considers the conclusions of the sciences to be insufficient for metaphysics for many reasons: they are less accessible than other data and more likely to lead to confusion or intellectual indigestion "than to a world view" (p. 302), and they "look more like collections of items than a structural unity

of any sort" (p. 302). Moreover, one must not rule out from the elements of metaphysics "material drawn from art, poetry, religion, personal observation, and common sense" (p. 303). As a starting point for metaphysics, the author suggests "common sense guided by key insights" (p. 309).

But here the question arises, for one thing, where these key insights come from and whether they are not metaphysics in themselves, and, for another, what is common sense if not some generally accessible data of science and of man's everyday experience transformed into accepted postulates. Why then should a modern philosophy be based on such a shaky, and, shall we say, backward foundation?

4. Hahn, "What Is the Starting Point," p. 294.

5. F. Engels, *Ludwig Feuerbach and the End of Classical German Philosophy* (Moscow: Foreign Languages Publishing House, 1950), p. 64.

6. V. I. Lenin, *Philosophical Notebooks,* in *Collected Works,* vol. 38 (Moscow: Foreign Languages Publishing House, 1961), p. 189.

Chapter 2

Objective Foundations of Scientific Method

V. V. MSHVENIERADZE

Professor V. V. Mshvenieradze is head of the department of contemporary Marxist Philosophy in the Institute of Philosophy of the U.S.S.R. Academy of Sciences in Moscow. A former scientific secretary of the institute, he is a specialist in dialectics, methodology of science, and contemporary philosophy of history. He is the author of several books, among them *The Philosophy of Neopositivism and Semantics* (1961), *Main Trends of Contemporary Bourgeois Philosophy* (1961), *Contemporary American Philosophy* (1966), and *The Role of Ideology in the Life of Society* (1969).

The topic of the symposium, formulated by the Society for the Philosophical Study of Dialectical Materialism, i.e., "Metaphysics and Dialectical Materialism," invites discussion of a wide range of questions. My paper emphasizes one aspect, based on the understanding of metaphysics and dialectics as two mutually exclusive and directly opposed methods of investigation[1] employed in the process of knowledge. Scientific method is an instrument of investigation that provides us with true knowledge when applied to cognition of objective reality. However, truth is not an end in itself. The ultimate goal of knowledge consists in finding objective laws of development of reality in order to transform it in the interests of man.

Objective reality, the world, should be cognized as it really

18

is. This assertion hardly will provoke any disagreement. But at the same time this assertion implies that objective reality must be cognized with all its intrinsic complexity and oppositions, with the endless diversity of its connections and transitions. The assertion implies also not *invention,* but *disclosure, discovery* of the objective laws of the development of reality. Specific features inherent in the objective world exert influence upon the method of its investigation. But the questions arise: What is the objective world? What is the correct method of its investigation? What is the nature of the connection between a general theoretical conception and its method? What is the relation of the dialectical method to the methods of the particular sciences? What are the specific features of scientific method as such? My paper deals with only a part of questions mentioned above. There are two more preliminary questions; they refer to content and scope.

First, with regard to defining the philosophical aspect of the problem in question, I would like to point out the following. In particular sciences there are diverse methods of understanding the phenomena studied. Concrete application of these methods is the business of the respective particular sciences. However, when the method itself becomes the object of a special analysis, then the problem of *methodology* arises, which exceeds the bounds of the particular sciences. When scientific method is studied, it becomes the subject matter of philosophical investigation. And I will try to show that materialistic dialectics as an integral component of dialectical materialism is both a scientific *method* of thinking, and scientific *methodology,* thinking about scientific method.

Second, the investigation of the objective foundations of scientific method implies on the one hand determination of those specific features that distinguish it from nonscientific methods, and on the other hand the qualitative peculiarity that is the common feature of a scientific approach in any branch of scientific knowledge.

Finally, I would not ignore a famous saying, according to which truth comes out of controversy. Along with a positive exposition, I will make some critical remarks.

A historical approach to the problem may help to clear it up to a great extent. The history of philosophy, if one thoroughly studies it, appears to be always a history of struggle of diverse opinions, very often contradictory opinions on the problems of the universe, on ways and methods of cognition of the outside world, on ways of attaining true knowledge, and on the possibilities of its verification. It is a history of systematic overcoming of different difficulties that are placed by life before the inquisitive mind of man. The complexity of the process of knowledge and the discrepancy between our knowledge and the outside world are determined first of all by the complexity and peculiarities of the subject matter of investigation. In our age of progress in scientific thought this assertion hardly needs special arguments to be acknowledged. Meanwhile, the history of philosophy shows also that if the *complexity* of the process of knowledge and of the material world as a rule was beyond any doubt, the *discrepancy* between the outside world and what emerges in our knowledge was and sometimes is still quite evident.

This fact is seen, clearly in the Eleatic school, particularly in the conceptions of Zeno. The arguments raised in his well-known paradoxes and puzzles were directed against the possibility of movement and diversity. Zeno, to the degree permitted by the level of development of knowledge of that time, revealed the objective contradistinction between quality and quantity,[2] of sensory and logical knowledge, of finity and infinity of space,[3] of the one and many, and of motion and nonmotion.

Zeno cast doubt upon the reality of motion because of its contradictory nature. Here we see one of the most essential features of metaphysics as a method: *there is not and cannot be truth, where contradictions and discrepancies are; truth is incompatible with contradiction.*

Certainly, it would be quite naive to suppose that Zeno denied movement generally, that he rejected the existence of things that move. The real difficulty which he faced here and tried to overcome consisted in his understanding of the question: how is it possible to reflect the outside world, which is full of various internal objective contradictions, which is in a state of constant *changes* and *movement?* How is it possible to reflect this *contradictory* world in man's concepts, which, in Zeno's opinion, are *unchangeable* and *noncontradictory?*

V. Lenin made a significant remark: "It did not occur to Zeno to deny movement as 'sinnliche Gewissheit' [sensuous certainty], it was merely a question 'nach ihrer (movement's) Wahrheit' (of the truth of movement)."[4] And this was not a fictitious but a quite genuine difficulty, which pre-Marxist philosophy could not overcome because it had not been able to apply the principles of materialist dialectics to the theory of cognitive reflection.

Even those philosophers who lived much later raised a similar problem though they did not always formulate it with sufficient strictness. This was exemplified by Kant's antinomies, which essentially reflected the objective nature of contradictions in thought. However, Kant could not go further than a simple statement of the contradictions. Hegel, who tried to solve these contradictions from the idealistic point of view, created a rather grand speculative construction of idealist dialectics, which, however, in its primordial form was not suitable as a scientific method because of its mystical nature. Proceeding from the idealist principle of the identity of being and thought, Hegel described the objective contradictions of thought, and on the other hand he ascribed to reality certain contradictions which are specific only to thought.

The possibility of the metaphysical isolation of thought, of its separation from objective reality, lies also in the contradictory nature of the very process of knowledge, since thought inevitably separates those sides of the reflected object which, as a matter of fact, are closely connected with each other.

Contrary to metaphysics, materialist dialectics recognizes precisely *the contradictory nature of the objective world,* as well as *the contradictory nature of the process of knowledge, recognizes the truthfulness of objective contradiction,* considers the process of knowledge to be the process of reflection of the world by thought, involving the unity of opposites. Dialectics in the proper sense is the study of contradiction in the very essence of the object. It is very important to point out that materialist dialectics admits the necessity of reflecting the objective contradictions in *specific* contradictory forms that are inherent in thought.

V. I. Lenin was deeply right when he wrote: "We cannot imagine, express, measure, depict movement, without interrupting continuity, without simplifying, coarsening, dismembering, strangling that which is living. The representation of movement by means of thought always makes coarse, kills,— and not only by means of thought, but also by sense perception, and not movement, but of *every* concept.

"And in that lies the *essence* of dialectics.

"And precisely *this essence* is expressed by the formula: the unity, identity of opposites."[5]

In these words of V. I. Lenin, one should pay attention not only to the real difficulty that is indicated as arising in the process of knowledge, but also to the strict dialectical analysis that can be applied to any process of knowledge, because every such process inevitably is a case of the overcoming of diverse contradictions.

Perhaps it would not be a strained interpretation if we assume that the process of knowledge in a separate individual in its most general features repeats, though in miniature, the way of knowledge taken by mankind. No science can begin where there is not sufficient courage, daring, ability, and skill to divide that which is closely connected, first comprehending one side of the phenomenon, then the other, etc. This is a necessary condition of knowledge, but it is not quite sufficient. And to remain at this level means to deny the objective world as it really is. Analytical splitting of the object of knowledge must be followed by synthesis, which reunites its parts and aspects. However, this knowledge is based on a new foundation made possible by negation of negation, because the first separation of one side of the object has been the first negation, the negation of the whole.

The history of philosophy shows that in ancient times a primitive, naive, but intrinsically correct dialectical view predominated. These spontaneous dialectical conceptions later on were replaced by metaphysics, which in its turn was replaced by dialectics, the latter becoming scientific, materialist dialectics. Hence we can say that the history of philosophy in a certain respect is a history of struggle between dialectics and metaphysics; it is a history of a growing dialectical comprehension of phenomena and processes of the objective world. The naive dialectical conception was conditioned by the elementary level of development of science and the immaturity of social relations. But even in those times there existed very interesting and significant conjectures about the struggle and unity of opposites as a motive force of development.

According to the views of one of the founders of dialectics, Heraclitus, who by the way lived before Zeno, everything is and is not, for everything is fluid, is constantly changing, and is constantly coming into being and passing away. Heraclitus wrote: "The world, an entity made up of everything, was

created by none of the gods or men, but was, is, and will be
eternally living fire, regularly becoming ignited and regularly
becoming extinguished. . .". The struggle of opposites is a
source of the development of everything: "Everything becomes through struggle and according to necessity," said
Heraclitus. Though his conception was spontaneously dialectical, Heraclitus raised the problem of division of a single whole
and the cognition of its contradictory parts. The solution of
this problem as developed by dialectical materialism has made
a definite place for itself in the field of scientific philosophy.
In the course of history, this spontaneously dialectical approach
to the study of nature and human knowledge has suffered
many changes. It began with a denial (Zeno); had a one-sided
development in an idealistic manner (Kant, Fichte, Hegel); and
also a one-sided development in a materialistic manner (Aristotle,
J. Toland, F. Bacon, R. Descartes, B. Spinoza, D. Diderot,
V. Belinsky, L. Feuerbach, A. Herzen, N. Chernyshevsky, and
others).

A given period in the development of philosophical ideas is
conditioned by at least three factors: *the general level of
theoretical thinking, the level of development of the natural
and social sciences, and the maturity of social relations.* A
definite level of development of these three components was
necessary in order to make it possible to create the scientific
dialectical method of investigation. This level was reached in
the middle of the nineteenth century. By this time a number
of great discoveries in natural sciences had been made.

1. *The law of conservation and transformation of energy,*
which convincingly demonstrated the material unity of the
world and the indestructibility of matter and motion. At the
same time this law also showed that matter and motion are
qualitatively diverse, variable, and capable of passing from some
forms to others.

2. *The theory of the cellular structure of animal organisms,
of living tissue,* which showed that a material element, the cell,
is the foundation of any living organism. By demonstrating the
ability of the cell to change, this theory opened the way to a
proper understanding of development of organisms.

3. *Darwin's theory of evolution,* which put an end to the
view that the species of plants and animals are accidental,
unconnected with anything, are god-created and immutable.

It was scientifically proved that the complex, higher organisms had been formed from the simple, lower ones—not, moreover, by divine will, but through the action of the laws of selection inherent in nature itself. It was demonstrated that man too is a product of prolonged evolution of living matter.

Other natural sciences also underwent a spontaneous revolution and imperatively required *dialectical* generalizations. Dialectics, so to speak, knocked at the door.

The metaphysical method of investigation and thought, which had been dominant in the natural sciences and had a good deal of historical justification in its day, became an obstacle in the further development of science. It was even less useful for penetration into the essence of social processes. The idealistic dialectics of Hegel, as was noted above, could not be serviceable for science. It was *a method of investigation that combined dialectics with a scientifically mature conception of materialism,* which was necessarily required by the further development of science and social life.

To jump a few steps ahead, I would like to point out that dialectical materialism requires a dialectical approach also to the dialectical method itself, as well as to metaphysics. For example, contrary to Hegelian idealism, dialectical materialism by no means makes metaphysics an object of mockery. Nor does it deny absolutely the Hegelian idealist dialectics, generally neglected by metaphysically oriented philosophers. Dialectical materialism requires a concrete historical approach and objective evaluation of any phenomenon, material and spiritual. In this connection I cannot help recalling Engels, who said:

The old method of investigation and thought which Hegel calls "metaphysical," which preferred to investigate *things* as given, as fixed and stable, a method the relics of which still strongly haunt people's minds, had a good deal of historical justification in its day. It was necessary first to examine things before it was possible to examine processes. One had first to know what a particular thing was before one could observe the changes going on in connection with it. And such was the case with natural science. The old metaphysics which accepted things as finished objects arose from a natural science which investigated dead and living things as finished objects. But when this investigation had progressed so far that it became possible to take the decisive step forward of transition to the systematic investigation of the changes which these things undergo in nature itself, then the last hour of the old metaphysics occurred in the realm of philosophy also. And in fact, while natural science up to the end of the last century was predominantly a *collecting* science, a science of finished things, in our century it is essentially a *classifying* science, a science of the processes, of the origin and development of these things and of the inter-connection which binds all these natural processes into one great whole. Physiology, which investigates the processes occurring in plant and animal organisms; embryology, which deals with the development of individual organisms from germ to maturity; geology, which investigates the gradual formation of the earth's surface—all these are the offspring of our century.[6]

This was written by Engels at the close of the nineteenth century. At the beginning of the twentieth century, dialectical materialism as a whole and the dialectical method in particular were essentially developed in connection with new data in the natural sciences, and especially in modern physics.

In the development of dialectical materialism in accordance with the new requirements brought about by the natural sciences, V. I. Lenin played the great role.

When we speak about the development of dialectical method *in compliance with* the new data of the natural sciences, this should be understood not only in the sense that the dialectical method includes generalization and philosophical comprehension of new processes, *absorbing* new data, *enriching* and *concretizing* itself. There is included simultaneously another and quite different process: the influence of dialectical method upon the correct comprehension and interpretation of the things and processes of the outside world. Here we may witness the *heuristic* significance of dialectical method in the *search* for and *finding* of objective laws that govern natural processes.

This process comes to light in contemporary natural sciences and new branches of knowledge (cybernetics, information theory, bionics, relativity theory, quantum theory, the physics of elementary particles, and so on), which utilize basic principles and laws of dialectical materialism generally and rules of dialectical method in particular.

Let us consider relevant examples, one of them methodological (epistemological) and the other theoretical. First, the notion of *probability* is one of the most important concepts of modern physics. And it is impossible to understand the concept of probability deeply and in detail without a dialectically materialistic interpretation. Certainly, this concept might be simply described and systematized on the plane of theory. But in order to comprehend its *heuristic* significance, probability should be studied as an objective category and in close connection with such concepts as *possibility* and *reality*, *necessity* and *accident* (chance), *cause* and *effect*. Only in such a dialectical framework can the category of probability become operatively effective. Second, whether consciously or unconsciously, if a scientist creates a genuinely scientific theory which promotes the modern progress of knowledge, then he follows essentially the principles of dialectical materialism. Some scientists in this category acknowledge the principles and laws of dialectical materialism though they do not say even a single word about dialectical materialism as a world outlook and the necessity of its application. An eminent physicist of our day, Niels Bohr, while discussing the quantum theory, speaks of "profoundly true statements the opposites of which likewise contain deep verities."[7] It is well known that in classical physics light was regarded as a set of electromagnetic waves, and matter as a discrete structure. When modern physics discovered and experimentally proved that light has corpuscular properties and matter displays the properties of waves (in atomic-scale phenomena), it became necessary to solve a dialectical problem posed by dialectical reality. It was necessary to explain a phenomenon of objective dialectics by dialectical method. Metaphysics was absolutely useless here. As a scientist Bohr felt it and formulated the problem in a very interesting way in the form of antinomies. He wrote:

Suppose that a semitransparent mirror is placed in the path of a photon in such a way that the further progress of the photon is possible in two directions. Then of two photographic plates placed across these directions far apart from each other one and only one can record the photon. Now, if the plates are replaced by mirrors, interference phenomena will be observed due to two reflected waves. Any attempt to represent the behavior of the photon clearly will meet with the following difficulty: on the one hand, we should naturally state that the photon will always choose one of the two ways yet on the other, it behaves as if it were traveling along the two ways simultaneously.[8]

Bohr appeals to the complementarity concept. But the point is that he really felt the dialectical nature of the photon and recognized the necessity to use two opposite, mutually exclusive, yet mutually inclusive notions in relation to a single object. That is dialectics, not metaphysics. In like manner, the corpuscular and undulatory properties of an atomic object represent a unity of opposites.

Thus we must say that the metaphysical method, justifiable and necessary as it is in a number of domains whose extent varies according to the nature of the particular object of investigation, sooner or later reaches a limit, beyond which it becomes one-sided, restricted, abstract, lost in insoluble contradictions. In the contemplation of individual things, it forgets the connection between them; in the contemplation of their existence, it forgets the beginning and end of that existence; preoccupied with their repose, it forgets their motion. And, in this sense, dialectical method becomes the overcoming of the metaphysical method. And return to the latter would only mean a step backwards.

Dialectical materialism does not throw off achievements of previous philosophical and theoretical thinking, which were expressed in German classical philosophy (Hegel, Feuerbach), but considers these to be one of the theoretical sources of dialectical materialism. Other sources were certain economic, historical, and socialist theories. However, this is no occasion to dwell upon this matter in detail. I would like only to point out that to transform these theories into science, it was necessary to make a revolution, which manifested itself in the fact that these theories were comprehended in a new scientific fashion on the foundation of a *materialist understanding of history and a dialectically materialistic method of thought and investigation.*

By the middle of the nineteenth century, parallel with the achievements in natural and social science, social relations developed to such an extent that it became possible to discover objective laws of social development. The maturity of social relations manifested itself in the aggravation of the class struggle between bourgeoisie and proletariat. Further social progress of a spontaneous kind became impossible, and the historical necessity of *conscious scientific* activity arose. This maturity of social relations was one of the necessary·conditions of working out scientific dialectical method, because the latter is inseparable from, can exist only in indissoluble integral unity with, materialist theory.

Thus, by the middle of the nineteenth century, there had been quite distinctly revealed the whole complex of problems posed by the development of natural and social sciences, and by the development of theoretical thought and social life. These problems required a definite and scientific answer; the answer was given by Marx jointly with Engels. That was a genuine revolution in theoretical thinking, in the creation of the scientific method of investigation. Materialist dialectics as well as the philosophy of dialectical materialism was essentially enriched by V. I. Lenin, who developed and concretized Marxist philosophy and created a whole stage in its development.

Thus materialist dialectics as a method of thought and investigation is not at all *pure invention* created in the mind of a genius. It is a method *discovered* on the basis of the deepest and most thorough study of the objective world, which takes shape as a result of the data of science and is a product of the critical and careful comprehension of all the history of mankind, of all achievements of human knowledge. The force of dialectical method consists in its truthfulness, in the fact that it truly reflects the objective laws of development of reality, the objective dialectics of the material world, that it is in a state of constant improvement in connection with discoveries in natural and social sciences, and in social practice.

In order to secure the objective foundation of scientific method it was necessary to make fundamental social discoveries, and such discoveries were made. I shall briefly dwell upon one of them, the materialist conception of history. The chaos and arbitrariness that had been dominant in pre-Marxist sociological and historical theories were replaced by a scientific approach to social processes. The material unity of the world was confirmed on a new ground. Also confirmed were the interrelation and interconditionality of all the processes of nature, society, and man's consciousness.

In discovering the laws and categories of materialist dialectics, it was also revealed that a most important feature of scientific method is that it is conditioned by the objective laws of reality—nature, society, and human thought. The unity of all these three domains of reality, based on the material unity of the world, as well as the most general features inherent in them, essentially influenced and determined specific features of the dialectical method that is synonymous with scientific method. Engels defined it in the following way: "Dialectics, so-called objective dialectics, prevails throughout nature, and so-called subjective dialectics, dialectical thought, is only the reflection of the motion through opposites which asserts itself everywhere in nature, and which by the continual conflict of the opposites and their final passage into one another, or into higher forms, determines the life of nature."[9]

Today dialectics, as the scientific theory and method of investigation, represents a whole, the unity of theory of knowledge and logic, of principles, laws and categories, a unity which facilitates the effort to comprehend and investigate the world in the contemporary scientific level.

NOTES

1. This paper does not touch on the question of the polysemantic meaning of the term "metaphysics," the etymology of which goes back to disciples of Aristotle, and which now is often used as: (1) a theory which consists of unverifiable propositions and statements, which for this reason are considered to be referred to the realm of faith or belief (cf. empiricism); (2) a theory which takes for granted some theological principles and deduces the universal essence of being from them (cf. Thomism).

2. Zeno's paradox, "A millet seed," asserts that if a grain falls to the ground we would not hear any sound. But if such a grain falls to the ground we must hear a sound. As for our reason, it asserts, that either only one grain makes a sound, or a sack of grain does not make any sound. Otherwise the sum of zeroes would give us a certain positive number.

3. Take "Dichotomia": a body cannot budge, it cannot begin movement and finish it, it cannot change from repose to motion because if it moves toward a goal it has to pass half way towards it first; but it has to pass half way through that first half, and so on. Essentially for the same reason, Achilles cannot overtake the tortoise, and "a flying arrow rests."

4. V. I. Lenin, *Philosophical Notebooks*, in *Collected Works*, vol. 38 (Moscow: Foreign Languages Publishing House, 1961), p. 256.

5. Ibid., pp. 259-260.

6. F. Engels, *Ludwig Feuerbach and the Outcome of Classical German Philosophy* (Moscow, 1934), pp. 55-56.

7. Albert Einstein, *Albert Einstein als Philosoph und Naturforscher*, ed. P. A. Schilpp (Stuttgart, 1955), p. 150.

8. N. Bohr, "Discussion with Einstein of the Problems of the Theory of Knowledge in Atomic Physics," in Bohr's book, *Atomic Physics and Human Knowledge* (Moscow, 1964), p. 214.

9. Frederick Engels, *Dialectic of Nature* (Moscow, 1964), p. 214.

Chapter 3

Reflections on Economic Determinism

BRAND BLANSHARD

Sterling Professor of Philosophy Emeritus of Yale University,
Brand Blanshard has been a Gifford Lecturer and president of the
Eastern Division of the American Philosophical Association. He
has taught at the University of Michigan, Swarthmore College, the
University of Minnesota, and Yale University, and is the author of
The Nature of Thought (1939), *Reason and Goodness* (1960), and
Reason and Analysis (1961).

Exchanges of views between Soviet and American philosophers
should be commoner than they are. It is true that there is no
international language in which the exchanges can take place,
as there is in music and mathematics; and it is unhappily also
true that, if the discussion even approaches politics, there is
a wide range of value-charged terms such as "democracy,"
"imperialism," "freedom," that must either be avoided or
else defined with elaborate care. But such obstacles should not
be insuperable as between persons with a common aim. And
philosophers do have a common aim. Put roughly, it is to
discover the fundamental truth about the world. Truth, if
it is really truth, must be the same for all men, and the methods
and standards of seeking it must also be the same. An argument valid in Moscow cannot be invalid in Boston. No one
would say that there is an American or Soviet chemistry or
physics; there is only chemistry or physics—period—whose

facts and laws are the same everywhere. And surely there
ought to be no American or Soviet philosophy if that means
philosophy whose conclusions have been warped to suit local
interests or desires. Philosophy no less than science must order
itself by objective fact, not veer about with hopes or wishes
or fears.

But here precisely comes the rub. To many western thinkers,
Marxism seems to rule out the pursuit of philosophy as they
have always conceived it. The difficulty is not that all philosophies other than the official philosophy are discouraged in
its homeland, though on that there would certainly be questions;
the difficulty is philosophical. It is that in Marxism, as officially expounded, there seems to be a built-in denial that in
speculative thought objectivity is possible. In their economic
interpretation of history, both Marx and Engels insisted that
the culture of an age was determined by economic conditions,
and ultimately by the mode in which the means of subsistence
were produced. Let me cite a few characteristic statements.
Marx says:

The mode of production in material life determines the general character
of the social, political, and spiritual processes of life. It is not the consciousness of men that determines their existence, but, on the contrary,
their social existence determines their consciousness.[1]

Engels in his preface to the *Manifesto* says:

The prevailing mode of economic production and exchange, and
the social organization necessarily following from it, form the
basis upon which is built up, and from which alone can be explained,
the political and intellectual history of that epoch.[2]

Writing jointly, Marx and Engels say:

Morality, religion, metaphysics, all the rest of ideology and their
corresponding forms of consciousness, thus no longer retain the
semblance of independence.[3]

In *A Textbook of Marxist Philosophy* prepared by the
Leningrad Institute of Philosophy, we have a report of Lenin's
views on philosophy. Regarding idealism, under which communist writers seem to include most western philosophies,
his attitude is reported in the words:

... that idealism is really superstition, that it is really myth-making, and the only purpose of such thinking (i.e., what the theory means in practice) is to justify things as they are in the interests of the owning class and to betray reformers into paths of folly and futility.[4]

Professor J. D. Bernal, Britain's Marxist scientist, writes of priests and philosophers, whom he groups together:

... for the most part ... their function was to cloak over the inequalities of wealth and power in society by mythological or metaphysical theory.[5]

Such statements are scattered through communist literature, and we need hardly multiply them. They are important because they supply from authoritative sources the Marxist conception of what philosophy has been in the past and what it is still conceived to be in non-Marxist communities. Let me spell out a little further what I take these statements to mean.

They mean that the philosophy of a people belongs to its ideology, and that its ideology is what in these days would be called a rationalization. It may seem to its followers to be a theory logically worked out and freely accepted, but it is really a by-product of the class position of its authors. Philosophy in the past has been a creation of the bourgeoisie, since they alone had the leisure and freedom to cultivate it, and their philosophy has justified and even glorified the bourgeois class and its activities. In Plato and Aristotle and Spinoza, it made pure contemplation the highest work of man; in St. Augustine and St. Thomas, it embodied and praised a religious retreat from social responsibilities; in the thought of Locke, it turned social philosophy into a defense of private property; in Hegel, it made history a march of God on earth, with his own nation leading the van. The tremendous apparatus of St. Thomas sugar-coated an opiate for the people in the form of an assurance that God's in his heaven and all's right with the world. The vast machinery of Hegel's categories was an attempt to show that the world is governed by the sort of thought and values to be found in his own bourgeois head. The true nature of these undertakings was for the first time made plain by Marx. They are all parts of some ideology whose character is in the end determined by economic pressures.

This, I take it, is the crucial point at which Marx's explanation of philosophy differs from that of the west.

What are we to say to our Russian colleagues about this view? The things that suggest themselves are so obvious that I confess to some hesitation in giving voice to them. But I will try to put a few of them frankly.

The first comment is that this view seems to make objective philosophizing impossible. By objective philosophy, I mean the sort of reflection that starts with facts, either empirical or self-evident, and proceeds by logical inference from these facts. That is what all the great philosophers have attempted. They have assumed that it is possible to follow the line of implication and to arrive at a conclusion warranted by the evidence, and accepted solely because the evidence requires it. They have been tempted like the rest of us to believe what would fulfill their hopes or appease their fears or justify their class prejudices, but they assumed that with honest and self-critical effort they could hew to an objective line. None of them would have claimed that they had wholly succeeded. But unless such thinking is possible and can be achieved at least in some measure, philosophizing is surely futile. If, when we try to think straight, we are still puppets pulled by class interests, if our conclusions are not functions of the evidence but of our modes of getting a living, then the attempt to see things as they are is hopeless, and philosophy is defeated before it begins. In short, if philosophy is ideology governed by economic facts, as Marx and Engels said it was, then it is a conscious or unconscious fraud.

That suggests a second point. Is not economic determinism itself a philosophy? Surely it is. It is the philosophy of culture elaborated by the Marx of the 1840s. And thereby hangs a paradox. Marx was not one of the proletariat; he was a journalist and scholar with a university education, married to a member of the minor nobility, inept with his hands, and, from time to time, in a small way, an employer of labor himself. He was a bourgeois. Now his theory tells us that, when bourgeois people theorize, their theories are the by-products of their bourgeois class interest. That raises an inevitable question: was Marx's theory itself the product of such interests or not? Neither way of answering this question leaves economic determinism standing. Suppose you say that his theory, like other such theories, is a product of class pressures; there is then no reason to believe it true, since a theory resting on subjective pressures rather than objective fact and reason could be true only by accident. On the other hand, suppose, as Marx clearly did suppose, that his own theorizing was the product of fact and reason, and therefore true. In that case, it is admitted that theory may play free from economic determination and follow the evidence. But then economic determinism has again been abandoned. If thought can in Marx's own case free itself from irrational leading-strings, it may do so in other cases. Philosophy is rehabilitated, but at the cost of Marxist theory.

Engels seems to have been troubled by the irrationalism of this theory, and attempted to obviate it by a distinction. He suggested that *science* could be objective, that physics, chemistry, and biology, for example, could be made answerable to fact, but that philosophy, together with law, morals, politics, art, and religion, was a form of ideology controlled by class biases. Straight thinking was possible in the first group; it was impracticable in the second. Now it must be admitted that philosophers have achieved less objectivity than scientists; they have never succeeded in gaining a like measure of agreement. And if Marxists based their depreciation of philosophy on the positivist line of argument, which says in essence that only science is meaningful, they would have a case which, though not I think valid, would at least be plausible. But Marxists have shown small interest in positivism or any other school of analysis. They deprecate philosophy in its traditional forms not because it is meaningless but because it is inevitably twisted, biased, and, as Lenin said, implicitly dishonest. I see no good ground for this charge, nor can I hold it consistent with their admission that we can think objectively in science. Thought does not abruptly change its character in passing from science to philosophy; incorruption does not suddenly transform itself and put on corruption. Bacon and Hobbes and Descartes and Leibniz and Locke and Newton and Einstein were both philosophers and scientists; they were not aware of any break in their thinking as they passed from one province to the other, nor was there in fact any such break; the laws of thought, the standards of relevance, the meaning of rigor and demonstration, are the same in both. Surely when Aquinas tried to prove the existence of God or Locke the existence of matter, their arguments were as objectively valid or invalid as the reasonings of Darwin about the origin of species. If it is possible to think objectively about stars and atoms, it is incredible that the same thought should be helpless to follow the evidence about free will or the meaning of causality.

No responsible historian would now deny that the wealth or poverty, the privilege or underprivilege into which one is born, may profoundly affect one's outlook on the world, and it is very largely to Marx that we owe a proper appreciation of this fact. But it is surprising that neither Marx nor Engels nor, so far as I know, any other communist writer has ever worked out in detail how these factors operate in molding thought; and it is notorious that Engels, at the end of his life, confessed that he and Marx had misled their followers into overrating the importance of these factors.

Surely in that he was right. Of course the likelihood that a person born in poverty will have the chance to turn his attention seriously to philosophy is far too small, though in the United States it has frequently occurred; he will be pre-occupied with more pressing business. But assuming that he does turn his attention to it, is it plausible to say that the way his thought develops will be controlled by his economic status? I cannot see that this is either antecedently probable or in accordance with known fact. Granted that Leibniz and Newton might have accomplished little if their bourgeois background had not permitted them access to books; still, once presented with certain problems of pure theory, they went on to develop a new branch of mathematics, the calculus, by way of solving them. Why did their thought take this line? Because the problems logically required it and because they had first-rate heads. Their economic status had nothing to do with it. Besides, their economic status was different, while the theory they developed was the same. One would have supposed it obvious that, in any branch of thought, the better one's head— that is, the more able one is to follow the logic of the case— the less likely one is to be the puppet of any kind of strings. Hence, so far as economic materialism is true at all, it applies to the second- and third-rate thinkers rather than to the first.

What is suggested by reflection is here borne out by fact. There seems to be no fixed relation at all between the class status of the major philosophers and the conclusions they have arrived at. The great philosophers have come from all classes. Bacon, Descartes, Shaftesbury, and Russell were members of the nobility; but Kant was the son of a leather worker; Spinoza was a lens grinder who lived in an attic; Rousseau was an engraver's apprentice. It is easy to show that philosophers of very different social classes have developed the same philosophy, and philosophers of the same class have developed very different philosophies. Marcus Aurelius was an emperor and Epictetus a slave, but their philosophies were almost identical. On the other hand, Bacon and Descartes were both aristocrats, living in the same period; one of them was the founder of modern rationalism, the other an antirationalist who was the father of modern empiricism.

Philosophers have a way of confounding their Marxist interpreters by developing in the most wayward fashion systems that will not fit into Marxist pigeonholes. Russell inherited an earldom, and ought therefore to have been an ideological apologist for capitalism and its class system; instead he has been a socialist critic of both nearly all his life; indeed he says: "I went to Russia a Communist; but contact with those who have no doubts has intensified a thousandfold my own doubts."[6] John Dewey was the son of a grocer, and was therefore presumably a bourgeois; and sure enough, we find that the Soviet specialist on American pragmatism, Yuri Melvil, represents Dewey as the philosopher of American imperialism. Those of us who knew Dewey find it a little difficult to recognize him in this guise, since he lives in our memory as the defender of the individual against every form of exploitation and repression; indeed his defense of Trotsky against the hounding of Stalin seems to be the strange ground on which he is now called an imperialist. Among American intellectuals who have been friendly to Marxism, there has been no one kind of background; if one reflects on the cases of Max Eastman, Granville Hicks, Sidney Hook, John Dos Passos, Norman Thomas, Harry Laidler, Benjamin Gitlow, Whittaker Chambers, James Burnham, John Chamberlain, and Malcolm Cowley, the one thing that leaps to mind as common to all is that through a succession of steps, of which the Stalin purges of 1936, the Hitler-Stalin pact of 1939, and the incidents in Hungary in 1956 were the most important, their communist sympathies gradually dropped away. Perhaps no American philosopher has striven harder to be fair to Marxism than Corliss Lamont, who is a scion, not of the proletariat, but of Wall Street.

One can anticipate the reply to all this. "You misunderstand Marx completely. You assume that his economic determinism was an account of how *individuals* come to think as they do instead of how *classes* come to think as they do. An ideology is a theory held by a class or people as a whole, and it was this only that Marx was attempting to explain."

The reply is inadequate. Classes do not philosophize; only persons do. When Marx says that metaphysics "no longer retains a semblance of independence," since it is the by-product of economic factors, whose metaphysics does he mean? I know whose metaphysics *I* mean when I talk about it historically; I mean the metaphysics of the great metaphysicians. And unless in explaining metaphysics one is explaining why *they* thought as they did, one is explaining nothing worth bothering about. No doubt the average man, proletarian or bourgeois, has some implicit speculative ideas; everyone does; but it is surely not vague ideas in the popular mind that the student of metaphysics is talking about. He is talking about explicit metaphysics, the thought of the great speculative thinkers whose systems stand out like mountain peaks on the horizon of history, of Aristotle and St. Thomas and Spinoza and Hegel and Whitehead. Of course these were all individuals. If Marxism does not explain why they thought as they did, it does not explain metaphysics at all. I have paid it the respect of assuming that in this case it is trying to do just that, which is the only thing worth doing. And it is easy to show—I think I have done it—that in this attempt it fails.

The attempt to explain the philosophy of the past as the by-product of the class system is so clearly at odds with facts as to make one wonder what is amiss with the Marxist machinery. I venture to suggest that something has gone wrong in the transmission. The economic pressure attendant on class member-ship is supposed to be the great powerhouse supplying the drive for men's action and speculation. But what of the belt by which this power is communicated? The fact that a man is a worker in a Ford plant does not affect his thought or poli-tics directly; it acts on him through his desires. And Marx seemed to think that the dominant desire of a class was always for what would better it economically. The dominant desire of the bour-geoisie was to secure its own status and extort more from the proletariat; the great hope of the proletariat was to slither out of the chains fastened on it by the bourgeoisie. But human nature is not so simple as that. The belt that carries the driving force frays out into a thousand strands of desire, turning a thousand different wheels. Some of these desires, it is true, are for economic status and security, but many of them are not. Indeed many of them have nothing at all to do with economic

interest; they may act, and often have acted, in flat contra-
vention of it.

Consider nationalism, for example. In eastern Europe after
World War I, the economic interest of the people was to unite
in a way that would promote trade and joint prosperity. But
in fact fanatical nationalism, confined to no one class, took
command, Balkanized and impoverished the people, and scattered
economic interests to the winds. This tragic tale of patriotic
Balkanization in scorn of economic consequence seems to be
enacting itself again in Africa. Or consider religion. Was it economics or was it religion that was behind the Crusades, the
Inquisition, and the Reformation? Is it economics or is it religion
that is behind the division of Ireland? One may argue that religion itself is an economic by-product merely. But it is easy to
show, as Tawney and Weber have shown, that this argument
works both ways, that economic developments are often determined by religion as well as the other way about. Dean Inge
has remarked of the American business man, with his thrift,
austerity, and hard work, that if he is not a son of the ghetto,
he is probably a grandson of John Calvin. Or take the pride
and animosity of race. After what has happened recently in
Mississippi, and then in reverse in the Congo, can anyone say
that the motives connected with race are weak among mankind?
Again, if we concede to Marx, as we plainly should, that
economic motives are powerful, must we not concede to Freud
that motives rooted in sex are also powerful, and have often put
to rout the desires for wealth and security? "Love treats lock-
smiths with derision." Think, finally, of the force in human
affairs of heroes and hero worship. Engels thought that heroes
were inconsequential and that, if Napoleon had never lived,
the dialectic process would have achieved the same end without
him. If personalities count for no more than this, one wonders
why Marxists have found it so hard and so important to represent
the cult of personality. To sum up: if economic pressure and
class membership are to produce the effects alleged, they must
do so through human desires, and human desires may as easily
flout economic interests as support them.

Here again one may anticipate the line of reply: "Marxism
never made economic interest the sole determinant of an ideology.
It would not deny any of these competing interests its rightful
place in the government of thought and action." But (1) the
preface to the *Manifesto* says: "the prevailing mode of economic

production and exchange, and the social organization necessarily following from it, form the basis upon which is built up, and from which *alone* [my italics] can be explained, the political and intellectual history of that epoch." Is that "alone" to be taken seriously or not? (2) Suppose, as is now urged upon us, and as Engels himself seems finally to have supposed, that it is *not* to be taken seriously. What does "economic determinism" then amount to? It says that economic factors are important, but that others are important too. Now is there anyone who would deny that? One had imagined that economic determinism was a distinctive theory, which sharply separated Marxist from other philosophies of history. The separation seems now to disappear. Western philosophers are quite ready to allow the importance of economic interests, and if Marxist philosophy allows that religious, patriotic, and other interests can play free of the economic, does it any longer have a position of its own? If, in view of this multiplicity of motives, Marx was justified in working out an economic view of history, was not Hegel justified in working out a rationalist view, and Toynbee a religious view? A mere difference in degree with which the various motives are stressed is hardly a basis for setting the Marxist view in radical opposition to all others. In criticizing Marxism, I have again assumed that it meant to say something distinctive, something different from what western philosophers are saying. Is this assumption unjustified?

Marx oversimplified human nature. He has therefore given us an unbalanced picture of the philosopher and what moves him. Just as he failed to credit the independence of other motives from economic factors, so he failed to give due credit to the distinctness and independence of thought. Thought, for Marx, was a tool of action. You will remember the famous statement of the *Theses on Feuerbach:*

The question whether objective truth belongs to human thinking is not a question of theory, but a practical question. The truth, i.e., the reality and power, of thought must be demonstrated in practice.
  Philosophers have only *interpreted* the world in various ways, but the real task is to *alter* it.[7]

Here the search for truth seems to be identified with the quest for power, and truth with effectiveness in transforming the world. This pragmatic notion of truth is of course familiar in the west; it has been repeatedly offered, respectfully examined, and by most philosophers rejected. They do not recognize in such a description the end they are trying to achieve.

The attempt to transform the world is one kind of activity; the attempt to understand it is another. Theory and practice, thinking and acting, are not identical. The man who tries to understand is seeking theoretical or intellectual satisfaction— the kind one gets from solving a problem and not from driving a nail. Marx is in essence trying to reduce the former to the latter, and it cannot be done. There is such a thing as the love of truth, as distinct from the love of getting things done, an interest in knowing for knowing's sake, the ancient elemental longing to understand one's world. This love of truth may, as Housman said, be the faintest of human passions, but it does exist, it has standards of its own, and in the great philosophers it has risen to passionate dedication.

Marx questioned the possibility of such disinterestedness and, in so doing, introduced the profoundest cleavage that exists between Soviet and western thinkers. Not only did he represent philosophers as driven from behind by economic pressures; he thought that for the most part they were deceived as to their own aim in thinking, for under the appearance of disinterested inquiry they were in truth grinding a practical axe. I suppose that is why Marxist philosophers can manage to believe of their colleagues in the west, however honest, liberal, and disinterested they may seem to be, that at base they are really stooges of capitalism and imperialism. This, if I may say so, is poisonous nonsense. Such servitude did not hold even of Marx, who, for all his unattractive hatreds, had a powerful intelligence and at times a very clear eye for the truth.

Nor do I believe it holds of our Soviet colleagues. When we come to discussing things in private they certainly do not sound like puppets, though the tendency of all of them to take the same line on every major problem is indeed disquieting. If Marx is right about them, if their thought draws its aim and standard from practical success, there is little hope of our understanding each other. To take a frivolous example, we shall be like the fishwives whom Sidney Smith heard abusing each other from opposite sides of an alley: "They will never agree" said Sidney; "they are arguing from different premises." But I find it hard to believe that, as we present our case to each other, we are governed by totally different ends. Truth, as was said in the beginning, is one, and the business of thought is quite simply to conform to it always. When thought abandons its own ends to become the tool of alien purposes, as it did under the Fascists, whom we equally detest, it may become a power for evil as readily as for good. Its business is to yield to no pressures of any kind, economic, religious, or political, but by understanding them to circumvent them, and stick to its line. Would our Soviet colleagues dissent? We can talk together in hope so long as our dialectical materialisms or dialectical idealisms or even dialectical theologies accept the lead of that dialectical philosophy from which all of them alike have grown. The imperative of Socrates, who started it all, is as valid today as it ever was: follow the argument where it leads.

NOTES

1. Karl Marx, *A Contribution to the Critique of Political Economy*, trans. N. I. Stone (Chicago: Charles H. Kerr, 1904), pp. 11-12.

2. Friedrich Engels, *Manifesto of the Communist Party*, ed. Friedrich Engels (New York: International Publishers, 1948), p. 6.

3. Karl Marx and Friedrich Engels, *The German Ideology*, pts. 1 and 3, ed. R. Pascal (New York: International Publishers, 1947), p. 14.

4. John Lewis, ed., *A Textbook of Marxist Philosophy*, trans. C. A. Mosely (London: V. Gollancz, 1937), pp. 38-39.

5. J. D. Bernal, in Hermann Levy and others, *Aspects of Dialectical Materialism* (London: Watts, 1934).

6. Bertrand Russell, *The Practice and Theory of Bolshevism* (London: Allen and Unwin, 1921), p. 42.

7. Bertrand Russell, *Freedom and Organization, 1814-1914* (New York: W. W. Norton, 1934), pp. 191-192.

Chapter 4

Reflections on Blanshard's Reflections

JOHN SOMERVILLE

John Somerville, professor emeritus of philosophy, City University of New York, and editor-in-chief of *Soviet Studies in Philosophy* was twice awarded Rockefeller grants and took part in three UNESCO projects. As a Cutting Travelling Fellow of Columbia University, he did research in the Soviet Union from 1935 to 1937, and wrote *Soviet Philosophy: A Study of Theory and Practice* (1946). He has also written *Methodology in Social Science: A Critique of Marx and Engels* (1938), *The Philosophy of Peace* (1949, 1954), *The Way of Science, Its Growth and Method* (1953), *The Communist Trials and the American Tradition* (1956), *The Philosophy of Marxism* (1967), and *Durchbruch zum Frieden* (1973).

Professor Brand Blanshard's clear and concise "Reflections on Economic Determinism" merits careful examination and invites explicit comment. Part of the comment that needs to be made he makes himself. After the first five or six pages of his paper, he says: "One can anticipate the reply to all this. 'You misunderstand Marx completely. You assume that his economic determinism was an account of how *individuals* come to think as they do instead of how *classes* come to think as they do. An ideology is a theory held by a class or people as a whole, and it was this only that Marx was attempting to explain.' "

It would be quite ridiculous to say that Blanshard misunderstands Marx completely. (And I cannot claim to understand Marx completely.) But I think there is some misunderstanding

43

of Marx on Blanshard's part. To be specific, I think Blanshard
is right when he acknowledges that Marx was not trying to
give "an account of how *individuals* come to think as they
do," but wrong when he construes Marx as intending to give
an account of "how *classes* come to think as they do," at
least in the sense Blanshard means this expression. Part of
his meaning emerges when he says: "The reply is inadequate.
Classes do not philosophize; only persons do." But there is
no reason to believe Marx would doubt that statement or its
implications. One feels that at this point a meeting of minds
just missed taking place. Let us try to see if this is so, and
if so, why.

The first thing to be borne in mind is that Blanshard's
main problem is to account for ideas; but Marx's main problem
was to account for history. While these two problems overlap,
they must be distinguished, and kept in perspective. Throughout, Blanshard refers to Marx's basic social theory as "economic
determinism." To say that the usual Marxian term is "materialist conception of history" might be merely a terminological
difference were it not for the fact that the latter expression
includes a valuable element missing from the former—specific
indication of *what* is being conceived materialistically or
determined economically, namely, history; not simply ideas,
ideologies, or metaphysical systems. Put differently, Blanshard
is mainly concerned about one specific area within the whole
field of history to which Marx's whole theory is meant to
apply—the specific area of the history of ideas.

I venture to point this out, not in order to suggest that
there is anything wrong with dealing chiefly with one aspect
of a large theory, but in the interest of perspective on the
matter as a whole. What I think becomes decisive in respect to
Blanshard's treatment of the aspect with which he is mainly
concerned—ideas—is that he misconstrues Marx's view of how
the whole theory applies to ideas. What disturbs Blanshard is
the thought that a fair implication of the theory Marx held
would be that economic pressures determine the work of all
philosophers, including the best, in the sense that the system
a given philosopher creates must be a mere rationalization of
the economic interests and privileges of the class to which the
philosopher belongs, and therefore must be devoid of significant objective validity. Blanshard rightly feels that such a
view would not only be demonstrably inconsistent with known

facts in the history of philosophy, but would be internally inconsistent with the claims of Marxist theory itself, since it would make the very theory created by Marx and Engels a mere rationalization of class interests rather than objective truth, with the additional paradox that in this case the economic interests in question were not even those of their own economic class.

The first thing I would wish to say about this is that my contacts with contemporary Marxism, here and abroad, lead me to the conclusion that practically all Marxists today would be as much disturbed as Professor Blanshard by this thought, on which they usually bestow the adjective "vulgar." No doubt in past years beyond a generation or so ago, there were some writers calling themselves Marxists who tried to adopt the view in question; but they were never more than a minority, and they certainly never included figures like Marx, Engels, or Lenin. However, since Blanshard quotes from precisely these three, it is the more necessary to examine what these writers say, and try to see their meaning in the context of their theory as a whole.

The first passage Blanshard quotes is a portion of the famous preface which Marx wrote to *Contribution to the Critique of Political Economy:* " . . . the mode of production of the material means of existence conditions the whole process of social, political and intellectual life. It is not the consciousness of men that determines their existence, but on the contrary it is their social existence that determines their consciousness." Engels' expression of the same thought in his preface to the *Communist Manifesto* is also quoted: "The prevailing mode of economic production and exchange, and the social organization necessarily following from it, form the basis on which is built up, and from which alone can be explained, the political and intellectual history of the epoch." Several other passages are quoted to the same effect. However, all the central issues of discussion emerge clearly from these two.

It should be noted that these passages do not speak of class membership determining a given philosopher's views; the units of thought are much larger, deeper, broader. These passages are not trying to answer the question, "what determined the specific views of this or that individual philosopher?" They are trying to answer the question, "what is the chief causal factor determining the course of human history?"

The answer they suggest is that this chief determining
factor is the mode of producing the material means of existence,
the prevailing mode of economic production and exchange
(the type of tools and relations of production). As Professor
Blanshard correctly notes, Engels himself acknowledged that
he and Marx were to a degree blameworthy for having in their
earlier work emphasized this factor so much as to give some
people the impression that they did not allow for the operation
of any other causal factors in the historical process, which
would be absurd; the materialist thesis is not that no other
factors play a role, but that this factor plays the strongest role.

At one point Blanshard comes very close to a direct con-
fronting of this central issue, but again misses, by a very narrow
margin. This occurs where he writes:

What does "economic determinism" then amount to? It says that
economic factors are important, but that others are important
too. Now is there anyone who would deny that? One had imagined
that economic determinism was a distinctive theory, which sharply
separated Marxist from other philosophies of history. The separation
seems now to disappear. . . . If, in view of this multiplicity of motives,
Marx was justified in working out an economic view of history,
was not Hegel justified in working out a rationalist view, and Toynbee
a religious view? A mere difference in degree with which the various
motives are stressed is hardly a basis for setting the Marxist view
in radical opposition to all others.

But if we could justifiably say this, how would any school
at all be left standing as a distinctive school? For example,
Toynbee stresses religion, while Freud stresses sex. But Freud
recognizes that religion plays a certain role, while Toynbee
recognizes that sex plays a certain role. Is this a proper basis
for concluding that the differences between them are not of
serious significance, that there is no reason to separate them
off from one another, and regard them as in opposition? Hardly.

Differences about matters of degree, about which factor
exerts a stronger and which a weaker influence in a complex
causal pattern, about which is primary and which secondary
over a long period of time, can be extremely important both
to an understanding of the situation as a whole and any attempt
to improve it basically. From Blanshard's paper we learn only
a part of his attitude toward this central matter. We learn that
he recognizes a number of factors operative in the process of

determining the course of history (e.g., nationalism, religion, race, sex, hero worship) and that he would agree with Marx insofar as Marx also recognizes more than one causal factor; but we do not know which factor Blanshard would single out as primary, nor do we know whether his reason for not singling out any one factor as primary is that he is not prepared to commit himself, or that he believes it is rationally impossible or meaningless to single out any one factor as primary.

In any case, Blanshard would argue against what he assumes are the implications of Marx's thesis relative to the history of ideas. We indicated above what Blanshard assumes these implications to be, and we stated that his assumption was erroneous. It is now incumbent upon us to try to clarify what we think the implications actually are, what we think Marx was saying about the history of ideas. If he was not saying that each philosopher was creating a mere rationalization of the economic interests of the class to which the philosopher belonged, what was he saying? First, that the general kind of world-view, moral code, system of law and political theory which is *predominant* in a given culture in a given period must be such that, (a) it does not condemn or pronounce as illegitimate the existing system of production and exchange (or is not so interpreted); and, (b) that it can and does exercise a cooperative function in relation to the needs of this system as a going concern. If (a) and (b) were not the case, either the predominant philosophy would cease to be predominant or the existing system would cease to exist.

The second thing Marx is saying is that the economic system (which he calls the base) changes, and the philosophy (which is part of what he calls the superstructure) changes, and that the interrelations between these two levels of change are such that it is the philosophy which changes in response to new developments in the economic system far more and far more strongly than it is the other way around. Causation can run both ways; but it runs far more powerfully one way than the other. It was much more a case of the economic system changing from a slave or serf basis, and that change inducing changes in the prevailing moral and legal principles (from justification of slavery and serfdom to condemnation of them) than it was a case of new moral ideas about slavery and serfdom bringing about a new kind of economic system, one which replaced slavery and serfdom with wage labor. Predominantly, it is much more a case of people cutting their philosophies to the pattern of their lives than cutting their lives to the pattern of their philosophies.

In other words, one thing that should be historically explained about ideas is their general quality, content, tone, and emphasis in a given epoch, that is, the general characteristics of the ruling, prevailing, predominant ideas of one epoch as distinguished from another. If differences of this kind can be found, as between one epoch and another, can any factor be singled out as the chief determinant of such differences? Marx said yes. After all, if human society is an interrelated complex, it is to be expected that its different levels, aspects, institutions, as they operate and develop in the ongoing historical process, in some way condition one another, exert causal influence on one another, but not necessarily to an equal degree. This related to what Auguste Comte called the question of historical *filiation*. His answer to it, completely in the spirit of idealism, is set forth in the first chapter of his *Positive Philosophy:*

It cannot be necessary to prove to anybody who reads this work that ideas govern the world or throw it into chaos; in other words that all social mechanism rests upon opinions. The great political and moral crisis that societies are now undergoing is shown by a rigid analysis to arise out of intellectual anarchy. . . . But whenever the necessary agreement on first principles can be obtained, appropriate institutions will issue from them, without shock or resistance. . . .

This is the kind of thesis Marx is denying when he says what was quoted above: "It is not the consciousness of men that determines their existence, but on the contrary it is their social existence that determines their consciousness."

What led Blanshard astray was his assumption that Marx must have meant this in the sense that no individual thinker could develop a consciousness contrary to the special interests of the economic class to which he belonged, or, to put it differently, that there could be no exceptions to class conformity. But Marx and Engels did not forget that they were not proletarians by class membership, nor does their theory stand in contradiction to this fact. Moreover, their theory is greatly concerned about precisely what Blanshard is concerned about— the exceptional thinker, the exceptionally great thinker, whose work makes a significant difference in the history of thought, and therefore in the history of human society.

Marx is, of course, through and through a historical, dialectical thinker, centrally interested in the nature and implications of change, development, progress. As Marxist theory construes the matter, every society is going through changes, the dynamics of which involve conflicts of opposing forces. At the philosophical level, this means conflicts of opposing ideas. What gives ideas historical significance is that they have an impact upon society; that is, they make a difference in human life, in the way people live, in their development or stultification, their happiness or misery. Now Marx is not denying that there is a sense in which it is true as a general proposition (of which many examples may be cited) that any kind of individual person can get any kind of idea. (There are obvious limitations, of sequence and the like, which we need not dwell upon, e.g., we do not expect ideas about the nucleus of the atom before there are ideas about the atom, etc.)

But what Marx was especially concerned to emphasize in this connection was his view that a new idea which is capable of playing a beneficial role in human life (irrespective of the standard of "beneficial") will not actually play its role if the class which controls the economic system feels this idea as a threat, and remains powerful enough to resist it, or if the idea, in order to play out its potential role in human life, is in need of a technology which does not yet exist. The idea will have to wait (or search) for a different controlling class, or technology. It is immediately obvious that such a view has very profound implications in relation to understanding the history of moral ideas and their impact, or lack of impact, on human life. Similar consequences also become evident in relation to social, political, scientific, and other ideas. Thus Marx didn't say that a capitalist could not get socialist ideas, but he did say that the idea of socialism, or any big idea, cannot be expected to play its role in human life until a number of practical conditions, relating mainly to the economic order, but also to other aspects of the existing social system, have been fulfilled.

If Marx's "economic determinism," or rather materialist conception of history, stood for what Blanshard attributes to it, we would indeed be justified in saying there was not much about it to call distinctive or impressive. However, when we consider the actual nature and full scope of Marx's theory, its distinctiveness is felt and its wide influence becomes understandable. In this connection the comparisons so frequently

made are not without warrant—that Marx did for social and
philosophic thought something similar to what Darwin did
for biology and Freud did for psychology. We are not here
trying to argue the complete validity of Marx's conclusions,
in terms of empirical content and detailed doctrine. Even if
one thought most of that was inaccurate, or should be superseded, one would still have to recognize that Marx's contribution
was monumental, for, along with Comte, he was one of the
first to try to construct through an elaborate body of doctrine
a strictly scientific theory about human society as a whole.
Like Comte, he saw that, to be scientific, such a theory would
have to take in the entire world, and would have to be essentially historical, because human society is so obviously world-
wide and in process of historical development. But Comte never
came to grips with the economic facts of social life, the significance of class conflicts, and the realities of political power.
In these matters he was incredibly naive, though his insight into
the methodological demands and structural relations of social
science (within itself, and in relation to natural science), worked
out in systematic doctrine, is superb. However, no one before
Marx (or since) ever dug so deeply into the relations between
economics and politics, or got so far with a causative and
predictive theory of social evolution, which is at the same time
tied up with practice and with political programs. For a long
time to come, it will remain impossible to ignore Marx.

Blanshard raises the question of Marxism's view of the
relation between philosophy and science. It was mainly
Engels who wrote on this theme, and I think his views come
to this: a great deal of what has been traditionally called
"philosophy," especially within speculative systems of
metaphysics, offers no possibility of objective proof or
disproof; it therefore makes little contribution to the search
for confirmable truth, and must be criticized in terms of the
social role it plays. What is most valuable about philosophy
are the functions it performs in relation to what we have
come to call science. This relationship began with the birth
process, as all the primary sciences were created by philosophy
and philosophers. Historically speaking, science is one kind
of philosophy—in the Marxist view, the best kind—which
still has a great deal of unfinished business on its agenda.
Contemporary Marxists usually call philosophy the most
general of the sciences. Science and good philosophy must

be objective but that is not the same thing as being socially neutral. Medical science must be objective, but not neutral as between health and disease, life and death.

Blanshard characterizes the task of the philosopher (or scientist) as the search for truth, the use of reason, the following of the evidence, but gives no critical attention to a specific decision which must be made prior to any of these operations: choice of problem. Shall one seek the truth about God or the truth about man? The truth about how to make human beings live longer or the truth about how to kill them quicker? The truth about what will help oppressed people to throw off their oppressors or the truth about what will help oppressors to continue their oppression? It would be fatuous to reply, *"all* truth." Even if all truths were equally significant (whatever that would mean), it is impossible in practice to seek them all equally and simultaneously. Inevitably, one must make selections and determine priorities, and in doing so one should face the fact that significant truth is never neutral, so that he who seeks and finds it is never objectively playing a neutral role or a "pure" role, though he may subjectively think he is. This is at the root of what the Soviet Marxists mean by the term *partiinost'* (literally, "partyness"—the objective relation of a given theory to the concrete political-moral struggles going on at the particular time and place).

Another way of putting the point is to say that in scientifically significant truth the factor of power is always present, not only in the moral sense ex post facto (how it is used), but in the cognitive sense, definitionally. Blanshard did not look closely enough at the historical relations between philosophy and science to see what was involved, for example, in the Baconian principle, "Human knowledge and human power meet in one. . . ." (*Novum Organum*, I, Aph. III.) That is, it is not only that *significant* knowledge, once found, will yield power, but that if one wants significant knowledge (what we have since come to call science), one must seek that kind of truth which, when found, will significantly increase human power—first of all, the power to predict, which in turn leads to the power to utilize, to control. This yielding of power is not only the link between theory and practice, between pure and applied science; it is the central element in the criterion by which complex empirical truth is tested for validity and significance as science, and is of course a matter of degree.

What we call a better scientific explanation or better scientific understanding is that which gives us greater power to predict the behavior of the subject matter. This is the objective distinction between irresponsible speculation and confirmable science. Before this distinction becomes a source of human power, it must function as a test of scientific truth. We need the one as much as the other, and the two are interconnected. "Truth therefore and utility," as Bacon put it, "are here the very same things; and works themselves are of greater value as pledges of truth than as contributing to the comforts of life." (*Novum Organum*, I, Aph. CXXIV.)

To say that if we need scientific truth we need an objective criterion by which to test and measure it (besides the analytic rules of formal logic), and that this criterion is power to predict, which leads to utility and control, is no longer, as it was with Bacon, to write a prescription. It is now to state a vast empirical fact, which expresses three centuries of the history of modern science. In the nineteenth century Comte, arguing that a scientific sociology was possible, based his case on what had already been demonstrated by natural science when he said, in his neat French formulation, essentially what Bacon had said: "Voir, c'est savoir; savoir, c'est prévoir; prévoir, c'est pouvoir." (To see is to know; to know is to predict; to predict is [to gain] power.) This essential thought was what Marx also was building on, in his remark that philosophers have only interpreted the world in various ways, but the point is to change it. Clearly, in his view, this could never be done without the proper kind of knowledge. The choice was not simply philosophy or action, but irresponsible philosophy accompanied by ineffective action or scientific philosophy leading to effective action in the social sphere. But the objective link between scientific truth and human power was not an invention of Marx. That is rooted in the very creation and growth of science.

All this is what makes it impossible to agree with Blanshard's simplistic picture of the great philosopher and the great scientist seeking a truth that is independent of human power. The most one can say of such a philosopher or scientist is that he might be unaware of the connection between the kind of truth he chose to seek and the accretion of human power created by that kind of truth. But is that lack of awareness good, either for him or for the society of which he is a part?

There is a further aspect of the matter of power which neither Bacon nor Comte followed out, but which Marx and Lenin did. That is, when scientific philosophy or a special science finds significant knowledge which yields human power, e.g., pathology, heliocentric astronomy, nuclear physics, cybernetics, ecology, to mention only a few scattered examples of a principle that is general, this power does not go directly to humanity in general. It cannot be given directly to humanity in general. It must be "given" to and through the social channels, agencies, and institutions of the time and place. These channels, agencies, and institutions will determine, in large part, who gets the power and how the power will be used. Neither in its genesis nor in its consequences could philosophy or science be independent of the prevailing socioeconomic system, and if the individual philosopher or scientist wants his individual search for truth to have human consequences which he considers humanly good, he must be realistic about his choice of problems and his stance in politics. He must be aware, to the extent normally possible, of what power consequences are likely to follow from the solution of a given scientific or philosophic problem in a given socioeconomic system. This awareness of the relation between these two sets of functions—the scientific search for truth, and the dynamics of the socioeconomic systems—may lead to their mutual betterment, that is, may lead both sets of functions to a humanly higher level. This is the hope and the aim of Marxism.

PART II

MARXISM AND THEORY OF LOGIC

Chapter 5

Ontology, Logic, and Dialectical Materialism

JOHN SOMERVILLE

In contemporary philosophic developments relating to the general theme of ontology, logic and dialectical materialism, at least three distinguishable positions have emerged which have played important roles. Let us try to define these positions, to identify the problems raised by them, and to explore their implications in relation to these problems.

One position is that ontology and logic have no interrelations of the kind which would make the content of logic as a study dependent on the content of ontology. The expression "logic without ontology" might be used to designate this position. That is, the intent seems to be to assert that the correctness or incorrectness, the adequacy or inadequacy of any given theory of logic is not determined by or derived from or affected by its relation to ontological laws, or what are considered to be ontological truths.

It would seem possible, according to this position, to make no commitments about ontology, either explicitly or implicitly, and still arrive at an adequate theory of logic. Put differently, one could be objectively as well as merely subjectively neutral about ontology, and still be an excellent logical theorist. (Perhaps it is not necessary to add that there is of course an important difference between merely subjective

For biographical information about the author, see page 43.

neutrality, in which the individual sincerely feels that by statement X he is taking no stand on issue Y, whereas in fact he is, and objective neutrality, in which the individual's statement actually does not involve the taking of a stand on issue Y.) In traditional Marxist writings, the "logic without ontology" position has been regarded as a part of what has usually been called "bourgeois" philosophy. I am not here concerned with any one version of it, or with the variable specifics in terms of which it has been developed by any one philosopher, but rather with its general character and orientation.

The supporters of this position further maintain that in the basic sense there is no logic other than formal logic, that it is neither necessary nor possible to construct a system of logic on any basis which would deny the principles of identity, noncontradiction, and excluded middle as asserted by Aristotle. Thus, in this view, there is and can be no such thing as dialectical logic. Basically, there is no meaning or value in the very concept of such a logic, irrespective, for example, of whether that concept be projected in a Marxist materialist or a Hegelian idealist framework. It is very important to notice that the non-Marxist version of the "logic without ontology" position, while it often presents itself as neutral about ontology, seldom presents itself as neutral about logic, although a "logic without ontology" position could easily be conceived (I think, in fact, more easily conceived) as allowing for a diversity of logics, even as it allows for a diversity of ontologies, than as allowing merely for a diversity of ontologies, while insisting on one logic. Again, it is at least conceivable that a "logic without ontology" position might insist that the one genuine logic was not formal logic; but no one appears to hold such a combination of views.

The second of the three positions mentioned at the outset as playing influential roles in this matter is what might be characterized as the traditional or classic Marxist view. Contrasting most sharply with the "logic without ontology" thesis, this position, as I understand it, is that there are relations between ontology and logic, and that these relations are such that the question whether the content of a given system of logic is correct depends on the relation between that content and the basic situation in ontology. That is, principles of logic, to be correct, right, adequate or true (these adjectives are here intended as synonyms) must reflect, conform to, fit in with, or correspond to (these verbs are here intended as synonyms) the basic conditions of existence, the basic ontological situation, whatever that actually is. Furthermore (and I state this additionally because it is conceivable that there are some who might agree with what has just been said, but disagree with the holding that is about to be adduced), the classic Marxist position holds not only that correct logical principles reflect or correspond to the basic conditions of actual existence, but that what makes them correct, the standard and measure of the degree of their correctness, is the degree of fidelity, accuracy, with which they reflect, conform to or correspond to the most general conditions of actual existence. It is the business of logic, as a field of study, to find out and express those basic rules and principles which it is necessary to use in the process of thinking about what exists in order to attain certain results in relation to existence. Logical fitness is thus determined by the nature of existence. Thinking is thinking *about* some form of existence. It is in fact always a process of conceptually relating some form or part of existence to another form or part of existence. Implicit in the classic Marxist position as I see it is the view that correct thinking means to think the correct relations, and that the correct relations are the ones given and pervasive in existence, as opposed to those not given and not pervasive in existence. The correct relations are given in and by existence generically, and discovered in and by thought. They are not arbitrarily invented by thought and imposed on the rest of existence.

If they were really invented by thought independently of what existence was already like, and then somehow imposed on existence, how would we know which of such inventions were correct, right, true or adequate? The classic Marxist position seems to me to be pointing out that if anyone is disposed to answer this question by saying that the correct logical relations, in the sense of the correct rules and principles of logic (for example, noncontradiction and excluded middle as asserted by the formal logician) are correct because they are the ones which fit in so well with the rest of existence, this answer is obviously another way of saying their correctness is judged by their conformance with the basic conditions of existence, which is not logic without ontology, but logic justified, certified as correct, by ontology.

If on the other hand the respondent answers by saying the basic logical principles are arbitrary rules of a game, the next question is obvious: why not more than one game? In that case we might still have logic without ontology, but we would have more than one logic (e.g., a logic that reverses all the basic rules of formal logic). We would also have a still unanswered question: why do so many display such a stubborn fondness for one set of rules (those of formal logic)? If the respondent chooses another tack, saying these rules and principles are just the correct ones, self-evidently, intuitively correct, so that they need be traced to nothing else, then it will be pointed out that nothing need be taken as self-evident which can be justified by reference to something else; nothing is primitive or independent if it is grounded in something else, to which it demonstrably conforms.

Old-fashioned philosophers used to speak of logical principles which had to be accepted as self-evident because their alleged intuitive certainty was so clearly and distinctly perceived by the mind, or because the mind was allegedly incapable of conceiving their contraries in any acceptable sense. But the history of knowledge makes one wary; so many self-evident principles have had to be modified in the light of other evidence. In this case the classic Marxist position suggests that the reason such principles as noncontradiction and excluded middle seem self-evident and universally inviolable is that all our experience, all actual things and events seem to express and conform to these patterns. (I deliberately choose the word "seem" because, for these principles to gain acceptance as self-evident and universally inviolable it is not at all necessary that the basic, pervasively inescapable and constantly repeated conditions of existence should actually be as these principles pronounce, but only that they should so appear.)

It would do no good at this point to invoke the distinction, as usually made, between the logical and the psychological. It would be a clear case of *petitio principii*, since the very issue is whether the logical does or does not derive its logical content, or vital aspects of that content, from outside itself, from another level. The issue is whether the essence of that content, in whole or part is or is not in the nature of a reflection, a summation, an expression of something that is not itself, of something to which it must finally answer in order to be itself, in order to realize its own essence. The issue is whether logic is derivative or nonderivative. "Logic without ontology" makes logic nonderivative, unless there is to be an as yet unhinted denouement in which logic will be derived from something other than ontology. Barring such unlikely surprises, logic, the correctness of correct thinking, is conceived as existent but underived. Is not this an immaculate conception, and have not immaculate conceptions long since been reserved to the gods? Is a finite, nonderivative existence explicable? If it is, what is the explanation?

It must be kept in mind, too, that the question here is not whether the mental process of thinking has a neurological origin. I suppose we now all grant that. The question is whether the correctness of correct thinking is genetically related to anything, whether the quality of validity attaching to logic has any genesis at all, not in the sense of a neurological impulse, a physiological system or a social stream of experience (all those things might conceivably have been fundamentally different from what they are, while the quality of validity attaching to logic remained the same) but in the sense of something which, when *it* underwent fundamental change, or were conceived fundamentally differently, would necessitate fundamental changes in the very quality of validity attaching to logic. The classic Marxist position says, it seems to me, that there is something of that kind, from which the most basic principles of logic are demonstrably derivative. This something may be summed up as the most basic ontological conditions. The rest of the story is of course that the classic Marxist position finds these conditions to be dialectically dynamic rather than formalistically static. The whole point about the effort toward a dialectical theory of logic is to try to do justice to those dynamics.

But the fact that must be noticed and emphasized at this point is that whether or not a single significant contribution has yet been made toward a detailed system and theory of materialist dialectical logic, in the sense that there is a detailed system and theory of formal logic, the issue that remains primary is whether there are probatively significant relations between ontology and logic, whatever kind of logic is right. In this connection, it seems to me very strange that proponents of the universal adequacy of formal logic, at least those in the so-called bourgeois world, often identify themselves with the essential position of Aristotle and at the same time seem to want to stand on the ground of logic without ontology. No doubt it seemed that logic would be purer, and its formal systematization easier to defend as eternally and universally valid if it were considered to have had a sort of virgin birth. But perhaps that is a naive notion of purity, and it certainly does not make anything easier to defend on a rational basis. Aristotle himself was made of sterner stuff, and never dreamed of standing on such tenuous ground. He was not the kind of positivist who feels comfortable in a vacuum. He saw his logic as based on his ontology; he saw a probative relation between the two, and defended his logic on that ground. If anyone needs confirmation of this, let him look at "Metaphysics," 1005^{b} 6-34 and 1061^{b} 17-19, to cite only two passages. The first reads:

Evidently then it belongs to the philosopher, i.e., to him who is studying the nature of all substance, to inquire also into the principles of syllogism. But he who knows best about each genus must be able to state the most certain principles of his subject, so that he whose subject is existing things qua existing must be able to state the most certain principles of all things. This is the philosopher, and the most certain principle of all is that regarding which it is impossible to be mistaken; for such a principle must be both the best known (for all men may be mistaken about things which they do not know), and non-hypothetical. For a principle which everyone must have who understands anything that is, is not a hypothesis; and that which everyone must know who knows anything, he must already have when he comes to a special study. Evidently, then, such a principle is the most certain of all; which principle this is, let us proceed to say. It is, that the same attribute cannot at the same time belong and not belong to the same subject and in the same respect; we must presuppose, to guard against dialectical objections, any further qualifications which might be added. This, then, is the most certain of all principles, since it answers to the definition given above. For it is impossible for anyone to believe the same thing to be and not to be, as some think Heraclitus says. For what a man says, he does not necessarily believe; and if it is impossible that contrary attributes should belong at the same time to the same subject (the usual qualifications must be presupposed in this premise too), and if an opinion which contradicts another is contrary to it, obviously it is impossible for the same man at the same time to believe the same thing to be and not to be; for if a man were mistaken on this point he would have contrary opinions at the same time. It is for this reason that all who are carrying out a demonstration reduce it to this as an ultimate belief; for this is naturally the starting point even for all the other axioms.

The second passage states: "Since even the mathematician uses the common axioms only in a special application, it must be the business of first philosophy to examine the principles of mathematics also."

In the light of what has been said, we see that the non-Marxist protagonists of formal logic or Aristotelian logic fall into two groups, relative to the question here being discussed. One group, including Aristotle himself, would say that what is correct at the logical level is determined by the situation at the ontological level, by what is true of all existence taken generically. This is logic with ontology. The other group says the correctness of formal logic is not dependent on the ontological situation—logic without ontology. In other words, "logic without ontology" is not the same thing as the Aristotelian logic of Aristotle. It is Aristotelian logic without Aristotle, at least in relation to the issue we are discussing— ontology and logic. In a way, Aristotle, on that issue, always stood closer to the classic Marxist position than to the position taken by positivist formal logicians oriented towards "logic without ontology." This situation has long been reflected in many ways in Soviet writings. An early example is the book about Aristotle written by Alexandrov.[2]

Perhaps we need not dwell at length upon the fact that the classic Marxist position does not represent a wholesale rejection of formal logic, which is regarded as fitting and proper for certain areas, certain types of problem, certain aspects of thought. What is rejected is the claim that formal logic is adequate for all areas, types, and aspects. Generally speaking, the situation appears to be that supporters of dialectical logic conceive of it as including formal logic, while many supporters of formal logic conceive of *it* as excluding the possibility of dialectical logic.

We come now to the third of the three positions mentioned at the outset. This is a position that has emerged within the Marxist world fairly recently, during the last two decades. In the course of the first project of philosophic research which the present writer undertook in the Soviet Union from 1935 to 1937, this position could not have been said to exist in any significant degree. Now it exists in the Soviet Union, not to a predominant, but to a significant extent, and in certain Marxist countries, especially Poland, to a large and predominant extent. A good example of the Polish approach may be seen in the work of Adam Schaff, some of which is available in English, e.g., his paper, "Marxist Dialectics and the Principle of Contradiction," in *The Journal of Philosophy* (March 31, 1960). By 1957-1958, when I spent another academic year of research in the Soviet Union, there was already a considerable group of younger logicians, a leading figure among whom is Zinoviev, whose work has this new orientation, as well as certain veteran philosophers of high academic standing and much-published work, like Bakradze and Kol'man, who were early champions of the new position. If one talks with those philosophers, and with Soviet philosophers of the more classic viewpoint, such as Rozental' and Kopnin, as well as specialists in various aspects of logic and semantics, like Brutian, Tavanets, Mshvenieradze, Narskii and Gorskii, whose writings are numerous, one sees that the new position, while not predominant, has affected the classic position, and influenced new developments in it. A 1962 Soviet work, *Filosofskie voprosy sovremennoi formal'noi logiki* [Philosophical problems of contemporary formal logic], a collection of papers under the editorship of Tavanets, published by the Institute of Philosophy of the U.S.S.R. Academy of Sciences, constitutes an interesting and substantial expression of aspects both of the new orientation and its influence on the classic position. Seven of its twelve papers appear in English in the translation journal, *Soviet Studies in Philosophy* (Summer-Fall 1963). The new position is, of course, openly promulgated in university courses, lectures and discussions, as well as in publications, and has continued its influence.

What does the new position assert? Basically, that there is only one logic, which, in all fundamental respects, is formal logic. This means, for example, that the traditional principles of noncontradiction must be accepted as universally mandatory. Contradiction, in the formal sense of that term, is simply inadmissible. It is logically impossible to introduce contradiction of that kind into rational discourse, and it is equally impossible that there should be objective contradiction in things themselves.

Of course, such a position taken by Marxists immediately raises a whole series of interesting questions, *ad hominem* and *ad rem*. In a very blunt summary, the dialogue proceeds somewhat as follows. Is not the Marxist literature, from Marx and Engels on, full of reference to contradictions objectively existing in things? It is, but careful examination will usually reveal that what is termed contradiction is not really contradiction in the formal sense, but is actually some sort of conflict, or clash of opposing forces, the truth of which does not violate the principle of noncontradiction. How about the passage in *Anti-Dühring* wherein Engels flatly states that movement itself is a contradiction, precisely in the sense in which formal logic construes contradiction? Engels was mistaken, having been misled by an erroneous conception of the nature of motion, derived largely from Hegel. (I was present at a well-attended lecture given by Bakradze at the Institute of Philosophy in Tbilisi where he stated this view explicitly and emphatically. I heard the same thesis expounded by Kol'man at the central Institute of Philosophy in Moscow and by philosophers in Soviet Armenia.) How about ontology? The only correct ontology is dialectical materialist ontology; but this does not mean that logic must be dialectical. Formal logic is in principle adequate to the expression and validation of the logical relationships found in a correct dialectical ontology.

As arising in the Marxist context, there is still much that is not clear about the nature of this position, as well as about the manner of its vindication. While, as William James once remarked, in the early stages of philosophic trends, a certain degree of vagueness is what best consists with fertility, clarity must be sought in turn. For example, are we dealing with another case of logic without ontology? In Marxism, surely there is no neutrality, either subjective or objective, about ontology. The general laws of dialectics represent sharp and clear ontological commitments, a typical manifestation of which may be seen with particular force in the debate on the relation of philosophy to science between A. J. Ayer and the Soviet philosophers Kuznetsov and Kedrov which appeared in the Russian journal *Voprosy filosofii* [Problems of philosophy], and is now available in English, unabridged, in the first and second numbers, 1962, of the translation journal, *Soviet Studies in Philosophy*. Is the new position to be taken as asserting that the strong commitment at the ontological level need not affect what is constructed at the logical level? Prima facie, this would be rather odd, since ontology, in being ontology, is naturally the sort of thing which is generalized, pervasive, which can be expected as Aristotle pointed out above, to affect everything.

If, alternatively, the new position is to be taken as asserting that the dialectical commitment at the ontological level does affect theory of logic, but not to the extent of making necessary a dialectical theory of logic, but only something that might perhaps be called a dialectical theory of formal logic, then precisely what would that be, in the view of those who would reject the conception of a dialectical logic? In other words, what would be the nature and extent of a dialectical approach to formal logic if it accepted the claims of formal logic to eternal, universal, unconditional and exclusive validity?

It should be noticed at this point that dialectical logicians have always spoken of a dialectical approach to formal logic in a way which recognizes great value in the systematized apparatus of formal logic, but denies its claims to eternal, universal, unconditional and exclusive validity. The general view taken by dialectical logicians is that formal logic can make truly great claims, but they are relative to area and problem. The attempt to absolutize them, whether made in terms of a particular ontology, such as Aristotle's, or in a vacuum, such as in the "logic without ontology" approach, has not succeeded. It is interesting and significant that one sees in contemporary Soviet writings a tendency to refer to aspects of what was traditionally called formal logic as mathematical logic, a tendency which is of course not confined to Soviet writings. The suggestion is that that type of logic might best be viewed as the methodology of relating abstractions at the mathematical level, a very broad level, but far from exhaustive.

A point of central importance in relation to the new position is the handling of Engels' thesis concerning motion. Engels said: "Motion itself is a contradiction; even simple mechanical change of place can only come about through a body at one and the same moment of time being in one place and in another place, being in one and the same place and also not in it. And the continuous assertion and simultaneous solution of this contradiction is precisely what motion is."[3] Implicit in Engels' reasoning is the conception that a moment of time, even the tiniest instant, is a duration, an interval during which something happens. Time is obviously a flow, in which things happen. If we could not say that much, then we would not be able to say that the world (or the self) had a history. In that case there probably would be no problem. The problem arises after we have perceived that there are events, happening in sequence. If this is real, what follows? It seems quite clear that if time were made up of moments or instants during which or at which nothing happens, then nothing would ever happen or move, as Zeno saw long ago. However, if things do happen and move, it must be that even the smallest instant or interval of time is a flow. What Engels is saying, then, is that motion of anything is a process during which the moving thing is both at a given point and beyond that given point (in the sense of "being in one and the same place and also not in it," not simply in the sense of one part being in and another part not) during the smallest possible instant of time; and that if this were not possible, then there would be no motion.

Now this assertion, that moving body X is simultaneously (during the same instant of time) at point Y and not at point Y, is recognized by all concerned to be a contradiction, as formal logic construes contradiction. But if body X could not manage that, then it could never move, since the only other alternative would keep it at point Y, or some other point, at every nonflowing instant. If all instants were instants at which a given thing is stationary, it is obvious there could never be a time at which anything could move, as time is by definition made of instants. The alternative is that time is made up of instants during which a change takes place, which means the possibility of a simultaneous A and non-A, the possibility of the same part of X simultaneously being at Y and not being at Y. Strictly speaking there are no instants *at* which, only instants *during* which. (But among these are instants during which the changes taking place in A make no difference to a certain problem, instants during which the motion of X makes no difference in relation to a certain point of view and a certain scale of measurement.)

Thus we must choose between the reality of motion and the adequacy of formal logic, assuming its adequacy to be bound up with this conception of noncontradiction. It seems hard to blame anyone for choosing the reality of motion; but it must immediately be emphasized that this does not mean that the dialectical logician is saying that formal logic is good for nothing. He is only saying that it is not good for change, motion. This again does not mean that formal logic cannot make a constructive contribution to the solution of problems where change or motion is concerned. It can make such a contribution because specific problems where motion or change is concerned also have other aspects and dimensions; and innumerable important problems can be and are raised in relation to which the change and motion taking place can be disregarded. For example, in a criminal trial, the answer to the question, "what is your name," might be a matter of life or death. To answer that question truthfully, one would have no need of dialectical categories; the categories of formal logic are quite adequate. That is the kind of problem which, in the sense raised, can be solved while disregarding the change or motion taking place. But if I am asked to give a true account of how something got to be what it is I will ultimately have to face the fact that a thing called A is continuously changing in all of its parts all of the time into non-A, which means it is non-A as well as A, which takes me beyond formal categories into dialectical categories.

Frequently critics of the concept of dialectical logic seem to assume that this logic would say that every judgment made in accordance with the principle of noncontradiction is to be thrown out (or every contradictory judgment admitted), as if it would challenge such judgments as, either my key is in my pocket or it is not; and insist that we must always say, my key is both in my pocket and not in my pocket. But we have seen that the concept of dialectical logic is not of this character. It says that contradiction must be asserted. It does not say that noncontradiction must not be asserted, that only contradiction can be asserted. There is also no point in adducing the fact that protagonists of dialectical logic use formal logic; they urge that it be used wherever fitting. There is in fact no reason whatever that formal logic should not be used, though not necessarily exclusively, in an argument in support of dialectical logic.

One further point before drawing to a close: it is interesting to note that contemporary writings of Soviet dialectical logicians, doubtless in part reacting to the challenge of the newer positions, emphasize the necessity of keeping discourse free from logical confusion, in the spirit of the principle of noncontradiction, combining this necessity with the equal necessity of acknowledging and expressing whatever contradictions are found in actual existence. The possibility of reconciliation is seen on the ground that if there be objective reason to assert simultaneously two contradictory propositions, then there is binding reason not to deny such a simultaneous assertion, thus implementing the principle of noncontradiction in respect of the pair of contradictions taken jointly. For example, M. M. Rozental', long a leading figure in the area of Soviet dialectical logic, wrote as follows in his 1960 book *Printsipy dialekticheskoi logiki* [Principles of dialectical logic] :

Thus in judgments reflecting contradictions inherent in dialectical existence, contradictions in the evolution of the phenomena of the objective world, there are no logical contradictions in the previously indicated sense of that term, and the law of formal logic concerning the inadmissibility of such contradictions is fully observed. If I, pronouncing the judgment that matter is continuous and discontinuous, at the same time asserted something directly opposite to this scientific truth, then I would have actually introduced confusion into my thought. But it is impossible to characterize the accurate reflection of real contradiction in things as logical confusion. One possibility or the other: either we acknowledge these existing dialectical contradictions, and necessarily, along with that, the inevitability of their reflection in the logical form of judgments, or we do not acknowledge them, in which case it becomes possible to assert whatever is convenient, since our procedure would already have passed out of the bounds of the scientific approach to reality.[4]

This paper has not tried to set forth systematically the evidentiary factors which point to the possibility and need for a dialectical logic. That would call for a great deal of detail, some of which the present writer has tried to supply else-where.[5] The fact is there is something prior to the problem of the adequacy of formal logic or the possibility of dialectical logic, namely, the problem of the interrelations of ontology and logic. The latter problem contains the key to the solution of the former.

NOTES

1. Richard McKeon, ed., trans. Ross, *Basic Works of Aristotle* (New York: Random House, 1941), pp. 736-737, 856. In the context of these passages "the philosopher" means, of course, the ontologist or metaphysician, as "first philosophy" means meta-physics or ontology, and "to examine" means with a view to validation.

2. G. Aleksandrov, *Aristotle* (Moscow: Sotsekgiz, 1940). This work has not been translated into English. An abstract of it by the present writer appears in *Philosophic Abstracts*, No. 10 (1941).

3. *Anti-Dühring*, trans. Burns (New York: International Publishers, 1939), chap. 12, p. 137.

4. M. M. Rozental', *Printsipy dialekticheskoi logiki* [*Principles of dialectical logic*] (Moscow: Izdatel'stvo Sotsial'no-Ekonomicheskoi Literatury, 1960), p. 314. Translation J. S.

5. See John Somerville, *The Philosophy of Marxism: An Exposition* (New York: Random House, 1967), especially chaps. 1-2.

Chapter 6

Comments on Professor Somerville's Paper

IRVING M. COPI

Irving M. Copi is professor of philosophy at the University of
Michigan and has taught at the University of Illinois and the
University of Hawaii. A Guggenheim Fellow and recipient of
other awards, he is the author of *Introduction to Logic* (1953,
1968) and *Symbolic Logic* (1954, 1967). He is the co-editor
of *Readings on Logic* (1964), *Contemporary Readings in Logical
Theory* (1967), and *Essays on Wittgenstein's Tractatus* (1966).

In discussing Professor Somerville's stimulating paper, I should
like to begin by acknowledging some broad areas of agreement.
First of all, I agree that ontology is a legitimate and important
area of study. I agree also that logic is importantly related to
it, perhaps even dependent on it in some sense. That sense,
however, is not easy to explain, because much broader and
deeper advances have been made in logic than in ontology. It
is tempting to say that ontology is prior to logic in the order
of being but not in the order of knowledge. However, I doubt
that this way of speaking is very helpful.

Although I share Professor Somerville's rejection of what he
calls the "logic without ontology" position, I do not share all
of his beliefs about it. I dispute his claim that supporters of
that position maintain that it is impossible to construct systems
of logic which would deny the principles of identity, noncontradiction, or excluded middle. Systems of many-valued

logics have been developed largely by logicians and mathematicians who either pay no attention to, or else explicitly reject, ontology. And many vexing issues centering around identity—especially in modal contexts—have been brilliantly discussed by such logicians.

It is good to hear of the emergence in the Marxist world of a "new orientation" against self-contradiction. I am delighted to learn that some Marxist philosophers may be ready to abandon the confusing jargon in which they used to assert the existence of "objective contradictions in things themselves." I have long held that the examples traditionally supposed to illustrate such contradictions are really conflicts, or clashes of opposing forces, rather than violations of the principle of noncontradiction.

Marxists were not the first to notice conflicts in human history, but their philosophy of history wisely emphasized the pervasiveness of such conflicts. I find much to admire in the insights of dialectical materialism: that change often occurs through conflict, and that innovations in the material means of production often underlie changes in the forms of society. Recent technological changes in both production and destruction, as well as in communication and control, seem to me to herald and to require new forms of political, economic, and social organization inconceivable to the nineteenth-century mind. It is surprising that dialectical materialists fail to appreciate this trend and thus break faith with their own basic philosophical position. Some cultural lag is to be expected, of course, but this constant dedication to century-old slogans and dogmas by self-styled apostles of change is remarkable.

I agree with Professor Somerville that Engels' thesis concerning motion is important, but I cannot agree that it is correct. It does not establish or reveal a contradiction, but rather presupposes one. If we speak only of finite time intervals, then no contradiction at all arises from the obvious fact that during one and the same interval a body can be both at a specified point Y and not at point Y. For it can be at Y earlier in the interval and not at Y later in the interval. The contradiction reached by Engels and Professor Somerville has nothing to do with motion but rather arises from what is referred to as "the conception that a moment of time, even the tiniest instant, is a duration, an interval." Any duration or interval has an earlier half and a later half, each of which is itself a

duration or interval. Hence, there can be no tiniest duration.
So "tiniest duration" is as self-contradictory as "round square"
or "extensionless area." If we want to speak only of durations,
there can be no "tiniest" part of time. If we want to speak of
a tiniest part of time, it must be an instant that has no duration.

To argue that because the whole of time is extended, therefore every part of time is extended, is fallacious. It is as
fallacious as Leibniz's argument that because the crashing of
a wave is audible, therefore the "crashing" of each single
drop of water must be audible as well. The fallacy involved is
that of division, in which what is true of a whole is wrongly
inferred to be true of each of its parts. One might as well
argue that because a family is made up of persons, therefore
each member of a family must be made of persons, or that because a chair contains seat, back, legs, rungs, etc., therefore each
part of a chair must also contain seat, back, legs, rungs, etc.

A more useful analysis of motion, time, and space involves
the mathematical continuum conceived as an ordered set of
extensionless points or instants. These least parts are not
spatial intervals or temporal durations, but indivisible entities
that have location but not extension. Given this conception of
an instant, we can see the mistake in the Engels-Somerville
dichotomy: must a thing be either in motion or at rest at
any instant? A thing is neither—*at an instant*: motion and rest
can occur only over a temporal interval. The thing is at rest
during an interval if it occupies the same position at every
instant of the interval; it is in motion during the interval if it
occupies different positions at different instants of the interval.
But how do we get movement from what are not movements?
No miracle is involved here any more than in getting families
from persons who are not themselves families, or chairs from
parts that are not themselves miniature chairs. Motion involves
no more contradiction than does a family. The latter may
involve conflict, but scarcely requires its members to be both
persons and not persons at one and the same time.

To point out the mistake in a doctrine is never the whole
story. One must also explain how it happened, what made the
mistake tempting. I think the history of mathematics provides
an answer. Early formulations of the calculus were radically
defective. They posited an "actual infinitesimal" supposed to
be at once greater than zero and less than any positive number.
Although criticized with great acuteness by Berkeley, it was

not replaced by the more satisfactory theory of limits until early in the nineteenth century. Itself absurd, this "actual infinitesimal" served admirably as a mathematical account of the nonsense of a minimum momentary or instantaneous interval of time during which a thing could simultaneously both be and not be at a specified position. But by Engels' time the "actual infinitesimal" had been banished. The mathematics of his day lent no support to his philosophy of motion, which was more closely related to the already obsolete mathematics of the seventeenth and eighteenth centuries. I suggest that it was ignorance of the science of his day that led Engels to this particular blunder.

There is something very odd about this new Marxist orientation against self-contradiction, as Professor Somerville explains it. The logic is to be consistent but the ontology self-contradictory. This is even more radical a separation of logic from ontology than that criticized by Professor Somerville in the early part of his paper. It signals a complete abandonment of ontology by Soviet logicians. And to the extent that Soviet ontologists are committed to the self-contradictions embraced by Engels, I cannot blame Soviet logicians for abandoning ontology in favor of mathematical logic. The official commitment to contradiction in ontology, I suspect, is political rather than philosophical. It certainly is not *logical.* What are the prospects for a reversal of this tendency, for a revived interest in first philosophy in Communist countries? I fear that they are minimal while politics determines ontological orthodoxy—or even while there is any ontological orthodoxy, however determined. It is much to be hoped that the Marxists' recent de-Stalinization of the party will be followed soon by a de-Engelsization of the party's philosophy.

Chapter 7

A Comment on Professor Somerville's Paper

MAX BLACK

Susan Linn Sage Professor of Philosophy at Cornell University,
Max Black is also director of the Society for the Humanities there.
He has been a Guggenheim Fellow and a Fellow at the Center for
Advanced Study in the Behavioral Sciences, and has held other
fellowships. Former president of the Eastern Division of the
American Philosophical Association, he is the author of *The
Nature of Mathematics* (1933, 1950), *Critical Thinking* (1946,
1951), *Language and Philosophy* (1949), *Problems of Analysis*
(1954), *The Labyrinth of Language* (1968), and other works.

Professor Somerville raises what he regards as the fundamental
question of the relations between logic and ontology. So far as
I can tell, he is asserting the following propositions:

1. Logic is not an autonomous discipline: the ground of
validity of logical truths is to be found in something outside
logic, *viz.* in the degree to which "they reflect, conform to or
correspond to the most general conditions of actual existence."
(For example, the evidence for the principle of contradiction
is grounded in the circumstance that "all actual things and
events seem to express and conform" to it.)
2. Familiar principles of logic, such "the principles of
identity, noncontradiction and excluded middle," are not

75

universally true: there are, for instance, situations in which "contradiction must be asserted."

The first of these assertions would convert logic (and I suppose mathematics also) into a branch of physics. The second would require us to view the principles of logic and mathematics as having only limited application—true for some domains of experience, false for others. Both assertions then seem to me to arise from elementary confusions about the character of logical and mathematical propositions.

I suppose the "principle of identity" might be rendered in logical symbolism as the proposition: (x) $(x=x)$. Suppose a student were to challenge me to give grounds for its truth. It would be the height of absurdity for me to answer: "Look around you! You will invariably find that the sun is the sun, a dime is a dime, your handkerchief is your handkerchief, and similarly, without any exception, that everything is itself." Far better to say nothing. If anything at all is clear about the "principle of identity" it is that it is *not* a generalization from experience. If it were, some verifiable sense would need to be attached to the form of words, "x is in fact not x but something else." But of course no such sense attaches to it. There is no such thing as verifying in experience that a thing is identical with itself. If Somerville had fully grasped this elementary point (which has, of course, been made a thousand times) he could have spared himself the writing of most of his paper. That the "principle of identity" should be a priori or necessarily true is, no doubt, puzzling to philosophers— especially to those with an exaggerated respect for the importance of sensory experience. But that is their affair. No amount of pretentious talk about the relations of ontology and logic, and no invocation of the dubious authority of Aristotle, can make any difference to this simple starting point. If anybody thinks, to vary the example, that the truth of $1 + 1 = 2$ is certified by looking at pebbles and lumps of sugar, he shows such a lack of understanding of what goes on in arithmetic that any serious discussion with him about the philosophy of mathematics would be pointless.

It would be startling indeed if examination of experience could show that the traditional principles of logic were sometimes false. Somerville's argument to this effect does not inspire confidence. He cites, with apparent approval, the hackneyed and muddled text from Engels in which it is alleged that "motion is a contradiction" and that a moving body is constantly "asserting" and simultaneously "solving" this contradiction. That an inanimate body should assert anything at all does not strike Somerville as being odd. At any rate, he himself is prepared to assert that the moving body "is simultaneously (during the same instant of time) at point Y and not at point Y." Well, what does Somerville mean by an "instant"? If he really means an instantaneous moment, then he really *is* contradicting himself, in the most elementary fashion (and with no more cause for self-complacency than in any other case of gross and overt inconsistency). But if by "instant" he means a small *interval* of time, then, of course, there is no logical contradiction in saying that during such an interval a moving body will at one instant be at Y and at another instant during the same interval will not be at Y.

There is evidence that Somerville is led into this confusion by thinking that unless a body both is and is not in a given position at a given instant, it cannot be moving, but must be at rest. But, *pace* Zeno, this is a nonsequitur. Whether a body is at rest or in motion is not determined by its instantaneous position but by its behavior during an extended time-interval.

If this is the kind of reasoning that "dialectical logic" encourages, the chief function of that pseudodiscipline would seem to be to facilitate conceptual confusion. It is encouraging to learn from Professor Somerville's report that some such realization is at last becoming moderately respectable in Soviet quarters (see his last quotation from Rozental'). It is time to let the ghost of Engels rest. There are better things to do than to trudge down these old ruts.

Chapter 8

Alienation and Dialectical Logic

HARRY K. WELLS

Harry K. Wells is now a practicing psychologist in New York City.
He has held positions in philosophy at Columbia University and
Hartwick College. He is the author of *Process and Unreality* (1950),
Pragmatism: Philosophy of Imperialism (1954), *Pavlov and Freud*
(1956-1960), and *The Failure of Psychoanalysis* (1963), and has
contributed to journals and encyclopedias at home and abroad.

In Western Europe and North America it has become fashionable to characterize the twentieth century by the descriptive
term "alienation." By "alienation" is meant the estrangement
of man from nature, from fellow men, from society, from
ethical and esthetic values, from reason—from, that is, the
entire range of human relationships and capacities that constitute human nature. The core of alienation is then said to be
the loss of identity of oneself as a human being.

The classified description of alienation in all its apparently
endless forms gives rise to one or another type of multiple
factor theory of the causality of the phenomenon. Alienation
is attributed to a nexus of factors including industrialization,
technology, science, the profit system of economy, urbaniza-
tion, mass man, mass media, the giant impersonal state and
corporation, conformity, individualism, collectivism, and so
on. These factors, with here more emphasis on one, there on
another, are said to form the class of alienating conditions.

They are the social, economic and historical circumstances that give rise to the individual feelings of estrangement characteristic of twentieth-century man: anxiety, hostility, aloneness, hopelessness, powerlessness, meaninglessness, and so on. These feelings comprise the psychological syndromes of alienation variously termed the "mal du siècle," "the age of anxiety," "the human predicament," or "the neurotic personality of our time."

Factorial conditions and symptomatic syndromes are the two most general classes under one or the other of which the subclasses of the phenomena of alienation are subsumed. This classificatory approach almost invariably leads either to the optimistic proposal of a romantic return to some presumably more integrated kind of social-individual community or to the pessimistic prediction of a garrison state with imposed integration leading ultimately to total atomic destruction. Even when the solution is seen to lie in some form of "socialism," the welter of variously classified phenomena of alienation provides no structural approach that could indicate how such a system could be achieved. The "socialist" solution of alienation thereby becomes utopian. The romanticism of the two optimistic solutions—the return to previous forms of integration and the advance to utopian socialism—readily give way to the pessimism of the totalitarian state and nuclear annihilation. The general conclusion from the classificatory analysis is that alienation is the price man pays for progress and therefore is a salient feature of the human condition. A historically constituted phenomenon is thus transformed into a metaphysical principle: the principle of absurdity, namely, that the more man adapts the environment to his needs and aspirations the more divorced he becomes from both the environment and himself. Such a conclusion is writ large and most graphically in the philosophy of existentialism, in the psychology of psychoanalysis, in the theatre of the absurd, and in the novel of the alienated man.

The first step in understanding any phenomenon is the classification of the subject matter. In a similar manner the first stage of any science is classification. For example, in botany and biology the first stage, lasting some 2,500 years, was concerned with the classification of plants and animals; in astronomy, with the classification of kinds of stellar bodies;

in history, with the classification of kinds of societies; and in psychology, with the classification of psychic qualities. The philosophical categories relevant to this first stage of science were, among others: the static or unchanging; isolation and analysis without distortion; space as the room in which things exist; time as simple duration; motion as limited to locomotion; and causation as an external relation of push or pull.

The logic relevant to the first stage of the sciences was rooted in the principle of identity—a phenomenon is what it is: A is A; the principle of contradiction—a phenomenon cannot be at one and the same time what it is and what it is not: A is not not-A; and finally the principle of excluded middle—a phenomenon is either what it is or what it is not, either A or not-A. These principles are minimal requirements for the purposes of definition and classification and do in fact reflect actual levels of objective reality, including the material world, language, logic, and thought. The logic based on the three principles was the logic of classification with its paired categories of class and member, genus and species, universal and individual, general and particular, quality and quantity, one and many, and so on. The structure of classes reflecting—in language—the structure of ontological levels was mirror-imaged in the classificatory syllogism: the major premise as the relation between genus and species, including and included, excluding and excluded classes; the minor premise as the relation between individual and species, member and class; and the conclusion as the inferred relation between individual and genus, member and including or excluding class.

Classificatory logic underlies the approach to the question of alienation as outlined earlier. It is thus the necessary first step of understanding the nature of the phenomenon. The organizing mutually exclusive classes of alienation and alienating conditions on the one hand, and under alienation the suborganizing classes of existential alienation of the individual and the states or feelings of alienation of the individual on the other, together with the wealth of detailed specific classes subsumed under each, constitute an indispensable beginning in the attempt to understand alienation. The analysis into parts and the synthesis into external classificatory relationships organize the myriad phenomena of alienation into a conceptual framework reflecting the various simultaneous

levels existing in the world and in the mind of man. The
classificatory approach, however, is not explanatory or causal
and does not therefore lead to understanding of alienation as
a process with a beginning, middle, and predictive end. It does
not, in short, provide a structure of temporal or spatial internal
interconnections which would guide man in dealing with the
phenomenon in such a manner as ultimately to transform it.
The point is not only to recognize and classify the varied
aspects of alienation as a static human condition, but to
know its causes and interval connections in order to change it.

The second stage of the investigation of any given phenomenon
is to understand its origin, development, and direction of movement, to understand it not only as a class with subclasses, but
as a process with subprocesses. The second stage of any science
is likewise characterized by concentration on process with its
equal emphasis on temporal and spatial intercommunications
and internal and external interrelations. Over the course of the
past 150 years, almost all the natural and social sciences have
made the transition from the reflection of the classificatory
structure of their subject matters to the reflection of their
developmental structures: in astronomy with Kant and Laplace;
in geology with Lyell; in logic with Hegel, Feuerbach, and Marx;
in history and political economy with Marx and Engels; in
biology with Darwin; in physics with Einstein; in physiology of
the higher nervous activity with Pavlov; and so on. As a matter
of fact, mathematics was the first to move into the structural
analysis of process with the development of the calculus by
Leibniz and Newton.

As formal or classificatory logic is the structure of classes in
general, so genetic or dialectical logic is the structure of
processes in general. In the attempt to understand alienation as
a process, then, dialectical logic is, to say the least, helpful as
a structural intellectual instrument. Here, however, intrudes a
peculiar situation, for dialectical logic has itself been a victim
of alienation.[1] In view of this fact, familiarity with it cannot
be assumed at any level, academic or otherwise. Before applying dialectical logic to the structuring of those sciences relevant
to an understanding of alienation as a process, this logic must
itself be structured.

What Hegel called "natural" logic, both classificatory and
genetic, is embodied in language. Language is the reflection
of reality in words (vocabulary of nouns, verbs, etc.) and in
sentence structure (grammar). Natural logic is the reflection

of reality in interrelated sentences structured into a line of argument (usually as an enthymeme syllogism). Over the 2 million years of human evolution, man has had to deal existentially with classification and change and has therefore had to develop linguistic and logical reflection of both classes and processes. The science of logic, like the science of linguistics, came into existence very late in man's development, only during the past 3,000 years. The semantic fact that in the case of language there is a separate and distinct name for the science, i.e., linguistics, while in the case of logic the term is the same for both the phenomenon and the science, has caused some confusion on this subject.

The historical fact that the initial task of the sciences was the classification of their respective subject matters, led to the development first of the science of classificatory logic. Thus the first stage of the development of the science of logic was classificatory or formal logic. The second stage of the sciences, based on the task of understanding their subject matters as processes, led to the second stage of the science of logic, genetic or dialectical logic. As sciences, classificatory or formal and genetic or dialectical logic constitute two successive stages in the development of the science of logic as a whole. The general science of logic, with its two historically constituted stages, is the science of the structure of the structure of reality, including both the structure of the structure of the material world and of its reflection in human consciousness by means of natural language and natural logic. If logic as a whole (as far as it has developed at this time) is the structure of the structure of the world and of thought, then classificatory or formal logic is the structure of classes in general while genetic or dialectical logic is the structure of processes in general. Each stage of the science of logic underlies and is expressed in the relevant stage of all the sciences, physical and social.

As the science of the structure of process or change in general, dialectical logic is concerned with the syllogistic reflection of beginning or origin, middle or development, and end or transformation that occur, barring catastrophic accident, seriatim in any process. Dialectical logic penetrates into the structure of this syllogism on at least four levels, moving from appearance to essence to deeper and still deeper essence.

The first level of reflection of the genetic or dialectical syllogism of process or change is concerned with the three stages of development—beginning, middle, and end—in terms of quantitative and qualitative changes. The syllogism here views the beginning or origin as the transformation of a qualitative change into quantitative change: a "new" thing or thought has come into being (originating obviously from a previous quantitative development) and begins to develop quantitatively. The middle phase of the syllogism is the quantitative development of the quality: the thing or thought remains the same only by changing and changes only by remaining the same. The end phase of the syllogism is the transformation of the quantitative change into a qualitative change: the thing or thought has remained the same only by changing and changing to the extent that it can change no more without changing into something else, a "new" quality.

There are several generalizations in regard to this first level of the dialectical syllogism. Among these are:

1. Every beginning is an end and every end is a beginning.

2. Between every beginning and end is a more or less extended development during which the quality remains the same in kind but changes in degree.

3. The concept of quantitative change includes in itself the principle of identity of formal or classificatory logic, but transformed in terms of process or change.

4. As a process, a thing or thought is an identity (A is A) only because it is changing in degree and changing in degree to the point at which it changes in kind, becoming a "new" identity (in which B is B).

5. The concept of quantitative change likewise preserves within dialectical logic the principle of contradiction since as long as a process is changing quantitatively it is not anything other than what it is (A is not not-A).

6. By the same token, the first level of the dialectical syllogism preserves the principle of excluded middle in the form of quantitative change during which the thing or thought is either this or that (either A or not-A).

7. While quantitative change preserves the three principles of formal logic, the dialectical syllogism reflects likewise the fact that identities come into being and go out of being, that they undergo qualitative change simply because they are what they are only by changing quantitatively to the point of transformation.

8. Finally, and by no means least important, what is a quanti-

tative change at one level of reality is a qualitative change at another and what is a qualitative change at one level is a quantitative change at another—this does not mean that it is arbitrary choice of abstraction that determines the kind of change involved, but rather that the abstractions of thought must, to be true, correspond to actual levels of reality.

The second level of the dialectical syllogism, penetrating more deeply into the structure of process, is concerned with the interconnections of content and form as a quality—thing or thought—moves from its beginning through its middle to its end. Involved here is one of the major categories of dialectical logic, namely, contradiction. The central feature of contradiction is that negation carries affirmation in itself and affirmation carries negation in itself. What is simultaneously negated and affirmed, and how these affirmations and negations take place, involves the interconnections between content and form.

In the beginning phase of the second or contradiction level of the dialectical syllogism, when a new quality comes into being and begins to develop quantitatively, this quality is viewed as a particular content united with a particular form, the particular form of that particular content. At the beginning, the relation of form to content is one of conformation. By conformation is meant that the form allows for the development of the content. In the middle phase of the contradiction level of the dialectical syllogism, as the quality develops quantitatively, the form still conforms to the content allowing the latter to develop, but this very fact brings the content closer and closer to the point of nonconformation of form to content. The identity of a thing or concept can now be seen to consist not only in quantitative change but also in the fact that content and form remain the same. However, they remain the same only by moving from original conformation toward ultimate nonconformation of form to content. This is part of what is signified by the term "contradiction." There is a developing contradiction between content and form. The two cannot exist apart, but at the same time they exist together only by moving from conformation to nonconformation. The change is quantitative so long as there is the same contradiction within a thing or concept, and the dialectical principle of identity consists in both these aspects. The end phase of the second level of the dialectical syllogism is the point of transformation of quantitative change into qualitative change, the point at which the form passes over into nonconformation with the content. The content breaks out of the old form and brings into being a new form, one which conforms to the new level of the developing content. This is termed the resolution of the old contradiction and the establishment of a new one.

There are a number of generalizations relevant to this second level of the dialectical syllogism, the level of contradiction. Among them are:

1. The course of movement of the contradiction from its inception to its resolution. If each step in this movement is a partial resolution of the contradiction—if, that is, the point of nonconformation of form to content takes place at the moment of closest unity of the two—then the resolution of the contradiction is said to be nonexplosive and the contradiction itself to be nonantagonistic. If on the other hand each step in the movement of the contradiction widens the gap between the form and the content—if, that is, the form moves in the opposite direction from the content—then the point of nonconformation of form to content takes place at the moment of sharpest disunity. In such an event the resolution of the contradiction is said to be explosive and the contradiction itself to be antagonistic.

2. Another generalization in regard to the contradictory level of the dialectical syllogism is concerned with the categories of negation and negation of negation. Both have to do with the point of qualitative transformation of form and content. The first negation is the bursting asunder or rejection of the form and the preservation or retention of the content. It is the "no" or negative of the form and the "yes" or affirmative of the content. This is the preservative or conservative aspect of the dialectic. The second negation, the negation of the first negation, is the sublation or raising and transforming of the content at a new level through release from the constricting confines of the old form and at the same time the establishment of a new form which initially conforms to the new level of content. This is the creative or emergence-of-novelty aspect of the dialectic.

3. The third and final level of the dialectical syllogism penetrates still further into the structure of process. Involved is the negation and negation of negation of the laws of classi-

ficatory or formal logic. Here the laws or principles are taken
in the classical sense as ontological as well as logical, as laws
of being as well as laws of thought, as, that is, laws of the
material world reflected through language and logic in the
laws of thought. Dialectical logic structures the two primary
laws of classificatory logic, the laws of identity and contradiction, into content and form. The law of identity is the
content and the law of contradiction is the form appropriate
to the classificatory content of identity. Thus the law that a
thing or thought is what it is, that A is A, is the content that
develops throughout the history of logic whether formal or
dialectical. The law of contradiction, that a thing or thought is
not what it is not, that A is not not-A, is the form this content
takes in the classificatory stage. So long as the primary task of
the sciences was classification of subject matters, this form of
the law of identity conformed to the content. The classificatory
form of identity stated that A is A and is not any unspecified
spatial or temporal not-A. A thing or thought is differentiated
from all things or thoughts other than itself. The A is a
specific and particular A, while the not-A is unspecified and
universal, including everything which A is not. It was not until
the classificatory structures of the various sciences began to
break down, when things were found that could not be classified as either this or that, that the classificatory form of identity
came into nonconformation with the content of identity. The
latter passed over from static class to dynamic process. In the
science of logic this meant that identity as process or change
required the rejection of the old form and the retention of
the content, namely identity. This break-up of the old form,
and the freeing of identity from it, constitutes the first negation of the laws of formal logic. It is the affirmation of the
content and the repudiation of the form. The second negation,
the negation of the negation, is the sublation of the content,
the raising and transforming of the old content of identity
as a static class to the new level of the content of identity as
a process having a beginning, middle, and end. This new
content of identity then requires and brings into being a new
form, one that conforms to process. This new form is the negation of the negation of the old form. It is on the one hand
the rejection of the unspecified, universal not-A and on the
other the sublation, the raising and transforming of the not-A,
the transformation of the universal not-A into a specific tem-

poral not-*A* of the identity *A*. The specific temporal not-*A* of
A is the particular past and particular future of *A* as it changes
from its beginning through its middle to its end.

The third level of the dialectical syllogism is concerned with
the negation of the negation of the laws of formal logic. The
principle of identity as process in its new form states that a
thing or thought is what it is because it is what it was and what
it is becoming. What it was and what it is becoming are specific
opposites in the sense that the past is the opposite of the future.
The new dialectical level of identity is then said to be an identity
of opposites: *A* is *A* because *A* is a specific past not-*A* and a
specific direction of change into the specific future not-*A*.
The content of identity is retained but in a new form. Instead
of being an identity excluding the universal temporal not-*A*,
it is an identity including the specific temporal not-*A*. The
cornerstone of dialectical logic is the principle or law of the
identity of opposites. Dialectical logic includes classification
within itself, but is the form of the classification of processes—
types or classes of processes. Dialectical logic is not a rejection
of formal logic, but is rather the negation and negation of
negation of it. The content of classification is preserved but
is sublated and given a new form. The dialectical syllogism
embodies this new conformation of form to content: the
structure of the process of change from one class to another
in which each class (or member) is itself a process with its
own specific temporal not-*A*, its own specific past and specific
directional future.

There are a number of generalizations in regard to the law
of the identity of opposites:

1. The opposites comprising an identity interpenetrate, enter
into, and are an internal part of one another, to such an extent
that the one cannot exist without the other. Separation is
impossible without the destruction or distortion of the identity.

2. While the opposites cannot exist apart they likewise cannot
exist together without changing one another. This is called the
conflict of opposites within an identity. The identity will
remain the same while changing quantitatively so long as it
is composed of the same opposites.

3. The opposites, however, interpenetrate, conflict, and
change one another ultimately to the point of transformation.
At this point of qualitative change the opposites destroy one

another and in so doing negate the identity. At this point the content of the identity is sublated and a new pair of opposites constitutes the new identity.

4. Every identity is composed of a single pair of opposites, but each of these opposites is an identity composed of its specific opposites.

5. Thus within any identity there is an entire structure of identities of opposites, levels within levels, stages within stages of processes.

6. Syllogistically this would be reflected as the interconnection of syllogisms moving from the more general to the more particular, from the more abstract to the more concrete—or vice versa. This structure of identities of opposites, which may be logically reflected in interconnected syllogisms, can be presented graphically.

7. Within each pair of opposites there is one that is the determining element: it brings about qualitative changes in the other, while the latter acts back again on the former to induce quantitative changes.

8. Within any structure of identities of opposites there will be a pair of opposites comprising an identity which constitutes the motive force of the entire identical process. When it moves all others will ultimately move.

9. The pair of opposites constituting the motive force will be found within the structure of opposites subsumed under the determining element. The motive force is the source of self-motion of the identity as a class, quality, thing, or thought.

There are many interconnections among the three levels of the dialectical syllogism. For example, the determining element in any pair of opposites is the content at the level of contradiction while the determined element is the form. Again, what is an identity of opposites at one level is a contradiction at another. Finally, what is an identity of opposites at one level and a contradiction at another is in both cases a quantitative change during which the class, quality, thing, or thought remains the same. Thus the content of the principle of identity is preserved, albeit in a sublated form, within dialectical logic.

The three levels of the dialectical syllogism, reflecting more and more essential levels of the structure of ontological process, are concerned explicitly with the temporal interconnections within a given identity between its specific past and specific future as they interpenetrate and conflict to comprise its ongoing present. The full dialectic, however, is found in the spatial interconnections between two inseparable identities. Each of these identities is a structure of pairs of opposites. Spatial interconnection of paired identities is concerned with the negation and negation of negation of the formal logical principles of identity and contradiction taken in their spatial signification. A class, quality, or thing is what it is, A is A, and is not anything else, A is not not-A in which the not-A refers to all things existing outside or external to A. The formal logical spatial not-A is universal. It is a distinction between A and all that is spatially not-A. The first negation of the universal spatial not-A is the rejection of the universal form and the retention of the content, the spatial not-A. The negation of this negation is the sublation of the spatial not-A, the raising and transforming of it into the specific spatial not-A of A. This new content induces a new form, the specific not-A of A is the environment of A without which neither A nor specific spatial not-A could exist.

In dealing with two identities of opposites, A and its environmental not-A, dialectical logic is concerned with the relation of categories reflecting levels of reality as subject and object, internal and external, attribute and property, necessity and accident, time and space. Each subject is an object—each A is itself an environmental not-A of its opposite—and each object is a subject—each environmental not-A of A is in itself an A. What is internal within A externalizes itself over against its environmental not-A and becomes internal to the not-A of A, and vice versa. The attributes of A and the attributes of the environmental not-A determine the properties of A in relation to not-A, and vice versa. Internal temporal necessity gives rise to external spatial accident which in turn is necessary for the internal temporal necessity of the not-A of A, and vice versa. Time is the internal development of A from its beginning to its end, but this temporal development acts spatially on, and becomes an internal part of, the temporal development of the specific spatial not-A, and vice versa. Here in the dialectic of the external or spatial interconnections of A and its specific spatial not-A, there is the reflection of the transformations of subject into object and object into subject, of internal into external and external into internal, of attribute into property and property into attribute, of necessity into accident and accident into necessity, and finally of time into space and space into time.

When these two identities in spatial relation, the A and its specific not-*A*, are viewed as opposites within an inclusive identity, they are transformed into an identity of opposites in regard to which all the laws and generalizations as well as levels of the dialectical syllogism, relevant to such identities, pertain. Therefore what is a spatial relation at one level is a temporal relation at another, and vice versa.

With the temporal and spatial negation and negation of negation of the laws of formal or classificatory logic, the entire dialectic is present, if only in outline form. Dialectical logic is seen to be the structure of the temporal and spatial interconnections of processes in general. This most abstract structure can now be applied to the more concrete, though still abstract, structuring of those sciences relevant for an understanding of the historically constituted conditions that give rise to the psychological syndrome of alienation.

Logical structure, whether of classes or of processes, is applicable to the structuring of the categories of any given phenomenon or science thereof because it is the reflection by human consciousness through language of the levels of reality at which society in its practical activity—for example in industry and in science—is dealing with the world. The practical activity of society is both the origin and verification of man's reflection of the structure of levels of reality. Logic is the reflection of the structure of the structure of reality at the level at which society is dealing with it. It is the generalization of the structure of classes and processes as they have been reflected and verified in and through the various sciences. The ultimate test of the truth of reflection is its effectiveness in guiding man's practical activity in the adaptation of the environment to man's needs and aspirations. Logic is a most abstract level of man's reflection of the world and of himself and is a true reflection in so far as it corresponds to the levels of the world at which man is working with it.

Underlying both classificatory or formal logic and genetic or dialectical logic is the reflection theory of knowledge and the correspondence theory of truth. These theories have always underlain man's practical and theoretical activity. The structuring of the categories of gnosiology—of, that is, cognition and epistemology—is one of the main tasks of dialectical logic.

Logic has ontological as well as logical reference. It is expressed in the sciences either implicitly or explicitly. Implicitly when the scientists are unaware of its employment; explicitly when they are aware of it—and to the degree to which they are so aware. Logic in both its formal and dialectical stages is fully applicable to the sciences because it is already embodied and expressed in them. The application makes explicit what is implicit. Sciences reflect levels of the world and these levels are both classes and processes at one and the same time. Thus the two levels of logic are always and everywhere embedded in the sciences, in so far as they truly reflect aspects of objective reality. The application of logic to the categories of the sciences is not a matter of forcing the latter into a mold, but of expressing the abstract structure concretely embodied in the scientific theories, laws and facts.

The sciences most relevant for understanding the existential conditions that have given rise to the psychological syndrome of alienation are history, political economy, and psychology. History in the broad sense includes the history of mind and economic and political organization. The most relevant history is the history of the production stage over the past ten thousand years. Still more relevant to the understanding of alienation is the history of capitalism and in particular the history of monopoly capitalism in the twentieth century. To grasp the nature of the production period as a whole, however, it must be set within the entire course of human history—past, present, and directional future.

The first stage of human history was the gathering stage lasting some 2 million years. In this extended period, man evolved biologically and physiologically as a species embodied genetically in the individual. But this biological and physiological evolution of the specific individual took place only over against and in inseparable connection with the development of a historically constituted society based on weapon- and tool-making with its concomitant skills. Forms of economic and social organization developed and along with them language and logic leading to reflection, in thought and emotion, of the environment at the level at which man was dealing with it by means of his skills and tools. Social consciousness, the consciousness of society embodied in institutions and social knowledge, developed in closest conjunction with social being.

In the gathering stage of human history, the basic laws of
evolution and historical development become apparent: first,
social being determines social consciousness while the latter
acts back again on the former; second, social being and social
consciousness are not only organizing classificatory categories
of society, but constitute the organizing pair of opposites
within the identity or quality which is society; third, the
structure of social being is a structure of paired categories
including the forces and relations of gathering with its tools,
raw materials, and skills on the one hand and its relations
of man to the means of gathering and to other men, on the
other; fourth, that the motive force of human history at the
gathering stage lies in the forces of gathering; fifth, that the
individual person becomes a human being only by means of
a double potentiality including on the one hand the specific
human innate biological and physiological structure and
function with which he is born and on the other, the inter-
nalization via physiologicalization through participation in
the externally existing social heritage (language, logic, thoughts,
emotions, institutions, arts, rituals, mores, skills, etc.) embodied
in the society into which he is born. The dialectical structure
of the society and of the individual as ongoing, closely interconnected processes characterized by pairs of opposites,
exhibit the features of nonantagonistic contradictions. The
common ownership of the means of gathering is the decisive
nonantagonistic contradiction. This is reflected in the social
consciousness and in the consciousness of the individual.
Psychologically, the emotions of the individual, internalized
from his society, conform to the ideas of their objects: fearing
what society confirms as fearful and expressing that fear
within the bounds of socially determined limits; hating what
is socially determined as hateful within the allowed forms of
expression; loving what is socially determined as lovable, and
so on. The syndrome of alienation as we know it today was
nowhere extant in the gathering individual. His fear, hate, love
were characteristically interconnected with the social knowledge
of the object of the emotion and with the socially determined
expression of the emotion. Hence, his fear, for example, did
not become objectless and transform into anxiety. He was an
integrated individual, in ideation and emotion, conforming to
the integrated, nonantagonistic social being and social consciousness of his society.

The direction of development of the gathering stage was toward its transformation into the production stage. While gathering, involving weapons and the animals to be gathered by their means, was the primary mode of supplying food, clothing, and shelter, production was a secondary mode. The weapons had to be shaped by means of tools skillfully applied to raw materials. During the two-million-year age of gathering, therefore, the next age of mankind was developing within it. The transformation from the gathering stage to the production stage took place at the point at which production became the primary mode, including gathering within itself—in the form of the gathering of raw materials as one aspect of production.

The very development of gathering weapons, together with the processing of what was gathered, brought with it the development of that which would eventually replace it. This movement of gathering toward production was at the same time the movement from absolute scarcity toward relative scarcity in which production gave rise to labor producing a surplus over and above the minimum amount of food, clothing, and shelter required for the continued existence of the producer. This relative scarcity as relative surplus brought into being relations of production in the form of owners and nonowners of the means of production, the tools and raw materials. This division in turn brought into being the classes based on ownership and nonownership, thus splitting social being into antagonistic contradiction. The owning class, a small minority, brought into being the state with its legal structure and armed forces to maintain its class position, thus splitting social consciousness into antagonistic contradiction between superstructure and human knowledge. The antagonistic contradictions in the social being of production society brought into being a range of antagonistic contradictions in the social practice and consciousness of the individual living within the society. Thus the transformation from the gathering age of mankind to the production age entailed the transformation from characteristically nonantagonistic contradictions to antagonistic contradictions.

The direction of development of production society is from the production of relative scarcity and relative abundance to the capacity to produce absolute abundance. The United States is rapidly approaching this capacity—if it has not already done so. At that point the forces of production strain at and

eventually break out of the private relations of production—
out of, that is, the ever more private ownership of the means
of production. The social ownership of the social forces of
production would transform the antagonistic contradiction
lying at the base of production society into a nonantagonistic
contradiction. The absolute surplus of useful products will be
made available to the people as a whole, meaning to each
individual. The abundant useful products include not only
food, clothing, and shelter, but also culturally useful products.
The reduction of the working day or week made possible by
automated, self-regulating machines, will provide the leisure
time necessary for creative and self-creative activity of the
individual. The age of production transforms into the age of
creativity.

Leisure and creativity have developed throughout the age
of production as a secondary feature of society and the
individual. This is seen in the development of professional
art and science from their beginnings in slave society to
larger and larger proportions in the final stages of capitalist
society. In the age of creativity, what was secondary in the
production age will become primary. At the same time, of
course, the age of creativity will carry within itself the production
on which it rests—just as the age of production carried within
itself the gathering on which it rested.

The transformation from the age of production to the age
of creativity will bring with it not only the abolition of
private ownership of the means of production, but likewise
the elimination of the division of society into antagonistic
classes and of the division of social consciousness into superstructure and human knowledge. The social consciousness
of creative society will ultimately become identical with
human knowledge in its artistic, scientific, and technological
forms, including the organization of production and distribution in the interests, needs, and aspirations of the individuals
living within the society. The motive power of creative society
will in all likelihood reside in the nonantagonistic contradiction
between specific levels of knowledge and ignorance constantly
transformed on more essential levels. The objective of the
creative age will at one and the same time be the advance of
social and of individual creativity—the one being the condition
for the advance of the other. The age of creativity will presumably be characterized throughout by nonantagonistic

contradictions, the form expanding with the expansion of the content, at both the social and individual levels.

The structure of the age of creativity has not yet come into being on our planet. The unconditional future tense is employed because we are on the threshold of this transformation and its coming is unavoidable. Once mankind can produce enough for every individual, then the age of creativity is at hand. The people of the United States have given proof over the past half-century that man can achieve absolute abundance—even though this very capacity looms as a colossal threat. It looms as a threat precisely because the capacity to produce an absolute surplus is squeezed within the narrow confines of private ownership of the means of production. Thereby American-human victory appears as defeat, and instead of being proud of our achievement, we cringe at its implications within our given society. Break out of the society and the achievement can be celebrated as the great human victory it is.

In such a perspective the age of production appears as a brief moment characterized on the one hand by exceedingly rapid change and on the other by sharp antagonistic contradictions that appear nowhere else in the course of human history. The relative briefness and rapidity of the changes brought about in the period of production suggests that it may be viewed as the moment of qualitative change from animal-human to human-human—in fact the transformation from animal to man. The creative society and the creative individual comprise the fully human society and individual. Anything beyond the age of creativity is inconceivable at this time—unless messages from outer space are received and decoded which could then conceivably indicate ages beyond creativity, if such messages could be understood at our earthly level of development.

The philosophical time-span, with its indication that antagonistic contradictions within mankind, social and individual, are limited to the age of production, carries with it the implication that the psychological syndrome of alienation, reflecting such contradictions, is likewise limited to this transitional age.

The syllogism of movement from the beginning of the production stage through its slave, feudal, and capitalist middle is characterized by a heightening and further heightening of antagonistic contradictions. For example, the relations of production become more and more private, more and more concentrated in fewer and fewer owners, until in monopoly capitalism this shrinkage reaches its apex. At the same time, the forces of production become more and more social, concentrating masses of workers and giant machines in one plant or complex of plants. Thus the content, the forces of production, moves in one direction while the form, the relations of production, moves in the opposite direction. Such sharpening of antagonistic contradictions are found in all spheres of monopoly capitalism.

The monopoly capitalist stage of production society is characterized by antagonistic contradictions in almost all its structure of processes with the notable exception of the forces of production. Even the latter are so interpenetrated by the private relations of production that they exhibit features of antagonistic contradictions, for example, in the separation of labor power from the means of production and their union only through hiring and wages. The means of production become capital and the labor power itself becomes a commodity, as does the product of the two. The product as a use value is interpenetrated with private ownership through expropriation and becomes inextricably interconnected with exchange value.

Marx in his early works tended to call antagonistic contradictions alienations, after Hegel. In his mature scientific works, however, he dropped the term "alienation" as applied to the contradictions within society. The scientific use of the term "alienation" is as a particular kind of distorted reflection in the human mind of the antagonistic contradictions characteristic of the production age. Alienation, therefore, is a category of individual consciousness and of ideological superstructural social consciousness within the productive period, but particularly in capitalism and more particularly in monopoly capitalism.

The alienation syndrome is a distorted reflection of the antagonistic contradictions in contemporary capitalist society. This distorted reflection is found first in the institutions and ideologies of the superstructure erected over the base, the particular relations of production characteristic of monopoly capitalism. The primary function of the superstructure is to serve and preserve the base. One of the forms of such service and preservation lies in the obfuscation of the reflection of the antagonistic contradictions of the society. The most effective and prevalent form of obfuscation is ideologically distorted reflections of these contradictions. Such reflection is the rationalization of and apology for antagonistic contradictions. An example would be the factor theory of alienation and its alienating conditions. Another would be the transformation of the very real historically constituted antagonistic contradictions into the metaphysical human predicament or human condition—or into the proposition that progress in civilization leads to neurosis and ultimately to psychosis.

In any event, the effect of all the varied superstructural fantastic and distorted reflections of the antagonistic contradictions in monopoly capitalism is to render the objects of knowledge into unknown objects, into nonobjects, and the corresponding emotions into objectless vague feelings. The objectless feelings, such as anxiety, hostility, aggression, aloneness, hopelessness, meaninglessness, despair, guilt, and so on, constitute the syndrome of alienation in the individual. In each symptom of the syndrome, there is the same transformation from a dialectically close interconnection between emotion and its object as truly known to a separation of these emotional and ideational opposites. This separation tears apart what in fact can only exist together. Thus the real emotion and the truly human object are transformed on the one hand into objectless feelings and on the other into unknown or misconceived vague objects. These feelings of alienation can lead to depression, panic, and paralysis of emotion, intellect, motivation, and activity—which in turn feed and reinforce the original feelings. Such feelings are, of course, an effective means of serving and preserving the base of society. This is particularly true when it occurs in the cultural and intellectual community. Our art, novels, theatre, and psychology, not to mention philosophy, are replete with just such a syndrome. In this manner a large section of the cultural and intellectual community serves and preserves the base by enhancing the fictional reflection of the antagonistic contradictions in our society.

Obfuscation of human knowledge occurs in many ways. First is the ideological and institutional inadmissibility of large areas of knowledge, including entire sciences such as materialist philosophy, dialectical logic, materialist history, political economy, the physiology of higher nervous activity, the science of human psychology, the science of ethics and morality, among others. Another is the undercutting of science by means of epistemological arguments directed against truth as correspondence, at once relative and absolute, of ideas to their existential objects. Once obfuscation of established human knowledge has been achieved, the way is open to all manner of fantastic reflections, theories and explanations, ranging from historicism through economic and social apologetics to psychoanalytical and existential psychologies and philosophies.

One of the outcomes of such obfuscation and fantastic explanation is the splitting of emotions from their objects as known at the level of knowledge of the individual. Emotions, the significance to the individual of objects as he knows them to be in themselves, cannot exist apart from such objects. Separated from their objects as known, the emotions cease to be emotions and are transformed into objectless feelings or states. The negative emotions when separated from their objects as known become the symptoms that together form the syndrome of alienation. Once split off from their objects the emotions (now objectless feelings or states) cannot be transformed into their opposite positive emotions which in turn could give rise to motivations and eventually actions to change the self and the society. The symptoms of alienation, as objectless feelings or states, immobilize the individual, blocking motivation and action purposefully directed toward self-change and social change. This immobilization is the ultimate product of ideological and institutional obfuscation.

Alienation is an identity of two sets of opposites, one external and the other internal. Alienation is the external opposite of the integration of emotion and its object as known. At the same time, it is the identity of opposites on the one side of vague feelings and on the other of unknown or distortedly reflected objects. The total effect of alienation is estrangement from and antagonism toward all possible unknown objects, including nature, world, society, other people, opposite sex, values, standards, knowledge, reason, emotional involvement, action, and finally, self. The effect of estrangement and antagonism as embodied in objectless feelings is immobilization: panic, hysteria, and paralysis.

The central symptom, the symptom that plays the organizing role in the syndrome of alienation, is anxiety. It is even said that we live in the "age of anxiety." An analysis of this symptom will serve to exemplify the meaning of alienation as a very real psychological phenomenon in contemporary society.

Anxiety is, in appearance, objectless fear. But fear separated from the fearful object ceases to be fear and becomes anxiety. Anxiety therefore is, more essentially, dread of an unknown and fantastically distorted dreadful object or complex of such objects. The identity of opposites within anxiety is on the one hand dread and on the other the dreadful object at the individual level of ignorance and misconception. The external opposite of anxiety, as of all the symptoms comprising the syndrome of alienation, is the superstructure of capitalism and more particularly of monopoly capitalism. The superstructure, through its institutionalized ideologies, fosters and inculcates obfuscation and distortion of the true reflection of the objects of fear. One of the ideological functions of the superstructure is to furnish rationalizations and apologetics for the fearful antagonisms inherent in the final phase of capitalism. These rationalizations and apologetics obfuscate and distort the fearful objective antagonisms into dreadful objects which in turn transform fear into dread. Dread is expressed physiologically and behaviorally as immobilization, panic, hysteria, and paralysis—of nerves, feelings, motivations, and activity. Dread cannot be transformed into courage, but leads rather to "fear and trembling" verging on self-destruction—literally suicide.

Anxiety, with its ideologically induced dread and dreadful object, can be transformed into courage only by first transforming itself into fear. The transformation of anxious dread into fear can be accomplished only by prior transformation of the dreadful object into the fearful object in which the fearful nature and effects (attributes and properties) of the object are known and evaluated as to degree of fearfulness. Deepening knowledge of the fearful object moving from abstract to concrete and from appearance to essence (through social participation) can transform fear to a level at which it can be overcome. This identity of opposites, fear and the overcoming of fear, is courage. Courage is the positive opposite emotion of fear, into which fear can be transformed.

To transform anxiety into fear requires first the breaking up of the ideological misconceptions comprising the dreadful object; and second the application of human knowledge to the dreadful object thereby, through a process of cognition and participation, transforming it into the fearful object. The transformation of fear into courage entails the further application of human knowledge, through a process of cognition and participation, aimed at transforming the little-known object of fear into the well-known object.

Human knowledge, the thus-far developed knowledge organized in all the sciences and the arts, can transform anxiety into fear and fear into courage. Superstructural ideology, the obfuscation of human knowledge and the substitution of apologetics, can transform courage into fear and fear into anxiety. The latter is the genesis of the organizing symptom of the syndrome of alienation, while the former is the genesis of courage which is the organizer of the human integrative emotions that can motivate and activate the individual to change himself and to help change the society. It is little wonder, then, that the superstructural preservation of the society requires the ideological transformation of courage into fear and fear into anxiety, dread, panic, hysteria and paralysis; or in general that it requires the transformation of the emotions of integration into the symptoms of alienation. Progress toward the transformation of the individual and society requires the reversal of this process.

The dissolution of the syndrome of alienation can be achieved on two levels, the individual and the social. The individual can dissolve the alienation syndrome by reuniting his emotions, each with its appropriate object. He can do this by breaking through the fantastic and distorted reflections of the nonobject and transforming it into a known object. He can transform it into a known object by mastering the social knowledge relevant to that object. The level of the emotion, in both its content and expression, will then conform to his level of knowledge of the object. When the emotion does not so conform, he will take this as an indication that he must strengthen and deepen his abstract and concrete mastery of the social knowledge available to him. In short, the transformation of the alienation syndrome at the individual level is a matter of reeducation. Reeducation involves a two-fold task of breaking through distorted reflection and substituting true knowledge. It requires, that is, the transformation of the levels of participation of the individual in society. More particularly, it involves rejection of fantastic ideologies and participation in the knowledge amassed down the ages by mankind—and, under the motivation engendered

by closely related emotion and knowledgeable ideation,
putting that knowledge to work.

The dissolution of the syndrome of alienation at the social
level entails the transformation of society. Such transformation
means the elimination of the primary antagonistic contradiction
between the private ownership of the means of production
and the social organization of the forces of production. All
the other antagonistic contradictions can then begin to be
eliminated as the new society develops quantitatively. The
new society will in time become the creative age of mankind,
built upon the achievements of the gathering and production
stages. Prediction of the creative age is firmly based on the
current and particularly American achievement of the capacity
to produce not only the food, clothing, and shelter in sufficient
quantity for all, but also the means of creativity—the cultural
means and the leisure to employ them. We in the United
States especially are on the threshold of this transformation.
Indeed it is the only resolution possible, not only of the syndrome of alienation, but more fundamentally of the intolerably
sharp antagonistic contradictions permeating our society.

The identity and interpenetration of the two opposite
resolutions of the syndrome of alienation are readily apparent.
The social resolution requires the individual resolution—the
freeing of the individual from ideological distortions and the
acquisition of the knowledge that, put into action, will build
the creative society.

NOTES

1. That dialectical logic has been a victim of alienation in the
Soviet Union as well is indicated by M. M. Rozental', *Printsipy
dialekticheskoi logiki [Principles of Dialectical Logic]* (Moscow:
Izdatel'stvo Sotsial'no-Ekonomicheskoi Literatury, 1960), in which
he states that "we have paid a great deal of attention to formal
logic and almost none to dialectical logic."

PART III
MARXISM AND PHILOSOPHY OF SCIENCE

Chapter 9

Critique of Dialectical Materialism
*A Few Points Regarding Epistemology, Ontology,
and Philosophy of Science*

HERBERT FEIGL

Herbert Feigl is Regents' Professor of Philosophy and director of
the Minnesota Center for Philosophy of Science at the University
of Minnesota. From 1925 to 1930, he was an active and critical
participant in the Vienna Circle of Logical Positivism. A former
president of the Western Division of the American Philosophical
Association, he is the co-editor of *Readings in Philosophical
Analysis* (1949) and *Readings in the Philosophy of Science* (1953),
and is the overall editor of several volumes of the *Minnesota Studies
in the Philosophy of Science.*

Much as I appreciate the invitation to speak in this symposium,
I must immediately admit, nay *stress*, that my qualifications
for the task are altogether insufficient. Although I have—in my
student days—read a good deal of Marx, Engels, and even Lenin,
my current recollections are rather dim. More recently I have
read with interest such expositions of the dialectical-materialist
doctrines as those written by J. D. Bernal, John Somerville,
Robert S. Cohen, and Walter Hollitscher, and such critical
studies as those by J. M. Bochenski, K. R. Popper, Philipp Frank,
and Sidney Hook. I have not read any of the recent Russian
philosophical publications, and I don't even know whether there
are any translations of recent Chinese philosophical works. I

did listen intently to the Russian delegates at the Zurich
International Congress for Philosophy of Science in 1954, and
even had some discussions with them. And I have had public
discussions with Ernst Bloch and Walter Hollitscher in Austria
in 1964. Otherwise my ignorance is regrettably large.

I have nevertheless accepted the invitation to speak on
dialectical materialism—first, because our chairman, and my
good personal friend, Professor Cecil Miller, assured me he could
not find anyone else as foolhardy as myself to undertake this
difficult job; and second (and this is surely more important),
because I think that the lines of communication should be kept
open, not only between East and West, but among all forms of
philosophies and ideologies. To the extent of my very limited
abilities I have tried on occasion to do my part not only in
regard to dialectical materialism, but also in regard to neo-
Thomism, Protestant theologies, Oriental philosophies, and
various types of metaphysics. I recognize the dangers of
dogmatic fixation and petrifaction, not only in the movements
and ideologies just mentioned, but also in my own point of
view which is that of a logical empiricist and a scientific
humanist. I might mention that I have been among the most
outspoken critics of logical positivism although, of course, I
owe a tremendous debt of gratitude for the stimulation received during my formative years in the Vienna Circle—most
notably from Moritz Schlick, Rudolf Carnap, Otto Neurath,
Hans Hahn, Philipp Frank, and from other Viennese scholars
outside the circle, especially Edgar Zilsel and Karl Popper. Of
the thinkers just mentioned, it is interesting to note that Carnap,
Neurath, Hahn, and Zilsel were certainly socialists, in the sense
of being—with varying degrees of radicalism—convinced of the
truths contained in the economic interpretation of history, the
essentially social-economic nature of man and of his moral
potentialities; and unanimous in regard to the imperative need
for a peaceful world order, based on world law. Speaking for
myself, and as a "bloody layman," I am impressed with the moral
ideals of socialism, but am inclined to think that an "*économie
dirigée*" (as the French call it)—in other words, a democratic
welfare state that allows for a certain measure of well-controlled,
but otherwise free, competition—might work out best in the
long run. By "working out best" I mean, of course, the sort
of socioeconomic system that will provide for the possibility
of maximal human happiness, coupled with a full recognition

of universal human rights, i.e., in the absence of special
privilege, of invidious discrimination of any kind, the equality
of opportunity in a world state that will guarantee permanent
peace and the conditions for progress in the arts and sciences,
in the ways of living together in friendship (if not with love),
in the extermination of the evils of disease, crime, and injustice.
Having avowed my own basic commitments, and realizing that
I have precious little to contribute along the lines of suggestions
for *practical social action*, I shall turn to philosophical matters
in which I feel a little more confident. (As to whether I am also
more competent in this sphere, I must leave that to you—the
reader—to decide.)

POINTS OF QUALIFIED AGREEMENT WITH
DIALECTICAL MATERIALISM

The contributions of dialectical materialism to economics,
to the philosophy of history, to a synoptic view of man's place
in nature and society, are still controversial. But in my view they
are at least as well (or as poorly) confirmed as the equally controversial contributions of Freud and his disciples to the psycho-
dynamics of the human individual. And if Alfred Adler—despite
his apostasy—may be considered a Freudian (or "ex-Freudian"),
we find in his work a genuine synthesis of a depth-psychology
and a socialist, i.e., at least partly Marxist, view of society. In
any case, the sort of scientific empiricism and humanism which
I advocate is in general agreement with the following theses of
dialectical materialism.

Realism (versus: Subjective Idealism, Phenomenalism,
Transcendental Idealism)

Although I consider Lenin's arguments against "empirio-
criticism" as resting in part on misunderstandings (especially
of Mach and Avenarius), I think his realistic convictions are
eminently sound. I think it takes the sophisticated perversion of
Berkeley's reasonings to lend any plausibility to a philosophy
of immanence. I think, indeed, that such reasoning inevitably
drives one toward a solipsism of the present moment, a position

no one has ever been able seriously to maintain. As to whether the arguments *for* a realistic epistemology and ontology need to be as crude as those of Lenin (or for that matter of G. E. Moore, who was not a dialectical materialist), and as to whether the dialectical materialists are right in thinking that only a realistic philosophy can furnish a basis for the economic interpretation of history and for a program of social(istic) action—this is a question which, in one interpretation—demands a quite trivial, affirmative answer. But if the question is understood in terms of the current and highly recondite epistemology and analytic philosophy, it seems hardly relevant for the basic intentions of dialectic materialism. Does it really matter, for example, in asserting the reality of the class struggle, whether one is a sophisticated phenomenalist, direct realist, critical realist, hyper-critical realist, semantic realist, instrumentalist, pragmatist, etc.? The existence and importance of the class struggle seem so obvious to me, that their denial on purely epistemological or metaphysical grounds would merely demonstrate the silliness of such a type of epistemology or metaphysics. What I mean to say is that the distance of such intricate and remote epistemological considerations from the sociological question of the existence of the class struggle is so great as to make the realism-idealism issue just as ridiculous here as it would be if the reality of mountains, rivers, and oceans were at issue! If, contrary to what I think in these matters, a clever phenomenalist *were* able to give an adequate and logically coherent account of what amounts to the existence of such physical (or geographical) entities, he would surely be able to give a similarly adequate account of the class struggle. In short, much as I appreciate the realistic convictions of the dialectical materialists, I think that the constant emphasis on realism in their literature—ever since Lenin's book—has been otiose and incongruous.

Nonmechanistic Materialism

Here again I find a large measure of agreement with current scientific empiricism. Most scientific empiricists consider theological or speculatively metaphysical doctrines at least fruitless, if not (in some of their claims) simply false, and, in some other of their formulations, even factually meaningless. Hence there is also a positive agreement regarding man's place in nature and society. The dialectical materialists discredit theological supernaturalism primarily by pointing to its plausible origins in anthropomorphic and wishful thinking, and its perpetuation by religious institutions in the light of their socioeconomic settings and functions. I consider arguments of this sort important and illuminating. They prepare the ground for and supplement the logico-analytic critique offered by the scientific empiricists; a critique which rests on distinctions any honest thinker must make between the cognitive and the noncognitive types of meaning, or the corresponding different functions of language. As soon as one grasps the difference between *information* on the one hand and *exhortation* (consolation, edification, fortification) on the other, it becomes clear that religious language (whether or not within the frame of a theology) at best conveys a moral message, but is devoid of informational content. Even if the notorious empiricist criterion of factual meaningfulness is not invoked (and perhaps dialectical materialists reject that criterion), many scientific empiricists would join forces with the dialectical materialists in maintaining that there is no good reason whatever for accepting the truth-claims of the theologians.

The agreement in regard to the positive doctrine of *materialism,* however, must be critically scrutinized and qualified. Regardless of whether it is ontology, philosophy of nature, or philosophy (including methodology) of science that is under consideration, the common assumption or (respectively) the working hypothesis or the research program is that of *naturalism.* This implies that the origin and the development of organic life, the place of mental phenomena and of social processes and institutions, are to be understood in an evolutionary manner. They are all conceived as levels or aspects of a universe whose ultimate constituents are *material.* What precisely is meant by such an assertion has, as far as I know, not been very precisely specified by the dialectical materialists. But it has been a major concern of recent philosophy of science, and of analytic philosophy. The issues involved here are by far too complex and manifold for a brief discussion. I can submit only a few terse statements and questions. If they sound dogmatic, it is only because I must not take your time for a more elaborate presentation.

The emphasis on a *nonmechanistic* form of materialism is surely justified by the advances in the empirical sciences. Democritean and Newtonian mechanistic explanations, their triumphant successes in parts of astronomy and physics to the contrary notwithstanding, have been successively supplanted, or at least incisively amended, by the introduction of the concepts and theories of electromagnetism in the nineteenth century; and by the developments of the theories of relativity, the theory of quanta (quantum mechanics and electrodynamics and nuclear theory) in the twentieth century. Moreover, while the vitalistic metaphysics has been rejected by most biologists, dialectical materialists, and logical empiricists, it has been supplanted by various doctrines of holism and evolutionary emergence, along with the related Gestalt theories in psychology. I must leave it to the historians of scientific and philosophic thought to decide to what extent (if any) these ideas were anticipated in the works of Marx and Engels. Personally, I would recommend great care lest too much be read into the rather vague and general principles of the dialectic. (More about this later.) In any case, it seems to me that some of the most fruitful and promising developments in recent science were not in any way anticipated by either the dialectical materialists or the logical empiricists. I am referring here to such "bridge sciences" as cybernetics and information theory, as well as to the still-controversial general systems theory and mathematical biophysics. Dialectical materialists should certainly welcome the contributions especially of cybernetics. For according to the achievements of this young and prosperous discipline, the *causal* mechanisms of *teleological* processes are becoming increasingly understood. It is no longer *contradictio in adjecto* to speak of "teleological mechanisms"!

Again, the recent developments in molecular biology, with its discoveries of the mechanisms of self-duplication, should be a most welcome denouement of the riddles of reproduction.

If I understand the basic ideas of dialectical materialism correctly, I think that the essentially statistical characters of some of the basic laws of modern quantum physics need not disturb their general belief in the objective order of nature. In any case, I doubt that philosophers can afford to dogmatize about determinism or indeterminism at the "rock bottom" or "ground level" of nature. This, for the simple reason that we have no criterion for deciding as to whether a given stage of scientific investigation has "hit rock bottom." (Conceivably, the universe is infinitely deep, and there is no rock bottom!)

More generally, I wonder whether in *our* age of science it can

any longer be a hopeful and proper task for the philosopher to
hazard guesses at the riddles that only the advance of science
can responsibly resolve. Most logical empiricists have in this
regard been more modest in their aspirations than the dialectical
materialists. This is not to say that there are not some scientists
with a genuinely philosophical orientation, or a few philosophers
thoroughly competent in some of the sciences, who could make
contributions of such an ambitious nature. But speaking socio-
psychologically for the moment, it is unlikely that philosophers
with their typical training, and from the vantage point of their
proverbial armchairs can, in this day and age, blaze the trail for
significant revolutions in science. It seems to me that it is a
sufficiently important, vital, and timely task to provide an
adequate *understanding* of science.

Consider for example the current penetrating and logically
enlightened discussions of the mind-body problem. Does a
doctrine of evolutionary emergence really solve this problem,
or does it perhaps only provide a verbal gloss on the findings of
psychophysiology? The general formulae and principles of
dialectical materialism seem to me here to furnish as little a
contribution as the verbal sedatives of the (in some circles
highly overrated) Jesuit Teilhard de Chardin. Only a pain-
staking logical clarification of the complexities of the concepts
of the "mental" and the "physical," of "scientific explanation,"
and of "emergence," etc., together with a thorough consideration
of the entire range of scientific theories and their confirming
evidence, promises to illuminate this central issue of modern
science and philosophy.

Sociology of Knowledge

The attempts of the dialectical materialists to view styles and
fashions of scientific and philosophic thought in the light of
the social and economic factors, to regard ideologies quite
generally as "superstructures" of more fundamental realities,
is quite acceptable to the extent that it is itself as free as
possible from special bias. In the historical-sociopsychological
context it is, of course, interesting and enlightening to discover
the determining factors of the *Zeitgeist* of a given period or
episode in the developments of the sciences and of philosophy.

As long as we avoid genetic fallacies, i.e., the confusion of questions of validity with those of origin, the sociology of thought and knowledge is a perfectly legitimate and highly important endeavor. Once awakened to this sort of analysis, it becomes possible to spot the countless rationalizations in which most of us indulge when confronted with important social, economic, political, and moral issues. The danger points of this enterprise are by now well known. Dialectical materialists seem to me to have often prejudged an issue by the technique called in logic texts "poisoning of the wells." It is altogether too easy and comfortable to dismiss or repudiate a point of view or a scientific theory because it is typically "bourgeois" or because it is "idealistic." It took the Russian philosophers quite some time to adjust to and accept Einstein's theory of relativity. Einstein was perceived as a subjective idealist because his early thought was (as he always admitted) strongly influenced by his reading of Hume and Mach. (While I consider this attitude of the earlier Russian philosophers far less atrocious than that of the Nazi scientists and philosophers, it is nevertheless to be rejected for not too dissimilar reasons!) And if my own criticisms of dialectical materialism (along with those published by Philipp Frank, Sidney Hook, or Karl Popper) are regarded (by "class angling") as typical expressions of "American bourgeois positivism and pragmatism" (I was thus criticized in a Russian periodical some years ago!), I shall take this calmly and look carefully into the justice of the accusation, and of course also into the logical validity of the criticisms. "Poisoning the wells" has been practiced by some Freudians too, in a quite similar manner. We are by now quite familiar with this technique, and have our critical rebuttals ready.

POINTS OF CRITICAL DISAGREEMENT

In sketching the partial and qualified agreements between the philosophies of dialectical materialism and of logical empiricism, I have already indicated some of the divergences as well. Perhaps as the most important preliminary and fundamental point of disagreement I should mention my reservations regarding the "unity of theory and practice." I think I am more realistic than the Marxists in thinking that the philosophers (at least the majority of them), in view of their typical training and background, are among the people most poorly prepared to "change the world." Very few of them are even able to understand it! I think it is one of the (perhaps deplorable) consequences of the division of labor and/or excessive specialization in our time, that typical men of action are rarely also men of critical reflection (and vice versa). But—and this seems philosophically important—the adequacy of knowledge claims in the sciences is not uniquely connected with the acceptability of the aims of social action. Basically, this is simply the repudiation of the "naturalistic fallacy," i.e., the confusion of evaluative with factual judgments. Since this is a well-known, though still controversial, contention, I shall merely assert that as far as my lights enable me to see, no amount of factual information about the (likely) consequences of our social actions can by itself determine the "truly desirable" ends toward which we may employ the scientifically optimal means. I have a notion that, in this issue, the dialectical materialists are apt to agree with such American philosophers as John Dewey or Stephen C. Pepper, and to disagree with the logical empiricists (R. Carnap, A. J. Ayer, C. L. Stevenson). By the way, I don't think this disagreement in the theory of values and in moral philosophy is as momentous or as disastrous as the Marxists seem to believe. Modern civilized human beings all over the earth aspire toward an equitable, peaceful world society. There is no crucial difference in the ultimate aims. The real issues seem to me to concern the *means*, i.e., by what procedures, policies, strategies, and tactics that aim ("whose consummation is devoutly to be desired") is to be attained. Here, the notorious "bourgeois" differs from the "Marxist." But this is an issue that involves (in addition to some ethical decisions) questions of fact— economic, political, sociopsychological, etc. And our information here is usually not as reliable as would be required for rational decision—alas! Hence I am inclined to agree with Karl Popper in that, on the whole, evolutionary rather than revolutionary steps in social change are more likely to succeed.

Turning finally once again to the more academic issues of the conceptual apparatus of dialectical materialism, I cannot help but think that its much-emphasized philosophy of "process" and "change" is severely handicapped by the remnants of Hegelian logic—or *illogic*, as I would put it. First of all, I fail to see the importance of stressing the obvious, namely that ours is a changing universe whether we view it in its physical or social aspects. The dialectical materialists, along with John Dewey, Alfred North Whitehead, and their respective disciples, seem to me to be running in open doors in this respect. The facts of change, evolutionary or revolutionary, in the world of facts as well as in the realm of thought, are manifest and conspicuous. It is the task of the *sciences* to find out *what* changes, in *which direction, how fast,* and *under what conditions and circumstances.* The verbal gloss provided by the various process philosophies does not really add any further information to that provided by the sciences. The notorious Hegelian triad of thesis, antithesis, and synthesis may at best be a rough outline of *some* of the changes occurring, particularly in the realms of social change, and in the historical sequence of attitudes and beliefs. But, as has been pointed out many times (perhaps most rigorously and vigorously by Karl Popper), these swings of the pendulum, far from requiring a new *logic,* can be described adequately only on the basis of the good old two-valued logic. Similarly, whatever the logical or mathematical form of the description may be, it had better be consistent, for any self-contradiction in such a description (or in the premises of its explanation) makes the description devoid of factual content. It is not just false to ascribe or attribute self-contradiction to the facts of nature or society—it is downright nonsensical. Good old ordinary logic is quite sufficient, and indeed indispensable, for giving an adequate and intellectually responsible account of polarities, antagonisms, or conflicts. That such oppositions exist, and that they are essential for explaining a good deal of whatever happens, is of course admitted.

Walter Hollitscher, a Viennese Marxist (and formerly professor of philosophy of science in East Berlin), in a book on the current outlook of the sciences, felt obliged to present (aside from a genuinely competent review of the problems and results of modern natural and social sciences) and always to interpret the regularities of nature, society, and thought in terms of the dialectical principles of Marx and Engels. The slogan about the transition of quantity into quality is just as vague as the triad, or the "negation of the negation." These alleged principles are not at all helpful in either their ontological or their methodological significance. That a modern philosopher of science should try to salvage them strikes one as strangely incongruous. Hollitscher and other dialectical materialists have yielded to the temptation of interpreting the notions of complementarity and duality in the light of the dialectical "inter-penetration and unity of opposites." This seems to me merely to make the scientific issue even more obscure than it is in the famous Copenhagen Interpretation of Quantum Mechanics. Max Born and especially Alfred Landé, who as theoretical physicists have had a great deal to do with the development of quantum mechanics, consider these dialectical interpretations as absolutely useless and misguided.

It is my impression that once one replaces the dialectical formulae (the Hegelian triad, the interpenetration of the opposites, the "negation of the negation") by straightforward modern scientific language, nothing of their intended scientific significance would be lost, and an enormous gain in conceptual clarity would be achieved.

In sum, it seems to me that the leftovers of Hegelian verbiage in current dialectical materialism have tended to petrify and fossilize their doctrines. This is something that should not have happened to a radical and revolutionary movement that prides itself on its forward-looking philosophy. One can only hope that once the fossils are removed, the thus enlightened repre-sentatives of dialectical materialism will get ready for one more revolution in their thought and join forces with the defenders of the *critical* approach, of the policy of the open mind, and of the open society!

Chapter 10

The Concept of Dialectical Contradictions in Quantum Physics

M. E. OMEL'IANOVSKII

An Academician of the Ukrainian Academy of Sciences and a corresponding member of the Academy of Sciences of the U.S.S.R., Professor Omel'ianovskii is at present chief of the department of philosophy of science of the Institute of Philosophy in Moscow. He was formerly director of the Institute of Philosophy of the Ukrainian Academy of Sciences in Kiev, and has served as vice-president of the Scientific Council for Philosophical Problems of the Natural Sciences, in the Academy of Sciences of the U.S.S.R. Dr. Omel'ianovskii is the author of *Lenin and the Physics of the Twentieth Century* (1947) and *Philosophical Problems of Quantum Mechanics* (1956, 1962), and has edited and contributed to *The Structures and Forms of Matter* (1967), *Materialistic Dialectics and the Methods of the Sciences* (1968), and *Lenin and Modern Sciences* (1969).

THE NOTION OF "COMPLEMENTARITY"

AND DIALECTICS

Contemporary physicists, in creating theories adequate to nature's patterns of movement and development, speak the language of dialectics whether willingly or unwillingly. Even those whose personal outlook is at variance with dialectical philosophy acknowledge this in their own way. Thus

116

Heisenberg states that inquiry into the foundations of the quantum theory, especially as carried out by Bohr, has features reminiscent of Hegelian philosophy.[1] And, to quote Pauli, "Dialectics is that mutual game of two opponents which is typical of the Copenhagen interpretation of quantum mechanics."[2] Bohr himself, while discussing the quantum theory, speaks of "profoundly true statements the opposites of which likewise contain deep verities."[3]

Notable in those statements made by eminent physicists is the link between dialectics and the notion of complementarity which lies at the center of the Copenhagen interpretation of the quantum theory. When, in atomic-scale phenomena, light (regarded by classical physics as a set of electromagnetic waves) was found to have corpuscular properties, and matter (regarded by classical physics as a discrete structure) displayed properties of waves, the problem of bringing the corpuscular and wave aspects of matter and field in unison with each other and with reference to atomic processes presented itself. The solution of this problem in the framework of classical physics was obstructed by the fact that no object could possibly be a particle (i.e., a body confined within a small volume) and a wave (i.e., a field spread in a space of large dimensions) simultaneously. This obstacle was to be overcome by the complementarity concept. Complementarity is understood by Bohr to be a peculiar relationship among the observational data concerning atomic objects secured by means of different experimental setups. Such data, says Bohr, may seem to be contradictory when an attempt is made to unite them into a single picture, but as a matter of fact they represent, taken in their fullness, what we can learn of the object.[4] The use of classical notions to describe atomic phenomena observed through experiment leads to contradictions which can be given the form of antinomies. Bohr shows this clearly by many examples. Here is one of them:

"Suppose," he writes, "that a semitransparent mirror is placed in the path of a photon under conditions wherein the further progress of the photon is possible in two directions. Then of two photographic plates placed across these directions far apart from each other one and only one can record the photon. Now, if the plates are replaced by mirrors interference phenomena will be observed, owing to two reflected waves. Any attempt to represent clearly the behavior of the photon will meet with the following difficulty: on the one hand, we should naturally state that the photon will always be found to travel along one of the two paths; on the other hand, it behaves as if it were travelling along the two paths simultaneously."[5]

Bohr overcomes this difficulty by means of the complementarity concept. The behavior of the photon cannot possibly be separated from the conditions of the experiment in which it is observed: under some conditions the photon behaves like a moving particle, while under other conditions it behaves like a wave. To generalize, Bohr's concept states that a study of the so-called complementarity phenomena requires the use of mutually excluding experimental setups and that only a complete set of phenomena affords a complete knowledge of an atomic object, which means, of course, that by adopting the complementarity concept we have the right to make two opposite, mutually excluding, statements concerning a single atomic object.

The philosophical meaning of the complementarity concept for a physical theory is the recognition of the logical necessity under the respective conditions to use opposite, mutually excluding notions relative to a single object. In this way the formal statements of the quantum theory can be interpreted to agree with the experimental data so that no formally logical contradictions arise in overall theory.

Although recognizing the dialectical nature of thinking, the complementarity concept is only the first step toward the solution of the contradiction between the corpuscular and undulatory properties of micro-objects. In Bohr's concept this contradiction solidifies, so to speak, in the form of a pair of experimental set-ups opposed to each other, with which the "complementary phenomena" are linked. While the objective nature of the quantum-mechanical description is emphasized by Bohr, he says nothing of the inherent contradiction between the corpuscular and undulatory properties of atomic objects. The complementarity concept fails to take into account the fact that atomic particles in experiments never behave exactly like "classical particles" or "classical waves." Because of this important deficiency the concept is at a serious disadvantage. Instead of concentrating on the philosophical interpretation of the new notions of the quantum theory, attention is paid solely to an analysis of the limits within which old classical notions can be applied to atomic objects.

To solve the contradiction between the corpuscular and undulatory properties displayed by the behavior of atomic objects we must consider the corpuscular and undulatory properties of an atomic object as a unity of opposites. This is why the concepts employed by the quantum theory, in reflecting the dual nature of atomic objects, cannot but differ qualitatively from the classical concepts.

ON DIALECTICAL CONTRADICTION

The dialectical principle of contradiction, or the principle of unity and struggle of opposites, affords all the necessary and sufficient prerequisites for the motion (and evolution) of the objectively real world to be expressed in abstract notions (and in a system of such notions). A logic which excludes the dialectical principle of contradiction, that is, a logic with stationary categories (as in the case of the classical formal and the modern formal, or mathematical, logic) is unfit to solve that problem. This could already be inferred from Zeno's paradoxes and Kant's antinomies; but the proof was given by dialectical materialism.

The dialectical principle of contradiction consists in recognizing the opposite, mutually excluding, contradictory tendencies displayed by all natural phenomena and processes (as well as by society and thought). Credit for the scientific formulation of this principle belongs to dialectical materialism, but in an undeveloped form it had been expressed by many thinkers of previous historical epochs. While establishing itself it had to withstand countless attacks by representatives of dogmatic philosophy (and also of philosophical relativism) and is attacked in our times.

In this connection it is worth while to dwell briefly on the arguments made by H. Reichenbach and S. Hook against the dialectical principle of contradiction. Reichenbach, a neo-positivist, tries to solve problems of the logic of motion without the aid of dialectics. To this end he has introduced the notion of "genetic identity" which connects the various states of a single thing at different instants. Differentiating between "substantial genetic identity" (e.g., water particles) and "functional genetic identity" (e.g., water waves), he expresses himself against Heraclitus's dialectics. He believes that instead of asserting that no one can put his foot twice in the same river Heraclitus should have recognized the idea of functional genetic identity, which permits one to say that the same river can be plunged into twice.[6] Yet a flowing river is not a set of waters stationary at the different instants, just as time is not a set of different "nows." In other words, motion cannot be properly expressed in terms of genetic identity.

Even less founded are Hook's arguments against the concept of dialectical contradiction. He denies the existence of dialectical contradictions in natural phenomena and their reflections in thought, confusing dialectical contradiction with a logical contradiction due to incorrect reasoning. Resting on this confusion is Hook's statement that if all that exists is contradictory and thoughts are reflections of things, then consistent thinking should be invariably the mark of falsehood, and the sciences would be unable to make any progress at all.[7] Hook would have been right only if classical mechanics did not contain Newton's third law or Maxwell's theory were devoid of the notion of electromagnetic field, or special relativity were devoid of the notion of interval, or elementary algebra were devoid of the notion of relative number, and so on. United dialectically in Newton's third law are action and counter-action, while the notion of electromagnetic field reflects the inseparable unity of electric and magnetic fields, as the notion of interval reflects the unity of space and time characteristics of a moving body, and the notion of relative number reflects the internal connection between positive and negative numbers, and so on. At the same time all of these theories are known to satisfy the requirements of correct thinking, such as definiteness, conclusiveness and consistency. Thus, Hook's statement substitutes logical contradiction for dialectical contradiction. This logical error hardly needs comment, for, of course, the unity of opposites does not coincide with logical contradiction.

Correct thinking, definite, consistent and conclusive, will lead to the knowledge of truth. Formal logic, either classical or modern mathematical, is insufficient by itself to ensure the definiteness, consistency and conclusiveness of thinking. This is because natural phenomena and processes display dialectical contradictions which must be and are reflected by thought, whereas formal logic with such principles as identity and non-contradiction considers concepts and forms of thought as something static, not connected with the content of cognition, and thereby transforms them into empty abstractions.

On the other hand, abstractions, though destitute of motion by themselves are indispensable for gaining a concrete knowledge of the objective world, considered as a unity of manifold processes, as matter in process of development. The abstract is an indispensable step towards knowledge of the concrete. Natural science has for a long time been exemplifying this thesis of dialectics. Considered from this angle formal logic serves adequately to gain truth so long as its principles and concepts are not extended into a region where the motion of cognition must be taken into account.

Formal logic deals satisfactorily with different aspects and relations of an object when they can be considered separately, although actually interrelated in the real world. Dialectical methodology knows no abstract separation lines; it determines the applicability range of the concepts and principles of formal logic, and connects opposites through intermediate links to form higher syntheses.

Let us now compare classical formal logic, the so-called quantum logic, and dialectical logic, with reference to the knowledge of truth.

Classical Formal Logic

Its statements imply the existence of only two valid values: truth and falsehood. These values are not connected with each other and their opposition to each other is absolute. Nor do they depend on the conditions under which the statements are used. In addition to the identity and non-contradiction principles the law of excluded middle is in operation. Take, for example, the fwo following statements: (1) "The bullet which hit the board has hit it at this point"; (2) "The bullet which hit the board has not hit it at this point." Either the first or the second is true, and either the second or the first is false, respectively. Any third possibility is excluded.

"Quantum" Logic

Implied by its statements is the existence of three valid values: truth, falsehood, and indeterminacy. The "indeterminacy" (or uncertainty) is not tantamount to "lack of knowledge," but rather describes a special kind of situation. Neither "indeterminacy" nor the other two valid values are interconnected, being abstract opposites. The law of excluded middle does not operate any longer, whereas the laws of identity and non-contradiction remain in force. Example: if an electron which passed through a diaphragm with two holes is stated "not to have passed through a certain hole" this statement does not imply absolutely that it has passed through the other hole. There remains a third possibility: the electron may have passed through the hole "indeterminately."

Dialectical Logic

Its statements admit the existence of an infinite set of valid values, each containing an element of truth. The value of a statement is determined by the conditions under which the statement is used; that is, the truth is concrete. Subject to such conditions, truth and falsehood are opposites and the principles of formal logic hold true. Thus in the broadest sense the opposition of truth to falsehood is no longer absolute; a statement is subject to change, acquires new content and assumes a new valid value, whereby the knowledge of the object to which the statement refers rises to a higher level. Corroborative data and examples from the field of quantum physics will be given in the section which follows.

SENSE PERCEPTION AND ABSTRACT THOUGHT IN THE REFLECTION OF NATURE BY PHYSICS

In a logically developed physical theory the object under investigation is reflected at once by sense perception and by thought. Sense data are obtained by means of instruments, whereas the mathematical apparatus of the theory (i.e., a system of mathematical abstractions) permits these data to be raised to the generalization level, so that the law of the phenomena can be disclosed.

No physical theory, if it reflects (as it should) an objective reality, can obviate the necessity of connecting its mathematical system with instrument records: in the absence of such a connection, that is, without disclosing the physical meaning of the mathematical abstractions employed, there will be no physical theory. To put it on a philosophical basis, nature, with which physics has to deal, is matter in motion and we cannot possibly get any knowledge of matter unless matter is made to act on our sense organs (directly or through instruments).

Physical notions, according to classical theory, are usually direct generalizations of the notions arising in everyday experience; they are formed from this source as the physicist proceeds from instrument record to mathematical concept, connecting them according to certain rules. For instance, from practical comparisons of perceived solids with reference to length we have arrived at the notions of a constant measuring rod and a unit length; further, we developed certain rules for bringing the measured lengths into correspondence with definite numbers. In this way the lengths of the perceived objects could be measured accurately, or generally speaking, the notions of everyday experience and those of mathematical abstractions could be synthesized in physical notions.

It is also possible to proceed the other way round, from the mathematical abstractions used in theoretical equations to perceived instrument records. This way indeed is typical of quantum physics, as it investigates phenomena of atomic and subatomic scale, which are not directly perceivable. Thus, the fundamental equation of quantum mechanics, first formulated by Schrödinger, contained the wave function, the most important concept of that theory, whose physical meaning was discovered later.

The rules used to connect mathematical concepts with observations and instrument records are different in quantum mechanics from those in the classical theory. In the latter the instrument records are connected with the values of variables mathematically representing classical quantities. In quantum mechanics, on the other hand, connected with instrument records are the *eigen*-values of (Hermitian) operators which represent mathematically the physical quantities of the quantum theory; the wave function characterizing the state of the micro-object permits, under certain conditions, the transition from the operators to the values of physical quantities observed in the experiment.

Corresponding to this distinction between classical mechanics and quantum mechanics is the difference in the mathematical tools employed by these theories: the equations of classical formalism establish certain relations between variables (numbers), whereas the relations established by the equations of quantum theory formalism are between operators—mathematical notions more abstract than numbers, which do not necessarily obey the commutative law of multiplication.

Two circumstances should be emphasized. First, the quantum theory cannot avoid classical notions since they are necessary to describe the experimental data with which the notions entering into the mathematical system of the theory are connected according to certain rules. Without this connection, as has been mentioned earlier, the quantum theory cannot possibly be a *physical* theory. Secondly, the rules for connecting formal mathematical notions with instrument records are different in the two theories, each proceeding in its own way. Therein is reflected the qualitative distinction between the laws valid in the macroscopic world and those governing atomic-scale phenomena.

When we pass from the mathematical notions used in the equations of classical mechanics to observations (instrument readings), no paradoxes arise or can arise because the instrument records are described by means of classical notions and the equations are established as a mathematical abstraction of a system of measurements of a set of classical quantities. In quantum mechanics the conditions are different. Here paradoxes inevitably appear when we pass from mathematical notions to instrument readings (the problem of reconciliation of the corpuscular and undulatory patterns in the behavior of micro-objects). Their source lies in the contradiction between the mathematical system of quantum mechanics and the description of instrument records by means of classical notions, the former reflecting the behavior of micro-objects whose dual corpuscular-undulatory nature distinguishes them qualitatively from macro-objects, while the latter have been developed by studying the macroscopic world.

The role of the mathematical system of a physical theory is not merely to reconcile instrument records; it reflects an objective reality, though not directly in its abstractions but rather in their synthesis with observational data. Therefore, we may properly ask: how are the paradoxes of the quantum theory to be solved? In other words, is it possible (and if so, how) to express in notions the physical meaning of the quantum theory formalism on the basis of instrument records described by means of classical notions?

This question is discussed in the following section. What we have emphasized up to this point has been that the element of sense perception and the element of abstract thinking both enter necessarily into classical notions as well as into those of the quantum theory. Physical notions result from a synthesis of perceptual and conceptual knowledge of objective reality.

QUANTUM THEORY AND DIALECTICAL CONTRADICTION

How can we reconcile the corpuscular and wave patterns in the behavior of micro-objects, seeing that they both agree with experimental evidence and at the same time exclude each other when viewed in the light of classical concepts? We discussed above the complementarity concept favored by physicists, which is an attempt at such a reconciliation. Setting aside other systematized views on quantum mechanics, let us turn to the concept which recognizes as a fact the dual corpuscular-undulatory nature of micro-objects.

Many physicists have analyzed various aspects of this dialectical concept.[8] Its philosophical core has been distinctly elucidated by S. I. Vavilov.[9] In terms of this concept, matter is neither a set of particles nor a set of waves as represented by classical physics. Nor is it a combination of corpuscular and undulatory properties united in some mechanical fashion. The corpuscular and undulatory properties of matter are opposite manifestations of a single entity; that is, the properties of particles and waves are simultaneously inherent in matter.

Consideration of matter in this light gives a new philosophic significance to statements that in quantum physics both the notion of particle and the notion of wave are fundamentally different from what they are understood to be in classical mechanics and classical field theory, respectively. The limitations imposed by quantum mechanics on the classical notion of particle (as expressed in the uncertainty relation) set no limit to the knowledge of matter, but rather refine the knowledge of its corpuscular properties by taking account of its undulatory nature. The statement that in the quantum theory a system of particles is described mathematically as waves in a multi-dimensional space is not evidence in support of the idealistic thesis to the effect that the observable universe is dissolved in mathematics. What is expressed by this statement is the truth that a field is at the same time a set of particles, and a set of particles is at the same time a field.

In quantum mechanics, the distinction between particle and wave is considered to be of a relative nature; these concepts lose their abstract opposition to each other. Accordingly, the concept of particle undergoes a change, receiving a new definition, since in quantum mechanics the notions of particle and wave have a meaning only in their interrelation. This is in agreement with the fact that the properties of micro-objects as revealed in experiments are never exactly those of a particle or of a wave, since it is only in the limit cases that micro-objects behave like particles or like waves according to the conditions of observation. It will be obvious that in describing atomic-scale phenomena the experimental conditions (fixed by instruments) must be taken into consideration. This relation to observational means is a distinctive feature of a quantum-mechanical description, and it reflects the unity of the opposing properties—corpuscular and undulatory—possessed by micro-objects. Accordingly, the quantities entering into the so-called uncertainty relations of quantum mechanics differ radically from their classical analogues; they are quantities *sui generis* and cannot be reduced to classical quantities.

Nothing paradoxical remains, then, about the uncertainty relation. For instance, the uncertainty relation between the momentum and the coordinate is a paradox only if these are considered to be classical quantities. But the fact is that the uncertainty relation in this case shows that the *eigen*-values of the operators for the momentum and the coordinate are incompatible; that is, it is expressive of the law which governs quantum quantities. It is just because a micro-object is an entity of a dual nature, both corpuscular and undulatory, rather than a particle in the classical sense, that its momentum and coordinate have no definite value at the same instant. In other words, the impossibility of describing a micro-object except by re-course to the notions of probability and potential possibility proceeds from the very nature of this entity.

The question arises: why is the statement of the unity of corpuscular and undulatory properties of matter serviceable only in studying the phenomena of the micro-world, while a study of macro-world phenomena requires the recognition of a rigid antithesis between matter (particle) and field (wave)? The answer to this question is briefly as follows. The universal constant h connecting corpuscular and wave quantities, and having the dimensionality of action (described as quantum of action), is very small compared to those quantities typical of macro-world phenomena which likewise have the dimensionality of action. Thus, h can be neglected in studying the phenomena of the macro-world; that is, the corpuscular and undulatory properties of matter can be considered separately without taking account of their unity. In this way the laws of quantum mechanics are subject to modification in the direction of the laws of classical mechanics. Why should h have the numerical value it has? This question is unsolved by modern quantum theory, which takes h as empirically given. Its solution requires a more profound investigation than that afforded by contemporary quantum physics.

In the literature of this subject the question we have just discussed is often replaced by a quite different one: what does the unity of corpuscular and undulatory properties of micro-objects essentially mean, or, as it is put sometimes, what is the essence of the corpuscular-undulatory dualism? It is frequently held that the quantum theory fails to disclose this essence, leaving this task to a theory to come. Now, this question has no sense just as the question of the essence and foundation of the atom has no sense for the atomist. In fact, the atom can have neither essence nor foundation since it is itself the foundation of all that exists. "The unity of corpuscular and undulatory properties of matter" is a principle which discloses the essence of micro-world phenomena and lies at the basis of the quantum theory. This is why from the standpoint of the quantum theory, which reflects the micro-world, the question as to the essence of this unity, which some new non-quantum theory is expected to disclose, has no sense whatsoever.

Of a different order is the fact that modern physics is no logically complete system of theories. While some of its theories (for instance, quantum mechanics) are logically closed systems of notions, others (for instance, the theory of elementary particles) are but in the making, and the search is going on for logical bridges between such theories as those of relativity and quantum mechanics. Yet the tendency of modern physics towards a logically complete system of theories is obvious; and, considering the philosophical aspect, one may safely say that the road to such a system will not lead through the "discovery of the essence of the corpuscular-undulatory dualism." Something quite different will come about.

It must be borne in mind that "the unity of corpuscular and undulatory properties of matter" is an expression in modern physics of the principle of unity between the discreteness and continuity of matter. In dialectical materialist philosophy this principle is logically connected with the principle of space-time unity, and also with that of world unity and with the principle of development, evolution. Modern physics has still a long way to go before reaching an adequate expression of the whole of this logical chain. Thus, in quantum mechanics the synthesis is more profound, combining into one the notions of field and matter. However, in modern physics no organic combination has yet been established between the quantum theory and special relativity (where the principle of space-time unity is expressed more completely than in classical physics). The beginning of such a synthesis has been initiated by Dirac's relativistic theory of the electron, but a long way lies still ahead. As for general relativity, which has integrated the space-time continuum and the gravitation field into a single whole, it still stands aloof from quantum physics, except for certain ideas expressed by a few writers.

Thus, modern physics awaits a comprehensive synthesis of its leading theories. Corresponding to this future synthesis is the unification of the philosophical principles stated above. These principles, interconnected as they are, open up philosophical prospects for modern physics to solve the theoretical problems which have arisen in the course of its development.

Very often the idea of unity between the corpuscular and undulatory properties of matter has been linked up with idealistic hypotheses and represented in a distorted form. So it was at the time when quantum mechanics was first taking form, and so it is now. In Marxist works on the philosophy of modern natural sciences, this point has been thoroughly dealt with.[10] Here it will suffice, in concluding the present section, to make a brief remark on the statement that "the interaction between object and instrument defies any control in principle." On the basis of this assumption, certain physicists believed themselves to have solved the paradoxes of quantum mechanics.

It was assumed that the uncertainties involved in a simultaneous measurement of the coordinate and momentum of a micro-object are caused by impossibility in principle of controlling the interaction between micro-object and instrument. But if we subscribe to this statement we reject the objectively real nature of the unity between the corpuscular and undulatory properties of micro-objects. This assumption naturally gave rise to idealistic conclusions to the effect that observations and measurements are somehow the source for quantum theory laws, that the micro-object has a different "degree of reality" compared to the instrument, and so on.

"Interaction defying control in principle" is philosophically a wrong notion when applied to natural phenomena. In fact, all phenomena (and laws) of nature can be known and, accordingly, none of them is beyond our control in principle. The formulation in question may be regarded as an incorrect expression of the truth that the newly discovered forms of matter and motion cannot be brought within the scope of classical theories, and that the laws of micro-phenomena are not reducible to the laws of classical mechanics, which, far from being absolute, are confined to a certain domain of natural phenomena. The physicists who made this formulation did not clarify its meaning, and idealist philosophers used this circumstance against materialism.

Logical positivists on their part have subjected the idealistic interpretation to criticism. Thus, H. Reichenbach expressed himself against the statement that "the uncertainty is due to the object being disturbed by the observer." He criticized those who believed that "quantum mechanics called for a return to idealistic philosophy, according to which the 'ego' created the world, or at least the world could not exist without the 'ego' that observed it." At the same time Reichenbach has come to the conclusion that "human knowledge of the microcosm is bounded by the uncertainty principle,"[11] and this is one of the idealistic inferences.

Because it considers the mathematical system of a physical theory merely to be a tool for establishing relations between observational data, logical positivism is unable consistently to criticize idealistic views in science and advocates in reality a subjective standpoint. The consistent criticism of an idealistic attitude towards philosophical problems in physics comes only from the side of dialectical materialism.

THE PROBLEM OF ELEMENTARY PARTICLES

In the quantum field theory, the synthesis of corpuscular and wave aspects is more profound than in quantum mechanics. Necessarily connected with this is a characteristic feature of the quantum field theory: it raises to the rank of fundamental law the discovery of the interconversion of elementary particles made by modern physics, while the classical theory could not conceive of this. Accordingly, the problem of elementarity of particles presents itself in a new light.

In pre-quantum physics this problem, as is well known, was handled as follows: serving as the foundation of matter are unchangeable, structureless particles which combine to form the structure of more complicated aggregates of matter. In chemistry this assumption justifies itself to a certain extent: Prout's hypothesis that chemical elements consist of hydrogen has come to be recognized as true, although the hydrogen function is supplied by the charge of the atomic nucleus, which determines the number of electrons in the atomic shell and the place of the element in the periodic table. From the chemical point of view the chemical element is an "elementary substance"; yet from the standpoint of atomic physics the chemical element is a complicated system, consisting of different ingredients (the atomic nucleus and the electrons of the atomic shell.).

Now that modern physics has found an abundance of elementary particles interacting with one another and exhibiting a set of varied properties, the elementary problem has come up again. Can it be solved in a familiar way, as was done before the discovery of elementary particles, or is some new approach necessary? To clear up the situation, it is well to note that highly stable particles which do not disintegrate without external influence, such as the proton, electron, photon, and neutrino, should not be described as genuinely elementary in the effort to distinguish them from particles termed elementary which decay spontaneously and on this account are regarded as complex. We must bear in mind that the neutron is not actually composed of a proton, an electron and a neutrino, although free neutrons decay to liberate these three particles.

It may seem that the elementarity problem can be reduced to a certain set of divisions (or levels) of matter, each constituting simultaneously an "elementary" step for the next division and a complex level relative to the division preceding it. This elementarity scale is embodied in Newton's concept of matter as a system of particles of gradually increasing complexity and, to a certain extent, in the modern representation of the structure of matter (level of elementary particles, level of atomic nuclei and atoms, molecular level—the scale continuing toward the macro-world and, possibly, toward the micro-world.)

Will the scale-structure concept of matter really solve the elementarity problem? Suppose the series of divisions to begin on the elementary side. Matter will be represented as a set of elementary particles and of systems of particles of varying degree of complexity composed ultimately of the elementary particles. We are here faced with a variant of the old atomic theory.

Now suppose the scale of divisons of matter to continue indefinitely on either side, forming an infinite series of transitions from "elementary" to "complex" and conversely. On this assumption "elementarity" is a relative notion, every object considered separately being complex. This will ultimately (I shorten the reasoning) lead to the conclusion that there are no "elementary" objects at all, that is, that matter does not consist of elementary particles.

There is one more approach to the problem. This is to discard the notion of purely relative elementarity while remaining at variance with the old atomic theory. As pointed out by Engels, the scale involving an infinity of divisions of matter consists of different nodal points which account for the · qualitative variety of forms in which matter appears. From this standpoint matter is no mere set of elementary particles and their combinations; neither is it all substance destitute of elementary particles, but rather presents a union of properties typical of the elementary and of the complex.

In the physics of the macro-world one can neglect the unity of the elementary and complex and consider them separately without coming into conflict with facts; yet in quantum physics the situation is very different. This is because the deeper physics penetrates into matter, the more its theory depends on the interconversion of elementary particles. In modern atomic theory the notion of *transmutation* comes to the fore, and in this new context the problem of elementarity and complexity cannot be handled in the way it was dealt with by the classical atomic theory (where the concept of transmutation is reducible to the conjunction and disjunction of some immutable elements).

When applied to the micro-world, the notions of elementary and complex lose their literal meaning and are no longer abstract opposites. Elementary particles are not elementary in the classical sense of the word. They are more like classical complex systems, but the likeness is by far not complete. As a matter of fact, they combine the properties of the elementary and the complex, presenting a higher type of synthesis. Accordingly, the word "consist" (or "be composed") loses its literal sense too, when applied to the micro-world. It does not mean here that anything is composed of something different.

Even in nuclear physics the notion "consist" undergoes some metamorphosis. When the atomic nucleus is said to "consist" of neutrons and protons the word "consist" has not quite the same sense as in the statement that the sand in the box consists of sand grains. As is well known, the atomic nucleus is not composed of neutrons and protons. The notion "consist" is still further metamorphosed, when applied to the complex structure of the pi-meson, composed of a nucleon and an antinucleon (Fermi's hypothesis). Here the enormous loss of mass occurring in the pi-meson reduces the nucleon masses to all but zero. So the word "consist" in the statement of Fermi's hypothesis has a very arbitrary meaning.

Still more essential is the change of meaning suffered by the word "consist" when it is used to describe resonance particles, recently discovered, which are elementary particles with an extremely short life (under 10-20 sec.). One of these particles, for instance, the nucleon resonance N, can be formed and can disintegrate into a nucleon and a pi-meson. This does not mean, however, that this particle "consists" of a nucleon and a pi-meson.

These examples show clearly that transmutable elementary particles cannot be described as "elementary" or "complex" in themselves, that is to say, without regard to the conditions under which the transmutation has taken place and with which their nature is organically connected. In experiments no elementary particle behaves exactly like an elementary entity or like a complex system. Only in some special cases elementary particles appear either as elementary entities or as a complex structure, depending on the conditions of transmutation.

Thus, the proton behaves like an elementary entity when colliding with particles having energies less than 100 Mev, but if the colliding particles have much higher energies, then the proton may be considered to consist of hyperons and K-mesons.

Here the word "elementary" does not describe a purely relative elementarity. If, indeed, we say of an object that its elementarity is purely relative, this implies that it is actually a complex thing. With the elementary particles the state of affairs is different. The proton, for instance, is neither elementary in itself, nor complex; it cannot possibly be assigned either of these properties without having regard to the conditions of its transmutation. In other words, to describe a proton as complex makes sense only if the energy of its collisions is duly taken into consideration (whereas we can speak of the complexity of the atom without taking into account its ionization energy). The relative nature of the "elementarity" and "complexity" of elementary particles is analogous to the relativity of the dimensions of a body and the duration of the process it is involved in (according to Einstein's theory), or to the relativity of the corpuscular and undulatory characteristics in quantum mechanics, although these relativities have different kinds of content. Without relativity entering the picture in this sense it would be impossible to apply classical notions, in duly refined form, to the description of such natural phenomena as refuse to enter the frame of the classical theories.

It will be evident that elementary particles of the kind described, elementary and complex at once as they are, cannot possibly be structureless objects. According to contemporary views, an elementary particle, the nucleon, for instance, is not conceived as a point, but as something possessed of structure (Hofstadter's experiments), though not of a structure in the sense in which that word was used in pre-quantum physics. When an elementary particle is said to consist of other elementary particles, which compose it not in a real sense, but in an approximate sense, this means that the words "structure" and "consist" have not the same meaning in quantum mechanics as in the classical atomism. The new meanings of such words as "elementary," "complex," "structure," and others, are due to the mutual transmutability of elementary particles, which is the principal feature of contemporary atomism.

ON STRICT PHYSICAL NOTIONS

Once quantum mechanics had established itself as a physical theory, the fact became generally accepted that the laws of classical mechanics hold only in the macro-world, breaking down in the micro-world, and so have no absolute or universal validity. In quantum mechanics, this way of construing the laws of physics has been consistently exemplified in its mathematical system. Not so consistent is the attitude of different writers toward the rules for connecting mathematical abstractions with instrument readings to give physical sense to these abstractions. All authors are not equally aware of the fact that the connection-rules should not be the same in the classical as in the quantum theory.[1][2] Indeed, we often find it stated that no new fundamental physical notions should be introduced in quantum mechanics and that the fundamental classical notions applied with limitations set up by the uncertainty relation should suffice. And attempts have been made to proceed further to the philosophical conclusion that the uncertainty relation imposes limitations on human knowledge. That such statements are incorrect has been shown above. The qualitative distinction between the laws governing the macro-world and those valid in the micro-world becomes evident especially in the fact that not merely the mathematical tools, but the rules of connecting the mathematical notions with instrument readings, are different in classical mechanics and in quantum mechanics.

In modern physics this attitude toward the relation between the laws of classical mechanics and those of quantum mechanics is generalized to cover the interrelations between all fundamental physical theories. The existence of closed systems of concepts, definitions, and axioms is recognized, each system presenting the highest logical abstraction of the respective theory describing a definite domain of natural phenomena. The first such system relates to *classical mechanics,* covering also acoustics, hydro-dynamics, aerodynamics, celestial mechanics and several other sciences concerned with mechanical processes. The second system has been formed in connection with *thermodynamics.* The third system has been formed from the studies of *electrical and magnetic phenomena* (built up by the work of Lorentz, Einstein, and Minkovsky). The fourth system relates to *quantum mechanics* and is also serviceable to the theory of atomic spectra, to the conduction theory, and similar theories. The appearance of a fifth system is possible in connection with the *theory of elementary particles,* which is yet in the making. And we can also speak of a sixth system, connected with *general relativity.* These closed systems of notions reflect the existence of discontinuities (leaps) in nature and testify to the fact that the motion-forms of matter, interconnected by transitions, differ qualitatively from one another.

As for the interrelation of these systems, this question, speaking generally, reaches far beyond the frame of the present paper. In the first place it may be remarked that classical mechanics is contained in special relativity and in quantum mechanics as their limit case. Similarly quantum mechanics and special relativity will enter as limit cases into the theory of elementary particles when it will have been built up. Secondly, the notions of classical mechanics and some of those of the classical field theory are necessary to establish the rules for connecting the mathematical system of the theory with instrument readings. The second requirement is not realized distinctly in general relativity, where the mathematical aspect pre-dominates.

Let us now see what the expression "a strict physical notion" means.

It has been emphasized above that in any physical theory a physical notion reflecting reality is neither an instrument reading nor a mathematical abstraction, the two being merged into a single whole reflecting an objective reality. *Strict* physical notions are strict because they correspond to an objective reality (the correspondence being established by experiment).

The so-called *abstract* physical notions should not be set in opposition to the so-called *directly intuited* physical notions, as regards their relation to objective reality and their accuracy. Both the former and the latter, so far as they reflect an objective reality (this question is ultimately settled by experiment), are accurate notions. Every physical notion is connected with some experimental data, but in the case of abstract notions the connection is effected through a more complicated logical chain of reasoning (suggesting a deeper penetration into the laws of nature), than in the case of directly intuited notions. Therefore, both abstract and intuitive notions use terms of habitual language in their definitions, yet of course not to the same extent: in the definitions of intuitive notions the connection with experience is easily seen (thus, the notions of ordinary language, which may be regarded as the limit cases of intuitive notions, are immediately derived from experience) whereas abstract notions are defined by means of a system of fundamental concepts and axioms, so that their connection with the experimental evidence is not immediate and often follows a rather tortuous way.

On the other hand, strict notions retain their *strictness* only within the limits of a definite closed system of notions. So they are only *relatively* strict, there being no all-inclusive closed system in existence. It stands to reason that every relatively strict physical notion includes some sensory element, owing to its connection with experimental evidence. Therefore, the notions of any theory (sufficiently developed logically to be constituted as a closed system of notions) contain an abstract-thought element and a sensory-intuitive element. This is true of nonclassical as well as classical theories in physics. Yet the notions of the classical theory are direct generalizations of experimental data (it can be said that the respective notions of ordinary language are raised in the classical theory to the first rank of abstraction), whereas the notions of the quantum theory are not; here the experimental evidence is generalized indirectly through the use of classical notions, which pass into more abstract, nonclassical, notions.

Thus, we arrive at the conclusion that classical notions are in no sense a priori statements relative to quantum theory; in other words, we cannot subscribe to the view that in quantum theory only classical notions are used with the respective restrictions. As stated above, quantum mechanics employs fundamental notions and principles of its own. Accordingly, its notions, though qualitatively different from classical notions, are not less accurate, definite and clear. In quantum mechanics there are new fundamental notions, such as "relativity to observation instruments," "probability as a measure of the potentially possible," and others.[13] This circumstance should be taken into account when considering the problem of accurate physical notions.

The following illustration may here be useful. Reflected in the classical notions of velocity and position, clearly and accurately, is the fact that classical mechanics investigates the slow (compared to light) motions of macroscopic bodies.

In the oscillation theory, which investigates the motion of waves, quite accurate notions of phase velocity and group velocity are used, which must not be identified with the notion of velocity as used in classical mechanics. Even more complicated is the state of affairs in quantum mechanics since the electron does not exactly behave like a particle or a wave, but simultaneously exhibits corpuscular and undulatory properties. Here we cannot speak of velocity and position as independent of each other, so that new accurate notions are employed, which differ widely from the conventional classical notions, yet are still connected with them.

To conclude, let us examine a certain tendency observed in physical science which seems to run counter to the tendency toward accurate notions just discussed. The latter, indeed, does not ensure an adequate knowledge of nature. You cannot exhaust nature or any part of it. Accordingly, science, with its theories and notions reflecting nature more and more fully and deeply, cannot but change and develop indefinitely. Old notions (and theories) become inaccurate when applied to a new sphere of natural phenomena; new accurate notions and theories are developed to correspond to the new domain. Thus when physics penetrates into a new domain of phenomena, the applicability range of its old notions and theories reaches a limit, and all along the line new notions and theories are developed. These two processes merge into a single process— that of the evolution of science: first the inadequacy of the old notions in the new domain is established empirically, whereby hindrances and paradoxes arise in the attempt to use the existing theory—the period of travail before the birth of a new theory; then the development of knowledge leads to a strict delimitation of the applicability range of the old notions and theories, and this delimitation goes hand in hand with the development of a new system of notions. Thus a new theory comes into existence. Traversing the whole length of this road is in a sense what led to quantum mechanics, which at present is a closed system of notions, and the same course is being followed by the contemporary theory of elementary particles. Here again the presence of hindrances and paradoxes leads to the necessity of developing a new system of notions, or "mad ideas," to use the graphic expression of Bohr.

So we come to the conclusion that science, when in process of development, cannot manage to forge ahead on the basis of accurate notions only, and never could. Under certain conditions, when the new theory is still in process of construction, and has not yet developed its own system of notions, science cannot but use inaccurate notions without which the building of a rigorous, consistent and complete theory is practically impossible. Thus, the tendency of a developing science to strict notions interlaces and merges with an opposite tendency, characterized by the use of loose notions. Every advance of science entails their employment. Notions of this character disappear when a certain development cycle of science has been completed, and reappear at a further stage of development.

To summarize, quantum physics is permeated by dialectical contradictions. It implies the recognition of contradictions and oppositions in the very objects and phenomena of nature, their union and transitions to new levels, the solution of old contradictions and the appearance of new ones.

NOTES

1. W. Heisenberg, "Planck's Discovery and Fundamental Philosophical Problems of Atomic Theory," *Uspekhi fizicheskikh nauk* 66 (1958): 169.

2. W. Pauli, "Wahrscheinlichkeit und Physik," *Dialectica* 8 (1943): 118.

3. Albert Einstein, *Albert Einstein als Philosoph und Naturforscher*, ed. P. A. Schilpp (Stuttgart, 1955), p. 150.

4. N. Bohr, "Quantum Physics and Philosophy," in his *Atomic Physics and Human Knowledge* (Moscow, 1961), p. 144.

5. N. Bohr, "Discussion with Einstein on the Problems of the Theory of Knowledge in Atomic Physics," in *Atomic Physics and Human Knowledge* (Moscow, 1961), p. 74.

6. H. Reichenbach, *Time Direction* (Moscow, 1962), p. 302.

7. S. Hook, "Dialectical Materialism and Scientific Method," special supplement of *Bulletin of the Committee on Science and Freedom* (Manchester, 1955), p. 7.

8. D. S. Rozhdestvensky, "Analysis of Spectra and Spectral Analysis," *Uspekhi fizicheskikh nauk* 16 (1936); I. E. Tamm, "New Principles of Bose-Einstein Statistical Mechanics," *Uspekhi fizicheskikh nauk* 6 (1926); D. I. Blokhintsev, *The Foundation of*

Quantum Mechanics (Moscow, 1949); V. A. Fock "On the Interpretation of Quantum Mechanics," in *Philosophical Problems of Modern Natural Science* (Moscow, 1959).

9. S. I. Vavilov, *The Micro-structure of Light,* 1959; *The Eye and the Sun;* see also his papers on philosophical problems of physics in *Collected Works,* vol. 3 (Moscow, 1956).

10. See, for instance, *Philosophical Problems of Modern Physics* (Kiev, 1956; Moscow, 1958; Moscow, 1959); *Philosophical Problems of Modern Natural Science* (Moscow, 1959).

11. Reichenbach, *Time Direction,* p. 302.

12. L. I. Mandelshtam seems to have been the first to point out the necessity of using different rules of transition from mathematical notions to experimental data in classical theory and in quantum theory. Lectures on "Foundations of Quantum Mechanics" in *Collected Works,* vol. 5 (Moscow, 1950), p. 354.

13. The essential theoretical significance of "new primary notions" in quantum mechanics has been noted by V. A. Fock. (Notes on Bohr's discussions with Einstein. *Uspekhi fizicheskikh nauk* 66 [1958] : 599-600.)

Chapter 11

Marx's "Science" of History

QUENTIN LAUER, S. J.

Quentin Lauer is professor of philosophy and chairman of the
department of philosophy, Fordham University, New York City.
He has written articles on nineteenth-century philosophers,
especially Hegel, Feuerbach, and Marx, and has been active in
Christian-Marxist dialogue. His writings include *La phénomèno-
logie de Husserl, The Triumph of Subjectivity* (published also
as *Phenomenology: Its Genesis and Prospects*), and, with Roger
Garaudy, *A Christian-Communist Dialogue* (1968).

With the disappearance of Josef Stalin and, hopefully, of the
Stalinist dogmatic interpretation of Marx's thinking, two
changes have taken place in the approach of scholars to
Marxism (apart from what political and attitudinal changes
may have taken place in those portions of the world which
are dominated by Communist ideology). First, scholars now
have an opportunity—previously either not available or not
considered likely to be fruitful—to re-examine the sources
of Marxism and thus come to a more nuanced understanding
of its philosophical subtleties. Second, the Western scholar
who would approach Marxism objectively is in a far less
defensive position than he was as recently as fifteen years
ago. Formerly the problem was, in fact, that of being objective
and of showing that Marx's own thinking was philosophically
(if not politically) respectable. Today it has become more

fashionable to say nice things about Marx, the "humanist" philosopher, and to reserve one's critical barbs for contemporary Communist perversions of authentic Marxism. Thus, the question of objectivity has been to an extent reversed, and the problem of philosophical respectability is not a problem at all. Not least among the reinterpretations made possible by these changes in attitude is that of the "scientific" character of Marx's theory of history as an explanation of socioeconomic development and, more particularly, of the genesis and inevitable decline of capitalist society.

The problem regarding Marxist "science" arises out of the fact that philosophers have tended to be more naive in their attitude toward the very meaning of science than have scientists themselves. If we read, for example, Conant's *Harvard Case Histories in Experimental Science* we find that the experimental scientists of the seventeenth and eighteenth centuries were truly giants in their ingenious capacity to devise and interpret experiments which would permit them to penetrate the secrets of nature. They were, however, as Cassirer shows, in *The Philosophy of the Enlightenment,* far more modest than were philosophers in regard to the "scientific" character of their discoveries. To the extent that scientists as scientists (and not as part-time philosophers) have a theory of science at all, it is scarcely epistemological in character; they are little concerned with methods of refutation or even of partial validation; still less are they concerned with the character of the knowledge they have or with its certainty. Rather, they are concerned with discovering and employing the most economical method of concept formation, knowing that concepts are the most important instruments at their disposal in research and knowing, too, that, through the concepts they form, they will force nature to give up its secrets.

Philosophers, on the other hand, have always felt it their vocation to tell the scientist what he is about. At no time was this more in evidence than at the end of the eighteenth and in the early nineteenth centuries. The philosophers of the Enlightenment had bequeathed to Kant and to his followers an admiration for scientific "laws" which was little short of idolatrous; not only did the establishment of scientific laws tell us (with certainty, no less) how things do in fact come about, but the laws themselves told us how things *had* to come about; nature, so to speak, was *obliged* to observe them—otherwise they would not be universal and necessary and, hence, not scientific. Unfortunately, however, if we accept as knowledge only what has been scientifically established, and if we accept as scientifically established only that which has been apodictically verified, then, strictly speaking, we are denying the possibility of a history of science. There can be a history of the process of arriving at scientific verification, but, according to the naive conception, at no point along the way can we justifiably speak of "science," since only at the end of the process does it make any sense to speak of apodictic verification; if there is a history at all it is of that which is not yet science. Logically, however, such a conception should lead one to deny that there is any science at all, since what is still corrigible has not been apodictically verified, and it is questionable whether we would want to call any scientific theory incorrigible. Scientific "laws" are constantly being modified, corrected, or replaced, but they do not by that fact cease to have been scientific—unless, of course, one wants to look upon science as the "possession" of knowledge rather than as the process of approaching the ideal of knowledge.

The problem of Stalinist dogmatism, then, is not that it ignored or suppressed the earlier, more philosophical—and, hence, more tentative—writings of Marx, but rather that it refused to admit that the "discoveries" of later Marxist "science" are corrigible. It agrees that there can be further advances in science but denies that they can be such as to require a new look at what has already been scientifically established.[1] There is, incidentally, a certain naiveté in thinking that the late discovery (1932) of Marx's early philosophical manuscripts has contributed disproportionately to our understanding of Marx. This is particularly true with regard to the concept of science, which is nowhere more clearly expressed than in the *Contribution to a Critique of Political Economy* (1859) and in the preface to the first volume of *Capital*. The same might be said of Engels' elucidations of Marx's thought in *Anti-Dühring* and in *Ludwig Feuerbach and the Decline of Classical German Philosophy*. What has happened, then, since the inauguration of a policy of de-Stalinization in 1956, is not so much that new evidence has become available; rather it has become possible to examine the old evidence with new glasses.

Marx's primary aim was not to *know* but to do., i.e., to change the world[2] and, thereby, the human situation in accord with what history tells him that situation is to be.[3] His secondary aim was to accomplish this transformation on the basis of "science" or of a "scientific method for the construction of this society"[4] wherein man is to become what history has destined him to be. In this framework, then, it is "historical" science which enables Marx to know both what man is destined to be and how to bring this about.[5]

Without going into the question of what meanings or connotations the term "science" has taken on in our contemporary and particularly English-speaking world, it might be well before going on, to look at the meaning which the term *Wissenschaft* had for a German in Marx's day. Originally the term was quite vague and indicated either something so indefinite as "information" or the subjective state of having knowledge in this or that particular area. Until late in the eighteenth century it was difficult to distinguish this meaning of the term from that of "art." Only gradually did the term begin to take on the meaning of a body of knowledge in the theoretical sense, and only at the end of the eighteenth century did it appear primarily in the singular as designating the sum total of what is objectively known, in the strictest sense of the word "know," which in German is *wissen*. Thus, to know "scientifically" was to know in the best possible sense of that term. With Hegel, however, who in this area had the strongest influence on Marx, *Wissenchaft* became the whole process of coming to knowledge in the strict sense, such that any stage in the process was knowing in a relative sense, and was thus in connection with the whole process "scientific."[6] It is important to emphasize Hegel's influence on Marx precisely from this point of view. For Hegel human knowledge is always on the march, and to be scientific is to follow the line of march faithfully. The dialectic was not conceived as a "method" which would enable the scientist (or philosopher) to compel reality to give up its secrets; it was a description of the process through which both mind and reality go in coming to the identity which is at once true knowledge and true reality. What Marx took from this was the conviction of process and of a truth which only gradually (historically) reveals itself, because it is constantly in the making.

It should be pointed out here that in the tradition of the

Enlightenment and of early nineteenth century philosophical
thinking, the concept of "science" was largely negative in
the sense that stressing the autonomy of human reason in
"scientific" thinking involved denying the validity of authority,
tradition, the supernatural, etc. Thus, a natural explanation
of what had been previously explained supernaturally, even
though it might on our terms be considered only plausible,
was in the eyes of the "enlightened" a scientific explanation.
It is true that they demanded for science that what it claimed
to be true also be seen as *necessarily* true, but the concept
of "necessity" was at best a vague one. This is particularly
the case where the science in question is historical and where
the "objective necessity" of scientific laws is thought to
govern historical process.[7]

Against this background, we can, perhaps, understand what
Marx was trying to do in his endeavor to study man and
society "scientifically." From the Enlightenment, he had
inherited the demand that reality be explained on the basis
of rationally discovered "objective laws." From Kant, Fichte,
and Hegel, he had inherited the realization that these laws
are not contained in nature but are the product of human
thinking—as a human response to facts in an endeavor to
account for them rationally. From Feuerbach, he had inherited the conviction that there is no going beyond the
evidence presented to the senses in doing this. His own unique
contribution was to synthesize all three elements of this
inheritance, basing his synthesis on a concept of man as truly
human only in the context of society, which society was
constantly the product of human material activity governed
by dialectical laws intrinsic to the process itself.[8]

To understand Marx, then, we must begin with the socioeconomic situation which he observed in nineteenth-century
industrial Europe. This in turn demands an awareness of a
number of factors—political, economic, social, and religious—
which characterized the world in which Marx lived.

Political. The French Revolution (although it was not unique
in this) had given the impetus—however vague—to the ideal of
political self-determination. The best German thinkers were
fascinated by the attempt to realize a society based on a
rational concept of man. By the time Marx came on the scene,
however, the rise and defeat of Napoleon had apparently
manifested the weaknesses of doctrinaire liberty, equality, and

fraternity. Finally, the dominance of the Prussian state had reinstated the framework of political absolutism, not merely by restoring the status quo but also by seeking to bolster the absolute state with the support of both reason and religion.[9]

Economic. The Industrial Revolution, which, although most advanced in England, had a strong influence on European life in general, was in the process of intensifying a movement which had begun at the end of the Middle Ages: the power of wealth was supplanting that of the feudal aristocracy, and the impersonal power of the national state was replacing the relationship of individuals to a personal monarch. The obvious cleavage between those who produce and those who profit by what is produced was rendered more acute by the private ownership of machines which were becoming an increasingly important factor in production. With this an extremely important "economic fact" imposed itself: with a quantitative increase in production the margin of profit on each individual item became smaller, and the need of weighing carefully the costs of production became paramount. From this it followed that labor—the human work force—was considered one of the "costs" of production and, thus, a commodity governed by the "law" of supply and demand. The result of all this was that the very logic of production produced a "class" of people whose only asset was work itself (an asset only while they were working) but for whom the absolute necessity of subsisting made a favorable bargaining position impossible.

Social. The massive industrialization of society resulted in a clearly defined division in relation to the process of production between those who owned the necessary instruments of production and those who were forced to sell their labor to such owners. One could still speak of various *levels* on the social scale, but more and more there were only two *classes* cutting across the whole of world-society.[10] With increasing industrialization (worldwide) the structure of society became hardened in such a way that political, economic, and social inequalities were given a permanence impossible to breach.

Religious. To top it all off religion was turning into a supernatural and supra-temporal justification of the status quo. No matter what the purposes of religion in itself may be, the political powers were employing it as a support of their own domination. At the same time, to all intents and purposes religious teaching, with its emphasis on safeguarding the rights of individuals, was serving simply to solidify the socioeconomic structure with its inequalities—when rich and poor are face to face as individuals, equality of rights is the grossest of inequalities. In addition, the emphasis which Christian religion put on the provisional character of the earthly pilgrimage was influential in persuading those on both sides of the socioeconomic divide to accept the situation with its inequalities—the hereafter could take care of equalizing.

Against this background we can now, perhaps, see more clearly Marx's task as he saw it himself. In his own age he observes a situation in which man has become dehumanized, "alienated" from what is truly human in him.[11] This is true not only of the vast majority, the working class which is cut off from the product of its own labor, but also of the owner class which has turned what it owns into a vast impersonal "capital," which it too serves without knowing it. In the spirit of his age Marx cannot be satisfied with observing a set of facts or even with criticizing the inhumanity of the situation he observes. Nor can he simply look for a program of reform which would ameliorate the situation. He had to have a "scientific" explanation of the situation as he saw it, and had "to account" scientifically for the only possible way to remedy the situation. To do this he had to elaborate a practico-scientific explanation of social development. As Marx saw it, in human affairs (or, for that matter, in human nature) there are no "givens," in the sense that any situation or relationship is essential either to human nature or to the human condition. If a situation exists it may be "given" to those who are in it, but it has been brought about, produced, by previous human activity. By the same token, if the situation is to be changed, the change must be brought about by human activity. What was peculiar to Marx's approach to the situation, however, was his determination to establish a "science" of the human activity which brought the situation about, a science which would also provide the rules for the human activity which would change the situation. Such a science would be a science of history; ultimately it would be scientific history, in the sense that the science would determine the history rather than history (or mere events) determine the science. For the accomplishment of his task Marx brought with him both a vast erudition and a messianic consciousness which would stop at nothing short of a recreated world.

As Lenin said of Marx, he combined in his thinking "all

that was best in German philosophy, British political economy, and French socialism."[12]

To change Lenin's order, Marx was influenced strongly by the effort of the economists to explain "scientifically" economic (and, hence, social) structures. What he found significant in their work was the endeavor to determine the "laws" which govern economic processes. They were not at all unaware of the ambiguity introduced into the overall picture by the arbitrariness of human behavior, and yet they were able to predict with considerable accuracy the movements of the economy by observing and describing the interrelations of the major factors in the productive process. Where they failed, Marx felt, was in their unphilosophical—and unscientific—acceptance of the contemporary structure of society as a given, as the necessary framework within which economic laws were operative.[13] Marx simply could not accept the Enlightenment presupposition—which was that of the British economists—that any factual situation is a "given" in nature. What is "given" has been produced, and the task is to understand its production.[14] This is where "the best in German philosophy" comes in. The gigantic philosophical endeavor, which began with Kant and—in a very real sense—ended with Hegel, had highlighted two essential features of the relationship between human thought and concrete reality: (1) the "objectivity" of thought can be meaningful only if it can be reconciled with the subjectivity of thinking; and (2) the objective world which thought thinks is a world in process, a science of which must be able to account for process. The first of these features made Marx reject the Enlightenment notion that the "laws" which science "discovers" are simply inscribed in nature independently of human thinking. Most important in Marx's thinking is his refusal to see in man or society an essential "nature" which can be arrived at by abstract thinking.[15] The second convinced him that the only real science—science of the concrete—would be a science of development. If, then, science was to discover laws, they had to be laws which took into account the thinking subject, and they had to be historical, in the sense that they gave an account of the coming to be of what was. Such a science Marx found in the Hegelian "dialectic," which sought to account both for the interrelatedness of thought and reality and for the developmental character of thought's object. Marx would go beyond Hegel in recognizing only what man had produced through action as the true object of knowledge. Thus, the object of knowledge is never a "given," not even man himself, since he is only to the extent that he produces himself. [16]

All of this, however, could have remained empty and formalistic, had not Marx also included in his thinking "the best in . . . French socialism." He could not be satisfied with a thought which sought merely "to understand the world." He required one which would "change it." It was characteristic of the French social thought of his day that it sought to *do* something about the situation which thought analyzed.

Here it seems necessary to indicate the prephilosophical— or prescientific—character of the insight which enabled Marx to see in the socioeconomic situation of his day a dehumaniza- tion or "alienation" of man. It has often been objected that to speak of man's alienation involves an ideal, a priori decision as to what man *should* be. There is unquestionably much of the idealist in Marx. Marx's own answer to the objection, however, would be that even before the elaboration of a *theory* of history the observation of historical development has revealed an orientation which the present situation of man contradicts. To see this situation as one of alienation, then, can be ascribed to what we can call a "historical insight," an insight into what the observed process demands. It will be important to recognize as we go along that without this insight the "science" of history does not make much sense. Although, like Bergson, Marx rejected vehemently any notion of "teleology" in historical development—the very term raised the specter of a spiritual providence—he was thoroughly con- vinced, as was Bergson, that development does have a direction and that deviations from that direction are a possibility (otherwise "alienation" would be meaningless). The point is that Marx sees history revealing its direction "realistically," not in terms of an abstract ideal which human thinking sets for it.

Out of Marx's "historical insight" comes a scientific theory of history which will back up the insight in two ways. It will explain on the basis of necessary "objective laws" of history the development which has brought about the present situation, and it will provide the key—again based on the operation of these "objective laws"—for a further development which will mean the reappropriation of what has been alienated. In the final analysis

Marx will have combined the economic "science" of the British, the "philosophy" of the Germans, and the "socialism" of the French in a science of history which reconciles theory and practice. The theory is Hegelian in its dialectical character; it is peculiarly Marxist in its materialistic character, not only in the sense that he sees only material development as susceptible of scientific investigation, but also in the sense that he sees the transforming activity of man as the labor which at one and the same time changes nature and makes man himself into what he is to become.[17] It is not that Marx denied the relevancy of ideas—he would have been intolerably inconsistent had he done so, since his own contribution to the movement of history was in the realm of ideas—but that he saw ideas as having their source in activity, not activity having its source in ideas. What Marx sought was "concrete science," and, as he saw it this demanded that he reject Hegel's "system" while retaining his method.[18]

Although it may be difficult for us to see what Marx can mean in insisting on a "science" of historical process or on "laws" which govern overall social development—especially when this insistence is accompanied by a refusal to accept the given as simply given—we may be able to grasp the whole thing better if we approach it from a different angle. The very notion of "science"—which we trace back to the Greeks, and which found its first articulate formulation with Aristotle—is based on two fundamental considerations: (1) the fact that we do observe certain regularities in events; and (2) the conviction we have that such regularities are susceptible of rational explanation in terms of "laws" (however loosely that term may be construed). Thus, as Aristotle says, when we observe that nature "always or nearly always" acts in a certain way, we conclude that there is a reason in nature itself for its acting the way it does. This is what Archimedes was doing when he determined the specific weight of gold; it is what Galileo was doing when he determined the rate of acceleration of falling bodies (even if the only experiments he performed were thought experiments); it was what Boyle was doing when he determined the laws which govern the expansion of gases. By the same token, however, it is what Gresham was doing when he tried to determine the law which governs the economic flow of gold and silver, or what Marx was doing when he sought to establish the relationship between surplus value and the accumulation of capital. We know, of course, that scientific "laws" are always corrigible; but they are always corrected in the form of other "laws"—which might be interpreted as new and better ways of formulating the same "laws" governing observed regularities. It is also significant that we are scientifically convinced that the laws which have been formulated will also be verified in events we have not observed—or have not yet observed (always remembering that further observation may demand modifications in the formulation of any law). Significant also is our basic conviction that given other regularities which we have not (yet) observed, it will be possible to formulate laws which will explain them.

We are, it is true, not quite so naive as was Marx with regard to either the formulation or the operation of these "laws," but we must remember that Marx was a child of the early nineteenth century (heir of eighteenth-century scientific optimism) and that we are not. In any event Marx was convinced that the "facts" he was able to observe exhibited the kind of regularity which demanded the formulation of laws governing their regularity. More than that, he was convinced that once these laws were formulated they enjoyed the kind of universality and necessity which made them operative throughout the entire process of history. At the same time, however, Marx was not so naive as to think that the laws of history correspond exactly with the laws of nature—as conceived in his day—according to which the future is already written in the past. He sought to formulate laws which would always take into account human initiative in a process where novelty was constantly emerging.[19] In so doing he was aware that ongoing reality is inexhaustible and not reducible to the knowledge we have of it. He was aware, too, that any scientific model is provisional and that, therefore, we must always look for richer, more effective—and, in a sense, truer—models.[20] In this connection it would be missing the point to think that Marx (or any Marxist, for that matter) would attempt to give a scientific account of individual behavior. Like the British economists, what he sought was an overall account of collective free behavior which would explain scientifically the genesis of social structures. Where he differed from the economists was in the significance he attributed to long-term historical processes, refusing to see in any particular stage of the process a model for the whole process.[21]

Now, although it would not be mistaken to say that Marx would extend his concept of science—*mutatis mutandis*—to all science (he is not known to have raised any objections to Engels' project of *Dialectics of Nature*), the fact is that his own aim was the development of a scientific socialism, wherein he determines the laws that have governed the development of human social relations and which will provide the possibility of planning the future of society—without predicting in detail what that future will be and without constructing a univocal model to which all future societies must in all circumstances correspond. He was convinced that class society as he knew it had to go, that only revolution would put an end to it, and that the rules for that revolution were to be found in the science of history as he conceived it. He did not believe that the way to do this was to conceive of the ideal rational society—somewhat after the fashion of the French Revolution—and then to institute the reforms which would bring it about. As Engels put it: "The task no longer consisted in constructing a social system perfect as possible but in studying the historical development of the economy which had necessarily engendered these classes and their antagonism, and in discovering within the economic situation thus created the means of resolving the conflict."[22] The key expression here is "necessarily engendered." For Marx the socialism he preaches is "scientific" precisely because it contains the only possible and, therefore, the "necessary" means, of resolving the contradictions of society—which contradictions, incidentally, are dialectically necessary for the development of society to the point where they need to be resolved. Methodologically this consists of an analysis of bourgeois society—[23] a "given" in the sense that it has been produced by the forces of history—which reveals the scientific laws operative in that society's development and which will bring about its destruction. Practically this science will channel the operation of those real forces capable of realizing the necessary social transformation.[24]

If, then, we are to understand Marx's concept of science (scientific socialism) we must see the manner in which he derives its laws and then the manner in which those laws operate to bring about the society of the future. As in any science the procedure begins with an observation of "facts" (regularities, of course, since no number of isolated facts can serve as a basis for scientific formulation). These facts are then seen as the result of a historical process, and the science consists in determining the necessary laws of whose operation these facts are the necessary result. It should be pointed out, incidentally, that this position is based on a presupposition which is itself not scientific nor, properly speaking, philosophical. It is that, if there is to be explanation (and explanation there must be, except of how matter and motion, the only givens, came to be), the explanation will be natural (material) *and* historical.[25]

One would have to rewrite *Kapital* to describe all the "facts" and to determine all the "laws" operative in necessarily bringing them about.[26] Actually Marx begins with the contemporary "fact" of human alienation and argues back to a complete explanation of human history, beginning with the production of food as that whereby man distinguishes himself from the animal, i.e., dialectically fulfills the need he has for the food which nature does not adequately supply, thus developing consciousness in order to plan, speech in order to communicate, division of labor in order to produce more efficiently, private property in order both to expand production and to satisfy the interests of the class which has become dominant as the result of the division of labor, etc.[27] We can, however, show in a more summary fashion how the thing operates by simply analyzing the functions of capitalist society which is the necessary product of the unplanned operation of productive forces down through the ages.[28]

As a first observed fact, then, we can take the situation of the worker (the producer of value) who has sunk to the level of a commodity to be bought and sold on the market.[29] This fact is a regularity, such that it must be the necessary result of laws operating to produce it, and the laws are those of capitalist economy, which by simply following out its own logic must make the rich get richer and the poor poorer. As a second fact we might take the paradoxical observation that the worker becomes poorer the more wealth he produces and the more his production increases in power and extent.[30] This is true, because, as we saw before, a condition for profitable mass-production is the lowering of the unit cost of production, a saving which is realized by lowering the share of the cost allotted to the labor force. This, too, is an "objective law" of capitalist production, sometimes called the "law of progressive pauperization."[31]

A third fact (not necessarily in the order of importance) is that labor, as an activity (a quality) which distinguishes man as man, produces goods which take on a greater importance than the labor itself and, than man himself. Thus, labor, whose end becomes the product and not the producer, actually degrades rather than dignifies man. It is here that the concept of "alienation" enters in; the product stands over against the producer and becomes his master, and man is master neither of the product nor of his labor—*a fortiori* nor of himself. Simply by following the laws of capitalist economy the worker produces surplus-value, i.e., that part of the value he produces which does not accrue to himself and which is left over after his subsistence and his contribution to the ongoing labor force by reproduction has been paid for. By the same laws surplus value accumulates and becomes capital, a kind of impersonal personality to which the worker is subject, which means that he necessarily produces an alien force to which he is subject. Thus, the labor whose dialectic function is to transform nature and so to transform man has been diverted into producing an alien force which enslaves him; in exchange for his creative effort which produces use-value the worker receives money, which is exchange value and in no way proportionate to the value he has produced.

The purpose of this summary description of Marxist methodology in one area has not been, obviously, to give a complete picture of the vast synthesis of theory and practice contained in *Kapital*—to say nothing of Marx's earlier, more philosophical works. Nor has it been to criticize the adequacy of the anslyses, which are unquestionably very keen. Rather it has been to give some idea of just what a "scientific law" means in a Marxist context and to show briefly how such a law can be derived. As Marx himself says, "the ultimate purpose of my work is to discover the economic law of development of contemporary society,"[32] which is but a global way of expressing the various "laws" which cannot but function, so long as capitalist society persists. It would defeat our purpose to give here (or elsewhere) a list of the dialectical laws of which Marx speaks. They are conceived of as emerging in the process itself and are not, except in general fashion, to be formulated definitively.

Here, however, we must go back to the more general notion of a science of history and of its laws. Even though it is true that Marx's primary concern from the theoretical point of view was to give a scientific explanation of *economic* development and from the practical to prepare an economic revolution, if all he did were to analyze the necessary laws governing *capitalist* economy he would not escape the criticism which he himself had directed against the British economists of not having pushed the science far enough and of having limited themselves to discovering the laws peculiar to a *given* situation.[33] If the revolution he proposes, whereby man is to reappropriate what has been alienated under the capitalist mode of production, is to have a genuinely scientific underpinning, the scope of his scientific contribution must be the whole of history and not merely the industrial revolution or the period of capitalist domination. To get this overall picture we can, I think, turn to Engels, not because he has expressed the scientific theory more clearly than Marx has, nor because he has made an original contribution which is not to be found in Marx's own work, but because he has concentrated into one book, his *Anti-Dühring* (cf. also *Utopian and Scientific Socialism*), a concise explanation of what "scientific history" means to Marx. The book is, so to speak, the classic textbook of Marxism, and it was written for Marxists.

Marx himself had said, in a letter to Kowalewski, "It is impossible to think logically except on the basis of the dialectical method."[34] What this says is that the developing nature of reality is such that only dialectical thinking can give a scientific account of it. Engels, in his work, is trying to show that Marxism is not, properly speaking, a philosophy at all but rather a dialectical method which alone permits science to be scientific. Apart from Engels' rather naive application of this principle to mathematics and to the natural sciences (which he repeats in the *Dialectics of Nature*), what he is saying is that a thinking which is other than dialectic must inevitably fail to see that the truths which science discovers are not eternal truths whose validity was always there to be discovered but rather are historical truths which are simply not true until historically they become true.[35] This is the "real basis" without which socialism never could have become a science.[36] At the same time there is no philosophy distinct from or embracing the particular sciences: there is only the dialectical method, which is what gives the scientific character to any investigation, which is but a way of saying that reality in process can be grasped only in a thought which is dialectical.[37]

Thus, there is only one law to which all conforms, the law of dialectical development. Actually the paradigm of science is the socioeconomic science of Marx, which became possible only when Marx had discovered the principle of a nonmechanistic, i.e. dialectical, interpretation of history, whose key concept with regard to an understanding of capitalism was that of surplus value. "These two great discoveries—the materialistic interpretation of history and the uncovering of the mystery of capitalistic production by means of surplus-value—we owe to Marx. With them socialism became a science, and it is now a question of working it out in all its details and connections."[38]

To work out this "science" in "all its details and connections," however, is not a matter of deduction; rather it is a question of determining the (derivative) laws of the socioeconomic process on the basis of the observed process of history.[39] This must be, since there is only one "given" to which science as such can appeal, i.e., matter, whose manner of being is motion, and this will reveal its real possibilities only as in the process they become realities.

What comes out of all this is not science—or any particular science—but rather a criterion for determining whether what is called science is truly science. Be it physics, biology, or socialism, if it traces the real connections whereby reality becomes the reality it is, we have science, otherwise we do not. As has been pointed out more than once, what the Marxist scientist *does* in no way differs from what a non-Marxist scientist does—nor, except for the "science" of history, is his conception of this or that science noticeably different. His conception, however, of what it is to be scientific is different, for he feels constrained to show that what he does and what he thinks must be subsumable under dialectical laws, or else fail to be scientific. Marx, as we have said, had no interest, as did Engels, in showing that his conception of science was true of physics or biology (although the theory itself did manifest to him the necessity of evolutionary development): his sole interest is to trace the necessary development of social forms and economic structures, which are what they are through the working out of history's discoverable necessary laws. Science, then, is "critical knowledge of historical movement."[40] Here there are no fixed natures of which static science would be a knowledge, but there is "historical necessity,"[41] which is exemplified in the "natural laws of capitalist production . . . working with iron necessity towards inevitable results."[42] Fortunately for Marx the revolutionary, to whom science would be meaningless, it did not reveal the changes *to be* wrought in the socioeconomic structure; an examination of the given situation reveals the "necessity of the present order" which "points to the necessity of a subsequent order."[43]

Now, if all we had were the foregoing, the whole thing would remain extremely vague, precisely because we should have no criterion for determining what is and what is not an inexorable law of history. Marx is certainly not so naive as to say that whatever happens necessarily happens; that would be the sheerest fatalism and totally incompatible with Marx's conviction that human initiative is operative in the working out of history. Marx was unalterably opposed to Hegel's dictum, "whatever is real is rational, and whatever is rational is real"[44] (at least to the common interpretation of it).[45] There has to be a sense in which some things *should* happen and others *should not*, or talk about revolution is nonsense. It is meaningless to say that historical development is the criterion of truth, unless there is some sense in which development can be unhistorical and, hence, untrue. Marx was no proponent of the policy of "folded hands," which simply awaits passively the working out of history's inexorable laws. Nor could he abide Hegel's "trickery of reason," which simply carried out its pre-conceived plans despite men's illusion that they were acting freely.

There must, then, be a way in which history can be read such that it reveals not merely what *does* take place but also what *should* take place. Engels said with regard to the "science" of history in general that, in it, the categories of good and bad, right and wrong, were no longer viable, only the categories of "historical" and "unhistorical."[46] One could almost say that Hegel's identification of the real and the rational had been transformed into an identification of the "historical" and the rational. Here it is, then, that the theory of dialectical "contradiction" enters in. That the contradictions in question are not the abstract contradictions of formal logic, but the concrete, dynamic contradictions of history should be clear; they are "surds" in the forward progress of historical development.[47]

The dialectic of need and fulfillment such as Marxism sees it working itself out in the historical process is one in which genuine development always means the resolution of contradictions in a given situation. The basic contradiction, of course, is found in the relationship of the forces of production to the product. Whether the stage of development be that of the most primitive production of food to fulfill the needs of purely biological life or that of capitalist production with its attendant division of the entire world into antagonistic classes, there arises a contradiction between the form of production which actually exists and the needs of man which require to be fulfilled. Contradiction, then, exists wherever a stage in the development of man has turned into *the* "chains" which impede further development.[48] Now, according to Marxism, where this contradiction arises it must be resolved, and it must be resolved by human activity. If the contradiction persists, the activity of man has by that very fact become unhistorical. The point is, however, that in the very contradiction itself is revealed the only true means of resolving it, and any other means reveals itself as untrue by either perpetuating the contradiction or being in itself contradictory. Thus, although there may seem to be many possibilities of solution, there is only one possibility of *real* solution—and that is the truly historical development. What this real possibility is, is not inscribed in history from all eternity but reveals itself only in the actual process of development,[49] and to look for change *before* the historical stage which calls for change has arrived is as unhistorical as is resistance to change when it is called for.[50]

Because in the last analysis Marx has a kind of Hegelian confidence in the rationality of history he can look at the past and see all those developments which have contributed to the present structure of society as genuinely historical (he can also see that there have been deviations or retardations). Thus, history itself reveals what is and what is not truly historical. Only when the contradictions of history have been genuinely resolved, it is true, can he say what precise form the resolution *had to* take, but he does know that the resolution was the result of the working out of "necessary laws." By the same token he does *not* know the precise form which the resolution of the present contradiction must take, but he is able to say what forms would merely perpetuate the contradiction or simply introduce new contradictions. Thus, he is quite sure that the contradiction will not be resolved until the division of society into classes has been overcome. Moreover, he is

equally sure that only revolution—communist revolution at
that—will resolve the present contradiction. Despite all his
efforts to avoid it there *is* an element of (somewhat illegitimate) prediction in this, but even this contradiction he
resolves in a twofold way: 1) he sees the collapse of capitalism
and the triumph of socialism as not an event in the future
but as a development already in process;[51] and 2) by a process
of elimination he has exhausted all other possibilities.[52]

   Nowhere, perhaps, do we find expressed more clearly the
Marxist notion of dialectical necessity in the historical process
than in Engels' interpretation of Hegel's dictum, "Whatever is
real is rational, and whatever is rational is *real.*"[53] The
proposition, he tells us, has been gratefully accepted by con-
servatives and angrily rejected by liberals, by both for the
wrong reasons. What both failed to see, says Engels, is that,
historically speaking, there is neither reality nor rationality
without necessity. The real is rational only when it is historically necessary that it be (or come to be); and the reality of the
rational is the historical necessity of its coming into being.
This means, according to the very rules of the Hegelian
dialectic, that the real as given contains within itself the very
irrationality which necessarily demands that it be superseded
by what is truly rational and, thus, historically real. The proposition, then, becomes the foundation stone of revolutionary
thinking (and action). Its meaning is, "Whatever *is* given
deserves to disappear."[54] There are no absolute truths to be
held on to dogmatically, precisely because truth lies in the
process of the developing knowledge which is science.

> The truth which philosophy had as its function to grasp was with
> Hegel no longer a collection of completed dogmatic propositions,
> which, once they have been discovered, demand only to be learned
> by heart. Truth was now to be found in the very process of knowing,
> in the long historical development of science, which climbs from
> lower to ever higher levels of knowledge without ever, through the
> discovery of so-called absolute truth, arriving at a point where it
> can go no further; where there is nothing more for it to do but fold
> its hands on its lap and marvel at the absolute truth it has attained.[55]

   The application, of course, is primarily to history, and it
embraces not only the process of thinking but also the course
of events and the human action necessary to bring about what
is historically "necessary." This process has no ideally perfect

human situation as its goal, but every stage in the process of development is rationally necessary in a process which has no term. The process is rationally necessary, and it is possible to know scientifically the inner dialectical laws of this process— in fact this is what science is.[56]

Admittedly this is not what Hegel himself said. The point is that it is what Engels sees as a necessary consequence of his dialectical method, and it describes what in fact the Marxist dialectic is. The Hegelian "system" is a dead end; but the method describes "scientifically" the necessary march of history.[57]

Despite whatever weaknesses this theory may reveal we can see that they are the weaknesses of Stalin's univocal interpretation of the form which the revolution had to take. I venture to say that the same is true of Lenin (at least in his most influential pronouncements)—and even of Engels—both of whom "dogmatized" Marxism to an extent incompatible with the more tentative approach of Marx himself.[58] In any event the non-dogmatic interpretation makes more intelligible the efforts of Marxists in Czechoslovakia, Yugoslavia, and Cuba, and in the non- (not yet) communist countries of France, Spain, Italy, etc., to realize "scientific" socialism in a manner which is not dictated by the univocal interpretation of the most powerful communist nations.[59]

Although it is difficult to subscribe to the opinion of some contemporary interpreters—usually proponents of some sort of non-communist Marxism—who emphasize the differences between the early and the late Marx,[60] it is nevertheless true that the language of the later works is more susceptible of the sort of dogmatic interpretation which until recently was current. We are, therefore, fortunate to have available the earlier, more philosophical writings, against the background of which we can understand the later insistence on "science" with its "objective laws." It is, of course, difficult to see what it can mean to speak of history's "scientific" laws, if one does not assume in history a sort of built-in teleology, but it is clear enough—and this many recent commentators stress—that Marx himself intended a historical process which was neither teleo-logical nor rigidly deterministic and yet susceptible of the kind of scientific knowledge which would enable him not only to criticize the aberrations of society but also to remedy them. The all-important point to remember—and here Marx harks back to the "transcendental" viewpoint of Kant and Fichte—is that the necessary antecedent condition for transforming the present situation of society is that there be "scientific" knowledge of the genesis of that situation. In the last analysis the reason why Marx calls this "science" is that for his purposes it *had* to be science—otherwise "revolution"[61] would be only "reform." What tends to make the whole thing suspect, precisely as "science," is that it is difficult to conceive of what—for Marx or for a Marxist—could even hypothetically count as evidence *against* the theory. If we know antecedently that any evidence which can be discovered will count as evidence *for* and not *against* a theory, are we talking about a "scientific" theory at all?

NOTES

1. It is significant that some contemporary Marxist thinkers—outside the Soviet Union—are emphasizing the need to conceive Marxist "science" more along the lines of knowledge in process, constantly being modified. Cf., e.g., Gajo Petrović, *Marx in the Mid-Twentieth Century* (New York: Doubleday, 1967), p. 11.

There is no particular point here in distinguishing between scientific certitude and probability, since it was not a concern of nineteenth-century thinkers, least of all Marxists.

2. Cf. Marx, *Theses on Feuerbach*, #11.

3. Cf. Petrović, *Marx*, pp. 22-23.

4. Roger Garaudy, *Marxisme du XXe siecle* (Paris: La Palatine, 1966, p. 8.

5. Cf. Engels' remark, in the Preface to the *Communist Manifesto*, that Marx's science was "destined to do for history what Darwin's theory has done for biology."

6. Jacob Grimm and Wilhelm Grimm, *Deutsches Wörterbuch* vol. 15, pt. 2 (Leipzig: Hirzel, 1960).

7. For German philosophers of the nineteenth century, the classical distinction between freedom and necessity was contributed by Kant in his *Critique of Practical Reason* and *Fundamental Principles of the Metaphysics of Morals*. Roughly, Kant would say that man is spiritually free but materially determined. Thus, he can choose to act, but once he goes into action, his activities are

governed by the necessary laws of material activity. Marx seeks to synthesize freedom and necessity in terms of "laws" of history which govern material activity.

8. Cf. *Theses on Feuerbach*, #1, where we are told that Marx's materialism differs from all other materialism (particularly the "mechanistic" materialism of the eighteenth century) in giving a materialistic account of man's subjective activity—called "praxis," i.e., purposeful activity). In *Capital*, vol. 1, trans. Samuel Moore and Edward Aveling (Chicago: Kerr, 1908), Preface, p. 13, Marx distinguishes between the "natural" development of capitalist production, which is manifested in Germany, and the situation in England, where at least an attempt had been made to curb the operation of "natural" laws by legislation. Cf. further, Marx, *Zur Kritik der politischen Oekonomie* (Berlin: Dietz, 1951), p. 237, where he assures us that individuals are what they are only in society which develops according to its own dialectical laws.

9. Cf. Franz Schnabel, *Deutsche Geschichte im neunzehnten Jahrhundert*, vol. 1, *Die Grundlagen der neueren Geschichte*, vol. 2. *Der Aufstieg der Nationen* (Freiburg: Herder, 1964).

10. Cf. *Manifest der Kommunistischen Partei* (Berlin: Dietz, 1951), p. 7, where we are told that modern bourgeois society has "simplified class antagonisms."

11. The concept of "alienation" is certainly not original with Marx (or with Hegel and Feuerbach). It is a religious concept of ancient vintage, indicating man's estrangement from God and, hence, from his own true humanity, through sin. It is from Hegel, however, that Marx derives the notion of "alienation" as an essential negative movement in the historical process of human development.

12. "Three Sources and Three Component Parts of Marxism," *Selected Works* (Moscow, 1936-1939), vol. 11, p. 3.

13. "In so far as Political Economy remains within that Horizon, i.e., as the capitalist regime is looked upon as the absolutely final form of social production, instead of as a passing historical phase of its evolution, Political Economy can remain a science only so long as the class-struggle is latent or manifests itself only in isolated and sporadic phenomena." *Capital*, vol. 1, p. 17; cf. pp. 17-19.
It would seem that Marx himself is guilty of a similar "unscientific" procedure. In deriving the "necessary natural laws" of capitalist production from the British industrialist stage in the history of capitalist production, he is taking it as the "absolutely final form" of this sort "of production" instead of a passing historical phase of its evolution.

14. Cf. *Die deutsche Ideologie* (Berlin: Dietz, 1953), pp. 40-41; *Theses on Feuerbach*, #10.

15. Cf. *Zur Kritik der politischen Oekonomie,* pp. 12-13. There are not any "eternal natures"; there is only historical process (cf. ibid., p. 236).

16. *Die heilige Familie* (Berlin: Dietz, 1953), pp. 84-85.

17. Cf. *Theses on Feuerbach,* #9.

18. *Die heilige Familie,* pp. 14-15.

19. Cf. *Theses on Feuerbach,* #2.

20. We are not, of course, saying that the term "model" was familiar to Marx.

21. As was pointed in note 13 above, Marx might have been even more scientific (and certainly more historical) had he not uncritically taken the England of the Industrial Revolution as the model for capitalist society.

22. Engels, *Anti-Dühring* (Berlin: Dietz, 1953), p. 31. Marx himself takes economico-historical development out of the realm of individual initiative into that of "natural" process: "My standpoint, from which the evolution of the economic formation of society is viewed as a process of natural history, can less than any other make the individual responsible for relations whose creature he socially remains, however much he may subjectively raise himself above them." *Capital,* vol. 1, p. 15.

23. *Zur Kritik der politischen Oekonomie,* p. 237.

24. Ibid., p. 13.

25. Cf. Marx, "National Okonomie and Philosophie," *Die Frühschriften* (Stuttgart: Kroner, 1953), pp. 246-248. It could be argued, of course, that no other form of explanation would be scientific, since no other form of explanation is susceptible of the kind of verification which science requires. It cannot be argued, however, that the only acceptable explanation is a scientific one (in this limited sense of the term) or that a scientific explanation is ever more than partial.

26. It is not for the philosopher (not even the philosopher of science) to judge the accuracy with which Marx presents economic "facts"—that is the task of the economist. What the philosopher can do is to judge whether the de facto presentation justifies a theory of "necessary laws"—and to what extent.

Marx's "Science" of History **163**

27. For all this, cf. *Die deutsche Ideologie*, pp. 17-30. It should be noted that each need-fulfillment leads at the same time to the engendering of another need to be fulfilled. Ibid., p. 25.

28. *Zur Kritik der politischen Oekonomie*, p. 14. Because, up to this point, development has been unplanned it is "prehistorical." This comes out strongly throughout *Capital*, where emphasis is constantly put on the "necessary" character of development up to bourgeois society.

29. Cf. *Capital*, vol. 1, pt. 6, pp. 586-617.

30. Cf. ibid., pt. 7, pp. 671-711.

31. Roger Garaudy, *Karl Marx* (Paris: Seghers, 1964), pp. 232-233. Cf. *Capital*, vol. 1, pp. 686-687. 706.

32. *Capital*, vol. 1, Preface to First Edition, p. 14.

33. Cf. supra, notes 13 and 21, where we have pointed out a certain contradiction in Marx's treatment of the situation in England as the "given" of capitalism.

34. Letter to Kowaleski, quoted by Garaudy, *Karl Marx*, p. 184.

35. *Anti-Dühring*, pp. 20-22.

36. Ibid., p. 22.

37. Cf. ibid., p. 29.

38. Ibid., p. 32.

39. Cf. ibid., p. 40.

40. Marx, *Das Elend der Philosophie* (Berlin: Dietz, 1952), p. 43.

41. Cf. *Theses on Feuerbach*, #6, where Marx accuses Feuerbach of having missed the whole point of "real science" by looking on humanity as a "natural" genus and thus failing to see that what makes one is not logical classification but historical activity.

42. *Capital*, vol. 1, Preface to First Edition, p. 13; cf. p. 15, where he calls the description of this process "natural history."

43. Ibid., Preface to Second Edition, p. 23.

44. Hegel, *Grundlinien der Philosophie des Rechts*, ed. Johannes Hoffmeister (Hamburg: Meiner, 1955), p. 14.

45. Cf. Engels, *Ludwig Feuerbach und der Ausgang der klassischen deutschen Philosophie* (Berlin: Dietz, 1951), pp. 7-10, for a nuanced Marxist interpretation of Hegel's dictum.

46. *Das Elend der Philosophie,* Engels' Preface, p. 27.

47. In *Capital.* vol. 1, Preface to Second Edition, p. 26, Marx tells us that the "contradictions" of which he speaks (in economic history) are "cyclic crises."

48. Cf. *Die deutsche Ideologie,* pp. 72 ff.; *Zur Kritik der politischen Oekonomie,* p. 13.

49. The similarities between the kind of verification envisaged here and that of pragmatism are too obvious to be detailed.

50. Cf. *Zur Kritik der politischen Oekonomie,* p. 14.

51. Cf. *Capital,* vol. 1, p. 14.

52. Cf. *Communist Manifesto,* pt. 3.

53. *Ludwig Feuerbach und der Ausgang der klassischen deutschen Philosophie.*

54. Ibid., p. 7.

55. Ibid., pp. 7-8.

56. Ibid., p. 8.

57. Ibid., pp. 9-10.

58. There is, of course, a suspicion—which applies more obviously to much contemporary Marxist writing (e.g., Garaudy's *Marxisme du XXe siècle,* pp. 62-63)—that "non-dogmatic" is in itself sufficient guarantee of "scientific."

59. Petrović, *Marx*, p. 56. It is true, of course, that the present phenomenon of Soviet intervention to suppress "counterrevolution" in Czechoslovakia and *Pravda*'s saber-rattling with regard to "neo-nazism" and "militarism" in West Germany cast some doubt on the ability of the theory to work itself out, where the univocal interpretation has all the military power. But here we are concerned with the theory as such.

60. Cf. ibid., pp. 31-34.

61. This does not mean, of course, that "science" would give Marx absolute certainty that any particular revolution would be successful. It is not the function of science to eliminate risks.

Chapter 12

Metaphysics and Marxist Philosophy

STANIŠA NOVAKOVIĆ

Staniša Novaković is head of the sector on methodology in the Institute of Social Sciences in Belgrade, Yugoslavia. He has been editor-in-chief of *Philosophical Theories*, the journal of the Serbian Philosophical Society. In 1964-1965, as a recipient of a Ford Foundation grant, he studied in the United States. He is the author of *The Problem of Demarcation Between Science and Metaphysics in Contemporary Empiricist Philosophy* (1965), *The Problem of Metaphysics in Contemporary Analytical Philosophy* (1967), and other works.

I still consider that disposing of the remnants of some rigid patterns of thought, and overcoming the fear of using some words, are important aspects in these endeavors that are oriented towards the open, free, and critical development of Marxist thought. This is especially so, since this thought spent quite a long period of time in a dogmatic standstill, under the total domination of current political ideology.

Metaphysics, of course, was, and unfortunately in the Soviet philosophy of today still is, one of those words with the worst possible ideological connotations. In fact, it seems to me that the meaning of some words in Marxist philosophy is still emotional rather than technical, and loaded with ideological and political implications (e.g., idealist, agnosticist, or even semanticist, on the negative side, and dialectician, or genuine

165

materialist, on the positive side). Calling a work of philosophy "metaphysical," or finding elements of metaphysics in somebody's philosophy, was some time ago nearly equal to proclaiming somebody an enemy of socialism and the state order. But what was it in the term "metaphysics" in dogmatic Marxism that made it such an unpopular and objectionable epithet?

Its clearest exemplification is in Stalin's short pamphlet "Dialectical and Historical Materialism" (originally the fourth chapter of the *History of the C.P.S.U./B./* (1938), where the metaphysical mode of thinking was all black and evil contrasted with the dialectical mode of thinking, which was all white and good, i.e., the possible and the only proper method of human thought.

Metaphysics, according to the characterization in that pamphlet of Stalin, (1) "regards nature as an accidental agglomeration of things, of phenomena, unconnected with, isolated from, and independent of, each other"; (2) "holds that nature is a state of rest and immobility, stagnation and immutability"; (3) "regards the process of development as a simple process of growth, where quantitative changes do not lead to qualitative changes"; and (4) "does not see internal contradictions in all things and phenomena of nature, does not see that the struggle between their positive and negative sides, the struggle between the old and the new, between that which is dying away and that which is being born, constitutes the internal content of the process of development, the internal content of the transformation of quantitative changes into qualitative changes."[1]

So, for more than two decades this was the only meaning of metaphysics that one could find in Marxist philosophy, and it is still the one that dominates in Soviet philosophy.

In what follows I would like first, to show that there are other meanings of metaphysics, i.e., that there are different meanings of the term "metaphysics" even in the papers of Marx and Engels; second, to try to bring out the essential meaning of the term in the entire historical development of philosophical thought, the meaning which is also most dominant in all non-Marxist philosophy today; and third, to explain what may be the consequences of these considerations for contemporary Marxist philosophy.

1a. In the first phase of their philosophical development, in the papers that are usually published under the title *Early Writings,* Marx and Engels are starting from Feuerbach's anthropological conception of philosophy. Feuerbach's conception of philosophy is not anthropological in the sense of anthropology as a separate science, but in the sense of being human, or humanistic. As a strong critic of theological views, Feuerbach pointed to the anthropological or human origin of all religious belief. Criticizing Hegel's philosophy as still having its seat in illusions of a religious type (as it started from the standpoint of the absolute, and considered that the general is more real than the individual), Feuerbach maintained that the subject matter of philosophy is not that self-developing process of the absolute idea, where man and his history are only a dependent phase, and that "the only, universal and supreme subject matter of philosophy" becomes just "man, including nature as his basis." However, Marx and Engels do not accept Feuerbach's antidialectical orientation. Relying on Hegel's dialectics materialistically interpreted, they try to develop a new dialectical anthropological philosophy.

The main subject matter of Marx's philosophy in that period was the concrete self-alienated man, i.e., the man living in a society based on private property, class exploitation, and a state apparatus. The main task of this philosophy was entirely concrete too; it was conceived as the material instrument for the liberation of the proletariat, of the class which, in the society of the self-alienated man, acts as the real basic force in the fight for abolition of alienation, for the realization of the general human emancipation.[2]

It was also the period when Marx (in his *Economic and Philosophical Manuscripts*) denied the possibility of an objective dialectics, in the sense of such fixed dialectical laws which eternally exist in nature, independent of man as a knowing subject. On the other hand, Marx said that dialectical laws originate in and arise out of human history. Trying to go beyond man and his history would be a speculative, metaphysical attempt. This speculative *attempt to go beyond the historical man* may be said, I think, to be the *first sense* of metaphysics which we can find in Marxism.

1b. Starting from their humanistic standpoint, in·their joint work *The Holy Family*, Marx and Engels severely criticized the speculative metaphysics of Hegel, having in mind Hegel's universal empire of reason (*Vernunft*), which transcended and overcame all dialectical opposites that understanding (*Verstand*) got entangled in, and in which the absolute truth was attained, all problems solved, and the process of acquiring knowledge completed.

It ought to be noticed that Marx and Engels had been inclined, in that period, to differentiate between such a speculative metaphysics (as in Hegel), and ordinary metaphysics of understanding (as in Descartes, Malebranche, Spinoza, or Leibniz). As the ordinary metaphysics, Marx and Engels had in mind that direction of thought of seventeenth-century philosophers who tried to build philosophical systems comprehending the whole of reality, but who did not take note of the development of scientific knowledge, dealing mainly, in Marx's words, with "abstract beings and heavenly things," and doing so in such a time "when all the interest began to shift to the real beings and earthly things." So, the *second sense* of the term "metaphysics" would be *the speculative attempt to go beyond concrete scientific knowledge, and to speak of transcendent beings and heavenly things.*

1c. But, trying to build a materialistic and anthropological philosophy, Marx and Engels were more and more inclined to an empirical rather than rationalistic approach to the determination of the role of the proletariat. They held the view that the social movement of the proletariat was not to realize some natural human order, but to fulfill a historical task springing out of the reality of capitalistic society. So, they suggested that it was not enough to try to determine the role of the proletariat philosophically, i.e., rationalistically, but that it must be determined through an empirical analysis of capitalistic society. Such an empirical orientation imposed the necessity of urgent and thorough scientific investigation of the existing economic and social order. It was this task then to which Marx devoted the main part of his life.

But, the same orientation yielded some doubts about the good reasons for the existence of any philosophy at all. This skeptical and positivistic interlude in Marx and Engels' thought expressed itself especially in the second work they wrote together—*The German Ideology*. In this book Marx and Engels wrote:

Where speculation ends—in real life—there real, positive science begins: the representation of the practical activity, of the practical process of development of men. Empty talk about consciousness ceases, and real knowledge has to take its place. When reality is depicted, philosophy as an independent branch of activity loses its medium of existence.

At best, its place can only be taken by a summing-up of the most general results which could be abstracted from the observation of the historical development of men.[3]

Holding such a radically antiphilosophical "philosophy," Marx and Engels almost identified philosophy and metaphysics, though they had not discussed explicitly what the subject matter of philosophy is, or how metaphysics ought to be understood. So, the *third position* would be: *identification of metaphysics with the whole domain of philosophy—identification being a negative assessment of both.*

In the mature works of Engels (Marx later devoted himself only to the economic and political sphere) there are still many positivistic formulations.[4]

But still, one can say that Engels, in spite of the above mentioned kind of statements, basically accepted Hegel's conception of philosophy as the knowledge of reality in its totality. And, rejecting Hegel's idealistic system from the materialistic standpoint, he tried to keep and develop further the so-called "rational kernel" of both dialectics of Hegel— subjective and objective.

It seems that Engels, as a matter of fact, had primarily in mind that old speculative idealistic philosophy would disappear, but that, over a long period of time, philosophy in general may also be overcome. It would no longer be a separate form, something over and above empirical science. It would, however, be preserved in its real content, because particular sciences should accept and incorporate in their body "the results of the development of philosophy during the past two and a half thousand years."[5] In that sense, modern materialism, which Engels thought is dialectical, no longer needs the philosophy that is over and above empirical sciences. "As soon as each separate science is required to get clarity as to its position in the great totality of things, a separate science dealing with this totality is superfluous. What still *independently* survives of all former philosophy is the science of thought and its laws—formal logic and dialectics. Everything else is merged in the positive science of Nature and history."[6]

It is especially important to find out what Engels meant by dialectics. It seems to me that Engels never reduced dialectics to the subjective dialectics, as "the product of human mind." He conceived subjective dialectics as "the product of nature, growing in and together with its surroundings," in other words, as part of objective dialectics.[7] So, although Engels was rather strongly anti-philosophically minded, dialectics included both subjective and objective aspects.

For dialectics conceived in such a way, or at least for its ontological component, it can be said to belong to metaphysics as the discipline which tries to transcend all partial scientific knowledge of reality, which tries to get knowledge of the whole of being. At the same time, we must bear in mind that Engels could not subordinate metaphysics to logic (or dialectics), as did Hegel, because this could be done only in idealistic systems, which identify concepts with reality. If one considers reality material, as did Engels, it is only possible to subordinate logic to metaphysics.

This being so, it is curious how Engels came (in *Anti-Dühring*) to a completely new conception of metaphysics, which later came to be the only conception of dogmatic Marxism.

1d. According to this last conception of Engels, metaphysics would be a theory that considers being only as the aggregate of unconnected objects of investigation, which are "isolated, rigid, fixed, given once for all," "to be considered one after the other apart from each other." It was such a mode of thinking, according to Engels, which, "considering individual things, loses sight of their connections; in contemplating their existence, it forgets their coming into being and passing away; in looking at them at rest, it leaves their motion out of account; because it cannot see the wood for the trees." This metaphysical mode of thinking (i.e., this method of investigation) was plausible and even necessarily related to certain stages in the development of human knowledge. To it Engels opposed the dialectical mode of thinking, which always tries to give "the picture of phenomena as a whole," and "grasps things and their images, ideas, essentially in their interconnections, in their sequence, their movement, their births and deaths."[8] Now we can formulate the *fourth sense* of the term "metaphysics": *a static mode of thinking, losing sight of the necessity to put everything in the complex and changeable whole.*

Why do I think Engels' conception of metaphysics curious? Its divergence from Marx's, or, still better, from their mutual conception, expressed, for example, in *The Holy Family*, is not the only reason that it is curious. The main reason is that the complete historical development of metaphysics as a philosophical discipline, regardless of some vagueness in its definition, does not support such an interpretation. It does not allow this meaning of the term "metaphysics."

Furthermore, Engels' claim that "the old Greek philosophers were all natural born dialecticians"[9] is also very strange, as well as historically unjustifiable and implausible. Equally unjustifiable and implausible is his inclusion of Descartes and Spinoza among the "brilliant exponents of dialectics,"[10] when in *The Holy Family* they are listed with Malebranche and Leibniz, as typical examples of metaphysicians; or *vice versa*, his inclusion of Bacon and Locke among the exponents of the "rigid metaphysical way of thinking,"[11] when in *The Holy Family* they are listed with Gassendi, Hobbes, Condillac, Voltaire, Bayle, as antimetaphysicians. As for Hegel, regardless of his dialectics, Marx considered him a speculative metaphysician (evidently he did not ever think of opposing dialectics to metaphysics); Engels, however, took the whole classical German philosophy as an example of dialectics in the tradition of ancient philosophy, and of Descartes and Spinoza.

Finally, it is also somehow queer that Engels took the metaphysical way of thinking as a mode of thought "transferred from natural science into philosophy" instead of trying to find its roots in ancient or medieval philosophy.

But, we must also ask ourselves: what is the main source of Engels' conception of metaphysics? The main source we can find, of course, is Hegel's description of the mode of thinking of our understanding, which Hegel also calls old metaphysics or metaphysics of the understanding (not, of course, metaphysics in general). However, Hegel did not oppose the procedure of the understanding to dialectics, but included it in logic, i.e., subordinated it to dialectics as one moment of dialectics.

So, this means that Engels' idea of opposing metaphysics thus defined to dialectics in fact does not come out of Hegel. It can only be traced back (as noticed also by Tacatura Ando in his book *Metaphysics, a Survey of its Meanings*) to a specific definition of metaphysics in Bacon. In his classification of knowledge, Bacon did not identify first philosophy with metaphysics. Instead, he took metaphysics as a special part of natural philosophy, which deals not with that which is transitory (that belongs to physics), but with that which is abstract and fixed. So Bacon opposed metaphysics, the investigation of the abstract and fixed, to physics, the investigation of the transitory empirical world. And this is very much like what Engels did in opposing metaphysics to dialectics.

Unfortunately, just this special and very limitedly justifiable conception of metaphysics, that one can find in later works of Engels, has come to dominate, and has turned out to be one of the main dogmas of, uncreative Marxism.

As for Lenin, it seems that he accepted the view of Engels,[12] though he nowhere insisted on such an opposition. Stalin, however, as the reader may have noticed, especially stressed, overemphasized, dogmatized, and vulgarized this opposition of the metaphysical and dialectical methods, so that he deprived it of any philosophical relevance.

2. The second task I put before myself, was to point to the meaning of the term "metaphysics" which is in greatest accord with the whole historical development of philosophical thought, and which is still dominant in non-Marxist philosophical literature.

I will not be able now, of course, to enter into any historical considerations (as I did in the first chapter of my *The Problem of Metaphysics in Contemporary Analytical Philosophy,* following the problem of the meaning of metaphysics from Aristotle up to present-day philosophical movements). But I believe that Kant—in a language that is not far from the one we now use— made explicit that meaning of metaphysics which prevailed before him. At the same time, since we may, with good reason, call the problem of metaphysics Kant's problem, I believe that in one way or another all philosophers discussing this problem after Kant had to take into account, and in fact took into account, Kant's view and his meaning of the term "metaphysics" (the second sense in Marx and Engels).

Kant thought that human reason is and will be forever (to the end of time) oriented toward metaphysics in the sense of the eternal aspiration of human mind to embrace the whole of being, the whole of reality, in the sense of the human need to try to solve problems transcending all possible experience, to make sense of the absolute totality of everything around us. Kant defined metaphysical statements (in his *Prolegomena*) as those statements in human knowledge that tend toward a total synthesis, as those ideas that are not given in experience and those principles that cannot be verified or falsified in experience. Yet they are set as a task before human reason just because it is in its nature to tend towards unification of the conclusions of understanding, to tend towards a supreme synthesis, transcending all possible experience.

Kant's concept of metaphysics, however, was in the main one of subject matter, and no subject matter determination can ever be exhaustive and precise in such a degree as to enable us to judge not only the character of a theoretical system as a whole, but the character of particular theoretical statements.

If we are interested in the latter, i.e., in the problem of demarcation, as K. R. Popper defined it,[13] in that case we need also the logico-methodological characterization of metaphysical statements.

In present-day empiricist philosophy, of course, different criteria have been proposed that can be considered to refer to the problem of demarcation. These are, as we know, (1) verifiability criteria (or later on: confirmability criteria); (2) translatability criteria; and (3) falsifiability criteria. All these criteria have been thoroughly and critically examined in the literature, and it seems to me that the most fruitful will prove a criterion which would be basically along the lines of Popper's falsifiability criterion. Namely, I think that one ought to consider as metaphysical those statements which can neither directly nor indirectly attain such a degree of testability, i.e., degree of empirical decidability, that can provide a decisive criterion for accepting them; we always have to make our choice between several metaphysical theories, to decide which one to adopt. The most significant advantage of this criterion I consider to be as follows: it not only allows close associations of metaphysics with scientific knowledge, but it emphasizes the significance and the role of metaphysics in scientific knowledge. There are some difficulties in it, but thus far this criterion has suggested the most adequate solution to the problem of demarcation between empirical sciences and metaphysics, in so far as metaphysics would be understood to stand for all that does not belong to the empirical sciences.

Naturally, I presume that nobody expects that we can ever draw a sharp line between the statements of the empirical sciences and metaphysics. Moreover, I think that in theoretical systems, both of empirical sciences and of philosophy, we can find different levels of statements with regard to their empirical decidability. I regard statements of theoretical systems as making a continuum: at one pole of this continuum we find clearly unphilosophical scientific statements, and at the other those philosophical creations which are beyond scientific testability.

Therefore, when we are dealing with some concrete system in the empirical sciences or in philosophy, then it is only possible to grade conceptions according to their empirical background or their scientific status. That is, it is only possible to find out in which segment of that continuum the centre of gravity is, in which segment the kernel or the bulk of the content of such a system is. Nevertheless, when we are considering some statements of a certain system, taking as the main criterion the degree of testability, it is possible to distinguish several levels of these statements, and among other levels the level of metaphysical statements as I have defined them.

3. Now, suppose we in Marxism throw away that one-sided but still held (or at least unquestioned) conception of metaphysics. (We can find many good reasons to do so: losing sight of the manifold positive function of metaphysical doctrines in science, as well as in satisfying some basic human needs; causing some unnecessary misunderstandings and communication difficulties in the dialogues of Marxist philosophy with other contemporary philosophical trends, etc.) Suppose we recognize that the official Marxist conception is limited and harmful. And suppose we accept as the main meaning that wider, traditional meaning (but one that—as we have seen—also prevails today and which we find in Marx and Engels too). If we do this, then we can recognize that the fundamental propositions of Marxist philosophy, i.e., the principal convictions of Marxists, are doubtlessly metaphysical too.

There is, of course, nothing harmful in characterizing the Marxist presuppositions as metaphysical. "Metaphysics" is a pejorative term in dogmatic Marxism. But dogmatic Marxism was not alone in trying to liquidate metaphysics.

Metaphysical statements are most distant from those registering direct experience. Metaphysics is a discipline only indirectly based on the results of sciences, and makes, if at all, only limited use of the methods of the empirical sciences. Therefore it remains on a relatively very low level of testability and certainty. Metaphysical statements and metaphysics in general have always been most exposed to doubt and to any kind of skeptical attacks, which have always tried to deprive it of any sense. The history of philosophy knows of many attempts to deny metaphysics.

It is, however, characteristic that these attempts were very often results of various misunderstandings. In many cases, these attempts did not deny what metaphysics really was, if one keeps in mind the meaning most adequate to the history of thought. These attempts, in fact, denied only "bad metaphysics," or that which was bad in otherwise "good metaphysics." Looking back to dogmatic Marxism from this standpoint, it seems that it attempts to draw out one side of metaphysics, to identify the whole of metaphysics with that aspect, and then to criticize it severely.

As a matter of fact, more serious attempts to deny metaphysics in contemporary philosophy are coming from the side of the majority of the logical positivists, as well as from the side of some linguistic analysts. But as some of the most eminent empiricists of our age have noticed (e.g., Bertrand Russell), it is useless to try to reject metaphysics from the standpoint of empiricism, since it is impossible to hold a pure empiricism. As for the standpoint of linguistic analysis, which limits all possible philosophy to the analysis of language, it pretends to reject not only metaphysics, but many other philosophical disciplines too. This conception of philosophy cannot have a wide influence, because, together with some other extreme limitations of the task of philosophy, it cannot satisfy all the complex human needs.

Therefore, it is not only impossible to show the illegitimacy, senselessness, or archaism of metaphysics. But out of the aggressive controversy going on within the world of contemporary empiricist philosophy, it has clearly emerged that there is no knowledge without some metaphysical presuppositions, as well as that these metaphysical presuppositions may have, and really often have, very positive functions in the development of human scientific knowledge. For example, metaphysical presuppositions give a conceptual framework and bring order into the explanation of things, and into the formation of a world picture. They present a vision of the universe, which sometimes reveals new perspectives for scientific investigation. They provide a system of theories that tries to say something about the ultimate, i.e., the human significance of scientific achievements.

In spite of the relatively low degree of their testability and certainty, metaphysical presuppositions are still open to rational discussion. We can discuss metaphysical statements rationally by examining their coherence, simplicity, fruitfulness, and clarity; by inquiring into the explicative precision or the logical connection of their elements; by investigating whether they are making any progress in resolving controversial problems. We can also usefully consider their adequacy from the standpoint of humanistic values, because it seems that we can, in the long run, determine the rationality of anything only from the standpoint of man.

I am sure that humanistically directed Marxism counteracts the flood of scientism and technicism threatening a neglect of all genuine human values. I am convinced that it ought also to rise openly and comprehensively against the tendency in modern culture to underestimate and reject metaphysics.

NOTES

1. J. V. Stalin, *Dialectical and Historical Materialism* (Calcutta: Burmon, 1943), p. 9.

2. Cf. especially Karl Marx, *Toward the Critique of Hegel's Philosophy of Law: Introduction,* in *Writings of the Young Marx on Philosophy and Society,* trans. and ed. Loyd D. Easton and Kurt Guddat. (Garden City: Doubleday, 1967), pp. 249-264.

3. Karl Marx and Friedrich Engels, *The German Ideology* (New York: International Publishers, 1939), p. 15.

4. Cf. especially F. Engels, *Ludwig Feuerbach and the Outcome of Classical German Philosophy* (New York: International Publishers, 1941), p. 25; his *Dialectics of Nature* (New York: International Publishers, 1940), p. 243-244; or his *Herr Eugen Dühring's Revolution in Science* (New York: International Publishers, 1939), pp. 45-46.

5. Cf. F. Engels, ibid., p. 19.

6. Cf. ibid., p. 32.

7. Cf. ibid., pp. 44-45, 160.

8. Cf. ibid., pp. 27-29.

9. Cf. ibid., p. 26.

10. Cf. ibid.

11. Cf. ibid., p. 28.

12. Cf. V. I. Lenin, *What Is the League of Nations?* or *Materialism and Empiriocriticism,* in *Collected Works* (Moscow: Foreign Languages Publishing House, 1960).

13. K. R. Popper, *The Logic of Scientific Discovery* (London: Hutchinson, 1959), p. 34.

PART IV

MARXISM AND HUMANISM

Chapter 13

Marxist Humanism[1]

ADAM SCHAFF

Adam Schaff has served as president of the board of directors of the
European Center for Coordination in Social Sciences in Vienna.
He has been professor at the University of Warsaw and director
of the Institute of Philosophy and Sociology of the Polish Academy
of Sciences in Warsaw. A recipient of a Ph.D. degree from the
Institute of Philosophy of the Academy of Sciences of the U.S.S.R.
(1945) and an honorary Ph.D. from the University of Michigan
(1967), he is the author of several books, among them *The Marxist
Theory of Truth* (1951), *Introduction to Semantics* (1960), *A
Philosophy of Man* (1963), *Language and Cognition* (1966),
Marxism and the Human Individual (1965), and *History and Truth*
(1970).

By humanism we mean a system of reflection on man which,
regarding him as the supreme good, aims at providing in practice
the best conditions for human happiness. Within this broad
framework, there is naturally room for various currents of
thought which, depending on their interpretation of the
individual, society and human happiness, may not only differ
considerably but even be mutually exclusive. Hence the
controversy about which of the rival varieties of humanism is
"true" or right. Naturally, this depends on what definitions
are accepted, and these in turn form part of the accepted
philosophical system and its related system of values. It is
therefore a debate which cannot be decided on its own merits, in

isolation from a wider theoretical context and from practice. On the other hand, what can be done is to compare arguments concerning the means offered to attain the ultimate end, which is the creation of the best conditions for human happiness.

Marxism is a radical humanism. Marx wrote: "To be radical is to grasp things by the root. But for man the root is man himself. . . . The criticism of religion ends with the doctrine that *man* is *the highest being for man,* hence with the *categorical imperative to overthrow all conditions* in which man is a degraded, enslaved, neglected, contemptible being."[2]

Here the character of humanism is clearly associated with the concept of the individual, which Marx chooses as his point of departure: if the basis is a real, concrete individual (concrete from the point of view of his social ties as well) then this humanism is real; but when we start from idealist speculation about "self-knowledge," "spirit" and the like, a humanism based on such premises is spiritualist. With which of them Marx sides is obvious—it is only real humanism that can be coherently related to his views of the world and society.

Closely connected with the reality of Marx's humanism is another of its characteristic features: it is a consistently autonomous humanism. This question has been dealt with in detail in an earlier account, and need only be briefly recapitulated. Because it starts from the real individual and real society and because its doctrine is based on the assumption that man, in the course of transforming objective reality, creates his world and indirectly influences his own development, Marxist humanism is consistently autonomous in the sense of interpreting the human world as a result of the play of its own forces, without resorting to any ultrahuman and thus heteronomous forces. This divorces Marxist humanism not only from all speculation of a religious nature, but also from objective idealism which, for instance, takes a heteronomous view of the world of objective values. Man, real man, is not only the point of departure but also the autonomous forger of his destiny, the maker of his world and of himself. Only a humanism which denies interference in human affairs by forces over and above man, can be described as consistent. This is the only possible humanism *sensu proprio.*

It is to this fundamental, one might say ideological, feature of Marxist humanism that a further characteristic is wedded: it is a militant humanism.

Objections are often raised, particularly by Catholic philosophers, to the appropriation of the adjective "militant" for Marxist humanism alone. Cannot, for example, a humanism which is based on Catholic thought be described as militant? Certainly, and one could even quote examples. But what matters in this case is whether the attitude of a militant humanist is a logical consequence of his theoretical assumptions or is independent of them, an accidental or loose appendage.

Viewed from this angle a humanism based on real individuals and their social relations and recognizing man as the supreme good must challenge everything that debases man. The attitude of militant humanism is in this case resolutely logical: to abstain from the struggle would mean a lack of conviction. On the other hand, if humanism proceeds from "spirit," "person," "self-knowledge," and the like, it may, but need not, oppose evil in practical life, since it is not such work, but rather intellectual speculation which is its province.

In this respect Marxism is a full-blooded humanism and is deeply rooted in practice: it not only preaches certain principles but draws practical conclusions from them. This is precisely why Marx as a young man had already made revolutionary struggle a corollary to his humanism: "As philosophy finds its *material* weapons in the proletariat, the proletariat finds its *intellectual* weapons in philosophy. And once the lightning of thought has deeply struck this unsophisticated soil of the people, the *Germans* will emancipate themselves to become *men*."[3]

This trend of Marx's thought culminates in his criticism of Feuerbach's philosophy, and the famous eleventh Thesis on Feuerbach contains his credo: "The philosophers have only *interpreted* the world in various ways; the point is, to *change* it."[4] With such an approach to philosophy, Marx could not, naturally, be satisfied with a humanist contemplation of human destiny. A man to whom philosophy was the spiritual weapon of the proletariat and the proletariat the material weapon of philosophy was bound to opt for a militant humanism.

It must not be thought, however, that this trait of Marx's humanism was arrived at by deduction from his general philosophy. The reverse was rather the case, although it seems likely that this is a classic example of mutual interaction.

As already pointed out, militancy is the logical outcome of Marx's humanism, primarily of its starting point, a consequence of the fact that this was a real humanism which interpreted the human world as an autonomous world, created by social man and only by him.

If the world of man and man himself are products of self-creation, then man cannot and should not expect to be liberated from his sufferings by some superhuman force—good or evil—but must set about freeing himself. In other words, belief in self-creation means that one must also accept the idea of self-emancipation. And it is precisely the idea of the self-emancipation of the proletariat which, to liberate itself as a class, must liberate the whole of mankind that is at the foundation of Marx's socialism; consequently, his humanism must accept the principle of struggle for its fulfillment, and thus it becomes a militant humanism.

It is only on the basis of the idea of self-emancipation and militant humanism that one can understand the Marxian theory of class struggle and of the historic mission of the proletariat in the formation of a classless society—so masterfully summed up in the *Communist Manifesto*. And it is only through this idea that we can grasp the dialectics of classes and of the supraclass nature of the public interest, as it appears in Marxian socialism, as well as the dialectics of love and hatred which manifests itself in the course of its realization.

Man is the point of departure of Marx's socialism; and man is also its point of arrival, its goal.

We know already that man is no abstraction to Marx—indeed, he criticized such an approach—but a concrete, real individual, involved in social relations and the resulting conflicts and struggles. Thus, in proceeding from real individuals, Marx at the outset predicated his argument on actually existing social classes and strata. In this way he made his discovery of the proletariat and its universal function.

But Marx's point of arrival, the object of his endeavors, is man in general, the happiness of every human individual. This is where the profound meaning of the dialectics of his humanism lies: without any unction about "love thy neighbor" or about "integral" humanism, it strives precisely in that direction, since it embraces the whole of mankind and is concerned with the full development of every personality. More than that: thanks to its realism and its stipulation of fulfillment through struggle, only this humanism can truly be called integral by virtue of its aims—although it is resolutely opposed to the catchword of integral humanism in the sense of a repudiation of genuine struggle for accomplishment.

With this dialectic of struggle, this interaction between what is proper to class and what is proper to humanity is connected with the dialectic of love and hatred in the pursuit of universal ideals. Since socialism—in every form—takes man and a revolt against the dehumanization of life as its point of departure, it starts with love of man and a sense of distress at man's dehumanization, debasement, unhappiness. Socialism is in a sense identical with love of man, while a socialism which hated man would be a contradiction in terms. Yet Marxian socialism shuns all wishy-washy and abstract injunctions of the "love thy neighbor" brand; it is a doctrine of struggle and so enjoins hatred of the enemy in the cause of love of neighbor. A contradiction? Only on the surface. In fact this is a much more consistent, and so authentic, attitude than the insipid watchwords of "integral" humanism which, even if sometimes subjectively honest, are in most cases sheer hypocrisy.

Socialism is a doctrine of love both in its point of departure and in its objectives. But since it approaches the problem of love not in an abstract but in a concrete way—that is, on the hard ground of struggle for its related ends and postulates— Marxian humanism must struggle against what is contrary to and incompatible with this love and so against all that debases, oppresses and exploits man—in short, against everything that makes him unhappy. But struggle is not simply a phrase; it means action to frustrate and remove from power all those who, in the name of their private interests, bar men's way to happiness—and so deny love. For in a class society there have been and still are enemies of this love—whether their behavior is conscious or unconscious. To perceive this is also to understand that the enemies of love among men, the enemies of the cause of man, must be fought—and this requires feeling hatred towards them in the sense of hatred directed against certain types of values and actions. Love of man, far from excluding, in fact presupposes abomination of those who act objectively, and still more if this goes with a subjective consciousness, in the name of hatred. The Nazis are the classic example of men acting in this way. Despite appearances, anyone who in such a contingency disclaims the necessity of struggle—and so of hatred of the enemy—is not a humanist but a typical antihumanist. By preaching a love of man which forbids harming another human being under any circumstances, one does harm to thousands and millions of innocent people who are victims of class, national, racial or other kinds of oppression and violence. That no sensible person would behave like this in practice is a different matter; but the very profession of such principles—and they are often put forward in self-interest to sow intellectual confusion and discouragement among one's enemies—is tantamount to asserting antihumanist ideas. On this point there should be absolute theoretical clarity.

Thus we have a love of neighbor, a love of man which does not exclude hatred, since it does not exclude struggle, but, on the contrary, postulates it. But having adopted such a position and following it through in practice, we must exercise particular caution, which is also indispensable in the development of the theory surrounding it. In both cases, the most important thing is to remember that the crux is man and the furtherance of his good, while hatred is always to be subordinated to something that serves another cause—the love of man. Unfortunately, in matters like this it is always difficult to keep within the proper limits. Here again, as on many other occasions, the idea has been best expressed by a poet; it was Bertolt Brecht who wrote these beautiful and profoundly humanistic lines:

Even the hatred of squalor
Makes the brow grow stern.
Even anger against injustice
Makes the voice grow harsh. Alas, we
Who wished to lay the foundations of kindness
Could not ourselves be kind.
But you, when at last it comes to pass
That man can help his fellow man,
Do not judge us
Too harshly.[5]

Finally, there is one other characteristic that distinguishes Marxist humanism, particularly in our days: it is an optimistic humanism.

Reading the classic Marxist texts on man under communism one sometimes gets an impression of utopianism. No doubt they do contain some such residue. But it may also be that, limited as we are by the narrow perspective of our own time, we lose sight of the more distant vistas adumbrated by the founders of the system. If it is advisable to beware of too bold flights of the imagination, it is equally necessary to avoid the mistake of keeping our feet too leadenly planted on the ground. In the light of the modern technical revolution, with its automation and harnessing of atomic energy, should we not take a different view of such goals as the elimination of the disparities between manual and nonmanual labor, between work on the land and in towns, or the possibility of a practically limitless satisfaction of human needs—all of which several decades ago belonged to the realm of fantasy.

Modern industrial technique certainly gives rise to a number of new problems, some of which were never envisioned. But in the right social context, it also offers possibilities of solving certain ancient problems as well, such as shorter working hours, to look no farther.

It is interesting to see, particularly as regards social psychology, how the same social phenomenon—industrialization and technical progress—can be interpreted in different ways according to the social point of view of the observer.

On the one hand, it forms the background of a philosophy of despair which treats society as a sum of isolated, atomized monads, moving meaninglessly on the stage of life in a setting of a depersonalized mass culture totally devoid of any human values. This is a grotesque exaggeration of certain features of the modern social and cultural situation in bourgeois society. That only these traits are perceived is undoubtedly due to a preoccupation with the "dehumanized world"—to use a phrase of the young Marx. But this point of view makes for a pessimistic vision of the world. If existentialism is humanism—as Sartre with justice claims—it is the humanism of a dying world and therefore tragic and doomridden.

But the same phenomenon can be seen in another light, as a harbinger of the new things the future will bring. This is the attitude of socialist humanism whose vision is determined by a completely new social situation—or at least by the prospect of such a situation. The technical revolution, which is eroding the old world, also holds out the possibility of creating a new one. For the first time in history there is a real chance of making mankind's age-old dream—a happy life for all men—come true. Can this dream be fully realized? This remains to be seen: personally, I am skeptical. But there is certainly a possibility of a better, happier life; this is already a great deal and no more can surely be expected. When things are viewed in this light—and this is only feasible given the necessary social perspective—the vision of the future development of the individual and society at once changes.

This does not mean that the vision of Kafka's *Castle* or Sartre's *La Nausée* must be replaced by the "soc-realist" brand of optimism in which virtue always triumphs like the sheriffs in American Westerns. Matters here are certainly—and fortunately—more complicated. But it is undoubtedly an optimistic humanism not because it irrationally believes that man is good and that good must triumph, just as Sartre's existentialism holds, or held, the opposite, but because of its conviction that the world is a product of man and man himself is a product of self-creation; consequently, since his possibilities of transforming the world are practically boundless—as proved, among other things, by the present technical revolution—man has in practice boundless possibilities of transforming himself. Such optimism is not an act of faith but a conviction based on facts. Thus it is not an axiom but a working hypothesis with a great degree of probability and tremendous practical importance. Such a hypothesis is a component of ideology, but its heuristic value is no less great than many propositions in the social sciences. And this is enough.

Every fully developed system of humanism contains its own theory of happiness. Marxist humanism is no exception to the rule.

The problem of happiness can be approached in one of two ways: from the angle of its positive features—what we call happiness—or from that of its negative ones—what we describe as unhappiness. The difference is essential, particularly from the point of view of practical conclusions, and cannot be reduced to the simple operation of inserting a "not" in certain affirmative propositions.

The first method is the traditional one, tested in the various theories of happiness which have made their appearance in the history of human thought. But experience has shown that approaching the problem of happiness from the positive angle does not—and cannot—yield any results, or only very modest ones. What a wealth of pronouncements we have had on this subject and how different, even contradictory, have the attitudes behind them been! No wonder: a condition which basically consists of subjective feelings, responses and sensations cannot be defined apart from definitions which are so general as to be practically meaningless and still less codified by means of norms and injunctions. I may go on for years telling somebody that he should be happy in a given situation,

seeing his circumstances through my eyes, or thinking of one
of the standard definitions of happiness (that of the Stoics,
for example) and yet this will make no difference whatsoever:
the person in question will continue to be unhappy and may
even commit suicide because, in his mind, the situation has
become intolerable. It is in this discrepancy between my and
your idea of a situation—one that cannot either be ignored or
skirted—that the crux of the matter lies. For what is involved—
and philosophers have often forgotten this—is not an abstraction,
but living, real men who often enough differ from each other
fundamentally as well as in details and constitute specific
structures, specific microcosms. The problem of happiness may
not be fully reducible to the subjective factor, but it is so
closely, so organically, linked with it that to take no account
of this when trying to construct generally valid—and thus
abstract—definitions is bound to be self-defeating. We all
know—and need not be surprised—that what makes one person
happy can make another unhappy, even within the same social
framework, the same historical period, and the same system
of social determinants. Some rejoice in exercising power, while
it would make others suffer deeply; some delight in permanent
leisure, while others are driven to despair by want of an occu-
pation; one man will exult in promiscuity, another would regard
it as intolerable drudgery. And so on and so forth. It is also
psychologically true, paradoxical as it may seem, that to feel
contented some people must be unhappy, or at least have
something to grumble about—and they go out of their way to
find a cause for dissatisfaction. In a word, people are not alike
and cannot find gratification in the same things. And since the
feeling of happiness is always an individual sensation which is
organically connected with the psychophysical structure of
the sentient subject, any attempt to settle the problem in a
"general" way, by means of sweeping definitions or, even
worse, by laying down when and in what circumstances people
should be happy is doomed to failure; and in the case of a
state embarking on practical activity to this effect it may
bring real human misery.

A socialist society should pay particular attention to this
problem—not only because the possibilities of centralized
action are greater under socialism than in other systems of
government, but also because the temptation of trying to
decree the conditions for human happiness is a real danger.

It is relevant to point out that it is precisely this formula that has provided the basis for various anticommunist utopias: a society which, to achieve a fusion of individual and public interests, strives to enforce a generally binding model of human happiness must inevitably end with a horrifying tyranny that suppresses the individual, and with a totally dehumanized life. Let me illustrate this with the example of a little known book, Zamiatin's *We*, probably the most original of its kind. I have chosen this novel not because I approve its tenor but because, like Orwell's *1984*, it takes to their logical extreme some of the elements running through socialist ideology and certain developments in socialist countries, and thus helps us visualize the possible dangers.

The message of Zamiatin's book is as follows. When the idea of a complete fusion of individual and society is carried to its extreme (note that the Marxist postulate of a fusion between the interests of individual and society has been twisted into a non-Marxist notion implying the disappearance of individuality; without this device, the novel would not work), this must necessarily result in a denial of the right to individuality and individual happiness. By abolishing individual identity the state imposes on everybody the same stereotype of happiness (in the book this is carried as far as the compulsory removal from the brains of all citizens of their "imagination center" which is responsible for their individualistic tendencies). This is where hell begins. Do not deprive individuals of their individuality, the author seems to be telling us, and do not enforce your own ideas of happiness, for in doing this you can only dehumanize human existence and make man unhappy.

Zamiatin may be right, although it could easily be objected that he is fighting shadows since nobody has ever sought to bring about the situation he describes, or that he has deliberately distorted the Marxist ideals by talking of a fusion between individual and society in terms of the liquidation of individuality. These criticisms are to the point, but even so, a hard core remains in the book which offers food for thought.

Working with a specific convention Zamiatin reduces to absurdity certain observed tendencies and shows what would happen if they were given full reign. Later, the same procedure was adopted by Orwell. It is true that this results in a grotesque or tragicomic distortion of things as they are. But the fact remains that this mirror reflects a certain reality—which deserves closer inspection.

Although Zamiatin's anticommunist utopia is false, there are some elements of truth in this falsehood and these should not be ignored. When definitions of happiness begin to be elaborated and are made the source of a code of behavior binding on all men (for their own good, of course; how many excesses have been perpetrated in history in this cause!), then people are threatened, under socialism too, with the danger of being "made happy" by decree, forcibly, according to the accepted model of happiness, and this may lead to general unhappiness. After all, a certain restriction of human freedom is then required—and every such constraint tends to reduce rather than increase the chances of happiness. Fortunately, experience has shown that such tendencies are a typical symptom of the teething pains of left-wing communism and usually fade away with the stabilization of life under the new system of government. Consequently, it is enough to conclude these remarks with just one warning: since there is not, and fortunately cannot be, a single type of happiness for everybody any attempt to construct identical stereotypes should be avoided. Socialism does not oppose human individuality; on the contrary, the reverse is the case. Let us then give this individuality free play in the pursuit of happiness and let everybody be happy in his own way—even if what he needs for this purpose is a hobby, or if he insists on being slightly eccentric or different. That's his own business. Recognition of this freedom, which can do no harm to socialism, is one of the conditions for a genuine, authentic happiness of all men.

Thus, if the positive approach to the problem of human happiness does not yield any results—and even holds a danger of doing mischief—our interest should be all the greater in the opposite method: an inquiry into the causes of unhappiness and the characteristics of this condition.

While no generally binding definition of human happiness can be given, since in view of its individual nature such a definition is simply impossible, it is fairly easy to name the causes of human unhappiness: hunger, death, disease, imprisonment, all kinds of exploitation and oppression, etc. People have various requirements and they cannot be codified positively from the point of view of general happiness. But they can be codified in the negative. No normal man can be happy unless he can satisfy a minimum of his own and his family's needs, if he is threatened with death in war, when his country is enslaved, when he cannot enjoy his freedom, etc.

Here is a reasonable basis for action on behalf of human happiness—not in the sense of making man happy but of eliminating the causes of general unhappiness.

The militant character of Marxist humanism is closely connected with this concept of happiness: it urges an uncompromising struggle against the causes of human misery as a mass phenomenon—and thus against its social roots. This is a realistic objective, the aim being to create the chances of a happy life. Nothing more can be achieved by any system since no one can guarantee happiness. This after all is an individual matter. Even in ideal social and economic conditions people can be unhappy—no economic or social system can protect them against disease, the death of their near ones, unrequited love, personal failures, etc. Nor is this the point—it would be as impossible and impracticable an objective as trying to make people happy by force or eradicate all sources of individual misery. But it is fully possible and practicable to root out the causes of widespread misery—whose sources lie not in the individual but outside him, in social conditions and relations. Thus Marxist humanism does not promise any utopian paradise and does not claim to provide a key to individual happiness for everybody. It does not even offer any insurance against the emergence of new barriers to human happiness in the future; even this cannot be guaranteed although a high degree of probability can be lent to the prediction that a rationally organized society will consciously combat such situations. But Marxist humanism advocates something else: the liquidation of the existing social causes of human unhappiness. This is a great deal—and is what gives this humanism its appeal to all those who suffer because of the prevalent social relations. It is this that determines its rebellious and militant character as it strives to implement Marx's words: "The criticism of religion ends with the doctrine that *man is the highest being for man,* hence with the *categorical imperative to overthrow all conditions* in which man is a degraded, enslaved, neglected, contemptible being."[6]

NOTES

1. Professor Schaff treats this subject in more detail in chapter 4 of his book, *Marxism and the Human Individual* (New York: McGraw-Hill, 1970).

2. Karl Marx, "Toward the Critique of Hegel's Philosophy of Law," in *Writings of the Young Marx on Philosophy and Society,* ed. Loyd D. Easton and Kurt H. Guddat (Garden City: Doubleday, 1967), pp. 257-258.

3. Ibid., pp. 263-264.

4. Ibid., p. 402.

5. "To Posterity," from *Selected Poems,* trans. H. R. Hays (New York: Harcourt, Brace and World, 1959).

6. Karl Marx, "Toward the Critique of Hegel's Philosophy of Law," pp. 257-258.

Chapter 14

The Economic Basis of Marx's Humanism

DONALD CLARK HODGES

Donald Clark Hodges, professor of philosophy at Florida State
University in Tallahassee, is also director of The Florida Center
for Studies in Social Philosophy there and associate editor of
Social Theory and Practice. He has taught at the University of
South Florida, the University of Hawaii, the University of
Nebraska, and the University of Missouri. He is the author of
more than one hundred articles, ten contributions to anthologies,
and *Socialist Humanism: The Outcome of Classical European
Morality* (1973).

In this essay I want to reconsider the relationship of Marx's
humanism to his economic writings. The latter not only have
policy presuppositions, but also continue to serve socialists as
the basis of their policy statements. Marx was perhaps the first
to recognize and dwell upon the full extent of this interdependence.[1] On the one hand, different economic theories express
different interests and corresponding policies; on the other hand,
for these policies to be enlightened, they must be predicated
upon the social sciences inclusive of economics.[2] Actually, if
we can call policies reasonable at all, it is because they are based
upon a knowledge of man's potentialities and upon the economic,
as well as social, conditions of human growth.

More often than not, contemporary philosophers have been

skeptical of the possibility of philosophical ethics becoming an applied social science, and their view has been increasingly shared by professional economists. Commenting upon the relationship of ethics to economics, Joan Robinson argues that traditional economic theory has built-in moral presuppositions, but that no amount of scientific refinement will ever help to bridge the gap between the economic "is" and the moral "ought."[3] Ethics has no scientific content precisely because its statements are ideological in character; metaphysical statements, she contends, are incapable of ever being tested, hence are beyond truth and falsehood in any scientifically meaningful sense.

But if ethical statements are unscientific, perhaps they can be translated into rough approximations of empirical ones. As a matter of fact, it is possible to reformulate ethical sentences without the surd elements represented by normative and metaphysical terms like "good," "right," etc. Such translations, like poetry into prose, are seldom faithful to the original, but at least they make the kind of sense that can be understood and communicated. Although we cannot bridge logically the gap between the "ought" and the "is," at least with the help of operations research and the theory of games we can move from traditional ethical problems to the consideration of contemporary problems of physiological fulfillment and the strategy and tactics of vital interests. In any case, we can pose the same dictum to moral philosophers that scientists have characteristically presented to theologians; so-called intuited truths cannot contradict the evidence of the sciences, but can only supplement it. A similar limitation can be set upon policy commitments, for what the social sciences tell us about human welfare cannot reasonably be contradicted. In the event of conflict between practical norms and social science propositions, the former need to be adjusted to the latter. Otherwise, we shall find ourselves acting *as if* warranted statements about human well-being are false.

In an important sense, then, a policy theory for successful living may be considered as an applied economic science. As such, it considers a variety of problems, notably the contribution of marginal utility theory and welfare economics to problems of self-fulfillment; the relevance of classical and recent theories of economic growth to the problem of self-development for persons and classes without economic, social, and cultural advantages; the bearing of equilibrium models upon cooperation and compromise; the significance of theories of imperfect competition for human conflict; and the contribution of operations research and game theory to the solution of strategical problems involving class antagonism. Clearly, what Marx called the rich human being is in important respects a function of economic wealth. Although occasionally the more we have, the less we are, it is more than accident that "wealth" and "weal" have the same roots.

As a matter of fact, there are two kinds of economic criteria for measuring personal growth: quantitative criteria, for which fulfillment is a function of the number and plurality of needs; and qualitative criteria, for which growth is a function of freely developed needs rather than biologically necessary ones. Both sets of criteria play a distinguished role in Marx's youthful *Economic and Philosophic Manuscripts.* First, the rich personality is the human being *"in need of* a totality of human life-activities."[4] As an example of the impoverished human being, there is the exploited Irish laborer, who no longer knows any need "but the need to *eat,* and indeed only the need to eat *potatoes—*and *scabby potatoes* at that, the worst kind of potatoes."[5] Actually, the more you eat, drink, and read books, the more often you go to the theater and dance hall; the more you think, love, sing, theorize, paint, and so forth, the less one-sided, stunted, and frustrated you are likely to be, the less bored and satiated with the pleasures of life. Second, some needs have a greater power to bring fulfillment than others. Such are the pleasures of the cultivated person emancipated from the pressures of survival, from vulgar egoistic needs that consider only the self instead of other people.[6] For Marx, the realm of personal freedom or optimum gratification does not begin until the point is passed where labor under the compulsion of external forces is required.[7] Since it lies beyond the sphere of material production and reproduction altogether, the "shortening of the working day is its fundamental premise."[8]

In an affluent society where the quantitative economic problem has in principle been solved, these qualitative considerations are especially important. The necessary or biological needs force themselves upon us and are quickly satiated; the corresponding pleasures are transient instead of lasting, simple instead of complex, cyclical instead of cumulative. In contrast, the pleasures to be had from the exercise of freely chosen skills are not only more interesting, but also grow like compound

interest, so that the more proficient we become the greater
is our enjoyment. Just as activities involve a greater number of
variables and are proportionately more challenging when the
materials acted upon are animate or fellow human beings
instead of simple physical objects, so the corresponding pleasures
are more attractive. To live at all has pleasures of its own; to live
intelligently leads to still futher pleasures, to pleasures that are
also free. On the one hand, a necessary condition of personal
growth is exemption from routine and long hours of unchal-
lenging labor. On the other hand, this leisure may then be used
to develop our uniquely human capacities, which is precisely
what distinguishes free activities from those required merely
to survive.[9]

Underlying Marx's theory of practice was an economic
sociology focusing upon problems of industrialization under
capitalism and the effects of exploitation upon the working
class. One of its premises was that the vital needs of life, health,
and security are more urgent than any others. Marx provides
evidence indicating that the struggle for a livelihood was in fact
the chief concern of wage-earners during the initial stages of
industrialization. If man does not live by bread alone, at least
he must have sufficient bread in order to live at all. Economic
security is not by any means either the laborer's ultimate goal
or, for that matter, even the most immediately rewarding one,
but it has been his most constant preoccupation and continues
to be the most urgent problem facing the labor movement.
    The worker's concern for economic protection was of special
importance to Marx, who gave preeminence to it in volume
one of *Capital*.[10] The disastrous effects of economic insecurity
upon the worker's physical well-being are traced to three
principal sources: an extension of the working day, the effect
of machinery and modern industry on the workman, and the
so-called general law of capitalist accumulation. Of the 33
chapters of volume one, the three chapters explicitly covering
these topics constituted almost one-half of the entire book.[11]
Where there are no social or legal limits to the working day,
the production of absolute surplus value leads to premature
old age and to compulsory working to death, not to mention
the effects upon health of continuous overwork.[12] And where
there is no legal protection against the effects of machinery,
the production of relative surplus value through the intensifi-

cation of the working hour has similar results.[13] As Marx notes, one effect of machinery is to wear out and exhaust the laborer in less time than formerly: "Every organ of sense is injured . . . by artificial elevation of the temperature, by the dust-laden atmosphere, by the deafening noise, not to mention danger to life and limb among the thickly crowded machinery, which, with the regularity of the seasons issues its list of the killed and wounded in the industrial battle."[14] Add to this the unemployment and pauperization due to the general tendency of capitalist accumulation, and it would seem that "the lot of the laborer, be his payment high or low, must grow worse."[15] Thus Marx's critique of capitalist society was directed first and foremost against the violation of the producer's vital interests and need for physical protection, and only secondarily against offenses to his socially conditioned needs and his sense of dignity.

It is remarkable how very few of Marx's commentators have considered at all carefully the influence of Hobbes upon his social theory. Yet his immediate concern for the producers was how they could effectively defend their lives, health and security against the injurious effects of accumulation. For Hobbes, these are inalienable rights in protection of which rebellion, sabotage, and personal violence are justified by his first rule of prudence and the vital interest of self-defense.[16] Although Marx speaks a different language, he agrees with Hobbes that these interests, if not inalienable, are nonetheless of foremost concern to workers. For protection against the "serpent of their agonies," they must organize as a class to compel the capitalist leviathan to pass laws limiting the legal length of the working day and regulating the conditions of work.[17] Such laws are needed to "prevent the very workers from selling, by voluntary contract with capital, themselves and their families into slavery and death."[18] For these and other reasons, the producers need the protective organization of their own trade unions, without which they "would be degraded to one level mass of broken down wretches past salvation."[19]

Following Hobbes, who defines the value or worth of a man as his price or what is actually given for the use of his powers, Marx notes that this price depends upon the relative abundance or scarcity of laborers.[20] At the same time, it depends upon historical and social factors, such as the cost of maintaining a family and producing a new generation of workers.[21] Since the supply of laborers generally exceeds the demand, their price can be pushed below the minimum necessary to their health and vigor unless they organize for their own protection. On the one hand, the laborer's wife and children can be made to work by paying the laborer himself barely enough for self-maintenance. On the other hand, he can be sweated at a near-starvation wage until he falls from exhaustion and is replaced by another. The experience of the last century shows how industrial capitalism seizes and wastes the vital power of the producers, "how the degeneration of the industrial population is only retarded by the constant absorption of primitive and physically uncorrupted elements from the countryside. . . ."[22] Given the relative abundance of cheap and easily replaceable manpower, owners and employers have grounds for ignoring the sufferings of the myriads of laborers and for being "reckless of the health or length of life of the laborer, unless under compulsion from society."[23]

In his concern for the immiserization of the producers it should now be evident that Marx gave precedence to their absolute or physical degradation rather than to their relative social and cultural alienation. The same order of precedence was recognized by the workers themselves, whose initial struggles were chiefly of a defensive nature. These were directed first and foremost against the effects of superexploitation and surplus profits in the effort to secure for themselves the bare minimum of food, clothing, and shelter. The immediate aim of the labor movement in its early days was to regulate the supply of labor, so that labor-power might be paid at its value, i.e., what it cost the laborer to maintain and reproduce himself. Labor unions sought to regulate hours of labor and conditions of work in order to defend the workers against injuries to their life and health. Although these struggles helped to raise wages, they were not directed against exploitation itself. Indeed, before the workers could hope to abolish exploitation, they first had to secure the physiological minimum necessary to live at all.

A rudimentary social psychology or model of human nature was the proximate basis of Marx's decision theory. However, Marx was an economist rather than a social psychologist in his basic approach to social problems. This does not mean that economic factors were for him the sole necessary conditions or sufficient explanation of human behavior. Speaking for Marx, Engels notes that the mode of production is not the sole determinant of social change, but rather that economic variables are less bound than psychological ones and, to that extent, more influential.[24] Since Marx's psychology is predicated upon his economic theory, it is a superficial view, to say the least, that finds in his concept of man the ultimate basis of his humanism.

Yet this is precisely the view of several prominent self-styled Marxists as well as of Marx's critics and revisionists. In fact, they argue that Marx's class orientation was only a special instance or adaptation of his humanism to the interests and circumstances of the working class. For them, the initial basis of his humanism was not a political economy of scarcity, but human nature considered independently of its subsequent articulation or modification by social, class and specifically economic conditions. In this light, his humanism appears as a superstructure based upon common biological needs and a corresponding universalistic ethic. His humanism is predicated not only upon the vital interests of the workers as defined by the science of physiology and the social conditions peculiar to a laboring class, but also upon moral considerations.

Authority for this interpretation has been found in a footnote to volume one of *Capital:* ". . . he that would criticize all human acts, movements, relations, etc., by the general principle of utility, must first deal with human nature in general, and then with human nature as modified in each historical epoch."[25] On the basis of this quotation, Erich Fromm distinguishes man's constant drives, such as hunger and the sexual urge, from his relative appetites, or man's general nature from his class-conditioned characteristics.[26] With this as a starting-point, he concludes that the fundamental goal of Marx's humanism is the emancipation of all men from alienated activity, and only secondarily the emancipation of the working class from exploitation.[27] Fromm is not alone in this interpretation of Marx. Appealing to the same passage from *Capital*, Mihailo Markovic' notes that Marx did not reduce human nature just to its class nature, and that the corresponding class-centered ethics of labor and capital are only articulations and adaptations to particular social circumstances of "a whole set of moral norms which transcend limits of class and epoch and which, in various, sometimes disguised forms, reappear in all historical forms of morality."[28] In fact, he argues that the constant factors in human nature, and not those relative to particular classes, constitute the basis of all evaluation.[29]

Some critics, like Robert Tucker, hold that Marx's humanism represents those enduring values associated with human productivity and creativity that are likewise incompatible with a class-centered orientation.[30] On the one hand, the collective worker personifies the enduring powers of creativity, the fundamental human attribute or "incarnation of the real self"; on the other hand, "my lord capital" represents the insatiable acquisitive urges behind all forms of narrow and exclusively class egoism.[31] Since these forces are symptomatic not only of a dualization of man but also of a split personality, it is readily understandable why Marx dismissed the possibility of ever reconciling them.[32] Marx's humanism, according to Tucker, was decidedly on the side of the collective worker as the incarnation of man's constant human characteristics and corresponding universalistic outlook. In this account, the policies of the producers are not egoistic at all, but simply means to an end. Like Fromm and others, Tucker interprets Marx's humanism within the framework of a psychological instead of an economic materialism. Thus the "intra-personal situation inescapably remains the primary fact, and the alienated social relation . . . only a derivative fact and a result."[33]

Unlike Tucker, John Lewis argues that Marx's humanism is both relativistic and absolutistic, and that its very strength "lies in the way in which it unites these two aspects of moral values."[34] Yet he, too, interprets it in psychological and ethical terms rather than in economic ones. Marx's class-centered policies for the producers are justified only as means to the realization of values that are universal and predicated upon the elements of permanence in human nature.[35] Actually, Lewis argues that the workers' contribution to social protest "was always *right* by absolute standards, always contained these *permanent elements* of morality that Engels speaks about, was always universal and not merely a class morality."[36] In effect, he agrees with Tucker that Marx's humanism is universalistic rather than class-oriented. Since we have here a criterion outside class interests by which to judge behavior, so-called Marxist ethics "are not purely relative but have genuine ethical validity."[37]

Let us concede at once that if Marx's humanism is suited only to a particular class at a particular stage of history, then it cannot be expected to elicit the needed support for a revolutionary transformation of society. The foregoing interpretations of Marxism assume, for the most part, that a class-centered humanism lacks the requisite universality of appeal to bring about a major social change. However, Marx did not expect such a transformation from the workers alone, who must perforce unite with other social classes in order to accomplish their own objectives. A universalistic ethic may well serve as an aid to revolutionary reconstruction and may even be indispensable to it. But even in that capacity it is to be distinguished from Marxian humanism, to which it is ancillary in Marx's judgment.

The foregoing interpretations of Marx's humanism stand in sharp opposition to his own thesis that a condition of scarcity is the basis of the humanism of the class struggle, and that an economy of affluence is the foundation of policies appropriate to a classless society. As we have seen, Marx advanced arguments on behalf of two different kinds of humanism: first, socialist humanism, which presupposes a condition of economic scarcity and a corresponding model of civil discontent; secondly, communist humanism, as predicated upon an affluent society and a corresponding economics of welfare. However, since affluence is possible only in the course of overcoming scarcity, there is a sense in which Marx's strategy and tactics of the labor movement are not only more relevant to the past history of the workers, but also more basic to their well-being in any society.

In contrast to the predominantly psychological approach of his revisionists, Marx's humanism was decidedly economic. He assumed, for example, the relevance of the classical postulate of economic man for the entire history of scarcity and the corresponding forms of civil society. Economic man is dominated by vulgar needs, by appetites that all animals have. Only in the drive toward affluence do other needs begin to assert themselves, notably the need for status and the respect of other human beings. The struggle to abolish exploitation is itself an assertion of the social needs of the laborer, his sense of dignity vis-à-vis the autocratic power of capital. Finally, in an affluent society, higher cultural and intellectual needs become increasingly important along with the corresponding products, which in an economy of scarcity are ordinarily regarded as luxuries.

The sources of this classification of our fundamental human needs can be traced to Marx's economic writings, to his youthful theory of alienation and to his subsequent discussion of human needs in *Capital*. In the *Economic and Philosophic Manuscripts of 1844*, the most elementary form of alienation is that from our own products and laboring activity—the result of frustrating our basic biological need for security.[38] From the producer's standpoint, the problem of his vital interests is a continuing one, which explains why the labor movement concentrates first and foremost upon matters of wages and conditions of work. Beyond these needs and as a consequence of exploitation, the laborer also finds himself alienated from his fellow men and from his unique capacities as a human being.[39] In the first case, alienation involves frustration of our distinctly social needs. In the second case, the needs that are frustrated are preeminently cultural, i.e., intellectual and artistic ones.

Actually, the goal of cultural fulfillment is less urgent to the producers than the struggle to overcome social alienation and status inequality. Thus the first phase of socialist society is concerned with the abolition of exploitation, and it is not until the higher phase of communist society that the satisfaction of man's cultural needs becomes paramount.[40] The latter, having immediate relevance to an upper class whose economic and social needs are already satisfied, is obviously not the order of the day for those classes still struggling for their economic and social emancipation. As a matter of fact, the problem of social alienation rather than cultural self-development is of most immediate concern to intermediate classes, which have already solved the economic problem for themselves but as yet lack the necessary conditions for a life of leisure.

We have, then, a distinction in Marx's early manuscripts among vulgar need or the satisfaction of man's elementary biological wants, the need of social wealth or the respect of other human beings, and the need to become oneself a rich human being, rich not in material possessions but in a totality of human experience.[41] This particular sequence in human development is not accidental, but corresponds to the typical behavior of individuals and generations which are fortunate enough to solve their economic and social problems. Thus in Thomas Mann's *Buddenbrooks*, the first generation sought money to satisfy its simple craving for security; the second generation, born to money, sought social and civic position; and the third, born to social status, turned to a life of culture and to music in particular.[42]

In an important sense, this classification of needs is an economic one. In fact, Marx turned to industry and to the history of human labor for the "*exoteric* revelation of man's *essential powers.*"[43] The entire history of culture involves "the begetting of man through human labor."[44] This history is repeated for each social class that rises from a condition of oppression to become the ruling class. To take Marx's favorite example, the modern class of wage-laborers organizes initially in defense of its vital or necessary wants under the conservative slogan of "a fair day's wages for a fair day's work."[45] With the progressive conquest of the problem of scarcity under capitalism, the day arrives when the gratification of the workers' social needs becomes economically feasible. At that point, the more enlightened sections of organized labor begin to inscribe on their banner the revolutionary watchword, "abolition of the wages system."[46] On the supposition that a social revolution will eventually bring the working class to power and succeed in meeting the demand for a new social order, the chief economic problem then becomes how to free the laborer from toil altogether and how to educate him for leisure.[47] Only then does the producer enter a realm of freedom that transcends the entire system of commodity production and the conditions of economic scarcity—a stage corresponding roughly to Galbraith's affluent society and to Rostow's successor to the age of high mass-consumption.[48]

An economically based psychology can also be found in Marx's later economic writings, especially *Capital.* There Marx distinguishes between two constituents of the cost of manpower: first, the cost of providing for the worker's physical wants, such as food, clothing, and shelter, which vary according to the climatic, geographical, and other physical conditions of his environment; and second, the cost of providing for wants conditioned by the general level of civilization, the expenses of education, training in specialized skills, the "degree of comfort in which the class of free laborers has been formed," all of which are socially necessary to produce, develop, maintain, and perpetuate the labor force.[49] These costs and corresponding wants are economically, if not always biologically, necessary to the expenditure and restoration of manpower of a higher kind. The most that laborers can hope to achieve in an economy of scarcity is payment according to the full cost of their labor-power, itself a function of historical conditions, degree of civilization, level of skill, etc. Under conditions of scarcity, however, the struggle of wage-earners is initially directed against the tendency of employers to reduce wages to the minimum or purely physiological cost of manpower, in consequence of which acquired skills can be maintained and developed only in a crippled state.[50]

The abolition of exploitation satisfies a different set of needs from the so-called necessary ones. The relationship of exploitation is social rather than biological in character, involving a class struggle between exploiters and exploited rather than a merely physical struggle for survival. Among other things, exploitation accounts for the worker's sense of inferiority and alienation from his fellow men. If Marx's forecast is correct, the share of capital in proportion to the share of labor tends to rise, thereby issuing in a relative impoverishment of the workers.[51] At the same time, a fall in relative wages involves a corresponding "widening of the social chasm that divides the worker from the capitalist, an increase in the power of capital over labor. . . ."[52] Although the pleasures of the laborer are greater, measured in terms of the quantity of commodities he can now command, they have fallen in comparison with the increased pleasures of the capitalist.[53] The satisfaction of our social needs depends upon factors of social status, such as the comparative pleasures of others; thus whenever profits rise proportionately faster than wages, the material position of the worker improves but at the cost of his social position.[54]

Moreover, there are still other worlds to conquer. The effort to abolish exploitation cannot hope to be successful short of an affluent society. Should exploitation ever be overcome or even seriously limited by social legislation, one can expect its place to be taken by the increasingly important problem of education for leisure. This problem raises to preeminence the satisfaction of our so-called cultural needs, a concern for our intellectual and artistic development. In Marx's terms, the end of exploitation, itself a precondition of socialism, opens up new prospects for a higher type of communist society. The struggle for communism becomes the order of the day: instead of the socialist principle, "from each according to his abilities, to each according to his work," we have the communist principle of all-round development of the personality or "from each according to his abilities, to each according to his needs."[55] Unlike the former, which calls only for the abolition of exploitation, the latter is designed to satisfy not only the laborer's vital and social wants, but also his need for a cultivated life, the need to become a rich human being.[56]

In this light, the goals of the producers transcend the narrow material objectives of the labor movement. But instead of emancipating the workers from bondage to the sphere of production and the corresponding treadmill of consumption, the labor movement is likely to make them consumer-oriented.[57] The producers are in danger of forgetting that the most gratifying human life is not an easy and comfortable one, but one that has personal growth instead of growth in material opulence for its object. Despite the several eccentricities of her book *The Human Condition,* we may agree with Hannah Arendt that the most rewarding activities of which men are capable center upon the living deed and the spoken word, "activities that do not pursue an end . . . and leave no work behind . . . but exhaust their full meaning in the performance itself."[58] The greatest source of felicity to man is neither the act of consumption which leaves no trace, nor the fabrication of works of art more costly and enduring than the craftsman himself, but rather the perfection of his uniquely human characteristics. The ancients, we may recall, summarized this condition of happiness under the heading of "virtue." Actually, few persons with the opportunity to choose prefer the great labor or even the great work to the all-round development of the complete man.

What needs stressing is that the worker's current preoccupation with exclusively economic goals is conditioned by an economy of scarcity. Considering that the magnitude of desire is a function of the quantity of goods available, the larger the stock of goods, the less the satisfaction from each increment. The resulting diminishing marginal utility constitutes an argument for the decreasing importance of consumption under conditions of affluence. As Galbraith notes, one effect of increasing affluence is to minimize the importance of economic goals: "With increasing per capita real income, men are able to satisfy additional wants . . . [but] of a lower order or urgency. This being so, the production that provides the goods that satisfy these less urgent wants must also be of smaller (and declining) importance."[59]

To be sure, it has been argued recently that the utility or satisfaction from new products does not diminish appreciably. As long as the consumer seeks quality and variety instead of quantity and sameness, he may accumulate like a museum without diminishing the urgency of his wants. However, this argument overlooks the "obvious fact that some things are acquired before others and that, presumably, the more important things come first."[60] It is also urged that after the producer has satisfied his vital wants, then socially conditioned desires take over, which admit of no limit and are seemingly insatiable. However, "wants cannot be urgent if they must be contrived for him."[61] Indeed, the whole case for the urgency of production based upon the urgency of wants collapses when production itself creates the wants.

The greatest prospect currently faced by the labor movement, according to Galbraith, is "to eliminate toil as a required economic institution."[62] A new working stratum has emerged recruited to a large extent from the class of laborers, but one that *works* for a living instead of *laboring*. The failure to appreciate the emergence of this new stratum lies in the outmoded belief that all work, physical, intellectual, artistic, and managerial, is the same. Ironically, the "president of the corporation is pleased to think that his handsomely appointed office is the scene of the same kind of toil as the assembly line and that only the greater demands in talent and intensity justify his wage differential."[63] An incipient sense of guilt can be apparently assuaged by the rationalization that he, too, is a worker and that mental effort is far more taxing than physical labor. However, the occupations of workers, as distinct from laborers, are so intrinsically fulfilling that the pay is unimportant. Work becomes a privilege for this stratum, whereas only labor is a burden. According to Galbraith, "those who do this kind of work expect to contribute their best regardless of compensation."[64] Considering the greater desirability of work to labor, a major objective of the new working class is its own self-expansion through substitutes for drudgery and routine. To minimize the number of people involved in these operations is the counterpart of upgrading the entire labor force.[65]

Galbraith and Arendt both criticize the reductionistic tendencies within the labor movement which are designed to subordinate all other goals to that of making life easier and more secure. The labor movement characteristically confuses the immediate and ultimate goals of its members, means and ends, strategies and principles. However, Marx makes clear that the long-run goal of the producers is neither a laboring society nor even a society of artists and intellectuals, but rather a fully human society of well-rounded and many-talented individuals.[66] Although socialism is the immediate aim of the working class, the annulment of bourgeois property is not the goal of human development.

Actually, Marx's long-run views concerning the labor movement have more in common with Galbraith's forecasts than with those of Arendt. According to Marx, self-activity or the long-term goal of the producers has for its condition the subordination of all goals to the immediate struggle of the workers against immiserization and exploitation. For the bulk of producers still suffering from underdevelopment and underconsumption, the major unsolved problem of our times continues to be the struggle for a laboristic society of abundance for all. The advent of Arendt's *animal laborans,*[67] or in Marx's terminology a proletarian revolution, is a precondition of the humanization of labor, its upgrading or conversion into skilled and intellectual work. Only then does the major problem become that of making labor more meaningful, which in turn requires the transformation of a laboristic society, in Arendt's sense, into a society dominated by *homo faber.*[68]

This transformation of society involving the replacement of laborers by skilled workers and engineers means, in current Soviet diction, abolishing the distinction between manual and intellectual labor. Even today in the economically advanced countries, it is not unrealistic to hope for a time when the vast majority of laborers will have acquired the status of professional workers. And yet this goal of the professional worker is not an ultimate one, but only an intermediate one for the labor movement. More far-reaching is the transformation of a society of technicians into a fully human society in which men are, first and foremost, well-rounded and developed human beings, in which they are actors as well as craftsmen. Such is the ideal of the *vita activa,* although, contrary to Arendt, the man rich in humanized needs not only speaks and acts, but also perfects himself through the use of his hands and body.[69]

NOTES

1. K. Marx, *Economic and Philosophic Manuscripts,* trans. M. Milligan (Moscow, 1956), pp. 120-121.

2. Ibid., p. 121. See also the translation of the same work by T. B. Bottomore in Erich Fromm, *Marx's Concept of Man* (New York, 1961), pp. 146-147 (italics deleted).

3. Joan Robinson, *Economic Philosophy* (London, 1962), pp. 2-4, 10-14, 146.

4. K. Marx, *Economic and Philosophic Manuscripts*, pp. 111-112.

5. Ibid., p. 117.

6. Ibid., pp. 106-107, 112.

7. *Capital*, vol. 3, ed. F. Engels (Chicago, 1906-1909), 954.

8. Ibid., pp. 954-955.

9. Ibid.

10. *Capital*, vol. 1 (Chicago, 1906-1909), p. 256.

11. Ibid., chaps. 10, 15, 25.

12. Ibid., p. 260.

13. Ibid., pp. 456, 462.

14. Ibid., p. 465.

15. Ibid., pp. 707, 709.

16. Thomas Hobbes, *Leviathan* (New York, 1950), pt. 1, chap. 14; pt. 2, chap. 21.

17. *Capital*, vol. 1, p. 330.

18. Ibid.

19. K. Marx, *Value, Price and Profit*, ed. Eleanor Aveling (New York, 1933), p. 61.

20. For Marx's indebtedness to Hobbes, see ibid., p. 38, and *Capital*, vol. 1, p. 189, n. 2.

21. Ibid., pp. 189-192, 568-569, 611-612.

22. Ibid., pp. 295-296.

23. Ibid., p. 296.

24. See Engels' letters on historical materialism in *Marx & Engels: Basic Writings on Politics & Philosophy*, ed. Lewis S. Feuer (Garden City, 1959), pp. 395-412.

25. *Capital*, vol. 1, p. 688 n.

26. Fromm, *Marx's Concept*, p. 25.

27. Ibid., p. 50.

28. Mihailo Marković, "Marxist Humanism and Ethics," *Science & Society* 27 (Winter 1963): 27, 14.

29. Ibid., p. 3.

30. Robert Tucker, *Philosophy and Myth in Karl Marx* (Cambridge University, 1961), pp. 146-149.

31. Ibid., pp. 217, 220-222.

32. Ibid., p. 222.

33. Ibid., p. 149.

34. John Lewis, *Marxism and the Open Mind* (New York, 1957), p. 101.

35. Ibid., pp. 101-102.

36. Ibid., p. 122.

37. Ibid., pp. 128-130.

38. *Economic and Philosophic Manuscripts*, pp. 72-74.

39. Ibid., pp. 74-80.

40. "Critique of the Gotha Programme," *Karl Marx: Selected Works*, vol. 2, ed. V. Adoratsky and C. P. Dutt (New York, 1933), p. 566.

41. *Economic and Philosophic Manuscripts*, pp. 109-112.

42. For a somewhat different interpretation of the economic import of Mann's novel, see W. W. Rostow, *The Stages of Economic Growth* (Cambridge University, 1963), p. 11 n.

43. *Economic and Philosophic Manuscripts*, p. 110; see also p. 109.

44. Ibid., p. 113.

45. K. Marx, *Value, Price and Profit*, loc. cit.

46. Ibid.

47. F. Engels, *Anti-Dühring*, 2nd ed. (Moscow, 1959), p. 390.

48. See J. K. Galbraith, *The Affluent Society* (Boston, 1958), pp. 334-348; Rostow, *Stages*, pp. 90-92.

49. *Capital*, vol. 1, 190-191; see also *Value, Price and Profit*, pp. 39-40.

50. *Capital*, vol. 1, p. 192.

51. K. Marx, *Wage-Labor and Capital* (New York, 1933), p. 37.

52. Ibid., p. 39.

53. Ibid., p. 33.

54. Ibid., p. 40.

55. "Critique of the Gotha Programme."

56. *Economic and Philosophic Manuscripts*, p. 112.

57. Hannah Arendt, *The Human Condition* (New York, 1959), pp. 110-117.

58. Ibid., p. 185.

59. Galbraith, *The Affluent Society*, p. 145.

60. Ibid., p. 148.

61. Ibid., p. 152.

62. Ibid., p. 340.

63. Ibid., p. 341.

64. Ibid., p. 342.

65. Ibid., p. 346.

66. *Economic and Philosophic Manuscripts*, pp. 106-109, 111-112.

67. Arendt, *The Human Condition*, pp. 278-279.

68. Ibid., pp. 122, 140-141, 186-187.

69. Ibid., pp. 156-159, 172-173.

Chapter 15

Marxist Humanism and Ethics

MIHAILO MARKOVIĆ

Mihailo Marković is professor in the faculty of philosophy of the University of Belgrade. He studied at the University of London and in 1961-1962 did research in the United States as a Ford Foundation grantee. In 1969-1970 he taught philosophy at the University of Michigan. Among his many works are *Formalism in Contemporary Logic, The Dialectical Theory of Meaning, Logic* and *Philosophy, A Social Critique* (in press).

The aim of this paper is to explore the possibilities of building up an ethical theory, starting from general assumptions of humanism implicit in the philosophy of Marx, and taking into account the methodological achievements of modern ethics.

In accordance with this aim, answers to the following questions should be given:

1. Can anyone who accepts the basic ideas of Marx speak clearly and consistently about an ideal in general and an ethical ideal in particular?

2. Are there elements in Marx's philosophy which provide an adequate theoretical basis for the development of a humanist ethical theory?

3. What are the solutions to the fundamental ethical and metaethical problems from the Marxist point of view?

Critics of Marx claim that there is no place for a genuine ethical theory within the frame of Marxist historical materialism. The reasons they give follow.

1. The very concept of determinism rules out freedom of choice and moral responsibility. Without these two latter assumptions, no theory of morals is possible.

2. The idea that morality is based on the economic conditions of a given society tends to identify moral right with economic advantage. To say the least, then, such a moral theory applies only to a part of life—morality is conceived as a matter of property-interest. Even worse, the idea of moral "right" has no place in such a conception.

3. The thesis that morality, together with other forms of cultural superstructure, reflects the interests of a social class introduces a complete relativism. Thus, the universally human character of morals is denied, the moral problems of an individual do not exist. The problem, which of the conflicting sets or moral standards is preferable, is now reducible to the question, "which social class is more revolutionary?" This way of looking comes close to Hitler's view that right is whatever promotes the interests of the German *Volk*.

4. For the moral to be subordinated to the political eventually leads to the acceptance of the old Machiavellian principle that ends justify means, and, of course, this principle is incompatible with morals in any ordinary sense.

The conclusion of such arguments seems to be that on the basis of Marx's philosophy no ethical ideal and genuine ethical theory is possible. However, both the arguments and the conclusion are false, for they are incorrect presentations of the totality of Marx's thought.[1]

The apparent conflicts between ethics and historical materialism can be easily resolved in the following way.

1. The concept of determinism in Marxism has a different, much more flexible meaning than usual. It is clear from *Capital* and other writings that Marx (as well as Engels in *Anti-Dühring* and *Ludwig Feuerbach*) conceived social laws as *tendencies* only. Although they restrict the possibilities of human action, they still leave several more or less probable alternatives open. It is up to men to choose and realize by their practical activity one or other of the possibilities. Marx's idea from *Theses on Feuerbach*, that in speaking about the determination of men by historical circumstances and education one should not forget that circum-

stances are changed by men and that "the educator himself must be educated," is essential here.

Man, for Marx, is an active, relatively free being (free within the limits of a partial physical and historical determination). This freedom increases insofar as his knowledge and control of various operating, mutually neutralizing factors increase. As a consequence, there is not the slightest doubt that a normal adult person is morally responsible for his actions, the more so the more his awareness of various possible alternatives and their consequences prior to his action can be assumed.

2. In his last letters, Engels himself expressed his apprehension that Marx's and his own repeated insistence on the importance of economic factors had been misunderstood. And he has explained, first, that the economic factor is only in the last analysis the decisive social factor which determines directly or indirectly all other social phenomena (and here again the word "determines" should be taken in a flexible, statistical sense). Second, various forms of social superstructure have their own, relatively independent logic of development, and can, in their turn, influence the development of the productive forces and the mode of production.

In such amended form, this is quite a sound conception, and any serious sociologist would hardly wish to reject it, although he might demand much more methodological rigor and empirical evidence.

It is absurd to present Marx as a champion of the identification of moral values with economic advantages. The exact opposite is the case. A certain degree of material well-being is, in his view, only a means, a necessary condition for the liberation from all other forms of human misery. His ultimate goal was a free, creative life for each individual, rich rather in sensate and spiritual content than in the amount of possessed goods.

3. Though Marx laid strong emphasis on the class character of morals, this was due to a compelling practical need to castigate moral ideals current in his time (for example, the ideas of natural rights—including right of private property, divine law, etc.).[2]

In fact, there is no doubt that Marx did not reduce human nature just to class nature. He made a distinction between constant "fixed drives which exist under all circumstances and which can be changed by social conditions only as far as form and direction are concerned" and "relative drives which owe their

origin only to a certain type of social organization." (The drive
for maximal economic gain he included in the second category.)
Criticizing Bentham's utilitarianism in *Capital* (vol. I, chap. 24,
sect. 5) he says: "He that would criticize all human acts, movements, relations etc. by the principle of utility *must first* deal
with human nature in general, and then with human nature as
modified in each historical epoch." In *Anti-Dühring*, one can
find a section along this line, speaking about eternal truths in
the field of morals. These are very rare, in Engels' view, but
they exist.

It is therefore quite compatible with Marxism to speak about
a whole set of moral norms which transcend limits of class and
epoch and which, in various, sometimes disguised forms, reappear
in all historical forms of morality. Such would be, for example,
norms prescribing fundamental duties toward children, parents,
friends, and community; norms which tend to discount lying,
cheating, stealing, killing, and which tend to bring certain
elementary order into sexual relationships, etc.

Those elements in a set of moral standards which are relative
to the specific interests and needs of a given class constitute only
one layer of morals. However, these elements are particularly
interesting just because they give specific character to a morality.
The reason why Marxists avoided speaking about universal
human morals is that those general values do not exist isolated,
in themselves; they are always given in a specific form, con-
joined with many norms of a variable, class nature.

However, these two come into conflict in all periods of crisis
and degeneration in a society. There are at least two symptoms
which indicate such a conflict: (1) members of the ruling class
stop living up to their own morality—there is a widespread
demoralization, cynicism, hypocrisy; (2) a strong opposition
appears which criticizes the ruling class and the existing social
system from a universally humanist point of view; by this time
already, a new morality appears, which contains again all the
traits of the general moral background *plus* some of the most
important specific moral values of the descending class, *plus* the
new moral demands of a new class leading the revolutionary
movement.

No historical relativism is implied in this view. At any moment
in any particular class-struggle one of the classes may desire to
be more progressive, not only for economic or political reasons
(fighting for a society with a more rational system of production,
more economic and political freedom), but also for moral

reasons. A really progressive class speaks and acts in the name
of the whole of humanity; in its morality, it incorporates all
the universal human ideals which the ruling class is incapable of
realizing. The important point is that any average, normally
intelligent, and honest person confronted with such a morality
would accept it, at least tacitly, provided that a discussion with
him has not been conducted on an abstract level only, but in
a concrete way—giving descriptions of various situations and
types of action and asking for immediate moral reactions with
subsequent analysis of these reactions. Of course, all this holds
only on condition that the representatives of a new morality
live up to their own higher standards. Otherwise they themselves become cynics and hypocrites. As a consequence they
would lose any chance of convincing others of the value of
their supposedly new, higher morality. An ordinary man is
absolutely right when he expects first to see the examples of a
morally higher practice and not just to be taught morality in
a theoretical way. And for a philosopher, it will be no great
surprise to discover some new cases of the difference between
theoretical declarations and practical conduct, and the difference
between a general historical tendency and particular deviations.
Insofar as he prefers to say anything about general tendencies,
he can safely assert that the really progressive classes inherit
all the achievements of a long humanist tradition, including
all universally human moral demands.

In this perspective, it is not difficult to solve the problem
of how to bridge a possible gap between the humanist
aspirations of an individual and his loyalty to a class. When a
class is really progressive, which, besides other things, implies
that it fights for the realization of the humanist ideals of its
time, the conflict is not likely to arise. There will be a full
accord between the objectives of the individual and those of the
social group to which he belongs. If he cannot put his heart into
a particular cause which, he has been told, is the objective of
his class, he must solve the dilemma in one of the various
possible ways.[3]

In conclusion it might be said that a humanist conception
of morality involves a recognition that morals play a plurality
of roles at various levels.

1. In a society composed of classes, nations, groups and
individuals with overlapping and more or less opposed interests,

it serves to bring to life a certain necessary amount of harmony and cooperation.

2. It rationalizes the needs and goals of a social class. The prevailing morality in a society is, among other things, a justification of the way of life of the most influential class.

3. Morality, no doubt, plays an extraordinarily important guiding role in the life of the individual; it provides a set of standards without which his orientation in life would hardly be possible; even more than that, observance of these standards is one of the deepest sources of spiritual satisfaction and happiness.

4. In this epoch of revolutions and wars, hot and cold, politics has been occupying an increasingly important position in relation to all other forms of cultural activity. As a matter of fact, moral demands, as well as legal regulations, scientific objectivity, freedom of artistic expression, etc., have often been sacrificed to immediate political goals. This is true of both capitalist and socialist countries. And as a matter of fact, some Marxists (although by no means only Marxists) have been behaving as though they accepted "the end-justifies-the-means" principles.

Marxist humanism rejects both this principle and the practice of permanent subordination of morals (and science, and law, and art) to politics. The struggle for political emancipation of the oppressed social groups is just one of the fields in which human emancipation takes place. Cultural and moral revolution in particular are certainly not less important than the political reconstruction of a society. Certainly, morality itself, as an expression of the interests of a particular class, is politically colored. But, on the other hand, any political party which claims to speak in the name of the whole of humanity must follow moral values in its political struggle. And it certainly must not overlook how closely connected are the moral values of ends and means. Noble goals can be realized only by noble men. There is no doubt that the use of bad, degrading means morally degrades those who use them. Men change and their practical activity is the most important factor determining the evolution of their consciousness. Thus it may happen that, after a time, hardly anybody continues to fight for the *original* goal. What eventually comes into existence is likely to be something vastly different, and, for the most part, morally inferior to the initial idea.

This does not mean that friendly persuasion remains the only legitimate means of political struggle and that in principle no force and no revolution can be allowed from a moral point of view. That would be absurd. Very often the only morally good choice of action is the use of force against those who use it against the weak and helpless.

What follows from the emphasis on unity among goals and means is that the same moral standards must be used in both cases. Any different attitude is both morally indefensible and self-defeating.

The conclusion from these consideratons seems to be that a humanist ethical theory is wholly compatible with a sufficiently flexible and modernized interpretation of the main theses of historical materialism. The philosophy of Marx is a humanist philosophy. Its central problem is the place of man in the universe, what *is* and what *ought* to be his relation toward nature on the one hand, and toward other human beings and society as a whole, on the other.

This philosophy contains a number of notions and principles which are relevant to ethics. The key concept among them is that of disalienation. To be alienated means, in general, not to be what man could be and ought to be: a free, creative, fully developed, socialized being. That from which man is alienated should not be taken in the ontological sense—as a fixed human essence or nature, which man sometime in the past, perhaps in primitive communities, had possessed and then lost. That would be either a really bad metaphysics or an empirically false idealization of primitive society.

If taken as a *descriptive* or *explanatory* concept, general human nature is constituted by (statistically) permanent features of human behavior in history. This is a concept of *empirical* sciences—anthropology, history, social psychology, etc. When speaking about alienation within the frames of sociology and ethics what is meant is human nature as a *normative concept,* as a *value,* in the sense of what man ought to be.

These two are closely connected. In order to be realistic and applicable, any conception as to what man *ought* to be must be based on the objective estimate of the *real possibilities* of his evolution, which in its turn can be established only on the basis of a reliable knowledge about man as he actually *is.*

Man actually is a practical being; he tends to change his surroundings, and whether his activity will have the form of creation or destruction, or just dull routine work, depends on various circumstances. Man actually is a rational being, he acts with purpose and has reasons to believe that what he does will bring about the desired result (although he may be wrong or his desire may be bad). Also he actually is a social being—he cannot live except in society, and even when his interests are in sharpest conflict with those of society as a whole, he tries to establish at least their temporary unity in various forms of rationalization—in politics, ethics, philosophy, etc. Ideology is not created in order to cheat others but in a sincere craving for social justification. Further, it can be added to any description of actual human nature that man is a being who evolves rapidly; he develops his knowledge, he uses more and more adequate material objects in order to satisfy his basic needs, he develops more and more sophisticated cultural needs, he creates more and more complex and efficient forms of organization, etc. Lastly, man has, as a matter of fact, always been free (in a rather restricted sense). It is difficult to think of any kind of human communities in which people, at least in some situations, have not been aware of more than one possibility of action and have not been free from compulsion as to which to choose.[4]

Such empirical generalizations correlated with an objective description of contemporary society provide a basis for the analysis of various possibilities of further development of society and human conditions. Among the results of an analysis of this kind would be such general empirical hypotheses as the following: (1) If the present-day armaments race continues indefinitely, the destruction of modern civilization would be possible, even very probable; (2) if the bureaucracy became a new ruling class and if science and technology developed in opposition to all humanist considerations, a society similar to Huxley's and Orwell's vision would arise; (3) if private property in the means of production were abolished and various forms of self-management of producers were substituted for the state, a society without antagonistic conflicts among groups of people would emerge, etc. Predictions of this kind are scientific in the sense of being verifiable and falsifiable extrapolations of actual trends of development in present-day society.

It is typical of Marxist humanism that it is based on such scientific considerations.[5] In this conception there is no discrepancy between facts and values, knowledge and ideals, insofar as one takes as a value, as an ideal, something which is *really possible* and which one knows to be possible. It still has the character of a value, of an ideal, because it is an extrapolation into the future which has been *chosen* among other alternatives.[6]

This choice is based not only on knowledge but also on certain value considerations. One is likely to accept the ideal of thorough-going human emancipation only insofar as one is deeply disturbed and dissatisfied by all those negative aspects of human existence in contemporary society, which Marx has embraced by the term "alienation." These are as follows:

1. Man has lost control over the products of his own physical and mental activity. Instead of being a means to satisfy one of his needs, any such product (be it money, church, state, political organization, etc.) becomes an end in itself, a strange, unknown power above him, which enslaves him instead of being ruled by him.

2. Instead of participating in creative, stimulating work, instead of performing various social functions of which he is capable, man is forced to spend his best energy in dull, automatic work just to obtain the material means of existence.

3. He has no opportunities to fulfill his various potential qualities, to develop and satisfy various more refined needs. His existence remains one-sided, poor, animal-like—he remains at the level of his basic animal needs for eating, sleeping, sexual gratification, and the most primitive forms of entertainment.

4. In his struggle for more property and power, man becomes estranged from his fellow men. Exploitation, mistrust, conflict, envy, hatred dominate his relationship with other men.

All these tendencies on the moral plane lead to a narrow morality devised to rationalize and justify a limited, basically egoistic way of living. In order to give it a broader objective basis, its source is sought in an imaginary transcendent power, in God, not in man. But an alienated man, being essentially an egoist, will never live up even to that restricted morality imposed by the church—he will too often be a hypocrite, a desperately split personality.

When one has a feeling of revolt against a state of affairs in which man is so degraded, both one's criticism and one's ideal for the future are not an arbitrary and temporary reaction; they are based on some very old and deeply rooted and, at least *in abstracto*, almost generally accepted human evaluations.[7] They

can be verbally expressed in the form of such preferences as:
all other conditions being equal, it is better to be free than
enslaved, to create instead of to destroy, to act in a way which
would satisfy both individual and social goals than to pursue the
former only and to disregard the latter; it is better to live in
peace than in war, in love and friendship than in mutual hatred,
in harmony than in isolation; it is more just if people have equal
rights than if there are undeserved privileges, and also, it is more
just if certain goods can be enjoyed by all or a majority than by
a minority; it is more reasonable and more likely to lead to a happy
life if a man develops his abilities than if he neglects them, etc.
The humanist ideal of Marx corresponds completely to such
deeply rooted, tacitly assumed preferences.

Future man ought to free himself both from subjection to
external natural necessities and from slavery to blind social
forces—his own products. Future man ought to develop creative
forms of his practical activity and to free himself from imposed
degrading labor. He ought to stop the destruction of material
goods and human lives which particularly takes place in time of
war. He ought to bring his individual interests into harmony with
the interests of other people and society as a whole. He ought
not to have any economic, political and cultural privileges—
which implies the abolition of class and caste distinctions, even
if it does not also imply complete equality among individuals.
Future man ought not to exploit other men; in other words,
he ought never to treat a man as a means but always as an end.
Instead of making desperate efforts to *have* as much as possible,
he ought to try to *be* as fully, as richly as possible. Therefore
he ought to develop all his potential qualities, all his human
senses, and to affirm his individuality in a variety of relations
to the world.

This ethical ideal was expressed by Marx in his youth. It
is still unsurpassed in modern culture. Marx devoted the rest
of his life to laying down scientific foundations for it, to
showing that such a complete liberation of man could be
realized in the contemporary scene only through the emancipation of the proletariat and the abolition of private property
in the means of production.

This, in turn, is not a mere dream, a utopia, but the necessary
outcome of historical development *if* men act in that direction.
Now, this "if" makes a whole world of difference. Those who
quietly ignore it claim that ethics is incompatible with Marxism.

Those who know well that without it "Marxism" would have
little in common with the philosophy of Marx, have the right to
claim that hardly any other contemporary philosophy provides
such a rich and flexible theoretical basis for the development
of a satisfactory ethical theory.

From the main principles of such an activist and dynamic
philosophy, there follows a conception of ethics which not only
analyzes and explains what morality is (in the totality of its
forms, dimensions and relations), but also evaluates and proposes
what morality ought to be. Thus, ethics has both theoretical and
practical tasks. The theoretical tasks of ethics are: to clarify the
basic concepts of moral discourse, to establish general criteria
of moral evaluation and methods of settling moral issues, to
explain the relations of morality toward various other social
phenomena, to examine philosophical assumptions and conditions of applicability of various moral doctrines. The practical
task of ethics is to contribute to the moral improvement of
human life by criticizing existing morals and laying down moral
ideals appropriate to human society in the given epoch.

Many philosophers would certainly object to this conception
of the subject-matter of ethics as being too broad. But the natural
reply to this is that perhaps their whole conception of philosophy
is too narrow.

As a matter of fact, throughout the history of philosophy,
philosophers have been concerned, in one form or another, with
all the enumerated problems. What is even more relevant here
is the fact that these problems are still of enormous importance,
and that there is nobody who should be more concerned with
them—certainly not the specialized scientist, or politician or
newspaperman.

The rejection of all other tasks of ethics except the analysis of
the language of moral theories is based on the assumption that
philosophy is neutral toward all possible ethical theories and
moral systems, uninterested in their evaluation and, in general,
too pure to take any stand on moral issues.

Such an attitude is unacceptable to a humanist philosopher,
particularly one who, following Marx, seeks not only to explain
and understand the world but also to change it, to improve it.
And while he may be in great sympathy with all demands for
clarity, and particularly with the rejection of any form of
obscurantism, he does not feel that very precise trivialities would

be a great gain either. Therefore, he will refuse to accept any framework which leaves him as the only possible choice, the sacrifice of all those philosophical problems which are of real interest, and directly relevant for human lives. Fighting against various forms of alienation, he will not overlook this particular one: the alienation of the theoretician who has completely appropriated as his end what was previously designed to be only a means, who has reduced all richness and complexity of his subject to just one dull and rather sterile dimension, who has estranged himself from his fellow-thinkers who deal with his field from various angles, by deliberately closing himself in the ivory tower of his metaethical purity.

The most important metaethical questions for any contemporary theory are: (1) what is "value" in general, "moral value" in particular, (2) what are the meanings of basic ethical terms such as "good," "right," "ought," (3) what is specific for ethical judgments; how do they differ from statements of other types, and (4) what are the methods of settling moral issues?

1. The concept of value is one of the fundamental philosophical categories. Not only are the basic concepts of ethics, aesthetics, political science and law value-terms, such as "good," "beautiful," "progressive," "just"; even in the very foundations of logic and epistemology we find certain value-demands such as clarity, precision, exactness, simplicity, adequacy, objectivity, completeness, elegance, etc. Truth itself is a cognitive value of a statement or a theory.

The concept of value implies always a subject who evaluates—be it an individual (in which sense we can speak about a personal value) or a social group (family, class, nation, etc.), or man in general, in which case we can speak about a universal human value, at least for a given period of time. To say that an x is a value in relation to a specifiable subject means that x has properties such that they satisfy certain (cognitive or emotive or both) needs of the given subject.

What is specific for moral values is: (1) that they constitute a special kind of object—certain patterns of human actions; (2) that they are relative either to humanity as a whole or to very large groups of people (whole communities, social classes) for a considerable period of time—very rarely do individuals have their own purely personal moral values, different from those of other individuals and nations; (3) that actions with positive moral value are those which satisfy a particular kind of human

need—the need for social harmony, coordination, social endorsement of some types of behavior, and discouragement of some
other types; above all perhaps, a need, deeply rooted in every
individual, to have a certain set of standards in accordance
with which to live.

So conceived, moral values are neither objective nor subjective,
in the absolute sense of these terms. They do not belong to the
sphere of absolute essences in themselves (which only come to be
exemplified in a particular human moral code). They, like all
other values, are relative to man, since in a world without man
nothing would be either good or bad. On the other hand, moral
values are not purely subjective and arbitrary, varying from
individual to individual; insofar as they satisfy certain pervasive
and profound social needs, they are interpersonal, objective.

2. The terms most often used to express moral values are
"good," "right," "ought" which, though they have a wider
usage, we shall consider here only in the context of moral
discourse. They all have a common core of meaning, as pointed
out in the preceding paragraph. They differ only insofar as, in
in characterizing an action as "good," we emphasize the quality
of the object (action) in question, and in calling it "right"
stress conformity with the rules of the accepted moral code,
whereas in saying that something "ought" to be done, the
emphasis is on action, and we directly (and not only indirectly
as in the previous cases) try to encourage a certain kind of
practical activity.

3. Speaking about the difference in sense between moral
judgment and other kinds of statements, we should distinguish
among various dimensions of sense. The problem can be
analyzed into three different questions: (1) what kind of
mental states would the ethical judgments express, (2) is there
a specific kind of objects which they designate, and (3) what
is the practical function, what is the expected effect of their
assertion? Some ethical theorists disagree just insofar as they
lay emphasis on only one of these various dimensions of meaning
(emotive, descriptive, prescriptive). A theory constructed by the
dialectical method would tend (1) to take into account all these
dimensions as various aspects of a complex phenomenon, (2) to
avoid making hard and fast lines both among these various
dimensions and between the meaning of the ethical judgments
(and value judgments in general), on the one hand, and of all
other statements, including cognitive judgments, on the other.[8]

The solution, then, would be that ethical judgments differ from cognitive statements in all three previously mentioned aspects of meaning, but the difference is not too sharp; there is a continuity between them.

So, (1) there are certainly specific kinds of psychological processes which are associated with ethical judgments. They express our emotive attitude toward a given type of action, our approval or disapproval, our preference for one over the other, our feeling of guilt, etc. (2) There is a specific kind of social, cultural objects, moral values, to which ethical expressions are related. Keeping a given promise, care of children, the old and sick, loyalty to one's country, a friend, etc., are such objects—objects in the sense of being patterns of behavior which are intersubjectively approved. Also (3) there is a specific practical function which ethical judgments perform: they not only convey information, but also to a much greater extent try to evoke feelings of approval and sense of duty in others. They tend to encourage or discourage others to act in a definite way.

However, the demarcation between ethical and cognitive judgments should not be construed as very sharp. Not only are there many borderline cases which it would be difficult to classify as either purely ethical or purely cognitive statements; it is also the case that the former do not express only our effective attitude, nor do the latter describe only outside matters of fact. The point is that whenever we have a moral judgment and know the society (with its moral code) in which the judgment was made, we may give a reliable *description* of the kind of human behavior to which the judgment refers. This shows that to the members of the society, as well as to all those who are sufficiently familiar with the historical and cultural conditions of its existence, an ethical judgment conveys, among other things, a certain amount of information about the human action which is being evaluated. On the other hand, there are many perfectly good descriptive statements, particularly in social sciences and ordinary life, which contain an element of moral evaluation. For example: "In country X 3 percent of the landowners keep 55 percent of all land, whereas 78 percent of the peasant population own only 16 percent." "At the entrance to the gas chamber at Dachau, the sign on the door reads 'bathroom.'" "The degree of radioactivity above the place X is now three hundred times greater than normal," etc. What is specific for ethical judgments is only that what is here only implied—the tacit condemnation of a certain kind of human practice—is there explicitly stated and stressed using special moral terms.

4. How can moral issues be settled? The case where opponents share some basic moral principles and, consequently, some basic criteria of evaluation does not present particular difficulties. It can be more or less easily shown that one of the opposing moral judgments contradicts accepted basic norms and that it must be given up—unless the person who asserts it prefers to abandon one or more of his fundamental values.

Many moral philosophers, particularly emotivists, hold that in the case where opponents disagree in basic principles the settlement of a moral issue is impossible in principle.

There is a temptation to think that a Marxist should subscribe to such a view. If every morality is the reflection of the particular interests of a given social class, people who belong to different classes would necessarily disagree on basic values and could not possibly settle their differences in particular questions.

However, a Marxist need not hold such a simplified view. A certain cautiousness and flexibility concerning universal statements is in the very nature of dialectical thinking. Most empirical generalizations are only statistically true—an allowance for exceptions and for deviations must always be made. Besides, classes, like all other things, should be construed as processes, as objects in constant flux, which implies that there are always individuals who are materially or ideologically abandoning one class and joining another one—this holds particularly for intellectuals. So, what is accepted on the macrolevel does not preclude various possibilities at the microlevel. Settling a moral issue remains always such a possibility even for opponents who belong to hostile classes.

The method here should be *to explore the consequences* of the particular moral judgment in question and of the whole network of reasons, including the fundamental principles, behind it. While the two opponents examine what kind of moral attitude each one of them would take, acting in various situations, or judging various kinds of human actions under specified conditions, any one of several results can eventually be achieved:

1. It would be natural to expect each opponent to grasp better the meaning of his rival's verbal declarations. Each of them would probably find it necessary to add certain qualifications to the sentences in which he expresses his judgments and norms. And it might be discovered that they have had different kinds of situations

in their minds and that in spite of the apparent sharp disagreement between their statements they share a basically identical underlying moral attitude which finds its expression in different norms under *different social conditions.*

2. In the course of such examination, one of the opponents might experience an unbearable conflict between his belief in certain fundamental (more or less abstract) norms and his immediate moral reactions to certain described or actually experienced types of action. He might *play the role* of a cynic, or of an egoist, or of a puritan; he might try to defend the basic morals of the complete individualism of a *laissez-faire* society, or the means-justifies-the-end principle of a revolutionary à la Stalin. *In abstracto,* while conducting purely theoretical discussions, he might be convinced that he is playing his role sincerely and that his heart is fully in what he says. And still it might happen that *in concreto*, when confronted with particular cases in which he would have to decide how to act, he would find it utterly impossible to act in accordance with his own norms or to justify anybody's acting so. This can happen to anyone who has accepted a morality or pretends to have accepted it in a more or less verbal form without a practical challenge in his own life, in his own immediate moral experience.

In deciding moral questions, this immediate moral experience has an analogous role to the one which observation has in deciding cognitive problems. It is true that the former is much more variable. But it does not follow that one should underestimate the amount of uniformity which is much greater here than in the area of abstract verbal declarations. At any rate, the appeal to moral experience is by far the most hopeful procedure in settling moral issues between opponents who disagree in basic principles.

It is on this concrete level of immediate moral responses to various specified kinds of behavior that a Marxist humanist would expect very strong support both for his criticism of the existing human relationships in the contemporary world and for his ethical ideals of a future world.

NOTES

1. It can be granted that in many Marxist writings, even in those of Marx, Engels, and Lenin, there are some formulations which are too

rigid and one-sided and which (particularly when they are taken out of theoretical and historical context) can call for strong criticism. Even today, some Marxists disregard all the nuances, qualifications, and counter-instances in which Marx's writings are so rich, and there is a neglect of the earlier manuscripts which lay down a sufficiently broad humanist foundation for the whole of this philosophy.

2. Besides, Marx has never been in the position of having to develop a complete theory of morals and of having to formulate all those commonplaces which are shared by almost all ethical theories. So it was natural enough for him to lay stress on what he considered new and specific—his criticism of ideology, his thesis that the prevailing morality in every society reflects the interests of the leading class and serves only to rationalize its conditions of existence.

3. For some time he might think he is probably wrong and try to be loyal. That means that there is either too little self-confidence in him or a great confidence in the leaders of his class. However, this cannot last very long, if he wants to preserve his personal integrity. Once he loses confidence in his leaders or has a strong feeling or moral obligation to act in a different way than most of the members of his class, he has no other choice but to act in accordance with his own convictions. If he is wrong he will realize it later—but he might also be right and by his actions help to change things for the better. In any case, if the class to which he belongs is conservative or reactionary or has an inadequate leadership which tends to act in a morally wrong way, there is no question of loyalty; one has to rely upon one's personal feeling of moral obligation.

4. Processes in nature and society are regulated by laws. However, these laws are not strict in the sense of excluding any chance events and any possibility of human freedom. Laws should be construed as trends, as most probable patterns of behavior of things and living organisms. In relation to a relevant law an individual event may constitute a deviation (chance) because of: (a) the action of a more powerful law outside the ordinary frame of reference, (b) a change in the initial conditions of the system in question, (c) the action of a variable factor inside the system.

Living in a world in which there is both order and chance, man is able to behave as a free agent only in so far as he: (a) becomes aware of both classes of determining factors—those of the *external* situation (objective conditions, natural and social laws) and *internal* determining factors (traits of character, interests, belief) which delimit his possiblities of choice and action; (b) is ready to resist both external and internal compulsion and to take the decision which best corresponds to his basic convictions and values.

5. There is no other kind of knowledge which is so objective and reliable as scientific knowledge. Whatever *has been* and *is* can best be known by using the scientific method (i.e., by expressing our experiences and thoughts in clear, publicly communicable terms, by applying logical forms of reasoning, by testing all generalizations empirically). What the alternatives of the *future* course of events are and what the probabilities of the various alternatives are can also best be known by using scientific methods.

On the other hand, which one of these alternatives we prefer to realize, no matter how probable it might be, depends on our needs and interests, on our conception of what kind of human life and society are good for man.

6. This is an element in Marx's thought which has often been misunderstood. His philosophy is essentially an *activist* one, his determinism is not fatalism, his communism is not something which must come *no matter how people behave*—it is something for which they must struggle and make efforts and sacrifices. This presupposes that they must choose to do so—they are not automata governed completely by blind external forces.

7. Although all knowledge and evaluation are relative to the conditions of place and time, relative to the degree of development of human culture, there are, on the other hand, certain elements (truths, values) which survive through various epochs and have a lasting human significance. These human (not absolute) constants constitute the very basis of all knowledge and evaluation.

8. While we analyze objects we simplify them and tend to draw demarcation lines which are too sharp. It is essential to be aware of this process of simplification and to supplement analysis by a subsequent process of synthesis, of the re-establishment of continuity between different (and often opposite) elements of a whole. Provisionally making rigid distinctions and subsequently loosening them by the discovery of common points and transitional cases is an important dialectical regulative principle of controlled inquiry.

Part V
MARXISM'S IMAGE OF MAN

Chapter 16

Marx's Notion of Man

FREDERICK J. ADELMANN, S. J.

Frederick J. Adelmann, S. J., is professor of philosophy at Boston College. He has taught at St. Louis University and is the editor of *The Quest for the Absolute* (1966) and *Demythologizing Marxism* (1969). He has written *From Dialogue to Epilogue—Marxism and Catholicism Tomorrow* (1968) and is currently at work on a volume on the philosophy of Herbert Marcuse.

I think that it is necessary right in the beginning to make a distinction between communism which is an ideology and Marxism which is a philosophy. An ideology implements a philosophy in practice and often loses its philosophical reredos in so doing. A philosophy—even one that includes practice—is still speculative. Here we are discussing a philosophical question.

To be even more precise, this paper is limited to a discussion of the notion of man in the writings of the young Marx. Hence, we are not trying to understand the notion of man that is evolving among current Marxist scholars, interesting and valuable as such a study is. Nor are we going to get involved in political theory or economics from any intention of mine. Furthermore, I am not trying to decide what Marx's own notion of man was in his later writings.

The image of man that I am portraying is based on a textual study of Marx's early writings gathered under the general title: *The Economic and Philosophical Manuscripts*.[1] I am using, basically, the three manuscripts which bear the subtitles: *Alienated Labor, The Relationship of Private Property,* and the *Critique of Hegel's Dialectic and General Philosophy.* The text used is the English translation made by Thomas B. Bottomore of the London School of Economics and published in 1959. The accurate and precise text was first published in German in 1932. Thus, this particular section of Marx's works came relatively late into the hands of scholars. Bottomore's English translation appeared first for American readers in 1961 in Erich Fromm's *Marx's Concept of Man.*

I am presently confining myself to these research materials because they have come so recently into our hands and because they have stirred great interest among Marxist scholars.[2] Furthermore, for our project about the notion of man, they are particularly fruitful because they contain the seeds of so much philosophical thinking.

However, it should be noted that, among Marxist scholars, a kind of academic debate is going on as to the precise value of these manuscripts. Some regard them as the immature philosophical musings of a young man not yet embarked on the course of his life's work, for they were written in 1844, when Marx was only twenty-six years of age. Yet other commentators see in them a new philosophical dimension in the study and analysis of contemporary communism.[3] In this light these texts have acquired the aura of an apocalypse among the revisionists, even though they are chronologically prior to his other major writings. We should keep these different interpretations in mind as we advance in our own discussion. As a matter of fact, even in these texts Marx does not give us a clear picture of his idea of man. It must, therefore, be gleaned from a careful textual study which I have tried to do.

First of all, where shall be begin? This is a most important question, because to my mind, it is where and how a philosopher begins that gives the hint as to where he will end up. If one begins as Plato or Descartes did, he will never end up with the conclusions of Aristotle or Thomas. Likewise, if one starts his philosophical enterprise within the phenomenological "epoché," he will never be talking about the "real" in Karl Marx's terms. Marx himself writes: "Let us examine Hegel's system. It is necessary to begin with the Phenomenology because it is there that Hegel's philosophy was born and that its secret is to be found."[4] And again he says: "Socialism no longer requires such a roundabout

method; it begins from the theoretical and practical sense perception of man and nature as essential beings."[5] Thus, we see that
Marx begins as a realist in the sense that I exist and other things
exist outside of me and independently of my thinking of them.
Yet Marx is a very special kind of a realist for, although he has
inverted Hegel's idealism, he is adhering here in a very definite
way to the Hegelian dialectic.

We are faced in the beginning with a bi-polar notion of being
which always and necessarily includes subject being and object
being. In other words, his theory of knowledge does not include
the abstracting of an essence to get a universal idea but rather
his method is to discover the network of very real relations that
really explain existing things. Thus, in the case at hand, this
object being is related to the subject being as its object being.[6]
There is, then, necessarily a relation between any subject and
object. A being is only called object in relation to a subject and
vice versa. For this reason a nonobjective being is nonbeing.
An objective being is a being that has an object outside of
itself. It is a natural being for it has its nature outside of it. No
being can be explained isolated from the totality of nature. A
being is "real" in the sense that it is involved with the rest of
nature. No being can be understood in itself; it is fulfilled by
and directed toward other beings. It is entwined in a network
of being.[7]

Up to now we have been dealing with sensuous being, i.e.,
being that is experienced in nature, being that is active and
being acted upon. This is good realism and a very appealing
aspect of Marx's thought for me; but it is not good Hegelianism
because it disdains the abstract and the conceptual as only
mental modes and far removed from the existential order.[8]
Marx does not claim that such abstractions are valueless but only
that many philosophers take them for real modes of being—
which they are not.

Probing further into Marx's notion of man we find that, for
him, man is unique. He is different from material elements,
plants and animals; he is a species-being. He is a species-being
because he is self-conscious and free. Man can universalize and
reflect, and manipulate the natural beings around him. He not
only knows but he knows that he knows. He can and must plan
his future; he must create his existence. To do this he must be
free, responsible and autonomous.[9]

This idea is very similar to Heidegger's distinction between man as an ontological being because he is self-conscious and can universalize and all other entities called ontic. Thus, *Dasein* in the Heideggerian sense is equivalent to Marx's "species-being," and ontic reality to Marx's natural beings.[10]

A "species-being" is self-conscious and free and hence human. And, thus, in a very special way, man is an objective being; he needs others to be—at all. And, hence too, man is by definition a social being.[11] One cannot talk about man in isolation; he must work out his existence, in fact, create it in collaboration with others.[12]

To make this clearer, let us return to the two levels within man. First, there is the natural level where man is a thing among things.[13] Here from the laws of physiology and the other empirical sciences man is seen as a part of nature. He cannot even on this level be considered nondialectically. In a kind of McLuhanian sense, his nature is beside itself. He needs food, sex, and companionship to complete his being. But so, in a lesser degree, do animals.[14] He can fall downstairs but not upstairs. He can sit or kneel but never vanish. In this context, he is a part of the whole of nature and follows its ineluctable laws.

However, no other being save man is self-conscious and free in the sense that man alone can plan and oversee the whole realm of other beings. Being human is to be able to universalize and to transcend and if a person were not free to act according to his intentions, there would be a basic frustration within his very existent being. This power of liberty gives him his special prerogative over all nature and it is thus that Marx typifies him as human.[15]

A deeper analysis of this species-being reveals a spirit within him that energizes his whole species-being. Consequently, man is embodied; he is incarnate.[16] This means that he is one; not a Platonic dichotomy, or a soul plus a body or the Platonic "sailor in the ship" idea. His flesh is dynamized by his unique spirit. These hands are my hands. This body is energized by my spirit from my intentions to my toenails. In man, his powers and faculties of knowing, willing, desiring and acting in the world are all energized by his spirit and are consequently human activities and different from the activities of merely natural things.[17]

His ear is a human ear attuned to the beauty of the melodies of nature; his eye is a human eye magnified to detect the eyes of another, to seek the texture of order and teleology; his sex activities are not limited to genital action but are human acts of love between two persons that utter in each the response of commitment and beget a family of other loved ones.[18]

More than this, he must act. Man is not merely passive but passionate.[19] His powers are urges and drives and tendencies that seek the fulfillment of his needs in labor and in the creation of objects wherein he sees his image sealed in frozen form.[20] Furthermore, a man must work. Whether he is a surgeon or a carpenter, his intentions flow to the exterior in activity that leaves some image of his own creativity. This is because he is a person. Now when society encroaches on this process and forces him to make more and more for less and less in return; when exchange value determines what he will make and how and how much, with the result that he has little to say about the results or little return to enable him to share in human activities, then he is exploited and his spirit is alienated.[21]

With keen insight, Marx realizes that a species-being must be autonomous. Man differs from the animals because he can universalize and manipulate beyond his own species. Animals are concerned only with their own species. They never transcend their given natures.[22] But man is not ordained by nature to be a slave but a master. Proudhon's communism is inadequate because it believes that carving up the world and dividing all the wealth will satisfy man's quest.[23] But this does not touch the heart of the problem. This is mere quantitative equality. Man as self-conscious, reflective and free is autonomous, and this is what makes him a person. It is because of this autonomy within him that he should not be used as a means for something outside of him. When this happens, man suffers alienation. Consequently, man must have a special reserve within his being, untouchable by the exploiters—be they politicians, economists or religionists. For a man, to be a slave is to be a nonman, a nonperson. The man in his cave in primitive times was still a man and a master. But the man in his Manchester cellar cringing with anxious fear because he does not have the money to pay his rent is not a man; he is unman.[24]

Therefore, the man for Marx is a self-conscious, free, incarnate autonomous individual. Such is a person, a bearer of rights who should not be compelled to act or suffer alienation in his human activities.[25] Of course, Marx realizes that even the species-being is an objective being, a social being and functions necessarily within the structures of justice and order.[26] Marx really is not an anarchist, though he is a rebel; a rebel against those forces that would alienate and estrange his species-being.

Before concluding this exposition, I would like to indicate certain lacunae that seem to me to arise from this study. First of all, I think that Marx has radicated the blight of alienation too one-sidedly in nature rather than, at least partially, within the species-being himself.[27] History, for Marx at this time, is conscious history and hence man's estrangement resides, to my mind, partially within man himself. It is often caused by man's own frailty, weakness and evil intentions. Thus, the mutually exclusive bi-polarity between capital and labor is over-naive at least for our own day.

Second, I believe that he leaves vague his assertions that man is free. We find in his text no clear-cut analysis of freedom along causal lines. For example, if a man is free in Marx's sense of the autonomous person, then he is not determined—and here, indeed, we have a mystery.

Finally, I think that Marx leaves unanswered the question of the origin of this unique species-being, not only historically but as a spiritual being able to transcend the natural order.[28] Whence comes the special energy needed to dynamize human activities as self-conscious and free? Needless to say, I believe that the source of this energy is an existent God and that permeating the whole of being is that mental side of stuff that allows Teilhard de Chardin to speak of the Divine milieu. But Marx straddles this issue in the very texts where he introduces the problem. For Marx, when you ask about the cause of the first man (or of anything else), you abstract that being from its subject-object polarity and end up with an abstraction or non-being; hence, for Marx, the question is meaningless. But at least we can ask why there should be anything at all.

Yet the results of our study should point up for us the profound philosophical realization that man is not a thing. Marx's insights into the human aspects of all our activities make clearer than ever the crude materialism of our own culture. For example, sex today is sold in the field of entertainment and other media of personal intercommunication on the basis of man's quest for gold.

Again, all of our efforts toward helping the black man will avail little unless we get to the heart and soul of the problem by realizing that black men are species-beings. To give them better housing, integrated schools, and higher wages will never alone redeem their current alienation.

And finally, this same idea of man as a species-being must be extended to all men everywhere in "praxis" and not just in talk. All the foreign aid that is planned and all the dividing up of the world's material resources will ultimately fail in bringing about peace unless we respect in fact the human dignity man already possesses.

The person is not a thing, not even a fattened thing, nor an educated thing. A person always and everywhere is a free, self-conscious, incarnate, human, autonomous individual. He needs you and me in order to just be; and you and I need him.

NOTES

1. All these references are taken from Karl Marx's *Economic and Philosophical Manuscripts*, trans. Thomas B. Bottomore, and are found in Erich Fromm's *Marx's Concept of Man* (New York: Frederick Ungar Publishing Company, 1961), and hereafter cited as EPM with Fromm's pagination.

2. Cf. Oliva Blanchette, "The International Symposium on Marx and the Western World," in *International Philosophical Quarterly* 7 (March 1967): 129-137.

3. Ibid., p. 135.

4. EPM, *Critique of Hegel's Dialectic and General Philosophy*, p. 172.

5. EPM, *Private Property and Communism*, p. 140.

6. EPM, *Critique of Hegel's Dialectic and General Philosophy*, p. 182.

7. Ibid., p. 182.

8. Ibid., p. 174, 176.

9. EPM, *Alienated Labor*, p. 103.

10. Heidegger, *Being and Time*, trans. John MacQuarrie and Edward Robinson (New York: Harper and Row, 1962), p. 34.

11. EPM, *Private Property and Communism*, p. 130.

12. Ibid., p. 129.

13. EPM, *Critique of Hegel's Dialectic and General Philosophy*, p. 181: "Man is directly a natural being. As a natural being, and as a living natural being, he is, on the one hand, endowed with natural powers and faculties, which exist in him as tendencies and abilities, as drives."

14. EPM, *Alienated Labor*, p. 102.

15. Ibid., p. 100.

16. EPM, *Critique of Hegel's Dialectic*, p. 182: "The fact that man is an embodied, living, real, sentient, objective being with natural powers means that he has real, sensuous objects as the objects of his being or that he can only express his being in real sensuous objects."

17. Cf. n. 13.

18. EPM, *Private Property and Communism*, p. 132: "The eye has become a human eye when its object has become a human, social object, created by man and destined for him."

19. Ibid., p. 138.

20. Cf. n. 13.

21. EPM, *Alienated Labor*, pp. 98-99: "What constitutes the alienation of Labor? First, that the work is external to the worker, that it is not part of his nature; and that, consequently, he does not fulfill himself in his work, but denies himself, has a feeling of misery rather than well-being, does not develop freely his mental and physical energies but is physically exhausted and mentally debased. So the activity of the worker is not his own spontaneous activity. It is another's activity and a loss of his own spontaneity."

22. Ibid., p. 102.

23. Ibid., p. 107.

24. Ibid., p. 97.

25. Ibid., pp. 99, 100.

26. EPM, *Private Property and Communism*, p. 130.

27. EPM, *Critique of Hegel's Dialectic*, p. 183.

28. EPM, *Private Property and Communism*, pp. 138, 139; *Critique of Hegel's Dialectic and General Philosophy*, p. 183.

Chapter 17

Comments on Fr. Adelmann's Paper

HOWARD L. PARSONS

Howard L. Parsons, professor and chairman of the department of philosophy, University of Bridgeport, Connecticut, has taught at several colleges and universities in the United States and Canada. He has written numerous articles and contributed to twenty collective volumes in the fields of religious, anthropological, social, and east-west philosophy. He is author of *Humanism and Marx's Thought* (1971).

Man in abstract and concrete. Fr. Adelmann states that Marx "disdains the abstract and the conceptual as only mental modes and far removed from the existential order." Marx did not separate the abstract and the concrete. Man, like any other existent thing, is always concrete, but, through consciousness and language, can abstract out certain qualities and relations from his existing situation. Such qualities and relations *as such* do not exist apart from that existing situation. An abstraction of them is always a reflection of them in the mode of consciousness and is to that degree a distortion of the full and rich complex of existing qualities and relations. Abstractions such as those of classical metaphysics falsify to the extent that they represent realities as isolated and static instead of inter-penetrating and developing. Man can comprehend and control realities only as he correctly reflects in his abstracting consciousness their dialectical movement and, guided by such

241

reflection, which involves both memory and anticipation, acts concretely to change realities in accordance with the limits of things and with his own knowledge of them. Fr. Adelmann's interpretation gives the impression that Marx leans toward existentialism. This is incorrect. Marx rejected equally the anti-intellectual view that "ideas are far removed from the existential order" and are irrelevant to changing that order, and the view that ideas predominantly or alone will change the world. He rejected both the blind communism of Weitling and Bakuninist anarchism, and idealism and utopianism. He affirmed, in short, the dialectical unity of thought and practice, since practice, to be effective, must mesh with the dynamic structures of the world; the world is dialectical, and thought, in order to guide practice, must become conscious of what man is doing, can do, and desires to do.

Alienation. Fr. Adelmann says: "Man's estrangement resides, in my mind, partially within man himself. It is often caused by man's own frailty, weakness, and evil intentions." "Within man himself" can mean two things. It can mean that individual man possesses potentialities or actualities (qualities relations, processes) which are independent of and *not* dependent on external actualities, or it can mean that man possesses potentialities or actualities which are independent of and *also* dependent on external actualities.

Marx denies the first meaning. To be in the spatio-temporal order of nature, and especially to be there as a sensitive, responsive, free, and responsible being, man is both independent of and dependent on the things and events of nature and society. "Men make their own history, but they do not make it just as they please; they do not make it under circumstances chosen by themselves, but under circumstances directly encountered, given and transmitted from the past."[1]

Marx does not deny that many men have been and are now frail, weak, and evil. (The controversy over whether Marx was a moralist usually turns out to be a semantic one; for while Marx repudiated traditional morals and moral philosophies, his whole work is pervaded with a humanistic ethics.) But he does deny that these qualities are "within man himself" in the sense that in the potentiality of his generic being he possesses them, or in the sense that he is necessitated to have them by nature or by society.

It is true that Marx does not give us an elaborated anthropology describing man's potentialities, the generic needs and dispositions

of man, or indeed specific remedies for all the evils that beset
the human condition under capitalism or socialism. But all that
he says about man indicates that man is a bio-socio-ecological
being who, from a biological base of potentialities for a social,
creative life, develops in dialectical relations with the things,
events, and persons of his world. The developing child and adult
often deviate from this normative pattern as a result of un-
favorable natural and social conditions. Man's frailty, weakness,
and evil are thus traceable to the whole complex of these
dialectical relations between man and the conditions of his
environment. For Marx, contrary to the individualists and
anarchists, evil does not lie in a system of politics or thought;
and contrary to the idealists (cf. St. Thomas) and utopians,
evil does not lie in some defect or partiality in the individual
person. For Marx "the human essence is no abstraction inherent
in each single individual. In its reality it is the ensemble of the
social relations."[2] Hence for Marx the evils of the human
situation are to be located not in individual persons—who, to be
sure, participate in the causes, conditions and consequences of
evils—but in the whole set of basic relations which define the
society. For Marx such basic relations are ultimately economic
ones, i.e., relations of a ruling and exploitive class to a ruled
and exploited class. Economic exploitation, which is the root
of human evil, ramifies into many other forms of exploitation.
Thus the way to correct evil is not to concentrate on changing or
alleviating the frailty and weakness of men by individual treatment;
it is to alter radically the basic economic and social relations of
men through the free, social, political action of individuals. We
may use an analogy: When an animal body is attacked by bacteria
or viruses, individual tissues and organs display symptoms of such
kind that we call them "diseased"; but to speak accurately, we
should describe the whole body (or the whole relevant environmental context) as "diseased," since the relations between tissues,
organs, and environment have been disturbed in their normal
functioning. Disease, like other evils, is cured by properly changing
the things and relations of the whole situation within which the
conditions of evil obtain.

Dignity. Fr. Adelmann speaks of "the human dignity man
already possesses." Marx can accede to such a description only in
the sense that it indicates an impulse and a promise and not a
fulfillment. Christian thought has tended to stress the givenness
of such dignity, and hence requisite gratitude on the part of man.

For Marx, the ultimate meaning of human dignity lies in man's creative and social activity, in his individual commitment to the welfare of mankind—not in a supernatural quality sealed like an Egyptian mummy in the pyramidal recesses of the soul, or in an assured heavenly destination. It is true that in the depths of their degradation by others men do retain their dignity; they do rise from the shackles of their indignity to proclaim and secure their humanity and even to redeem the depraved dignity of some of their oppressors. But in those cases dignity is always known and defined as an action and a struggle against the conditions of indignity. Apart from such struggle, human dignity is meaningless for Marx.

Here again Fr. Adelmann tends to become abstract in his argument. The "bi-polarity between capital and labor is over-naive," he says. Does he not understand that the oppression of labor by capital, i.e., of the large class of men in capitalist or feudal societies by the minority of the owning class, is the central cause of imperialism, war, fascism, and racism in the world? Fr. Adelmann condemns the commercial nature of sex and the degradation of the Negro. But he fails to see that these indignities are the direct, though masked, consequences of a basic antagonism between exploiters and exploited. His emphasis on the preexisting (and eternal?) dignity of man is the cause, result, and rationalization of this failure.

Freedom. Fr. Adelmann states that Marx is "vague" in "his assertions that man is free." We have, he says, "no clear-cut analysis of freedom along causal lines." "If man is free in Marx's sense of the autonomous person, then he is not determined, and here, indeed, we have a mystery."

It is true that Marx once more has not given us a detailed analysis of freedom. But his general position on freedom and determinism is unequivocal, and for him there is no "mystery" in holding to both freedom and determinism. The "mystery" of the contradiction necessarily existed for those philosophies—various forms of idealism and supernaturalism, and mechanical materialism—which reduced everything to causes external to individual decision and action. As instruments of ruling classes, such philosophies conferred the power of determination on God or nature and hence, indirectly, on those who might know God or nature. The great mass of men were, in consequence, left unfree; their lives were determined by causes external to their thought, decision, and action. The "mystery," in short, was how so few could be free (privy to the secrets of history and the universe) while so many could be determined. To put it in another way, the mystery was how as a *human* being, man seemed to be generically free, while in the mass he was unfree. Following Hegel, Marx solved this mystery. Man becomes free as he develops insight into the movements of things and people around him and before him and after him, and as he acts to change things in accordance with the basic needs of his human nature. And all men—not merely the few men of a select class— can be free as all classes are destroyed and a single cooperative society is created.

Marx's writings on the question of freedom have not always been philosophically consistent. More than once, Marx in his polemical writings was given to hyperbole. In wishing to stress his opposition to relativism and idealism, for example, he wrote in his preface to the first edition of *Capital*: "It is not a question of the higher or lower degree of development of the social antagonisms. . . . It is a question of these laws themselves, of these tendencies working with iron necessity towards inevitable results."

Considerably later, however, in volume 3 of *Capital*, he wrote: ". . . in theory it is the custom to assume that the laws of capitalist production evolve in their pure form. In reality, however, there is always but an approximation." Other passages might be cited to indicate that Marx conceived of the processes of nature and society as *tendencies* which in themselves and in their relations to other tendencies are not strictly determined but allow some determined free play.

Man's freedom from the determinations of his past and his immediate environment is the actualization of his capacity to develop insight into the tendencies in himself and his world, to foresee and rehearse outcomes of those tendencies, to select on the basis of a principle of human value, and to actualize his decision through control of the necessary means. Such freedom is a process that is not rigidly determined (in the sense that a genuine choice is possible), but at the same time it does not come out of thin air. Both strict determinism and unrestricted freedom constituted for Marx the real "mysteries." They are mysteries that correspond to the brute routine of the ruled classes and the vacuous license of the ruling classes.

For Marx man's freedom is a function of three variables: the specific, concrete conditions or tendencies which he encounters outside himself; the specific, concrete tendencies within himself; and the generic, concrete tendencies defining his own species-being. We are not Platonic essences floating in a Platonic heaven; we are flesh-and-blood, historical beings with our own habits and sensitivities and powers. Most important, we are not tabulae rasae, so that freedom turns out to be doing as we please or getting what we happen to want in a particular time and place. We are rather *generic species-beings* with need-dispositions that define us as *uniquely human.* To be free from the dehumanizing constraints of our pasts, our environments, and our own personal histories, we must develop insight into the necessities of our own natures—i.e., our generic needs—and into the obstructions to their fulfillment, and we must act to remove those obstructions. As Marx put it: ". . . socialized man, the associated producers, regulate their interchange with nature rationally, bring it under their common control, instead of being ruled by it as by some blind power . . . they accomplish their task with the least expenditure of energy and under conditions most adequate to their human nature and most worthy of it."[3]

"Under conditions most worthy of it [human nature] " means that man has a generic nature. Alongside his polemical statements against those German thinkers who spoke of "not the interests of the proletariat but the interests of human nature, of man in general, who belongs to no class, has no reality, who exists only in the realm of philosophical fantasy"[4] —it should be stressed that for Marx man does have a human nature. C. Wright Mills, Lewis Feuer, and others have misinterpreted Marx on this most important point. If we do not bear in mind Marx's position on man, Marx's humanism can have no definite or universal meaning; and freedom is reduced to the capitalist notion of doing what you want as long as you can get away with it—a notion that clearly benefits those with social power, i.e., the capitalists.

Marx's notion of freedom is essential to the Marxist notion of world peace. To be free from the destructive and dehumanizing effects of war, man must understand two things—his generic species-being, and war as a major obstruction to that. And he must act socially to remove those obstructions. There are many causes of war, but a Marxist analysis claims that the major causes must be located in man, in his environment, and in the relations between the two. An economy such as the capitalist economy of the United States, disposed toward foreign wars as a means of securing resources and markets, at the same time tends to produce ideas which are bent toward justifying such wars. The answer is clear: strike at changing the economy by changing the ideas. Here again, to be powerful, concrete practice and abstract thought must be inseparable. "Theory also becomes a material force as soon as it has gripped the masses."[5] Theory is reflective consciousness embodied in particular persons, and it frees man when it leads him to act with others in the direction of their mutual fulfillment.

NOTES

1. K. Marx, *The Eighteenth Brumaire of Louis Bonaparte* (Moscow: Foreign Languages Publishing House, n.d.), p. 15.

2. K. Marx, *Theses on Feuerbach*, vol. 6, in F. Engels, *Ludwig Feuerbach and the End of Classical German Philosophy* (Moscow: Foreign Languages Publishing House, n.d.), p. 97.

3. K. Marx, *Capital*, vol. 3 (Chicago: Charles H. Kerr, 1909), p. 954.

4. K. Marx and F. Engels, *Manifesto of the Communist Party*, ed. F. Engels (New York: International Publishers, 1948), p. 36.

5. K. Marx, "Contribution to the Critique of Hegel's Philosophy of Right," in K. Marx and F. Engels, *On Religion* (Moscow: Foreign Languages Publishing House, n.d.), p. 50.

Chapter 18

Commentary on Fr. Adelmann's Paper

GEORGE H. HAMPSCH

George H. Hampsch is professor of philosophy at the College of the
Holy Cross in Worcester, Massachusetts, after a period of teaching
at John Carroll University in Cleveland. During 1969-1970 he was
acting president of the Ohio Philosophical Association. He has
written a number of articles on Marxism and educational philosophy;
contributed a chapter, "The Practice of Freedom: A Prerequisite
to the Catholic-Marxist Rapprochement," to *Marxism and Christianity*
(1968); and is the author of *The Theory of Communism* (1965).

Fr. Adelmann's paper is a rather straightforward presentation
of Marx's insight into the human person as a being of *praxis*, i.e.,
a free being, as found in the *Economic and Philosophic Manuscripts*. Because it is a straightforward presentation of what is
now generally accepted by Marxologists as the insights to be
gleaned from this early work, I find little room for criticism
of the main thesis, although I would have preferred Fr.
Adelmann to place stronger emphasis, as did Marx, on the
relationship between private property and alienation and the
removal of private property as a necessary condition for human
freedom. But my criticisms are mostly on what I might call
Fr. Adelmann's "asides" made during his exposition of Marx's
thought. Time does not allow me more than mere comments
on some of the difficulties I have with his statements.

Fr. Adelmann wishes "to make a distinction between

communism which is an ideology and Marxism which is a philosophy." Now a distinction between communism and Marxism can be made if one wishes to point out certain discrepancies between what an interpreter considers to be authentic Marxism and certain historical practices in socialist countries. And if that were Fr. Adelmann's intention, then he would have some of his staunchest supporters among Communists themselves (there is the Sino-Soviet dispute, the Yugoslav-Soviet dispute, as well as the struggle between the Communist party and Socialist Workers party in America). But this is apparently not what he means. "An ideology implements a philosophy in practice. A philosophy—even one that includes practice—is still speculative." Marx uses the word "ideology" in more than one connotation throughout his writings, it is true, and this has led to considerable difficulties in understanding his use of that word. One use is pejorative and refers to theories, especially social theories, that are not based on the historical analysis of the material forces of production. Hence, he entitles one of his works which he authored in union with Engels *The German Ideology*. But to consider that Marxist *philosophy* is characterized by its being *speculative* is to miss a central point, if not *the* central point made by Marx, regarding philosophy. In the past, the purpose of philosophy was to understand the world; but for Marx, the purpose of philosophy is not merely to understand the world (or the nature of the human person), but to change the world (and the nature of man, if you understand the nature of man as Marx did as the ensemble of social relationships). Speculative knowledge does not become true for Marx except through practice. Deeper insights into the understanding of reality, including man, evolve only through practice. There is no distinction to be made between Marxist philosophy and its practice. Hence in the eyes of the Marxist, to make a historical study of Marx's notion of man without at the same time trying to understand the notion of man that is evolving among current scholars, Marxist and otherwise, may be interesting, but hardly valuable or meaningful to the understanding of man as he exists in the present historical moment. Nor is that historical notion to be considered any longer Marxist. Marxist philosophy is philosophical only by being lived, not by merely being discussed. To see Marxist philosophy otherwise is to begin at a point different from Marx's starting point, and one will not

end with Marxist conclusions regarding the nature of the
philosophical enterprise.

Another objection: Fr. Adelmann seems to imply that Marx's
notion of man and his alienation is such that Marx would consider
the caveman in primitive times to be more of a man, more of a
person, than a proletarian in his Manchester cellar cringing in
fear of the impending visit of his landlord. I submit that if this
is the implication, it cannot be supported in Marx's writings,
and especially is it in opposition to Marx's notion of the
historical development of human nature through the successively
more humanizing modes of production, as set forth in the work
The German Ideology. The notion of the noble savage is more
Nietzschean than Marxian. It is true that Marx states that
alienation is *greater* under capitalism than under earlier modes
of production. But that alienation is greater *precisely* because
man is more humanized and more cognizant of the disparity
between his spiritual needs and his social fetters, in much the
same manner that a sensitive person is capable of greater
suffering than a coarse buffoon. Of course, this is not to say
that the most ignorant lumpen proletarian under capitalism
is more conscious of his humanity than was the cultured
feudal doge. It is to say that the social consciousness under
capitalism has expanded to the extent that men of all classes,
as alienated by their relations to production, are capable of
greater suffering and misery, than those in comparable classes
of a lower mode of production. Because of the recognition
of their need for freedom, they are capable of greater good and
greater evil, greater freedom and more intense exploitation,
greater humanity and greater frustration—but all because they
are *more* human, not *less.* And, incidentally, this alienation is
to be found in both classes under capitalism. In America, for
example, the Marxist would find the white bourgeoisie as
alienated in its own way as the black lumpen proletariat. Only
with socialism will come the power to diminish man's alienation
and control the sources of his unfreedom. And while the universal absence of poverty and private property will not, of
itself, guarantee the destruction of alienation, their absence,
as pointed out by the Polish and Yugoslav philosophers, is a
necessary condition for any real progress toward freedom on a
social level.

Let us move on. Fr. Adelmann says somewhat categorically
that Marx really is not an anarchist because he views man as a

social being that functions necessarily within the structures of justice and order. Now it is factually the case that both Marx and Lenin vigorously opposed the anarchist movement as it was represented by Blanqui, Bakunin, and Kropotkin. But the anarchists were opposed because they were proposing to bring about a free community of free men without taking into account the stage of development of the material forces within the society, without taking into account the social consciousness of the working masses, and especially without taking into account the social forces that had to be brought to bear to keep the proletariat, once in power, from being overthrown or coopted by the bourgeoisie (as actually happened in the Third Republic and then again in the Paris Commune). In other words, Marx and Lenin differed with the anarchists over the issue of the dictatorship of the proletariat. And incidentally, this, it would seem, is the issue that presently distinguishes the Marxist "old" left from the SDS and other groups of the "new left" in the United States, and probably distinguishes the Communists of East Berlin and East Germany from the leftist students of West Berlin and West Germany. But it is important to note that Marx did not oppose the anarchists' goal of a free community of free persons. The word "anarchism" has of late taken on a pejorative meaning in the minds of many. But anarchism as a historical-political position is certainly not opposed to justice, nor is it opposed to order insofar as that order arises spontaneously within the community—an order, in other words, based on a unity of values and interests. The anarchist is opposed only to a coerced, structured order. Now the evidence is quite strong that in speaking of the future classless society, wherein the state as a coercive, structural organ of class will have gradually withered away into a *Staatswesen*, "community" of free persons as found in the *Critique of Gotha Programme*, Marx is quite close to the position of anarchism. When eminent scholars such as the Marxian Maximilien Rubel and the American Marxologist Robert Tucker, among others, hold that the logical consequences of Marx's social theory reduce to a community based on the anarchy of comradeship and mutual respect, we must, at best, leave open the question of whether Marx was or was not an anarchist.

Another objection: Fr. Adelmann complains about the lacunae in Marx's thought because he leaves unanswered the question of the origin of man as a spiritual being able to transcend the world of nature, and fails to ask the question, "why is there being

rather than nothing?" But as I read Marx, I find no such lacunae
in regard to the origin of man *within* the dialectical methodology
he accepts. The origin of man as a free being is quite adequately
explained in the dialectical development of material reality
according to the three Hegelian laws of transition of quantity
into quality, the law of the unity of opposites, and the law of
negation. To ask the question "Why something rather than
nothing" *within* the dialectical methodology is about as
meaningful as to ask the scholastic metaphysician "Who made
God?" *Within* the dialectical methodology there are no such
lacunae. Now, of course, one is always free to argue the relative
merits of different methodologies, but this did not seem to be
the original intent of Fr. Adelmann's paper. If there is argument
about methodologies, the Marxist will be most happy to point
out the mystification he sees in a metaphysical or theological
position which has its supposition or conclusion that the
energy of human praxis has its source in an existent God. Even
Heideggerians would wish to point out the possible temerity
involved in raising the God question at this early stage of
philosophical development, as well as the inanity of the concept
of creation.

Finally, and this more of a comment than a criticism, Father
Adelmann complains that Marx leaves vague his assertions that
man is free, and offers no clear analysis of the cause of freedom.
If man is an autonomous person, says Father Adelmann, then
he is not determined, and here indeed we have a mystery— but
a mystery to which Marx *alone* does not fall heir. In which
philosophical explanation does not the question of human
freedom still remain shrouded in mystery? Certainly not in those
metaphysics that have been assimilated into historical Christianity,
where the notion of free will in man comes face to face with
those perennial Christian hang-ups called divine foreknowledge,
predestination, and divine providence. Certainly not in the
explanations of Spinoza and Hegel where freedom becomes the
recognition of necessity. Nor is the mystery overcome in the
behaviorist psychologies wherein the soft determinists see
freedom and necessity as distinct categories of the same
phenomena, and the hard determinists shift the problem from
the category of freedom to the category of responsibility. Nor
is the mystery overcome in the theory of Hobbes, who sees
freedom as the absence of external impediments to movement—

a freedom animals and men would have in common. Sartre does not remove the mystery, for his notion of free acts can include those acts that are destructive of the human person itself.

It is true that Marx left his notions of human freedom vague; but Marxist scholars have done much to make the notion more precise as well as to develop it in the light of contemporary insights into human activities. One of the most interesting essays on freedom is by Gajo Petrović, a Croatian philosopher who writes in the journal *Praxis* (International Edition No. 4, 1965). In this essay, Petrović attempts to show that for Marx the relation between necessity and freedom as these notions are found in such humanist works as *Economic and Philosophic Manuscripts* does not reduce to the simple Hegelian formula reiterated in Engels that freedom is the recognition of necessity. Petrović points out that if freedom is conceived as a knowledge and acceptance of fate, destiny, or universal necessity, then "freedom" is only another name for voluntary slavery. Freedom is neither submission nor accommodation to external or internal necessity. Only that action can be free by which man *changes* his world and himself. *Knowledge of necessity is only the knowledge of limitations to freedom* at the present historical moment, and the awareness of the extent of human creative possibilities. The essence of freedom is not in the subjection to the given, but in the creation of the new, in the development of man's creative abilities, in the enriching of humanity. Hence for Petrović, Marx's notion of freedom is to be understood neither as the absence of restraint nor as the knowledge of necessity, but more correctly as self-determination. Only that activity is free in which a man himself determines his deed. But not every action inwardly determined of itself is freed. *Only that self-determined activity is free in which a man acts as an integral, many-sided personality, in which he is not a slave of this or that special thought, emotion or tendency,* says Petrović. "Man is free only when that which is creative in him determines his acts, when by his deeds he contributes to an extension of the *limits* of humanity."

In conclusion I wish to say that this reevaluation of Marx's concept of freedom away from Engels' freedom as the recognition of necessity towards the notion of freedom as self-determination within the limits of necessity is of extreme importance vis-à-vis the Christian-Marxist dialogue. For if this

notion of freedom can be accepted by the Marxist it offers a
notion of freedom much more compatible with the best in
contemporary Christian thought, namely, the personalist
thought as represented by Mounier, the thought of Teilhard
de Chardin, as well as those Christian philosophers who wish to
see human freedom in terms of a Heideggerian Dasein.

Part VI

MARXISM AND ETHICAL THEORY

Chapter 19

Value and Mental Health in the Thought of Marx

HOWARD L. PARSONS

I shall describe what Marx meant by "value" and hence mental health, how man loses mental health, and what man must do to recover it. I shall then offer some critical remarks on these ideas.

All value for Marx has its source in human "self-activity"[1] or free labor. This self-activity or self-creation[2] is the creating of the human self, human society, and the human world of natural objects—known, used, and assimilated to the needs and purposes of human beings in society. It is "practical-critical" and is the productive interaction of man (as social) with circumstances, each changing the other.[3] Nature (soil, plants, animals, etc.) exists prior to the operations of man upon it.[4] Moreover, ape-man may subsist in and through nature merely by consuming natural objects directly for his own subsistence (as in gathering fruits). But man becomes genuinely human and objects acquire use-value (satisfy some human need) when proto-man "annexes [Nature] to his own bodily organs,"[5] creates instruments or means of production,[6] and exchanges socially the use-value that he produces.

Ape-man, like other animals, produces his existence; man produces the means for producing his existence. The former

---

For biographical information about the author, see page 241.

consumes nature in order to live (satisfy minimal needs). The latter consumes nature in order to produce, in order to live, in order to produce in order to live productively. Man becomes man as he interposes his productivity between raw nature and his own needs. In doing so he makes products whose use-value is not just immediate and intrinsic but is prospective and instrumental; he makes products that can be used to produce additional products.[7]

In summary, value is a process by which man, social in his origins and makeup,[8] interacts with natural objects (unprocessed or already transformed by human labor), produces for his own productive use instruments of production, thereby increases use-values, exchanges such use-values with his fellow man, consumes use-values to satisfy needs, fulfills the demands of personal and social systems, and employs such fulfillment to facilitate this same process. The material consequences of this value-process are products—use-values and, if commodities, exchange-values. These are precipitates of the value process— "crystalization[s] of social labor,"[9] "material expressions of the human labor spent in their production."[10]

The value process differentiates itself as the creation of the self of individual man, the creation (or humanizing) of natural objects (nature) in and through man's relations to them, and the creation of society in and through man's relations to other men.

The self is created in the following events:

1. The impulsion to live, develop, struggle with obstacles to living, and progressively order existence.

2. The satisfying of the demands of subsistence by the producing of the means of subsistence.[11]

3. The eliciting of man's "slumbering powers."[12]

4. The evoking of man's sensitivities, achieved through objectifying man's essence in human, social objects which in turn awaken specific senses.[13]

5. The emerging, shaping, and directing of man's needs over and beyond the needs of subsistence. "This . . . is the first historical act."[14] Further, needs are satisfied in a psycho-somatic-social system of needs and satisfactions.

6. The emerging of consciousness, self-consciousness, consciousness of others and of natural objects (objectivity), language, and purposes.[15]

7. The achieving of man's identity, his continuous self-

becoming, and his humanization. "Free, conscious activity is the species-character of human beings."[16]

The self's relations to others are created by and in:

1. The emerging of man's need for others.[17]
2. The humanizing of the man-woman relation.[18]
3. The creating of the family and family-relations, and the reproducing of man.[19]
4. The cooperative activity of human beings in production and reproduction.[20]
5. The developing of the self's relations with others—love and trust—through reciprocal influence.[21]
6. "The productive power of social labor," developing the capabilities of man as man.[22]

The self's relations to natural objects are created by and in:

1. The transforming of the natural object from a mere thing to "a human, social object, created by man and destined for him."[23] This is the assimilating of natural objects into the context of human objective understanding, subjective appreciation, and human use. It is the transforming of things into values.
2. The naturalizing or objectifying of human needs—the other side of the humanizing of natural objects.[24]
3. The actualizing by the self of the possibilities of nature in thought and practice. "Living labour must seize upon these things and rouse them from their death-sleep, change them from mere possible use-values into real and effective ones."[25]
4. The self's changing of the form of the materials worked over by man.[26]
5. The producing of means of subsistence[27]—instruments and skills—which in turn create relations of production and exchange and give rise to the superstructure of institutions.

Marx thought of the value-process as being natural and as having the character of a natural law. He thought it was obvious to "every child" that if men did not work they would not live for long.[28] The ultimate good of man is the fulfillment of man's powers through social production. Action that, of all practical alternatives, most contributes to this fulfillment is right, and action that does not is wrong. As a naturalist in his ethics, Marx does not concern himself with an unqualified distinction between nature and man, between facts and judgments, between things and values. He does agree with G. E. Moore that value-predicates cannot properly be applied to natural objects as such, though he uses stronger language—"fetishism"[29]—for this error. At the same time "value" for Marx signifies an objective process of productive interaction of the individual person with things and with other persons. As a naturalist Marx thinks that a description of this will suffice to show what value is. Although in a single paragraph he uses the words, "expropriation," "exploiting," "misery," "oppression," "slavery," "degradation," "revolt," "fetter," etc.,[30]—he considers that these words may have objective as well as subjective meaning, and his main intent is to show by description the process of value, the obstructions to it, and the ways to remove the obstructions. The primary mode of his language is designative, and its primary function or aim is to evaluate things and events and to incite human action with respect to them. When a recent writer states that "technological necessity had for Marx the qualities of a finally beneficent deity,"[31] he distorts Marx. *The human, natural process* of productive activity is the ultimate value—and reality[32]—for Marx. The technological class struggles at various stages of history are the ways in which this productive activity expresses its large-scale antagonisms and resolutions. Because man makes his own history[33] and "mankind always takes up only such problems as it can solve,"[34] it is *man*, making and using instruments of production, who creates the kind of society he has.[35] In *Capital* Marx repeatedly underscores the fact that labor has created tools, machinery, technology, capital, and private property, and the implication is continuous that the same labor can change the relations of private property.

Mental health for Marx is the progressive fulfillment of man's practical-critical capacities that comes with productive activity. It is psycho-somatic-natural-social health. The health of man is organic in this inclusive sense. Since ideas grow out of, organize, direct, and change the productive process,[36] all beliefs in a mechanistic fate or an omnipotent providence, or in a disembodied domain of ideas, are conditions of illness. Since "nature is [man's] body with which he must remain in a continuous interchange in order not to die"[37]—then philosophical idealism which denies the primacy and coerciveness of bodily needs is a sign of illness. Since man's productive activity is a natural transaction, wherein a part of nature, man, along with his objects, becomes humanized and man becomes more fully naturalized[38] —then religious supernaturalism is a symptom or cause of illness. Since man's productive activity is social and "the human essence . . . is the ensemble of social relations"[39] — then all isolation, enmity, subservience, and exploitation of man in relation to man are pathic. Since man's self-activity is always revolutionizing the conditions of his life[40] —then all fixation of ideas or forms of actions, all idolatry of the *status quo*, is indicative of illness. Since *man* is the locus and man's fulfillment is the measure of value—then all forms of "dehumanization" are conditions of sickness, both in the dehumanizer and the dehumanized.

In capitalistic society, man experiences ill health and the loss or "crippling" of his self-activity[41] when, as he cooperates with tools and machines and other men and produces his life, he comes into conflict with the relations of private property. Man's productive labor is social and cooperative but the products of his labor are exchanged according to the principle of private ownership and exploitation. Thus in the exchange of the commodity of his labor, he is returned less than the use-value he creates.[42] The difference is expropriated by the capitalist in the form of surplus value. This conflict, which takes the social form of class struggle, is the conflict between social productivity and the private appropriation of the products of productivity. (If we follow ordinary usage we cannot call it "stealing," for the term in law and religion alike does not apply to it.)

This conflict is the expression of man's "alienation." It means that man is split off from the product of his labor, no longer at one with nature and with it, no longer owning it; that human value (including man himself and his products) is "objectified" in the form or things, products, commodities, to be bought and sold according to the principle of making money in the transaction, rather than using the commodities to fulfill human need; that man loses his unity with his means of subsistence; that he is alienated from himself by the constricting, exhausting nature of his work, and the separation of his production from genuine self-activity and enjoyment; that man is forced to work, not for the joy of creating, but in order to get the means whereby to satisfy other needs; that man is alienated from his "species-life," being compelled to enlist his whole life-activity in the service of animal subsistence and in the dehumanizing tasks of "detail labor";[43] and that man is alienated from other men by the division of labor, the "mutual cheating,"[44] and the exploitation of private property relations.[45] In short, man experiences his own "devaluation"[46] for the sake of the power and glory of things. Money talks, through the mouths of those few who own and control it; and the mass of men listen and dance to those who call the tune. Thus Marx portrays the pathology of man's productiveness, the occlusions in the arterial stream of the otherwise healthy body of society.

Marx believes that since by man came alienation and death, so by man also will come the resurrection of the dead and the return of alien man to his true human home. The cure for man's illness is (1) the removal of the causative conditions and (2) the natural therapy of productive, social labor. To remove the conditions of illness, man must call upon the resources of health in his situation. Marx thinks man possesses at the roots of his being a natural impulsion to development and that this is elicited and exerted in the face of adverse circumstances. It is at this point of conflict that consciousness is generated[47] and is used to conduct man in recovering his lost unity with himself and the world of natural objects. The real is the rational—if by "rational" we mean the ordering process of man's productive activity. Man is ever impelled to "make sense" of his world and thus to remove the "contradictions" that appear in his practice. This must be done by practice,[48] guided by theory. Man's real, healthy nature tends to assert itself in the face of obstacles: this is the anthropological basis for Marx's thesis that the forces of production overcome the "fetters" of the relations of production. The dialectical process in history is the transforming power of human practice writ large. Individual men collectively make history.

The key ethical concept in Marx is "development."[49] Man has a definite structure, a "species-life," a character that defines his humanity as creative growth; man's problem is to recover this. C. Wright Mills overdoes Marx's "historical specificity" and is in error when he says that "human nature, according to Marx, is not an unchanging, inevitable anchor-point for any existing or possible institution."[50] When Marx speaks of "new men" and of founding "society anew,"[51] he has in mind a return to (or progress toward) man as he really is in all the many-sided fulfillment[52] of his productive potential. Marx's anthropological "premises" are "men, not in any fantastic isolation or abstract definition, but in their actual, empirically perceptible process of development under definite conditions."[53] The goal of ethical thought and political action is "an association, in which the free development of each is the condition for the free development of all."[54] We cannot now know the full concrete content of such future development, but we can know that it will express the "species-life" of man's developmental nature.

Man's immediate task is to break the bonds, to burst the "integument,"[55] of capitalist private property. It is to socialize the means of production and bring property relations into harmony with productive relations. The economic exploitation of the many by the few is the particular fetter from which creative man must now be freed. Capitalism is the particular "womb"[56] from which the new society must be delivered— "after prolonged birth pangs."[57] The root metaphor in Marx is productive labor, the joyful travail of the creator, the Promethean and Nietzchean suffering for the sake of a higher humanity, both here and now and in the future. This labor, moreover, is *social.* The primitive family, where the serpents of commodities and money have not entered, is also a root metaphor in Marx. The ideal is a world-wide family of creators. Marx rescued the stone that the liberal and capitalistic builders rejected—fraternity—and made it the cornerstone of society's new temple.

To criticize Marx for absolutizing the economic factor in history and the task of creating a socialistic economy now is to mistake his particular for his generic emphasis. Marx was a philosopher as well as a man of political action. The emergence of man from the dark ignorance and slavery of "prehistory" into the full light[58] of intelligent social control and freedom, the turning around of the manifold "inversions" and the removal of "contradictions" of past and present, issuing in the unitary health of man and restoring man to the productive center of his life—that is the generic goal for man. But in practice contradictions and problems must be solved step by step. The great task in capitalistic societies is to conquer and sublate the obsession with food and material goods by socializing and collectively controlling the means whereby these are produced and exchanged. That conquest by a social and industrial democracy is itself a manifestation of man's self-activity but it also paves the way for creativity at a higher and freer level.[59]

Egotism (status-seeking, the cult of the individual), tyranny (capitalistic or bureaucratic, centralized control of decision-making and the mass media), rigidity in belief and practice (authoritarianism or sectarianism), schisms between theory and practice, overpopulation, nuclear war, economically undeveloped societies, automation, are specific problems too, but they will not be solved with maximum value unless men collectively deal with them in democratic, creative ways for the sake of the release of man's creative capacities—"the capabilities of his species."[60]

Marx can be criticized for his failure to discern or foresee: the power of the noneconomic and nonpolitical factors in the life of man—biological and ecological forces; the symbolic origins and transformations of the minds and cultures of men; the force of social institutions and traditions, such as autonomous military and police powers; the sway of mass propaganda and advertising; instruments of destruction reared by technology—megaton negations to end all negations; the narcotizing effects of mass media; and the inhibitory, repressive, perceptually and conceptually distorting effects of unconscious anxieties and habits. He also failed to comprehend in the nineteenth century the limits of man's control over his own history and development. He was aware that ideas and modes of action grow up unbeknownst to man in their full effects and that circumstances change men in ways men do not imagine or will. He stood on the verge of seeing that if man does not arrest his social life at the level of an ant colony or blast it into oblivion, and if man has discovered and provided the proper conditions for optimum creativity—e.g., opportunities for individual initiative, responsibility, methods of consultation and consensus—then unpredictable perspectives will emerge opening the way for directing man into new forms of creative experience.[61]

What is to be the guiding factor in human evolution? Those emergent perspectives are most useful to man which enable him to know, and to relate himself effectively to, the conditions that control the further emergence of perspectives. Optimal freedom arises at this point, where man freely minds and effectively acts toward the conditions necessary to the further freeing of his minding and acting. Perspectives and actions called "free" that do not produce this creative feedback can become obstacles to freedom in the above sense, when men who possess them purport to represent final truths and values for man. Their illusion is to

mistake their own limited knowledge and control for the wider
power of a creativity that under certain conditions frees them
from such limits. When Engels says that freedom consists in
the knowledge of natural laws and decisive control over things[62]
he is correct so far as freedom is in part the displacement of
ignorance and subjection with knowledge and control. But he
does not recognize, except perhaps implicitly, that the natural
law of man's development (liberation of creative powers), as far
as some now have insight into it, issues in knowledge of things
and knowledge of that law itself, which knowledge man does
not now have.[63]

An examination of the concept of mental health in many
psychiatric and psychological writings in the United States
(e.g., Angyal, Cantril, Erikson, Frank, Fromm, Horney, Kluckhohn,
Lewin, Maslow, May, Murray, Rogers, Sullivan) will show their
similarities to Marx's concept of man's health and his concept
of man. These writings and Marx's are continuous with the
pro-human tradition in the Bible, Greek thought, the Renaissance,
the Reformation, the Enlightenment, and modern times. This
tradition stressed the natural goodness of man as a natural, productive, and social being, and the improvability of man through
man's own practical-critical, revolutionary activity. Marx articulated,
in a searching, passionate, detailed, persuasive, and powerful way,
this same general concept of man and man's fulfillment. He put
motion into materialism, gave body to liberalism, naturalized
Hegel, and humanized Christianity. He also was the first great
thinker to trace on a massive scale the economic causes of man's
alienation and to extend the analysis of man's health to society
and history as a whole. (Engels acknowledged that he and Marx
neglected the origin and role of ideas in history.)[64] If we do not
recognize a rich and intense concentration of our creative heritage
in Marx, it is because we, as aliens ourselves, have turned away
from either Marx, or that heritage, or both.

NOTES

1. Karl Marx and Friedrich Engels, *The German Ideology*,
pts. 1 and 3 (New York: International Publishers, 1946), p. 66
passim. (Hereafter cited as GI.)

2. Karl Marx, *The Economic and Philosophical Manuscripts*,

trans. T. B. Bottomore, in Erich Fromm, *Marx's Concept of Man* (New York: Frederick Ungar Publishing Co., 1961), p. 139. (Hereafter cited as EPM.)

3. K. Marx, *Theses on Feuerbach* in F. Engels, *Ludwig Feuerbach and the End of Classical German Philosophy* (Moscow: Foreign Languages Publishing House, 1950), I and III. (Hereafter cited as TF and LF, respectively.)

4. Karl Marx, *Capital: A Critical Analysis of Capitalist Production,* vol. I, trans. from the third German edition by Samuel Moore and Edward Aveling and ed. Frederick Engels (Moscow: Foreign Languages Publishing House, n. d.), pp. 177ff. (Hereafter cited as C, I.) See also K. Marx, *Critique of the Gotha Programme* (Moscow: Foreign Languages Publishing House, 1954), pp. 15-16. (Hereafter cited as CGP.)

5. C, I, p. 179; and see EPM, p. 100.

6. GI, p. 16.

7. C, I, pp. 177-184.

8. EPM, p. 129.

9. Karl Marx, *Value, Price and Profit,* ed. Eleanor Marx Aveling (New York: International Publishers, 1935), p. 31.

10. C, I, p. 74.

11. Ibid., pp. 179ff.

12. Ibid., p. 177.

13. EPM, pp. 131-134.

14. GI, p. 17.

15. Ibid., p. 19; EPM, p. 132; C, I, p. 178.

16. EPM, P. 101.

17. GI, pp. 19, 74; EPM, pp. 126, 130, 138.

18. EPM, p. 126.

19. GI, p. 17.

20. Ibid., p. 18.

21. EPM, pp. 126-127, 168.

22. C, I, p. 329.

23. EPM, p. 132.

24. Ibid., p. 133.

25. C, I, p. 183.

26. Ibid., pp. 71, 178, 180.

27. GI, p. 16.

28. Karl Marx and Frederick Engels, *Selected Correspondence* (Moscow: Foreign Languages Publishing House, n. d.), following the Russian edition, Gospolitzdat, Moscow, 1953, p. 251. (Hereafter cited as SC.)

29. C, I, chapter 1, section 4.

30. Ibid., p. 763.

31. Lewis S. Feuer in the Introduction to Karl Marx and Friedrich Engels, *Basic Writings on Politics and Philosophy,* ed. Lewis S. Feuer (Garden City: Doubleday, 1959), p. xvii.

32. SC, p. 498.

33. EP, p. 39; SC, pp. 41, 498, 549; LF, p. 72; TF, III.

34. Karl Marx, *A Contribution to the Critique of Political Economy,* trans. from the second German edition by N. I. Stone (Chicago: Charles H. Kerr, 1904), p. 12. (Hereafter cited as CCPE.)

35. GI, pp. 74ff.

36. SC, pp. 496, 505, 542.

37. EPM, p. 101.

38. Ibid., pp. 100-101, 127, 129, 132ff.

39. TF, VI.

40. Ibid., I.

41. GI, p. 66; C, I, chapter 14.

42. C, I, p. 193.

43. Ibid., chapter 14.

44. EPM, p. 112; C, I, p. 164.

45. EPM, pp. 96-103.

46. Ibid., p. 94.

47. CCPE, p. 12.

48. EPM, p. 149.

49. GI, pp. 15, 16; C, I, pp. 399, 484, 488, 490; EPM, pp. 98, 140; Karl Marx, *Capital, A Critique of Political Economy,* vol. 3: *The Process of Capitalist Production as a Whole,* trans. from the first German edition by Ernest Untermann (Chicago: Charles H. Kerr, 1909), p. 954.

50. C. Wright Mills, *The Marxists* (New York: Dell Publishing Co., 1962), p. 39.

51. GI, p. 69.

52. Ibid., p. 22.

53. Ibid., p. 15.

54. Karl Marx and Friedrich Engels, *The Communist Manifesto,* authorized English translation, ed. and annotated by Friedrich Engels (New York: International Publishers, 1948), p. 31.

55. C, I, p. 763.

56. CCPE, p. 13.

57. CGP, p. 26.

58. EPM, p. 142.

59. Ibid., p. 140.

60. C, I, p. 329.

61. N. P. Jacobson, "Marxism and Religious Naturalism," *The Journal of Religion* 29, no. 2 (April 1949): 95-113. I am indebted to this article for the general direction of the paper.

62. Frederick Engels, *Anti-Dühring: Herr Eugen Dühring's Revolution in Science,* 2nd ed. (Moscow: Foreign Languages Publishing House, 1959), p. 157.

63. Henry N. Wieman, *The Source of Human Good* (Chicago: The University of Chicago Press, 1946).

64. SC, p. 540.

Chapter 20

Marxist Ethics, Determinism, and Freedom

JOHN SOMERVILLE

If one wishes to discuss the role of determinism in Marxist ethical teachings, which is what this paper proposes to do, two sets of problems must be distinguished. The first concerns the question whether it is possible to have any genuine ethics whatever, Marxist or otherwise, if a pervasive, naturalistic determinism is accepted. While this question is relevant to Marxism, it is not peculiar to it, and would have to be discussed in much the same way if we were dealing with the ethical teachings of naturalistic philosophers like Spinoza, Mill, Aristotle, or Dewey.

The question central to this set of problems is the age-old one: If each thing that happens has antecedently determined causes, and thus could not be different, can there be any such thing as a moral choice, or even a moral value? The second set of problems concerns matters specific to Marxist ethics and determinism. That is, what makes Marxist ethics different from other ethical doctrines which accept the principle of universal natural causation? Let us deal with these questions in order.

In relation to the general role of determinism as it enters into the first set of problems, one should note that it is only from a rather restricted and special standpoint that any problem at all exists concerning the compatibility in principle of determinism and ethics. Two presuppositions must be at least

For biographical information about the author, see page 43.

tentatively made before any problem of importance can be posed in this connection: (a) that moral values by their nature depend upon "free" choices; (b) that "free choices" in the sense of choices free from a natural causal nexus, are somehow possible. We must not forget that these are local presuppositions, so to speak, in no way inherently mandatory. In fact, upon close inspection (b) is seen to represent pure mysticism, which we probably cannot avoid classifying as cognitively meaningless. I am not saying it is necessarily bad to be a pure mystic. Conceivably, it might be the most precious thing in the world. I am only saying that such a mystic can hardly present himself as holding a *rationally* arguable position.

Why? Because he is claiming to get something (a choice) from nothing: and this claim simply cannot be made within the bounds of reason. Nor is there any logical need to make it, since there is ample evidence that a human choice is a choice made by a human being through a complex human apparatus responding to natural causes. In short, choices are obviously caused, and the only way we can understand them rationally, that is, in terms of objectively convincing evidence, logic and proof, is to trace them to causes, each of which is part of a naturalistic chain. This is in fact what we do in much of daily life and in technical science. The only alternative to a naturalistic determinism in this context is to hold that human choices are exceptions to the rule of causation, that either they arise out of nothing, which would signify inexplicable mystery, or that they arise out of something "spiritual," but do so independently of natural or humanly understandable conditioning, which would signify equally inexplicable magic. Indeed, it seems doubtful that any alternative to a general determinism can even be stated in rational terms, let alone validated by rational methods.

In any case, it is probably fair to say that the strongly felt objections in our cultural tradition to accepting a pervasive determinism have seldom, if ever, been grounded in rational considerations. They have usually sprung from feelings of moral revulsion which might be expressed by saying, "If things were like that it would be just too horrible. We would only be cogs in a machine, or, as Dostoevsky's *Notes from Underground* puts it, piano keys or organ stops. We would not be free. We would have no free will. We would not be moral agents at all."

A moment's calm reflection will, of course, convince anyone

272 **Marxism and Ethical Theory**

that such statements, even if they were true, would not
constitute arguments or evidence against universal natural
causation, but are the expression of feelings genuinely
anguished at the possibility that a long-cherished image (or
phantasm) born of hope and grown into habit, may have to be
laid aside. But we all know that whatever the rationally
obtainable truth is, it must be faced as the rationally obtainable
truth, as the only basis of effective action in the natural world.
When it is faced it usually ceases to seem so horrible, probably
because the spirit is fortified and gratified by the very exercise
of courage. Hope will always seek a more viable framework, for
that is its nature, while habit builds anew at more complex
levels. And if the stubborn underground man of Dostoevsky's
Notes should continue to cry out that it is just reason which he
can never bind himself to accept, that if it is all a case of twice
two making four, this simply makes it all the worse, then we can
only remind him, as Aristotle would have reminded him (but on
our part with more democratic charity and more effective
remedies, let us hope), that he had already pronounced his own
diagnosis in the very first words of his remarkable underground
testament, which begins, "I am a sick man. I am a spiteful man."

Though the logic of the situation may thus favor the scientifically
oriented naturalist, he must still answer the old question: If
causation or determinism be accepted as the universal rule, how
are values to be construed? What is a moral act? Is "free will"
possible? The answers are not really difficult, nor have they ever
been. Values are values whether they are caused or not. If I value
life, logic, health, happiness, love, creativity, and operatively
above all, international peace (because it is in the greatest
jeopardy, and its jeopardy threatens all the rest), I am not in the
least discomfited by learning that all these values, and especially
international peace, have causes. On the contrary, I am encouraged, and sustained in hope, because it gives me something
to do as a philosopher. It invites the play of my reason. Where
there are causes, mind can operate; preventions can be worked
out. Now suppose international peace were the result of free,
undetermined processes, not rationally traceable to naturalistic
patterns of cause-effect. I should be reduced to something like
the meager scope indicated on one of the stamp cancellation
devices widely used by the U. S. Post Office: "Pray for peace."
I don't mean to condemn prayer, except to the extent that it
discourages thought and action. But I do condemn the Post Office

for singling out prayer alone, as if wars were acts of God, beyond the reach of any human control.

Now, what is a moral act? Naturally, it is one which serves to attain or embody the moral values. If values should conflict, the agent must of course decide which takes precedence; and he will decide in the light of his nature and the history of his mind and feelings. How can we tell which acts will attain or contain the desired values? In a context permeated by causation we tell through knowledge and intelligence. If the context of action were not a causative one, were unpervaded by natural law, there would be nothing to turn to save revelation, luck or prayer. Intelligence would be of no avail; in fact, it might even be a hindrance, diverting the individual into fruitless paths.

But what of free will? The question can be answered on condition that the terms be defined. What is meant by free? In other words, what do you want your will to be free from? If you want your will to be free from ignorance, cruelty, bigotry, spitefulness, intolerance, unfairness, arrogance, avarice, greed, conceit, ungratefulness, dishonesty, laziness, rashness, or anything else along these lines, a job can be done. And we have reason to think that a better job will be possible in the future than was possible in the past. The reason is, these factors have causes; and we can discover more and more about the causes, and then apply the knowledge.

But if you are not satisfied with this sort of thing; if, like the Dostoevskian underground man, you want your will to be free first and foremost from causation, how can any job be done? If your will were free from causation, it would not even exist in the natural world; if it exists, we can discover no way in which it can be free from natural causation.

Strangely, people often seem to think that their choices would not be "their own" if the choices were admitted to be products of causation. If such people were consistent, would they not reason, with equal melancholy, that their babies were not their own, that their eyes, ears, hearts, lungs and livers were not their own? You call your arm your own; yet you readily admit that every particle of it is the result of the lines of causation—through heredity, environment, nutrition, exercise and the like. Why, then, is it your own? It is your own because it is joined to your shoulder, and no one else's, and the whole wonderful growth took place in and through you. Your choices become your own in exactly the same way, because they take place in and through you. What we call a free will or a free choice is not and could not be free from causes. What happens is that we call it free if the operative causes involved are such as we accept or respect. In the end, it is as simple as that.

Ask anyone, including the most erudite philosopher, to specify some acts which he performed "of his own free will." Acts adduced in response could be small or large in scope, e.g., "I mailed a letter," or, "I took a trip," or, "I decided to write a book." Whatever the actual answers are, it will be safe to say that causes were operative through environment, heredity, education, training, conditioning, and the like to bring about the actual choice or behavior in each case. But the individual who feels the choices as "free" simply sees nothing to object to in the concrete causes, feels no revulsion, no resistance or rejection on his own part to the operation of those particular causes. On the other hand, if he had been threatened with death unless he mailed the letter, if he had been tricked into taking the trip, if he had been under the influence of alcohol or drugs when he said he would write the book, then he would maintain these acts were performed, or these choices made not of his own free will. Obviously, the difference is not between causes and no causes, but between causes acceptable to the individual and causes unacceptable to him. If a total absence of causes, acceptable and unacceptable, is demanded, it is hard to see how anyone could mail any letter, take any trip, or come to any decision to write a book. We sometimes say that free choices are "self-determined" choices, but we must remember that this means the choice is determined by the self; and it does not mean the self is determined by the self. The self cannot be free from antecedent causes any more than the choice can. The self as we speak of it here is a unified complex of causal forces brought into being by the action of preceding forces.

In this connection, a specifically Marxian formulation has been the occasion of frequent debate and question, partly because it smacked of the paradoxical. That is: freedom is the appreciation of necessity. This thought, associated in its pat form of expression with Engels' polemic against Eugen Dühring, has been variously translated into English. The Burns translation uses the word "appreciation," as above;[1] an alternative often used is "recognition of necessity." Engels' original German reads: "ist die Freiheit die Einsicht in die Notwendigkeit."[2] Clearly, it would be better to translate this as, "freedom is insight into necessity." In translation it sometimes happens that the more literal rendering is not the better one; but in this case there can be no doubt that it is better. The word "insight," much more pointedly than "appreciation" or "recognition," suggests, as part of its meaning, a basis for better understanding, action and control, which as we shall see, was central to Engels' thought. The other terms, more diffuse and weaker in this respect, can give rise to gross misunderstanding. For example, if a person were the victim of racial persecution, there is certainly a sense in which he might "appreciate" or "recognize" the causal factors, the patterns of necessity present, without having the genuine knowledge (insight) which is the key to effective action to counteract them, and thus attain his freedom.

In this connection it is instructive to trace the Russian translations of the passage. Lenin, in an early work, "The Economic Content of Populism," (1895) translated Engels' key term, "Einsicht," by means of the Russian word which most literally and unambiguously signifies "understanding," *"ponoimanie"*: "Svoboda est ponimanie neobkhodimosti."[3] (Freedom is the understanding of necessity.) In his later work, *Materialism and Empirio-Criticism* (1909), Lenin again translated this passage into Russian, using a different word to render *"Einsicht,"* the word *"poznanie,"* which has a technical philosophic flavor, and means "cognition." In the Kvito translation of *Materialism and Empirio-Criticism* into English, this passage appears as, "freedom is the recognition of necessity."[4] But "recognition" misses the point. It does not convey the philosophic sense of "cognition," of thorough, operative understanding.

Part of the difficulty has been that the brevity of this traditional formulation, so often repeated in bare and injudiciously blunt fashion by both advocates and opponents of Marxism, gives rise to vagueness and ambiguity, as extreme bluntness always can. However, when the context of Engels' exposition is seriously examined, the key to the paradox is found. It is the thought that the most dependable way to gain freedom from something, or freedom to do something, is to know and utilize the causal conditions relating to the things in question. Thus he follows up his blunt formulation with the following elaboration of his thought:

Freedom does not consist in the dream of independence of natural laws, but in the knowledge of these laws, and in the possibility this gives of systematically making them work towards definite ends. This holds good in relation both to the laws of external nature and to those which govern the bodily and mental life of men themselves—two classes of laws which we can separate from each other at most only in thought but not in reality. Freedom of the will therefore means nothing but the capacity to make decisions with real knowledge of the subject. Therefore the *freer* a man's judgment is in relation to a definite question, with so much the greater *necessity* is the content of this judgment determined; while the uncertainty, founded on ignorance, which seems to make an arbitrary choice among many different and conflicting possible decisions, shows by this precisely that it is not free, that it is controlled by the very object it should itself control. Freedom therefore consists in the control over ourselves and over external nature which is founded on knowledge of natural necessity. . . .[5]

The blunt formula was brought up by Engels in connection with Hegel, to whom in fact he traces it. "Hegel," he says in the language of the Burns translation," was the first to state correctly the relation between freedom and necessity. To him freedom is the appreciation of necessity."[6] We may note in passing that this involves a clear error on Engels' part concerning the history of philosophy, as Spinoza, long before Hegel, had worked out this whole relationship with superb logical precision. It is significant that Plekhanov, speaking as a Marxist, once observed that dialectical materialism could be considered as a form of Spinozism.

What is perhaps most specifically Marxian in regard to the role of determinism in ethics is the systematic and realistic working out of the whole set of social conditions, the social and technological etiology, necessary to the attainment of the basic ethical values on the part of the great majority in the concrete circumstances of the modern historical epoch. One has in mind here not simply the point that human ethics can be treated responsibly only in a social context. In its general sense Aristotle had kept that point in the center of his *Ethics* and *Politics* (which he conceived as one work, not two—it is we who have split up the work), and demonstrated its cogency in characteristically massive fashion. But Aristotle thought of this connection in local terms of irredeemably aristocratic limitations, including even a justification of slavery. It was necessary to work out the whole thing anew within the widened horizons of democratic aspirations, a recognition of social evolution and its relativities, a new level of science and an existing society of fluid industrial capitalism moving (partly spontaneously) in a socialist direction.

That this was a breath-taking, morally exhilarating enterprise is a fact almost impossible to avoid sensing in any extensive reading of the works of figures like Marx, Engels and Lenin, whether or not one agrees with their conclusions. It is well nigh incredible that philosophically experienced commentators have sometimes pronounced Marxism to be an amoral system. The connection with Christian values such as brotherhood, charity and the raising of the downtrodden is so clear that Marxism has just as often been characterized as only a thinly veiled secularization of the Judeo-Christian eschatology. In fact, Marxism has sometimes been chastised on both counts simultaneously by one and the same critic, such as Bertrand Russell in his *A History of Western Philosophy*.[7]

It is likewise almost impossible for anyone who has stayed for any length of time in one of the present communist countries to avoid sensing the strong moral, indeed often moralistic, tone which pervades the society, in spite of well-known and highly publicized discrepancies. In fact, many of those who have fled such a society have done so not because they found it immoral in relation to its own value framework, or essentially amoral, but because they could not accept the collectivist, mass-oriented value system, which they found all too insistently applied in practice. In my discussion with professional philosophers in the Soviet Union, I was in the beginning quite surprised at the extent to which they maintained that the basic values which they hold, such as full physical, mental, and emotional development of all people, and social justice as manifested in a classless society in terms of the principle, "from each according to his ability, to each according to his needs," are free from subjectivity, and capable of being proved objectively in the scientific sense.

Much has sometimes been made of the claim that there is an essential inconsistency in holding, as Marxism does, that the victory of socialism over capitalism is historically inevitable, and at the same time exhorting people to take part in the struggle to bring about that victory. We have already set forth the logic of the Marxist's reply. It is the same that a physician uses when he says to the patient: "You will certainly recover. The main thing is, follow my directions." The physician holds that recovery is inevitable because he is counting on the patient following the directions since the patient wishes to live. The Marxist holds that the victory of socialism is inevitable because he is counting on society following a certain program since it wishes to live. Either or both predictors could conceivably be wrong in fact; only time will tell. But neither the physician nor the Marxist is holding a demonstrably inconsistent position. Incidentally, neither one says the predicted outcome is good *because* inevitable. Each says it is good *and* is inevitable.

Here we can see also where Marxism draws the line between its type of naturalistic-scientific determinism, and fatalism. The fatalist says: "Since my recovery is inevitable, I need do nothing." The scientific determinist says: "My recovery is inevitable since I am caused to do something, and through knowledge to do the right thing." Fatalism is seen to spring from a form of determinism which Marxism rejects as "absolute" and "metaphysical." The Marxists have always pointed out, as Aristotle did, that there is a relative sense in which chance and accident exist (not as uncaused, but as unintended or unplanned). Most importantly, however, they disengage themselves from absolute and fatalistic determinism by their conception that, while causes create the will of man, man's will in turn and of necessity becomes itself a creative cause.

NOTES

1. F. Engels, *Anti-Dühring* (New York: International Publishers, 1939.), p. 130.

2. F. Engels, *Herrn Eugen Dühring's Umwälzung der Wissenschaft* (Stuttgart: Dietz, 1904), p. 112.

3. V. I. Lenin, *Sochineniia*, 4th ed., vol. 1 (Moscow: State Publishers, 1954), p. 400.

4. V. I. Lenin, *Collected Works of V. I. Lenin*, vol. 13: *Materialism and Empirio-Criticism* (New York: International Publishers, 1927), p. 154.

5. Engels, *Anti-Dühring*, pp. 130, 131.

6. Ibid., p. 130. The second is the full sentence, a portion of which was quoted above.

7. Bertrand Russell, *A History of Western Philosophy* (New York: Simon & Schuster, 1945), cf. pp. 363, 788.

Chapter 21

A Critique of Marxist Ethics

FREDERICK W. McCONNELL

Frederick W. McConnell is associate professor of philosophy and chairman of the department of philosophy at Moravian College in Bethlehem, Pennsylvania. His essay, "Berkeley and Skepticism," appeared as a chapter in *New Studies in Berkeley* (1966).

In what sense is an ethical theory true? The ethics of dialectical materialism is disarming because it is dialectical. Ideas, particularly ethical ones, are consequences of economic processes and their truth lies in their social effectiveness. If truth be defined in terms of practical consequences, the Marxist ethics certainly is true. But such a pragmatic, flexible theory renders a critical judgment difficult because its pragmatism destroys the basis of any rational interpretation of its truth.

This problem, however, is not peculiar to Marxism but is implicit in any theory which recognizes the potency of an idea. Assume that a person is good and this assumption will encourage goodness. Let a psychological law be made known and it ceases to be coercive. In short, social, psychological, and moral theories are tainted with ideology, and, insofar as they are colored, their truth must have a practical, not an objective meaning.

How much the Marxists regard their own work as purely ideological is controversial. Certainly Marx regarded many of his ideas as statements of the status and goals of the labor

movement. That he was not exclusively an ideologist is
evident not only in his respect for impartial scientific analysis
but in the several value assumptions he tenaciously held. This
is even more true of Lenin who vehemently opposed all
forms of relativism. This explains his attack on the "economical"
or pragmatic views of Mach, as well as the kind words he
occasionally had for clericalism (idealism). How a relativistic
theory concerning the source and consequences of ideas could
be squared with the dogmatism of Lenin and more recent
Marxists is a problem with which we are not concerned. What
this paper does purport to show is that the dialectical materialist,
in spite of his ideological orientation, postulates absolute
ethical norms, that these norms are the value-claims of a
nineteenth- and twentieth-century secular bourgeois liberalism,
and that the moral conflict between Russia and the West is
essentially a family quarrel about means and not moral ends.
A criticism of the secular value postulates of the Marxist is
simultaneously a criticism of the bourgeois naturalistic
American mind.

What are these ethical postulates? They are the goals which
are associated with materialism, a deification of science and
technological progress, and an historical optimism. Certainly
the materialism of the Soviet Union is no less conspicuous than
the secularism of the West. In both countries science, technology, and efficiency have dominated the outlook to the point
where work is alienated and a sense of vocation has all but
vanished. In both, significant craftsmanship and leisure are
disappearing and men are more and more subjected to impersonal bureaucracies.[1] As C. Wright Mills has so well stated:

In both, science and loyalty, industry and the national canons
of excellence are in the service of the war system. . . . In both the
Science Machine is made a cultural and social fetish rather than
an instrument under continual public appraisal and control; and
to the Machine's economic as well as military aspects, the organization of all life is increasingly adapted. . . . In surface ideology
they apparently differ, in structural trend and official action they
become increasingly alike. . . . This trend is no Bolshevik invention,
it is part of the main line of Western and especially of American,
industrial, and technical development. [2]

But are not these similarities insignificant in comparison with
the one radical discord— freedom or reverence for personality?

Again certainly Marx and many Marxists have acknowledged freedom and the importance of political democracy. In fact Karl Marx was terrified at the thought of applying socialism to what he regarded as a barbarian civilization, i.e., Russia. Dialectical materialism does not logically entail totalitarianism.

The remainder of this paper will be a brief analysis of the ethical postulates mentioned above in light of Marxism and its relation to the naturalistic mind of the West.

Materialism assumes three forms: a lust for material things, a lust for power made possible by the possession of material things, and a metaphysical view which reduces mind to matter. That the philosophical spokesmen of the American bourgeois attitude are materialists in some, if not all, of these aspects is hardly debatable. But how materialistic are the Marxists? Certainly the most vicious kind of materialism is one that reduces the majority of people to such a low standard of living that material needs assume by necessity supreme importance. Marxists rightly contend that higher values are meaningless without the fulfillment of lower needs, and a social system based on an unequal distribution of wealth is immoral. Marx did not express it in this way, for he had an aversion to morals. But this is what he meant, and the same idea is implied in all civilized forms of law—to sin against lower instrumental values is a greater evil than the failure to develop higher ones. Selfishness or dishonesty are not legally penalized but a state cannot tolerate theft or murder if it is to "hinder hindrances to the good life." The Marxians carry the principle a step farther and criticize the capitalist state for its failure to fulfill this function.

Again, the economic interpretation of history need not involve a commitment to materialism. In itself, it does not imply that men can live by bread alone, but rather that they cannot live without bread. At best, the doctrine is a statement of the logical priority of the community to that of the state. The state must codify the more pervasive features of a culture, particularly the relations which determine the production and distribution of economic goods, just as the religious institutions must conserve the values which a culture deems important. This is why both institutions are essentially conservative and why they must be targets for any radical social reform. Marx's contempt for spiritual "mystifications" was as much a contempt for religious hypocrisy as it was an aversion to things moral.

Certainly economic determinism was in part an attempt to get some of the fate out of history, and this worthy goal may be more imminent than commonly recognized when destiny is becoming more and more determined by the coalescing military, political, and industrial elite.[3] With the more dogmatic and metaphysically inclined Marxians, however, economic determinism is no longer a working hypothesis serving to organize historical data for the purpose of explaining certain cultural phenomena but a means of reducing all expressions of experience to the material aspects of life. In this sense the theory becomes ludicrous—logical classes are converted into ontologies. That all human activities have their economic conditions is certainly not to say that they can be reduced to material needs. That cats and dogs are animals is by no means to imply that a cat is a kind of dog; that all things mental and physical can be numbered is not to invoke, with the Pythagoreans, a theology or ontology of number. Marxists of this breed generally seem to ignore the fact that the connection of ideas is logical and the connections of physical events factual and the truth of ideas must be judged by their logical consistency, inclusiveness and coherence, not by their particular sources, physical or otherwise. Indeed the assertion that ideas have physical sources is itself a relation of ideas and its truth certainly is not determined by a crude theory of phantasms. Many recent Marxists betray almost an inhuman materialism in their historical interpretations with their abnormal pre-occupation with the mundane and their relegation of moral and religious motivation to the fringe. Will the same Marxists write Soviet history as mundanely?

Concerning the second type of materialism, the lust for property combined with the lust for power, the Marxians were quite adept at disclosing the vicious form this type of materialism assumes in a capitalist economy. A person can hardly desire an infinite number of material things but he can practically desire an infinite amount of money and in a money economy this spells power. Hence, the intensity of the profit motive, and the power which the possessor of credit exerts on the community. In a feudal society, possession did not entail power. The most complicated tool could be owned by most. But in a technology in which the possession of machines requires capital investment, the nonworking moneylender virtually controls work and the worker. Rights are divorced from duties;

power is separated from social responsibility and function. The rest is an old story.

If it is true that the industrialist wields power because he possesses and controls the machine, certainly economic and political power will reside in any group which controls the apparatus of a technology. In the Soviet Union, this is the state and the political bureaucrat has replaced the capitalist "boss." The Marxists seem to overlook the fact that power, particularly irresponsible power, will not disappear with the decline of free enterprise or a change in personnel. Unless democratically controlled, the irresponsibility of the intensified profit-minded employers could be supplanted by a vicious power-hungry bureaucracy.

If the Marxists are not conspicuously materialistic in the two senses discussed above there is no doubt where they stand ontologically, and it is in their naturalistic outlook that they particularly find fellow travelers in the West. Mind and life are the activities of matter—a flexible, dialectical, creative matter—but matter none the less. Performing many creative antics, it produces new forms and on occasion even does something along the mental line, and in very rare instances,[4] in the minds of dialectical materialists, it truly reflects about itself. And since truth is a reflection of physical processes, a conflict of ideas becomes a battle of nerves. In spite of the dogmatism of Lenin and his followers, it is puzzling to see how Marxists escape from skepticism. If mind is derivative and if the cardinal principle of naturalism is "the existential and causal primacy of organized matter in the executive order of nature,"[5] there is no reason why a rational ideal would be a determining influence, and if it were, how could we be sure when the physical conditions were appropriate to this task? On any ground, of course, we are not sure, but we are less so if we give matter a primary "causal efficiency" and mind a secondary function.

But skepticism is only one difficulty. Is the ontology of the Marxists explanatory in any sense? Like magicians, they seem to get all kinds of metaphysical rabbits jumping out of their ontological hats, but only because they were already put there in the first place. The complex is explained by the simple only because it is smuggled into the simple—the explanation is as complicated as the things to be explained.[6] Only a prejudice for names explains why they labeled this infinitely complex ontological principle "matter." Why not call it "being"—for then its inclusiveness would leave nothing to be explained.

The ethical implications are clear. If Aristotle is to be criticized for imputing mental principles to nature, certainly the Marxists can be criticized for applying physical principles to mind. The higher values are but reflections of the physical needs.

> The phantoms formed in the human brain are also necessary sublimates of their material life process. Morality, religion, metaphysics . . . . no longer retain the semblance of independence. They have no history, no development; but men, developing their material production . . . . alter their thinking and the products of their thinking. Life is not determined by consciousness but consciousness by life.[7]

The physical needs are fundamental only because they are necessary. Once they are secure, they are the least important of our needs. Certainly the higher values have their own source and satisfactions, and even the materialists we have been describing seek material things for what they can do in the way of social esteem and social power. A woman buys a fur coat certainly not for the purpose of keeping warm and she purchases beautiful, insipid, juiceless Red Delicious apples certainly not for nourishment. Aesthetic interests are at stake. Even the voluptuary, unlike an animal which spontaneously satisfies its sexual desires, pursues an abstract idea—pleasure.

But the Marxists are much better than their ontological views would suggest. Justice, respect for personality, social welfare, creativeness, happiness are acknowledged. It is for this reason that they can be called naturalistic humanists, and, implicit in their doctrine of happiness, is an individualistic element which is absent in their liberal counterparts, Mill and Dewey. In the latter rights and interests are emphasized only because they are instrumental to the common good. With the Marxists social welfare and justice are esteemed because they will bring greater happiness to the individual, in spite of their inconsistent emphasis of collectivism.

But does not a respect for personality require a "truth" about man and his cosmos? If the whole is purposeless, it is difficult to see how a man could derive any significance from his connection with it. We normally judge the worthiness of a person by the worthiness of his interests and his enthusiasm for these interests. But interests denote one's relations with the world and in a worthless world can we talk about worthy

interests? That the universe is worthless follows from the
Marxian ontology of naturalism. Worth presupposes an evalua-
ting mind and in the metaphysics of dialectical materialism
things are essentially physical. Certainly it is better that we
live but when the human species becomes extinct it is no better
for the universe simply because being unconscious it cannot
remember.[8] Can a humanism be sustained by naturalism? As
John Mothershead has well said:

> The moral ideal of the communist society is a distant goal . . . . Yet
> we are asked to sacrifice for this goal, the content of which cannot
> be made clear in the interests of generations of men yet unborn.
> Could a demand for greater unselfishness possibly be made? Yet
> in the next breath we are told that people act only in terms of
> their own interests. How can it be construed to be in my interest
> to act for the sake of the Marxist ideal? On a materialistic philo-
> sophy can the Marxist justify the great unselfishness he calls for?[9]

The idolatrous attitude that the American people and their
naturalistic spokesmen display for science and technology is
partly excusable, for they make no pretense of radical social
reform. But for a social movement which claims to challenge
radically the assumptions of a bourgeois mind, the Marxists
in their failure to examine the social and moral limitations
of science and technology have failed miserably. As Mounier
states:

> It [Marxism] is simply the infallible operation of scientific reason,
> elicited by industrial effort to make man the lord and master of
> nature according to the Cartesian ideal . . . . A revolution that is
> motivated only by the ideals of abundance and comfort and security
> can but lead after the first fervour of the revolt to an universali-
> zation of the abominable petty bourgeois ideal, and never to an
> authentic spiritual liberation.[10]

What needs to be challenged is not science itself but the
extravagant claims which the Marxists and their bourgeois
friends, the naturalists and positivists, make for it. While the
sciences may outline possible and relevant goals and put at
our disposal the means of their realization, they cannot give
us the ends themselves unless they are defined in terms of
actual wants. But certainly the moral philosopher has more
to do than to assume the function of a statistician of wants.
Even as means, the sciences are handicapped without a will

to realize them and obligation is a normative and not a statistical matter. Ironically, even John Dewey, while with one hand mapping out the unlimited possibilities of social science in resolving group conflicts, with the other was writing patriotic anti-German literature. The Marxists were more realistic in eradicating social barriers to an objective social science. But it is questionable whether science and technology should monopolize the whole of man's life and his metaphysics. Certainly men have more to do than dominate over nature and theologize about their conquest.

A reverence for technology religiously invoked by Marxists and the West generally can but signify one attitude: that happiness is a consequence of the mastery of nature and the comforts and security which this entails. As Mumford has stated:

If anything was unconditionally believed in and worshipped during the last two centuries, at least by the leaders and masters of society, it was the machine; for the machine and the universe were identified, linked together as it were by the formulae of mathematical and physical sciences; and the service of the machine was the principle manifestation of faith and religion, the main motive of human action, and the source of most human goods.[11]

Consequently the solution to the problems created by the machine is not simply, as Dewey contends, a social science developed to counter the social lag but a moral rebirth. The social lag is an essential ingredient of a culture which believes it can be redeemed by material comforts.

The mania for production and efficiency exhibited by Marxists and Americans alike is the consequence not only of a dim view of happiness but the illusion that vital needs are limitless. Certainly if the body requires three meals a day, its vitality will not be tripled by nine. As Mumford humorously states: "A harem of thousand wives may satisfy the vanity of an oriental monarch, but what monarch is sufficiently endowed by nature to satisfy the harem?"[12] Once basic needs are satisfied and a culture becomes oriented to the higher values, the extent of the "mechanical enterprise" would be limited. In short, the higher the value, the less can it be expressed in terms of money and the more in terms of goods that machines cannot produce. As life becomes mature, "the social unemployment of machines will become as marked as the present technological unemployment of men."[13] Certainly one cannot infer that, if a certain amount of technology is good, more is better, anymore than if one were to say that, if two aspirins are beneficial, ten are more so.

It is true that the Marxists have imposed one moral demand on technology: that it be geared to an equitable distribution of comforts. But what capitalist state has not followed the lead? In no sense is this radical. The confidence that a re-shuffling of ownership would resolve group conflicts and destroy power elites is a product of a nineteenth-century secular liberalism which saw in social structure the source of all evil. Certainly no mere formal manipulation of the means of production and distribution will alter the mass mind, ugly cities, centralization of power, the production of military weapons. Technical superiority itself creates differences of property, social status, and power. Again no mere change in personnel and ownership will restore to labor its proper dignity and its sense of vocation. The inhuman monotony of factory labor and clerical drudgery will still be with us.

Theoretical considerations alone convince us that the Marxists do not intend to control in any radical sense the machine. The dignity of labor is not the dignity of a craftsman or a farmer but that of the factory worker. The labor theory of value is itself an acknowledgment of the supreme importance the Marxists attach to economic values. Obviously if economic goods are the primary concern of men then unquestioned dignity must be bestowed upon those who create them. But from a moral perspective, what kind of dignity can much of our factory and office routine possess? What sense of vocation could possibly accompany the production of repetitious, need-less, wasteful goods? It was not vulgarity which compelled Walter Kaufman in a cynical mood to state that creativity in many quarters of contemporary civilization has been relegated to "creative" sex deviations.

I dare say that with automation perhaps technology is pregnant with at least its partial cure. The coming automation may destroy "the dignity of labor" and the labor theory of value by eliminating in time the factory worker.

NOTES

1. Cf. C. Wright Mills, *The Causes of World War Three* (New York: Simon & Schuster, 1958), pp. 15-19.

2. Ibid., pp. 17-19.

3. Ibid., pp. 1-73.

4. The phrase is Bowne's. Cf. his *Metaphysics* (New York: American, 1898), pp. 1-100.

5. Ernest Nagel, "Naturalism Reconsidered" in Yervant H. Krikorian and Abraham Edel, eds., *Contemporary Philosophical Problems* (New York: Macmillan, 1959), pp. 337-349.

6. Cf. B. P. Bowne, *Personalism* (Norwood, Mass.: The Plimpton Press, 1908), pp. 217-268.

7. Quoted in George H. Sabine, *A History of Political Theory* (New York: Holt, 1959), p. 763.

8. Cf. W. E. Hocking, *Science and the Idea of God* (Chapel Hill: The University of North Carolina Press, 1944), pp. 51-83.

9. John Mothershead, *Ethics* (New York: Holt, 1955), pp. 174-175.

10. Emmanuel Mounier, *A Personalist Manifesto* (New York: Longmans, 1938), p. 54.

11. Lewis Mumford, *Technics and Civilization* (New York: Harcourt, 1934), p. 365.

12. Ibid., p. 394.

13. Ibid., p. 426.

Part VII

MARXISM AND ALIENATION

Chapter 22

The Concept of Alienation in the Philosophy of Karl Marx

A. JAMES GREGOR

A. James Gregor, associate professor in the political science
department of the University of California at Berkeley, has
held positions at the University of Texas, the University of
Kentucky, and the University of Hawaii. He is the author of
A Survey of Marxism (1965), *Contemporary Radical Ideologies*
(1968), *The Ideology of Fascism* (1969), and *An Introduction
to Metapolitics* (in press).

The discussion of the concept of "alienation" or "estrangement"
and its role in the philosophy of Karl Marx has only begun.
While significant and interesting treatments have been forthcoming, there has been no universal agreement among scholars
as to the ultimate role the concept plays in Marxism as a
system. The concept functions in many ways in the work of
the young Marx and reappears in the manuscripts in which
Marx was working when he died.[1] Its use in the early writings
is vague and ambiguous. Certainly the interpretation here
will be tentative and subject to correction. What can be said
with some assurance at this point is that the concept of
"alienation" is of fundamental importance in the early writings
and that the concept underwent critical change in the course
of Marx's philosophical maturation. The concept underwent

marked changes during the quarter-century in which Marx employed it. Any simple treatment of "alienation" based only on the Paris *Manuscripts of 1844,* as though these documents contained the final essence of Marx's thought, is in error.[2]

Alienation as a concept is, of course, rooted in the vastness of German idealism. In Hegel it shoulders an enormous metaphysical burden. In the context of his general speculative cosmology, alienation is a descriptive title designating the universal process through which the idea articulates itself as "nature."[3] The creative life of the Spirit is an activity of self externalization (*Selbstentäusserung*) by which it takes an objective form. The Absolute Spirit is thus both the subject and the object of this process. Alienation becomes a logical necessity if there is to be any development at all. If there is to be anything at all the universal spirit must in some sense and in some fashion proceed to distinguish itself from itself. Alienation becomes a necessary process, a logical presupposition of the development of the world.[4] The Spirit posits its "other" as something "alien." This, without doing too much violence to the purport of Hegelianism, might well be termed the metaphysical or ontological dimension of alienation or estrangement.[5] It seems to function as a logically necessary antecedent to development and proceeds through logical categories. Since Spirit is one, if there is to be development at all, Spirit must posit the "other than Spirit" out of itself in a "self-estrangement."[6] "The very essence of Spirit is activity; it realizes its potentiality—makes itself its own deed, its own work—and thus it becomes an object to itself: contemplates itself as an objective existence."[7]

The ultimate fulfillment of the Spirit is mediated through the consciousness and will of empirical men.[8] Now, the Spirit as conscious subject, as man, becomes aware of the self-estrangement of the Absolute Spirit by experiencing the natural world as an alien and hostile thing, something opposed to himself. Such an estrangement for man is transcended (*aufgehoben*) through the realization that the empirical self and the objective world are but moments in the all-embracing self-subsistent life of the Spirit.[9] There is thus in history a dimension of alienation which is "empirical."[10] These two dimensions of estrangement seem to possess diverse emotional saliences. Hegel attaches little, if any, negative connotation to the process of the self-estrangement of the Absolute Spirit for such estrangement is necessary if development is to take place at all.[11] Alienations, on the other hand, which afflict men in the course of their history engender what is referred to in the *Phenomenology of Mind* as the "unhappy consciousness" of self-estrangement.[12]

There can be distinguished then, for the purposes of our discussion, at least two dimensions of alienation: (1) the self-estrangement, through logical categories, of the Spirit as a metaphysical process, and (2) the empirical estrangements which involve the consciousness of men as actors in history. As long as a Hegelian Idealism is maintained, there seems to be little difficulty in maintaining the distinction between the two dimensions of alienation. The metaphysical process of self-estrangement through logical categories has the Absolute Spirit as its subject. But with the inversion of the Hegelian dialectic that followed Feuerbach's revision, the Idea, the abstract, universal Subject is recognized as an alienation itself. Man has projected his species traits into a "pure" realm of logic and sees development as the movement of categories.

Feuerbach, and the young Marx as his disciple, rendered man himself and not the Absolute "the true subject " of the historical process.[13] This was the essence of the young Marx's reform of the Hegelian dialectic. The young Marx, pursuing the critical inversion of Hegelianism, rejected the abstract subject, the Absolute. Feuerbach had argued that Hegel had succeeded in projecting human qualities, determinate predicates, into some metaphysical realm, thus elevating them to the status of self-moving subjects. Predicates had been transformed into substantives, self-moving, mystical subjects. Hegel had made man's determinate traits independent subjects—and men were reduced to predicates of some absolute subject. If men had ideas Hegel stripped them of particularity and delivered the Idea—of which determinate ideas were but byproducts. Subject and predicate were inverted. Men with ideas became moments in the development of the universal idea, byproducts in the life-history of the self-moving Spirit.

This was the analysis the young Marx made his own. He rejected the Hegelian metaphysical subjects, reducing them to byproducts in the life history of determinate men. This was the

critical revision, or revolutionary humanistic inversion undertaken by Feuerbach as early as 1839 and consistently and
explicitly employed by the young Marx as early as 1841. Instances
of its application abound in the *Poverty of Philosophy*,[14] and in
his letter to P. V. Annenkov in December 1846, Marx specifically
identified the treatment of "estranged predicates," "abstractions,"
and "categories" as "self-moving subjects" as "entirely mystical,"
as "old Hegelian junk," and a "mystic inversion."[15]

Since Marx made real men the true subject of history, the
cosmic objectifications of the Spirit which constituted the world
of empirical things, the alienations in the metaphysical realm, had
no home. The alienations and objectifications which Hegel
ascribed to the life-activity of the Spirit could only be ascribed
to the "true subject" of history, man himself. So, for Feuerbach
and Marx, man, not Spirit, *was objectified in nature*. Nature was
the unity in which man defined himself through objects—objects
which were in some sense self-objectifications. Both Feuerbach
and the young Marx conceived the objects of the external world
as "objectifications," "self-projections." In some real sense, man
objectified himself in nature—in some sense created an external
world. Marx articulated this reform of the ontological dimension
of Hegelian alienation: ". . . man's *feelings*, passions, etc., are not
merely anthropological phenomena in the narrower sense, but
truly *ontological* affirmations of essential being. . . ."[16] He
contended that "the object of labor is . . . the objectification of
man's species life: for he duplicates himself not only, as in
consciousness, intellectually, but also actively, in reality, and
therefore he contemplates himself in a world that he has
created."[17] Marx simply followed the principles advanced in
Feuerbach's revision of Hegel. Feuerbach had expressed the
same ontological commitment by saying that "the object of
any subject is nothing else than the subject's own nature taken
objectively."[18] "The object is [man's] manifested nature, his
true objective ego. And this is true not merely of spiritual, but
also of sensuous objects."[19]

In effect, while Marx abandoned the mystic Subject of Hegel,
the Absolute Spirit, he found himself faced with the necessity
of providing some account of ontological alienation, that
development which in Hegel proceeds through concepts and
categories as logical abstractions. Marx's *Manuscripts of 1844*
contain at least that much residual Hegelianism. Marx continued
to speak the Hegelian language and referred to "alienation" as

though it were something logically antecedent to the specific forms of alienation which are the product of human enterprise in the empirical world. In the *Manuscripts of 1844* Marx commits himself to a conception of a universal and logically prior alienation from which all empirical alienations derive. He uses the concept of alienation in a broad, generic sense, as a "logical concept" which identifies the necessary process by which man objectifies himself as a species being and thereby creates his world. When Marx tells us that "the object of labor is . . . the objectification of man's species life . . . and therefore he contemplates himself in a world that he has created,"[20] and that "labor is only an expression of human activity within alienation,"[21] he is obviously using "alienation" as an abstract or metaphysical category in much the same way that Hegel might, as something logically prior to its particular, empirical manifestations.

Thus there remains in the *Manuscripts of 1844* a "logical concept" of "alienation" which designates the undifferentiated activity, or labor itself, by means of which man objectifies himself and creates his world. The young Marx conceived man's sensuous activity as having the same developmental and dialectical character which Hegel had attributed to the Absolute as Idea and Spirit. "Alienation" is human activity in which "man becomes objective for himself and at the same time becomes to himself a strange and inhuman object. . . ."[22] Man has objectified himself in nature and then faces that objective nature as though it were an alien reality. The young Marx refers to that alien reality as "private property."[23] Thus Marx sought to explain the origins of "private property" in its limited, determinate sense, as employed by political economy, by relating it to the broad and abstract "private property" which was a product of metaphysical or ontological alienation. Specific alienation in economic property was the "necessary consequence of alienated labor, of the external relation of the worker to nature. . . ."[24] "Alienated labor," activity within alienation, produces "private property" in the undifferentiated or abstract sense. "All human activity hitherto has been labor— that is, industry. . . ."[25] This activity, this "industry" produces, through alienation, the objective world which man conceives as "external." Once the product of his own enterprise is conceived as "external," its alienation in the ordinary sense becomes possible. "Private property," as it is ordinarily used in political economy, exemplifies only one specific form of the concept alienation. Marx conceived "private property" in this limited, economic sense as a consequence of alienated labor, in its abstract or generic sense—"[private property] *results by analysis from the concept of alienated labor. . . .*"[26]

Marx felt that this kind of analysis, Hegelian in its principal features, answered the fundamental question concerning private property: "How is this estrangement *rooted in the nature of human development*?"[27] The concept of "alienated labor" seems to refer to human sensuous activity as such. Its product, objective reality, is then spoken of as "private property" in a similarly broad or ontological sense. This "alienation" is "rooted in the nature of human development." It is the logical presupposition of human development itself. Only in such an analysis would it make sense to say: "Private property is thus the product, the result, the necessary consequence of alienated labor, of the external relation of the worker to nature and to himself. Private property thus results by analysis from the concept of alienated labor—i.e., of alienated man, of estranged labor, of estranged life, of estranged man. True, it is as a result of the movement of private property that we have obtained the concept of alienated labor (of alienated life) from political economy. But on analysis of this concept it becomes clear that though private property appears to be the source, the cause of alienated labor, *it is really its consequence. . . .*"[28]

For the young Marx the alienation spoken of in political economy is only understood when it is seen as one specific empirical manifestation of the broad and indeterminate concept of alienation which is in some sense its presupposition. Marx himself realized that the treatment of the empirical alienation of property through the "concept of alienated labor" was Hegelian. Marx tells us:

The outstanding thing in Hegel's *Phenomenology*, and its final outcome—that is, the dialectic of negativity as the moving and generating principle—is thus first, that Hegel conceives the self-genesis of man as a process, conceives objectification as loss of the object, as alienation and as transcendence of this alienation; that he thus grasps the essence of *labor* and comprehends objective man—true, because real man—as the outcome of man's own labor. The *real*, active orientation of man to himself as a species being, or his manifestation as a real species being (i.e., as a human being), is only possible by his really bringing out of himself all the powers that are his as the *species* man—something which in turn is only possible by man's *treating these generic powers as objects:* and this, to begin with, is again only possible in the form of estrangement. . . . Let us provisionally say just this much in advance: Hegel's standpoint is that of modern political economy. He grasps *labor* as the *essence* of man—as man's *essence* in the act of proving itself: he sees only the positive, not the negative side of labor.[29]

Thus according to the young Marx, man objectifies himself, alienates himself as an objective world. The very objective world he creates becomes a strange and alien object: private property. This is the positive alienation—conceivably the "free private property" to which the young Marx obscurely refers.[30] Marx is apparently using "private property" in a broad, undifferentiated sense, something quite other than private property in the narrow sense of political economy. This is evident when he speaks of the *positive* transcendence of private property.

[The] positive transcendence of private property—i.e., the *sensuous* appropriation for and by man of the human essence and of human life, of objective man, of human *achievements*—is not to be conceived merely in the sense of *direct,* one-sided *gratification*—merely in the sense of *possessing,* or *having.* Man appropriates his total essence in a total manner, that is to say, as a whole man. . . . The transcendence of private property is therefore the complete *emancipation* of *all human senses and attributes*; but it is this emancipation precisely because these senses and attributes have become subjectively and objectively, human. The eye has become a *human* eye, just as its object has become a social, *human,* object—an object emanating from man for man.[31]

This *positive* transcendence is a *complete emancipation of all human senses* and attributes and cannot refer to private property in the narrow sense employed in economics. That the young Marx has something like this broad dimension of alienation in mind is evidenced by the fact that the transcendence of alienation in political economy through the annulment of private property by collective ownership, communism as such, is only a preliminary to the next and final stage of man's liberation. "Communism is the position as the negation of the negation and is hence the *actual* phase necessary for the next stage of historical development in the process of human emancipation and recovery. *Communism* is the necessary pattern and the dynamic principle of the immediate future, but communism as such is not the goal of human development. . . ."[32] Thus the young Marx conceived the liberation of man much more broadly than is generally conceded.

Communism, as fully developed naturalism, equals humanism, and as fully developed humanism equals naturalism; it is the *genuine* resolution of the *conflict between man and nature* and *between man and man*—the true resolution of the strife between man and man—the true resolution of the strife between *existence* and *essence*. between *objectification* and *self-confirmation*, between freedom and necessity, between the individual and the species.[33]

For the young Marx, the subject of the historical development of man is man, rather than the Spirit, as it is in Hegel. But the process is the same: "individuals always project themselves outward [*von sich ausgegangen*], they forever go out of themselves. Their relationships are relationships of their real life processes."[34] In such a context the transcendence of estrangement is identified with the transcendence of objectivity itself. Such a transcendence is achieved through communism only *as a fully developed humanism.*

The tentative interpretation tendered here would suggest that the young Marx in the manuscripts before 1845 used the terms "alienation," "labor," "economy," "industry," "mode of production," and "private property" in vague and ambiguous ways.[35] There is certainly some evidence that one use of "alienation" as a broad and abstract concept, carries in its train an array of equally broad and abstract usages with respect to "industry," "labor," and "private property." Within the general and undifferentiated *concept* of alienation there are specific alienations. Some of these alienations are described in political economy.

We have considered the act of estranging practical human activity, labor, in two of its aspects: (1) The relation of the worker to the *product of labor* as an alien object exercising power over him. *This relation is at the same time the relation to the sensuous external world, to the objects of nature as an alien world antagonistically opposed to him.* (2) The relation of labor to the *act of production* within the *labor* process. This relation is the relation of the worker to his own activity as an alien activity not belonging to him; it is activity as suffering, strength as weakness, begetting as emasculating, the worker's *own* physical and mental energy, his personal life or what is life other than activity—as an activity which is turned against him, neither depends on nor belongs to him. Here we have *self-estrangement,* as we had previously the *estrangement of the thing.*[36]

A third aspect of estranged labor is "deduced" from the precedent two.[37] Since all of nature is "man's inorganic body," estrangement of man estranges him from his *species life.* This estrangement leads to his estrangement from other men. Only this ultimate and derivative estrangement of man from man leads to private property in the *narrow sense employed by political* economy: "the product of labor does not belong to the worker . . . it confronts him as an alien power, this can only be because it belongs to *some other man than the worker.*"[38] Thus we see, the young Marx concludes, "how in real life the *concept* of estranged *alienated labor* must express and present itself."[39] Through successive applications of a concept from the more general or abstract realm to the immediate, empirical realm, Marx has shown how *a concept* presents itself in real life.[40] Unfortunately, the successive applications, and the successive meanings of the term, all bear the identification "alienation" or "estrangement." These successive definitions do not bear identifying subscripts or identifying adjectives. Apparently Marx inherited this technique from Hegelianism, abandoning it only after considerable critical reformulation.

There seems to be a real confusion in the *Manuscripts of 1844* and only in 1845 was critical reassessment undertaken. In the spring of 1845 Engels and Marx resolved to "settle accounts with [their] erstwhile philosophical conscience"—to seek "self-clarification."[41] Their enterprise resulted in two large octavo volumes, which remained unpublished until 1932[42] when they appeared as *The German Ideology.*

In *The German Ideology,* Marx undertook a concerted effort to concretize the formal abstractions of German Idealism. He sought to establish his revolutionary world-view on the sure foundation of *empirical assessment* rather than abstract derivation. In *Manuscripts of 1844*, this program was as yet incomplete. His *specific* charge against the Hegelians after 1844 was that they "*comprehended* everything as soon as it was reduced to an Hegelian logical category."[43] They understood history as the imagined activity of imagined subjects and their analysis of empirical reality rested not on "existing empirical data," but on the implications of a "concept."[44] Thus Marx's criticism of Hegelianism extended to a radical

reconsideration of Hegelian explanatory devices he himself
had employed prior to that time. In his criticisms his analytic
eye fell on the Hegelian use and abuse of concepts. By the
time of the completion of *The German Ideology* the young
Marx sought explanation in empirical assessment rather
than in the "working out of a concept." Thus in *The German
Ideology* the young Marx sought to provide an *"earthly"*
basis for human history, to trace man's history *empirically
without recourse to the metaphysical concepts and categories
of the old and reformed Hegelians.* In the critical treatment
of Idealism Marx specifically eschewed treating history
through *"categories,"* abandoning even the Feuerbachian
category of the "essence of man,"[45] which figured so
prominently in the Paris documents. What he had called
the "category of alienated labor" received the same treatment.

The "materialist" assessment of history of *The German
Ideology* commences with "real" premises: men must produce
in order to live; they must reproduce in order to maintain the
species; and, as production increases, a division of labor
(originally no more than a division of labor in the sexual act)
arises on the basis of the natural distinctions among men—
differences in constitution, needs, accidents, and so forth.
"This division of labor implies the possibility, indeed the
fact, that intellectual and material activity—enjoyment and
labor, production and consumption—devolve on different
individuals," different classes. "The division of labor and private
property are . . . identical expressions," for "with the division
of labor . . . is given simultaneously the distribution, and indeed
the unequal distribution (both quantitative and qualitative), of
labor and its products, hence property. . . ." *Out of these
empirical conditions arises "estrangement," "alienation."*[46]
The order indicated in the Paris *Manuscripts* is reversed. In
those documents the division of labor takes place *"within* the
estrangement"[47] and private property is the *"consequence* of
alienation."[48] In *The German Ideology* the division of labor and
the subsequent private property *causes* alienation. What had
been a logical or speculative presupposition in the *Manuscripts*
became in *The German Ideology* an attempt at empirical
analysis, for history, Marx decided, "does not have to look for
a *category.*"[49] In the *Communist Manifesto* of 1848 Marx was
to mock the "true socialists" who conceived the real activity
of political economy in terms of the abstract concept or
category, "Alienation of Humanity."[50]

His mockery is evidence of a genuine reevaluation of his own position of 1844. In Marx's notebooks we find a fragment in which the transition from the abstract treatment of "alienation" as a logical category is reduced to the empirical assessment of fact. "How is it possible," he asks critically in 1845, "that man's relations become relations standing opposed to him? that the powers of his own life threaten to overpower him? In one word: *the division of labor*, the level of which depends upon the correlative development of the productive forces."[51]

After the critical reassessment of 1845, "alienation" never functions as a general or abstract *concept* or *category*. Where it does appear, it is almost invariably used in the sense the young Marx used it when speaking of alienation as a *consequence of the division of labor and the differential distribution of private property*. This was his use in the *Manuscripts* when he referred specifically to the "empirical" alienations discussed in political economy. "Economy," which in the *Manuscripts* intends "Industry" (meaning "human activity"), becomes specifically "political economy," the "anatomy of civil society."[52] Even in *The Holy Family*, written in the autumn of 1844, "alienation" has narrowed to that which is consequent upon the development of private property in the strictly economic sense.[53] "The French and English workers . . . these *massy*, communist workers . . . are most painfully aware of the difference between *being* and *thinking*, between *consciousness* and *life*. They know that property, capital, money, wage-labor and the like are no ideal figments of the brain but very practical, very objective sources of their self-estrangement. . . ."[54] As we have indicated, by the time Marx wrote his polemic against Proudhon in 1846-1847, he advocated a "profane history of the categories. . . ."[55]

Between 1844 and 1847, Marx systematically reduced the scope of "alienation" to real or empirical alienation. In its specific meaning it was conceived to be the *consequence* of the division of labor, of private property and the class structure which these antecedent conditions fostered, rather than their cause. This economic alienation was but one of the forms of alienation discussed in the *Manuscripts of 1844*.[56] It was the "alienation" "in the conditions dealt with by political economy. . . ."[57] At that time the young Marx had anticipated a similar treatment of alienation in the state, law, ethics, civil life, and so forth.[58] By the time *The German Ideology* was written (1845-1846), Marx was convinced that political economy constituted the study of the real basis of society. The other proposed critiques could no longer be thought of as distinct from the critique of political economy.[59] Alienation was the consequence of the processes inherent in the activity attending the material production of life and all other alienations were conceived as subsidiary effects.

The influence of Engels in this redirection, or more specifically, in this empirical and specifically economic reorientation on the part of Marx, has not as yet been determined.[60] Certainly, between 1842 and 1845 Engels had applied himself far more than Marx to the problems of economics and the influence of political economy upon the history of Europe.[61] Although Engels consistently minimized his influence on Marx he did report that, prior to his meeting with Marx in 1844, he had decided, as a consequence of his experience with the economic situation in England, that economic facts, long neglected in historiography, "were of decisive historical importance and were the foundation of the real conflict between classes . . . and that they were the basis . . . of all political history."[62]

In November 1844, after Marx had written the Paris *Manuscripts,* Engels admonished him:

We must begin with the ego, with the empirical, living individual. . . . "Man" is a spirit figure as long as [he] does not have empirical men as [his] basis. In brief, we must proceed from empiricism and materialism if our thinking and specifically our "Man" is to be something true; *we must derive the general from the particular, not out of itself or out of the air à la Hegel.* These are all trivialities, which are Feuerbach has already, in part, discussed, and I would not repeat them if not for Hess—who appears to me, to treat empiricism . . . so shabbily. Hess, where he speaks theoretically, proceeds always in categories. . . .[63]

Whatever the ultimate source there is certainly an abandonment of the use of antecedent logical concepts and categories in explanation on the part of the young Marx. This is nowhere more evident than in his treatment of alienation. After 1845 the concept is used almost exclusively to refer to alienation in the specifically economic sense. The concept occasionally reappears in his writings and it is consistently used in the "empirical" manner of *The German Ideology.* The most careful treatment of this specific use is found in the preparatory notes made by Marx for the *Contribution to the Critique of Political Economy* during 1857-1858. An entire section[64] is devoted to the "Estrangement [*Entfremdung*] of the working conditions of labor with the development of capital." Here alienation is discussed in the following manner:

> The objective conditions of labor take up against living labor an ever increasing independence which reveals itself through its very extent, and the social wealth in ever increasing dimension stands over and against labor as an alien and ruling power. *The emphasis is not applied to the objectification in reality*, but to the alienated, objectified, projected being, the "not-for-the-worker," to the personified productive conditions, that is, the enormous objective power that belongs to capital that social labor has placed against itself as one of its moments.[65]

Here Marx seems to be specifically abjuring his treatment of abstract alienation as it is found in the *Manuscripts of 1844*. The emphasis should not be applied to the "objectification in reality" but to the real economic conditions which render the social labor of the worker an alien capital that stands against him as an opponent.[66] Thus the sense of alienation which survives into Marx's maturity is the empirical sense of alienation which, in the Paris *Manuscripts*, was accompanied by the broad sense of abstract alienation, the "objectification in reality."

NOTES

1. Karl Marx, *Capital*, vol. 3 (Moscow, 1962), p. 259.

2. E. Fromm, *Marx's Concept of Man* (New York, 1961), pp. v-89. Cf. A. J. Gregor, "Erich Fromm and the Young Karl Marx," *Studies on the Left* 3 (1962): 85-92.

3. "As a living whole, nature is a total process of Idea; as contingency and externality, it is the same Idea in its otherness or self-estrangement." Hegel, *Encyclopedia of Philosophy* (New York, 1959), p. 166.

4. Cf. Marx's discussion in *The Poverty of Philosophy* (Moscow, n.d.), pp. 117ff.

5. This is how Engels in his maturity refers to "alienation." Cf. Engels, *Ludwig Feuerbach and the End of Classical German Philosophy*, Marx and Engels, *Selected Works*, vol. 2 (Moscow, 1955), pp. 362, 385.

6. "Spirit is only that which it attains by its own efforts." Hegel, *The Philosophy of History* (New York, 1956), p. 55.

7. Ibid., pp. 73ff.

8. Ibid., pp. 37, 55.

9. Cf. Marx, *Poverty*, pp. 181, 270.

10. "Spirit is always one and the same, but unfolds its one nature in the phenomena of the world's existence. This must, as before stated, present itself as the ultimate result of history. But we have to take the latter as it is. We must proceed historically-empirically." Hegel, *The Philosophy of History*, p. 10.

11. Ibid., p. 55.

12. Cf. Hegel, *The Phenomenology of Mind* (New York, 1949), pp. 251-267.

13. Marx, "Kritik des Hegelschen Staatsrechts," Marx, Engels, *Werke*, vol. 1 (Berlin, 1961), p. 286.

14. Cf. Marx, *Poverty*, pp. 117ff., 121. Cf. A. J. Gregor, "Marx, Feuerbach and the Reform of the Hegelian Dialectic," *Science and Society* 29 (Winter 1965): 66-80.

15. Marx to P. V. Annenkov, December 28, 1846 in *Selected Works*, vol. 2, pp. 441-452.

16. Marx, *Economic and Philosophic Manuscripts* (Moscow, n. d.), p. 136. (Hereafter cited as EPM.) Cf. A. J. Gregor, "Giovanni Gentile and the Philosophy of the Young Karl Marx," *Journal of the History of Ideas* 24 (April-June 1963): 213-230.

17. EPM, p. 76.

18. Feuerbach, *The Essence of Christianity* (New York, 1957), p. 12.

19. Ibid., p. 5.

20. EPM, p. 76.

21. Ibid., p. 129.

22. Ibid., p. 105.

23. Ibid.

24. Ibid., p. 80.

25. Ibid., p. 110.

26. Ibid., p. 80.

27. Ibid., p. 82.

28. Ibid., p. 80.

29. Ibid., p. 151.

30. Ibid., p. 135.

31. Ibid., pp. 105ff.

32. Ibid., p. 114.

33. Ibid., p. 102.

34. Marx, "Aus I. Feuerbach," *Werke*, vol. 3, p. 540.

35. This compares with the various ontological and empirical usages found in the writings of Moses Hess. Cf. "Ueber das Geldwesen," In *Philosophische und sozialistische Schriften*, 1837-1850 (Berlin, 1962), pp. 330ff.

36. Ibid., pp. 73ff.

37. Ibid., p. 74.

38. Ibid., p. 79.

39. Ibid., p. 78.

40. Ibid., p. 80.

41. Marx, *Contribution to the Critique of Political Economy, Selected Works*, vol. 1, p. 364.

42. Cf. editor's introduction to *Die deutsche Ideologie* (Berlin, 1953), p. 6.

43. Marx and Engels, *Die deutsche Ideologie, Werke*, vol. 3, p. 19. (Subsequent references will be to this edition.)

44. "The family which to begin with is the only social relationship, becomes larger, when increased needs create new social relations and the increased population new needs, a subordinate one (except in Germany), and must then be treated and analyzed according to the existing empirical data and not according to 'the concept of the family,' as is the custom in Germany." Ibid., p. 29.

45. Ibid., p. 38.

46. Ibid., pp. 28-35.

47. Ibid., p. 129.

48. Ibid., p. 80.

49. *Die deutsche Ideologie*, p. 38.

50. Marx and Engels, *The Communist Manifesto, Selected Works*, vol. 1, p. 58.

51. Marx, "Aus I. Feuerbach," *Werke*, vol. 3, p. 540.

52. Marx, "Contribution," *Selected Works*, vol. 1, p. 362.

53. Marx and Engels, *The Holy Family* (Moscow, 1956), p. 51.

54. Ibid., p. 73; cf. p. 111.

55. Marx, *Poverty*, p. 128.

56. Cf. the Soviet editors' introduction to EPM.

57. Ibid., p. 69.

58. Ibid., p. 15.

59. "Our conception of history depends on our ability to expound the real process of production, starting out from the simple material production of life, and to comprehend the form of intercourse connected with this and created by this . . . as the basis of all history; further, to show it in its action as state, and so, from this starting point, to explain the whole mass of different theoretical products and forms of consciousness, religion, philosophy, ethics, etc." *Die deutsche Ideologie*, pp. 37ff.

60. Cf. M. Adler, *Engels als Denker* (Berlin, 1925), pp. 37-49.

61. Cf. Engels' writings during this period in *Werke*, vol. 1, pp. 454-592, particularly Engels' *The Condition of the Working Class in England in 1844*.

62. Engels, "On the History of the Communist League," *Selected Works*, vol. 2, p. 343; cf. R. Mondolfo, *Il materialismo storico in Federico Engels* (Genoa, 1912), p. 132.

63. Engels to Marx, November 19, 1844, in A. Bebel and E. Bernstein, eds., *Der Briefwechsel zwischen Friedrich Engels und Karl Marx, 1844 bis 1883* (Stuttgart, 1913), vol. 1, p. 7. Later, Engels was to characterize the method of "pure ideology" as that which deduces "reality not from itself, but from a concept." Engels, *Anti-Dühring* (Moscow, 1962), p. 134.

64. Marx, *Grundrisse der Kritik der politischen Oekonomie* (Berlin, 1953), pp. 715-717.

65. Ibid., p. 715.

66. Compare here Engels' account of "alienation" in his "Outline of a Critique of Political Economy": "The immediate consequence of private property was the split of production into two opposing sides—the natural and the human sides, the soil which without fertilization by man is dead and sterile, and human activity, whose first condition is that very soil. Furthermore we have seen how human activity in its turn was dissolved into labor and capital, and how these two sides antagonistically confronted each other." EPM, p. 193.

Chapter 23

A Comment on Professor Gregor's Paper

IVAN BABIĆ

A docent in the faculty of political sciences at the University of Zagreb, Yugoslavia, Ivan Babić in 1964 was a Ford Foundation Fellow in the United States and in 1970 was an Alexander von Humboldt Fellow. He has headed a department in the Institute of the History of the Working Class Movement in Zagreb and is an ex-president of the Politological Society of Croatia. He is the author of *Philosophy and Science in the Works of the Yugoslav Marxists 1930-1941.*

In my comment I am not going to deal with tiny technicalities of interpretation. If I were to do so, I would ask such questions as: what is meant by "Marxism as a system"? Or I would probably object to describing Marx, even young Marx, as "a disciple" of Feuerbach, for since his doctoral dissertation, at least, it is evident that Marx was never going to be satisfied with the simple role of a disciple. Even when he is involved in philosophical discourse in the Hegelian or Feuerbachian manner, he has by way of approach, interpretation, and insight been enough himself not to be a mere disciple. But, as I say, I am not going to put under the microscope these and other more or less technical points.

I shall rather try to touch the gist of Mr. James Gregor's paper, as I understand it, trying somehow to bring it into a possible connection with the essential character of philosophic discussions concerning the topic of alienation in the country from which I come, Yugoslavia. I believe that a short comment of such a kind is more to the point than a minute technical analysis.

The core of Mr. Gregor's paper I find in his statement that "any simple treatment of 'alienation' based only on the Paris *Manuscripts of 1844* as though these documents contained the final essence of Marx's thought is in error." And, for my part, I gladly accept it in this formulation.

After having analyzed different usages and interpretations of the concept of alienation in different works of Marx and in some works of Engels of the period 1844-1858, Mr. Gregor comes to this conclusion: "After the critical re-assessment of 1845, 'alienation' never functions as a general or abstract *concept* or *category*."

The point is that it *never* appears, and in view of this point, the next sentence comes as a surprise. *"Where it does appear* it is almost invariably used in the sense the young Marx used it when speaking of alienation as a consequence of the division of labor and the differential distribution of private property." This is again repeated in the final sentence of the paper. "Thus the sense of alienation which survives into Marx's maturity is the empirical sense of alienation, which, in the Paris *Manuscripts,* was accompanied by the broad sense of abstract alienation, the 'objectification in reality.'"

It seems to me that this is the most that any fair interpretation of Marx's opus can give. At first sight almost contradictory (for in one sentence it expresses the essence of both "abstract and "empirical" content of Marx's theory of alienation), it is in view of Marx's works, in my opinion, the only fair and comprehensive interpretation, i.e., the interpretation which gives a full account of Marx's reflection on the subject.

And at this essential point I may be excused for alluding to the discussion on alienation in my country.

Before the last decade, but especially during it, there appeared in Yugoslavia a number of articles, essays, studies, and a handful of books in which the topic of alienation was central. These writings were chiefly nonphilosophical. A number of philosophic gatherings, some international in character, were mostly devoted to the exploration and analysis of different aspects of alienation. And after trying to recall all those materials and gatherings, I believe I am right in saying that all theses presented have, in one way or another, been caught between the Scylla of abstract, i.e., transcendental, treatment of Marx's usage of the term and the Charybdis of its empirical content and emphasis. After a period of dogmatic phraseology in philosophy, our philosophers, discovering all the multidimensionality and richness of Marx's thought, were in a sense especially keen on stressing the transcendental level of Marx's insight, e.g., interpreting dialectics in terms of "the critique of everything existent" and "alienation" in its universal philosophical anthropological meaning; while our politicians, primarily engaged as they are in the empirical world of tackling the "realization" of Marx's philosophy in the concrete, were criticizing this philosophic emphasis as an example of "abstract humanism."

In numerous controversies of such a kind, the crucial question for any sort of discussion of alienation in the sociocultural context of a socialist country appeared: "What is the relation of the empirical world of socialism in all its manifold features, discrepancies, contradictions, problems, and dilemmas, toward the essential content of Marx's philosophy, and in what way can we use philosophy as an instrument for dealing with the complexity of problems that disturb us today?" Politicians, as it happens, are stressing the empirical character of Marx's approach: if the basis of alienation is empirical, then all we as socialists can do is to reconstruct, revolutionize, transform this empirical, touchable, efficacious, historically and humanly meaningful basis. Professional philosophers were pointing to the other side of the coin: just this reorganization and reconstruction of the empirical basis of alienation with all its distortions, limitations, failures, dilemmas, show that besides all the efforts towards the "realization" of Marx's philosophy in the empirical world of socialist economy and politics there remains something universally valid, transcendentally normative and by necessity *abstract* in Marxism as a *philosophy*, and just this abstract character of its emphasis, just this *abstract humanism* and only this can save us from giving to the empirical world attributes of something in itself final, something to be praised, justified, sanctioned, and made sacred as such. There is not such an empirical realization of Marxism which in itself will be a guarantee that the world of humanistic values and strivings present in Marxism will be under all conditions saved. All the history of socialism in this century and all the complexities of its construction wherever it is present on the globe, either professedly Marxist or not, point to this.

So far as Yugoslavia is concerned, the essential feature of the most recent discussions on the complexity of the problems of alienation so far as I was able to follow them, is the interaction of the empirical and transcendental approach. It seems to me that the trend of the discussion is toward a growing interest of philosophers in the analysis of empirical features of the Yugoslav socioeconomic and political system and, less obviously in theory than in practice, a tendency of economists, politicians, and administrators to take into account the imperative need of a philosophically enlightened, politically more radical, and pedagogically self-critical approach to the aspects of socialism as it is expressed in the "concrete" empirical world.

Thus what Mr. Gregor was pointing to by way of textual philosophic interpretation, I am pointing to by way of connecting it with the Yugoslav experience in the struggle for socialism. Like all the other aspects of Marxism in its full and manifold intellectual ambitions, the aspect of alienation has *necessarily* both empirical and abstract features.

Chapter 24

Alienation, Empiricism, and Democracy in the Early Marx

LOYD D. EASTON

Loyd D. Easton is professor of philosophy and department
chairman at Ohio Wesleyan University. He has taught at Ohio
State University and Methodist Theological School in Ohio and
in 1961 received a grant from the American Council of Learned
Societies. He is co-author of *Values and Policy in American Society*
(1954), author of *Ethics, Policy and Social Ends* (1955) and *Hegel's
First American Followers—The Ohio Hegelians* (1967), and co-editor
and co-translator of *Writings of the Young Marx on Philosophy and
Society* (1967).

In Marx's early writings from 1843 to the *Communist Manifesto*,
"alienation" is a prominent and pervasive theme. In developing
this theme, Marx was concerned with the projections and
externalizations of human experience which are either mistaken
in respect to knowledge or harmful in respect to man's self-
development. In the first respect he used the idea of alienation
to attack Hegel's "self-sufficing speculation" from the standpoint
of Feuerbach's empiricism, the view that genuine knowledge,

Several passages in this essay have been incorporated in the Introduction to
Writings of the Young Marx on Philosophy and Society, ed. and trans. by
L. Easton and K. Guddat (New York: Doubleday Anchor Books, 1967) and
"Alienation and Empiricism in Marx's Thought" by L. Easton in *Social Research*
(Autumn 1970).

truth, is based on sense-perception. In the second he used the idea of alienation to assert the centrality and sovereignty of man emphasized in Feuerbach's humanism, a cornerstone in his commitment to democracy and socialism.

Marx's use of "alienation" in the Paris *Manuscripts of 1844* in relation to labor, communism, and Hegel's emphasis on action has been explored many times. But Marx's first and earlier use of "alienation"—in a detailed critique of Hegel's view of the state and derivative essays in the *Deutsch-Französische Jahrbücher*— has been neglected. This is unfortunate, because Marx's first use of "alienation" fundamentally illuminates his relation to Hegel and Feuerbach and the genesis of his views on empiricism, democracy, and socialism. The main concern in what follows is to explore this earliest use of "alienation," relate it to major themes in Marx's other writings, and touch on a resultant ambiguity and problem in Marx's thought.

Marx took note of the writings where he first used "alienation" in the preface to the *Critique of Political Economy* of 1859, the classical statement of his "historical materialism." A few years earlier he wanted to include the essays from the *Jahrbücher* in the first collection of his writings[1] along with earlier pieces on censorship and government—pieces which followed Hegel in the "liberal" direction of "criticism" as measuring the existing social world against the Idea, a task Marx set for himself in notes to his doctoral dissertation in 1840. Contrary to Engels' dismissal of the earlier writings as unimportant or unreadable, Marx regarded them as important in their own right and the basis of his mature thought. To explore his earliest use of "alienation" in relation to empiricism and democracy, then, is to come to grips with ideas germane to the Marxism of Marx regardless of their current use in criticizing institutional Marxism, their connection with sociological "anomie," or their existentialist overtones in relation to "depersonalization"—uses which have widely drawn attention to Marx's early writings.

Marx's first important use of the idea of alienation appeared in an extensive, paragraph-by-paragraph criticism of Hegel's philosophy of law written in the summer of 1843. Some of its main points were used in essays Marx was then drafting for the *Jahrbücher*, "On the Jewish Question" and "Introduction to the Critique of Hegel's Philosophy of Law." Marx's extensive

criticism of Hegel was a turning-point in his thought, his first
radical objection to the philosophy he had followed since 1837
when he became active in the Doctors' Club at the University
of Berlin and resolved to seek "the Idea in the real itself." In
his doctoral dissertation he had applied Hegel's thought to a
neglected aspect of Greek philosophy and committed himself
to "criticism," to measuring existing actuality against the Idea.
His essays in Ruge's *Anekdota* and in the *Rheinische Zeitung*
followed Hegel in main points or defended liberal positions
from Hegel's premises. For example, he opposed easier divorce
laws on the basis of the ethical nature of marriage. In defending
freedom of the press, he saw the state as "the great organism"
in which reason—not reason in the individual but "reason in
society"—is actualized as law and freedom. But this identification
with Hegel, qualified in the direction of liberal democracy, was
broken in 1843 over Hegel's theory of the state.

Marx's first use of "alienation" against Hegel appears in his
dissection of paragraphs 261 to 269 of Hegel's *Philosophy of
Law*. Marx charges that Hegel's view of the "dependence" of
family and civil society on the state is a relationship not in
experienced actuality but only in something external and alien
to them. "Actuality," Marx says "is not experienced as it is
itself but as another actuality. Common experience is not
subject to the law of its own spirit but to an alien spirit."
The "dependence" Hegel finds is an "alienation within unity."
His mistake is a result of reversing subject and predicate in
respect to the Idea and its content while "development takes
place on the side of the predicate," on the side of the content
which is the real meaning of the Idea. So Hegel, Marx objects,
"does not develop his thinking from the object but he develops
the object by a sort of thinking he manages, and manages in
the abstract sphere of logic."[2] As a result, Hegel's method is
through and through a "mystification" involving the alienation
of abstract concepts from the concrete connections of
experience.

Here Marx was following Feuerbach's attack on speculation
which had appeared in the *Anekdota* with his own first published essay on censorship. The speculative philosopher, Feuerbach charged, sees nature, religion, and philosophy itself as
mere predicates of the Idea, but "we need only to convert the
predicate into the subject to get at the pure, undisguised truth."
Feuerbach saw Hegel's idealism as the apotheosis of abstraction
which "alienates man from himself" because it inverts the real

relation of thought to its object.[3] Following Feuerbach against Hegel, Marx would look to "empirical actuality" and "common experience" for the content of the Idea. He would be an empiricist to avoid Hegel's mystification, his way of connecting things "in the abstract sphere of logic." In relation to other paragraphs, however, Marx firmly adhered to "the party of the Concept," to use his identification of 1840. He accused Hegel of uncritically accepting the status quo as the truth of the Idea, as being a genuine state. This was internal criticism of Hegel from Hegel's premises.

Further, Marx used the idea of alienation to criticize Hegel's paragraph 279 dismissing sovereignty of the people as incompatible with the idea of the state. With this criticism Marx put himself on the side of democracy. Hegel had repeatedly insisted that the idea of the state requires unity of form and content, universality and particularity. These conditions, Marx insisted, are met only in democracy:

> In democracy the *formal* principle is at the same time the *material* principle. Only democracy, therefore, is the true unity of the general and the particular. In monarchy, for example, and in a republic as only a particular form of state, political man has his particular existence as unpolitical, private man. Property, contract, marriage, civil society here appear as *particular* modes of existence alongside the *political* state.[4]

Without democracy the "far removed existence of the political state" merely affirms the "alienation" of property, family and civil society. Marx sees this alienation as esssentially religious. In *The Essence of Christianity* Feuerbach had interpreted religion as involving man's projection of his deepest satisfactions and values into an ideal, heavenly realm whose substance must be returned to man. Now Marx sees in the "state as such" an instance of this projection and alienation. In Marx's words:

> Up to now the political constitution has been the religious sphere, the sphere of the people's life, the heaven of universality in contrast to the particular *mundane existence* of their activity. . . . *Political life* in the modern sense of the word is the *scholasticism* of the people's life. *Monarchy is* the completed expression of this alienation. The *republic* is the negation of alienation within alienation.[5]

Though Marx's conception of democracy at this time presupposed freedom of trade and private property, he saw it as resolving the alienation of political life through popular sovereignty and self-government. In democracy there is "self-determination of the people," and the constitution is "man's and the people's *own* work." In democracy, to continue with Marx's words, "Man does not exist for the law, but the law exists for man. In democracy there is *specifically human existence*, while in other forms of the state man is a *particular legal existence*." With the achievement of democracy in this sense, the political state as such disappears as the alienation of ordinary life from a "heavenly universality" is overcome.

As a corollary of this commitment to democracy, Marx condemned Hegel's treatment of the civil service as "bureaucracy," a theological "illusion of the state," "something apart from and alien to the nature of civil society." The resolution of this alienation was simply the further application of democracy. In Marx's words:

> What counts in the genuine state is not the chance of any citizen to devote himself to the universal class as something special but the capacity of the universal class to be actually universal, that is, to be the class of every citizen. But Hegel proceeds from the premise of a pseudo-universal, an illusory unreal class, from the premise of universality as a particular class.[6]

For the implementation of democracy Marx insisted on "unlimited voting" whereby man's individual political existence would become genuinely universal, and the alienation between the "heavenly universality" of the state on the one hand and life in civil society on the other would be overcome. "Within the abstract political state," Marx concluded, "the reform of voting is the dissolution of the state, but likewise the dissolution of civil society."[7] It is the dissolution of civil society, because civil society—the realm of economic interests, social classes, and labor which Hegel, following Hobbes, well characterized as "the war of all against all"—is authentically universalized. It is absorbed into democracy, into "socialized man as a particular constitution." Here is Marx's first conception of socialism in outline. It includes the dissolution of civil society—the existing organization of labor and industry—with the achievement of democracy as self-government through unrestricted voting. Marx reaffirmed this position two years later in the notebook containing his "Theses on Feuerbach." After linking the French Revolution with the "presumption of the political sphere," after distinguishing between centralized "state admin-

istration and communal administration," Marx concluded with
a reference to "Suffrage, the struggle for the transcendence
[*Aufhebung*] of the state and civil society."[8]

In his published essay "On the Jewish Question," Marx further
developed the theme of political alienation from his unpublished
dissection of Hegel's view of the state. Substituting Feuerbach's
idea of man's "species-life" for Hegel's concept of "universality,"
Marx described the split between man's political life and his
life in civil society:

> Where the political state has achieved full development, man leads
> a double life, a heavenly and an earthly life, not only in thought
> or consciousness but in *actuality*. In the political community he
> regards himself as a communal being, but in civil society he is
> active as a private individual, treats other men as means, and
> becomes the plaything of alien powers.[9]

Thus Marx was becoming as much concerned with alienation in
civil society as with alienation in relation to the state. He found
alienation especially apparent in money which, like all religious
objects, becomes a fetish with an independent power that
diminishes man and detracts from his personal worth. As Marx
put it:

> As long as man is captivated in religion, knows his nature only as
> objectified, and thereby converts his nature into an alien illusory being,
> so under the domination of egoistic need he can only affirm himself
> practically, only practically produce objects, by subordinating both
> his products and his actuality to the domination of an alien being,
> bestowing upon them the significance of an alien entity—money.[10]

Marx saw Judaism and Christianity in practice as expressions of
this alienation. Hence full human emancipation, a full resolution
of this alienation, could not come with bills of rights making
religion merely a private affair. Such rights do not go beyond
"the egoistic man, the man withdrawn into himself, his private
interest and his private choice, and separated from the community
as a member of civil society." Political emancipation through
bills of human rights, Marx allowed, is a great step forward. But
it fails to answer man's social nature and fails to make his
species-life real. Full emancipation requires democracy where
the sovereignty of man has become "a tangible reality, a secular

maxim." With Christianity that sovereignty remains a "chimera, dream, and postulate." The basis of democracy is thus "not Christianity but the human ground of Christianity"—a statement revealing the positive content of Marx's criticism of religion. His conclusion specifies the nature of that full human emancipation which can end man's alienation in civil society:

> Only when the actual, individual man has taken back into himself the abstract citizen and in his everyday life, his individual work, and his individual relations has become a *species being*, only when he has recognized and organized his own powers as social powers so that social force is no longer separated from him as political power, only then is human emancipation complete.[11]

This conclusion has been identified as the point at which Marx became a socialist, but its substance had already been achieved earlier in his view of democracy whereby civil society is absorbed into "socialized man" through unrestricted voting.

With his "Introduction to the Critique of Hegel's Philosophy of Law" Marx further applied Feuerbach's view of alienation and found in the proletariat the lever for the full human emancipation he earlier identified as democracy. With Feuerbach, Marx saw man as the basis of religion but man must be understood concretely and socially as "the world of men, the state, society." Marx had already complained that Feuerbach was "too much concerned with nature and too little with politics." Hence "The immediate task of philosophy which is in the service of history," Marx insists, "is to unmask human self-alienation in its unholy forms now that it has been unmasked in its holy form."[12] This requires criticism of law and politics and transcendence of philosophy by putting it into practice with "the categorical imperative to overthrow all conditions in which man is a degraded, enslaved, neglected, contemptible being." Thus Marx formulated the resolution of man's social as well as religious alienation in terms of Kant's central ethical norm. But the actualization of philosophy in practice requires action against the German *status quo* by a sphere of civil society having a universal character, a universal human title, "which cannot emancipate itself without emancipating itself from all other spheres of society, thereby emancipating them"—namely, the proletariat.

Marx's selection of the proletariat as the key to full human emancipation was undoubtedly influenced by many factors—his reading in Lorenz Stein and Flora Tristan on the proletariat, his discussions with socialists in Paris, his own financial distress in exile, and his close contact with French workers. But his preoccupation with Hegel was also a factor. He had read in Hegel that with development of industry "a great mass of people sink down below a certain subsistence and thus suffer a loss of a sense of right and law and of the honor to exist by one's own activity and labor." This "produces the proletariat [*Pöbel*] which in turn again further promotes the concentration of riches in a few hands."[13] Further, Marx's discussion of the proletariat followed Hegel's dialectic—namely, a class in chains is to destroy all chains; a particular class is to end classes; the complete loss of humanity is to redeem humanity.

Thus Marx was beginning to supplement Feuerbach from whom he had derived the idea of alienation by using Hegel's dialectic of reason to formulate and resolve alienation. This is further apparent in an exchange of letters with Ruge to launch the *Deutsch-Französische Jahrbücher*, particularly in Marx's last letter composed after he had finished "An Introduction to the Critique of Hegel's Philosophy of Law." Criticizing the socialism of Weitling, Proudhon and others as one-sided "abstractions" from "the reality of true human nature," Marx called for criticism of existing political developments. In Marx's words:

Reason has always existed, but not always in reasonable form. The critic, therefore, can start with any form of theoretical and practical consciousness and develop the true actuality out of the forms inherent in existing actuality as its ought-to-be and goal. As far as actual life is concerned, the political state contains in all its modern forms the demands of reason, even where the political state is not yet conscious of the socialistic demands. . . . We develop new principles for the world out of the principles of the world.[14]

Thus Marx viewed socialism not as a dogmatic anticipation of the future but as the fulfillment of historical reason which criticism, the measurement of actuality against the Idea, was to bring to light. He had already arrived at his view of democracy and full human emancipation through such criticism of Hegel reinforced by the humanistic principle from Feuerbach.

By the end of 1843, then, Marx had reached the main outlines of his socialism through an application of "alienation" which

leaned heavily on Feuerbach to reject one aspect of Hegel's
philosophy while retaining another. Marx continued to use the
idea of alienation extensively in his writings up to 1848. It was
prominent in the *Economic-Philosophical Manuscripts of 1844*
where Marx criticized Hegel's speculative method as the "alienation of man's nature." He enthusiastically followed Feuerbach,
"the true conqueror of the old philosophy," and adopted
Feuerbach's empiricism—also called "materialism," a common
usage of the day—as the resolution of speculative alienation. As
opposed to speculation, genuine thought is rooted in sense-
perception, the object, nature, and such perception involves the
social relaton of man-to-man. On this basis, Marx concluded,
"Natural science will in time include the science of man as the
science of man will include natural science: There will be one
science."[15] This resolution of alienation has been taken—over-
hastily, in view of Marx's criticism of Feuerbach to follow—as
evidence that Marx's commitment to an empirical, scientific
sociology had decisively eclipsed his Hegelianism.

Further, the *Manuscripts of 1844* utilized the concept of
alienation to analyze in detail the characteristic sphere of civil
society related to man's economic life, labor and its relationship
to commodities. Marx found man alienated from himself both
in the process of labor and in its product. The *Manuscripts*
particularly leaned on Hegel's *Phenomenology of Mind* where
wealth and state-power are viewed as alienations overcome in
the movement of experience toward absolute knowledge.
Marx warmly endorsed Hegel's insight that man is the historical
product of his own work in a process of alienation and its
resolution.[16] Hegel's mistake was to treat that process speculatively, as a purely conceptual development of knowledge rather
than as a dialectical development in perceptible, historical practice.

Both of these themes of alienation—alienation in unempirical
speculation and alienation in the dialectical movement of labor
in the proletariat—appear in the esoteric polemics of *The Holy
Family*. But they are more pointedly and fully developed in
The German Ideology of 1845 which Marx and Engels wrote
"to settle accounts" with their philosophic conscience. Here
Marx and Engels observe that man's own activity in government,
wealth, and culture "becomes to him an alien power, standing
over against him instead of being ruled by him." The remedy
is "communism," a "real community" in which "the contradiction between the separate individual family and the interest

of all" has been overcome by healing the cleavage between production and consumption, between intellectual and manual labor, arising from division of labor in modern industry. This involves the abolition of the state, social classes, and all existing forms of association which express man's self-alienation. The alien and seemingly independent powers which fetter men—the state, class, industry, religion—are brought under their control so there is nothing independent of self-active, associated individuals.[17]

This remedy for alienation rounds out Marx's earlier view of democracy and full human emancipation. But it is not, we are now warned, a speculative conclusion. Quite the opposite. Its foundation is "real individuals, their activity, and the material conditions under which they live," and such premises can be verified "in a purely empirical way." This empiricism from Feuerbach, however, does not save him from criticism. Marx accuses him of having an "abstract" view of human nature, of seeing man's nature as something fixed and isolated rather than as an "ensemble of social relations," to quote the "Theses on Feuerbach." In view of Marx's previous reliance on Feuerbach, this criticism is somewhat surprising. Marx had praised and adopted Feuerbach's view of man as a "species-being." He had agreed with Feuerbach that "the essence of man exists only in community, in the unity of man with man." What then was Feuerbach's deficiency? Specifically, he lacked an historical view of man and particularly a dialectical view of man's development in relation to industry and labor.[18] Hence his remedy for man's alienation could only be an ideal to be contemplated, an idealistic "ought" as suggested in the preface to *The Essence of Christianity*. For Marx the overcoming of man's alienation in communism was something different. It was the dialectic of reason in history manifest in the movement of labor, industry, and the social classes within civil society. Thus Feuerbach's deficiency was corrected by the "rational kernel" from Hegel that Marx acknowledged in his preface to *Capital* in 1872.

Engels emphasized this debt to Hegel in a review of the *Critique of Political Economy* first published in America by August Willich in the *Cincinnati Republikaner, Organ der Arbeiter*.[19] Hegel's dialectic, Engels insisted, was scarcely less important in Marx's position than the economic basis of society. Willich, in turn, saw Marx's use of Hegel's dialectic as its proof and evidence that Hegel was "the greatest philosopher of the 19th century." With all his criticism of Hegel, then, Marx retained an essential aspect of his thought—the dialectic of reason in history—and used it to amend the empiricism he found in Feuerbach. As Franz Mehring asserted, Marx "went beyond Feuerbach by going back to Hegel."

Marx's earliest use of "alienation" highlights his commitment to democracy which was extended into "full human emancipation" and communism. But there is ambiguity here as to the status of the individual, an ambiguity made important by totalitarianism and the increase of conformity from increased social and economic organization. On the one side, Marx implicitly condemned safeguards for the individual in "the so-called rights of men" as pertaining only to "the egoistic man, the man withdrawn into himself and separated from the community as a member of civil society." They were characteristic of a republic which is still a form of political alienation to be superseded. Later they were treated as mere tactical concessions for political publicity or ideological reflections of the interest of the bourgeoisie which is to disappear under communism. On the other side, Marx insisted on unrestricted voting, warned against establishing "society" as an abstraction over and against the individual, and described communism not as a state but an *association* where there is nothing independent of self-active individuals. Later he identified the Paris commune as "fuller democracy" involving universal suffrage, free discussion, and "self government of the producers." Perhaps this ambiguity is a result of differing emphasis as required by different circumstances, but it certainly obscures the relation of Marx's thought to liberal democracy.

There does seem to be, however, a serious and unresolved conflict between the empiricism Marx took over from Feuerbach and the rationalism he retained from Hegel. With empiricism Marx criticized abstractions and speculative "mystification." In *The Holy Family* his analysis of the Hegelian idea of "fruit" would please the most ardent logical empiricist. On the other side, the "rational kernel" from Hegel led Marx to view social facts through the spectacles of a dialectical movement of "proletariat," "wealth," "civil society," and "bourgeoisie." From this perspective he later condemned the views of Auguste Comte as "miserable compared to Hegel's." When Joseph

Dietzgen, whom Marx introduced as "our philosopher," developed from Feuerbach a view of knowledge which strikingly anticipated Ernst Mach and recent logical empiricism, Marx criticized it precisely for not having absorbed Hegel. Marx's rationalism is strikingly apparent in Marcuse's *Reason and Revolution* where the socialist "realm of freedom" is seen as "reason determining itself."[20] The "rational kernel" from Hegel was the source of Marx's over-simplified view of class-conflict and the dialectical "cunning" whereby intensification of class violence is supposed to end violence and increasing the power of the centralized state, as in the *Manifesto*, is supposed to make it "wither away."

Possibly a cogent synthesis of rationalism and empiricism would have appeared in the treatise on dialectic Marx intended to write but never did. Such a synthesis would, of course, have a place for abstractions as general concepts without which knowledge is impossible. There is a hint of such a synthesis in Marx's linkage of theory to "practice" in his aphoristic "Theses on Feuerbach" and unfinished *German Ideology*, but it is little more than a hint, and the juxtaposition of rationalism and empiricism in his early use of "alienation" remains more a problem than a solution, more an invitation to further philosophical work than a place to rest.

NOTES

1. Cf. D. Rjazanov, ed., *Marx-Engels Gesamtausgabe* [hereafter MEGA] (Frankfurt, Berlin, 1927–), Abt. I, Bd. 1^1, p. xi; Engels on Marx's early writings, *Reminiscences of Marx and Engels* (Moscow, n.d.), pp. 300f.

2. Marx, "Aus der Kritik der Hegelschen Rechtsphilosophie [1843]," MEGA, Abt. I, Bd. 1^1, pp. 406, 404, 414.

3. Cf. Ludwig Feuerbach, *Kleine Philosophische Sshriften* (Leipzig, 1950).

4. Marx, "Aus der Kritik," p. 435. A few years later J. B. Stallo of Cincinnati, Ohio, defended democracy on the basis of a similar internal criticism of Hegel. Cf. Stallo, *General Principles of the Philosophy of Nature* (Boston, 1848), pp. 158-62, 517f.

5. Marx, "Aus der Kritik," p. 436.

6. Ibid., p. 460.

7. Ibid., p. 544.

8. MEGA, I, 5, p. 532.

9. Marx, "Zur Judenfrage," MEGA, Abt. I, Bd. 1^1, p. 584.

10. Ibid., p. 605.

11. Ibid., p. 599.

12. Marx, "Zur Kritik der Hegelschen Rechtsphilosophie. Einleitung," MEGA, Abt. I, Bd. 1^1, p. 608 passim.

13. Hegel, *Philosophy of Law*, S243-44.

14. Marx, "Ein Briefwechsel von 1843," MEGA, Abt. I, Bd. 1^1, p. 574.

15. Marx, "Okonomisch-philosophische Manuskripte [1844]," MEGA, Abt. I, Bd. 3, p. 123.

16. Cf. ibid., p. 157 passim.

17. Cf. Marx and Engels, *The German Ideology*, trans. R. Pascal (New York, 1939), pp. 22f., 74f.

18. Cf. ibid., pp. 35ff.; Feuerbach, *The Essence of Christianity*, trans. George Eliot (New York, 1957), p. xxxiv.

19. [Engels,] "Karl Marx, Zur Kritik der Politischen Ökonomie (Dem 'Volk' entonommen)," *Cincinnati Republikaner*, ed. August Willich, September 15, 1859, p. 2; Engels, *Ludwig Feuerbach* (New York, 1941), pp. 70-81; Franz Mehring, *Karl Marx*, trans. E. Fitzgerald (New York, 1939), pp. 306ff.

20. Cf. Marx and Engels, *Selected Correspondence* (New York, 1942), p. 210, on Comte's "positivist rot" and 252f. on Dietzgen; L. D. Easton, "Empiricism and Ethics in Dietzgen, *Journal of The History of Ideas* 19 (1958): 77-83; H. A. Marcuse, *Reason and Revolution* (New York, 1954), pp. 271 passim, 315-330.

Chapter 25

On Alienation and the Social Order

IRVING LOUIS HOROWITZ

Irving Louis Horowitz is professor of sociology at Rutgers University, director of Studies in Comparative International Development, and chairman of the sociology department in the experimental Livingston College of Rutgers. He has taught at Washington University and other American, as well as foreign, institutions, including the London School of Economics and the University of Buenos Aires. He is editor-in-chief of TRANS-action, has edited several volumes, and is the author of *Philosophy, Science, and the Sociology of Knowledge* (1960), *Radicalism and the Revolt Against Reason* (1961), *The War Game* (1963), *Three Worlds of Development: The Theory and Practice of International Stratification* (1966), *Professing Sociology* (1969), and other books.

(1:1) Despite the incredible degree of confusion which exists about the term alienation—a confusion which has caused many influentials in sociology and psychology to try to do without it[1] —there is a danger in a premature scrapping of the term. There are few enough words in the vocabulary of social science having wide generic implications. In some sense the very confusions about the word alienation represent an acute, albeit painful, testimonial to a conceptual complication which exists in consequence of the autonomous development of the social and behavioral sciences. The heavy freight placed on such words as "anomie," "aggression," "intuition," "instinct," and now "alienation" is a burden better met by clarifying the meaning

325

of the term than by urging premature abandonment on the grounds that any word admitting of multiple different definitions is meaningless, or the equally spurious aim of preserving formal symmetry.

(1:2) The problem of the use of alienation, like so many other theoretical issues, was a debt to the philosophical ambiguities of nineteenth-century German realism. Nascent within German philosophical sources were the current schisms and polarization of meanings in the word alienation.

(1:3.1) Hegel argued that the true meaning of alienation lay in the separation of the object of cognition from the man of consciousness, the philosopher. Hence, for Hegel the chief way of overcoming alienation is through philosophical understanding, an embrace of the rational world; as if to know the world is somehow to be at one with that world, to become identified with it. To be reasonable for Hegel is the same as being at peace. It was in this problem that the equation of reality with rationality was the resolution of the problem of philosophical alienation; just as the reduction of reason to reasonableness was the resolution of the problem of practical alienation.

(1:3:2) In the philosophy of Ludwig Feuerbach, alienation comes to be seen as an anthropological problem. The word "anthropology" was being used as a surrogate for "psychology," since Feuerbach neither knew of nor really appreciated anthropology in any exact, empirical sense. Feuerbach considered the problem of alienation as a separation out, a parceling out, of human consciousness—one part of man is invested (properly) in the material world, and another to the world of God, the projective ideal world. In effect the dualism in Feuerbach is almost Platonic. The material world being dreary and dismal gives rise to a set of projections about a spiritual world of perfection. As long as these two worlds remain separated there cannot be any resolution of the problem of alienation.

(1:4) One can say, curiously enough, that the idealist, Hegel, is closer to a sociological view of alienation than the materialist, Feuerbach. The reason is that Hegel conceived of overcoming alienation by means of a set of activities which would connect up the subject of being with the object of the world, whereas in Feuerbach, the resolution of alienation is psychological in that it means an overcoming of the projective neurotic aspects of belief.

(1:4:1) It is a disservice to consider Marx's notion of alienation within a strictly philosophical framework, since Marx insisted upon the necessity of a social scientific resolution of what had up to then been viewed as a metaphysical or humanist dilemma. It was Marx himself who made the clear and decisive break with the philosophical tradition of explaining alienation. No longer was alienation a property of man or of reason, but it became a specific property of select classes of men in factory conditions who were, as a result of these conditions, deprived of their reasons, which is another way of saying that the labor context of alienation itself represented a scientific break with romanticism; a rupture consecrated in the bedrock of political revolution.

(1:5) At its source, the word "alienation" implies an intense separation first from objects in a world, second from other people, third from ideas about the world held by other people. It might be said that the synonym of alienation is separation, while the precise antonym of the word alienation is integration. The main difficulty with the philosophical traditions is the assumption that those who are defined as alienated are somehow lacking and that they ought to be integrated. In both Hegel and in Feuerbach therapeutic values are assigned to alienation and to integration, to the distinct disadvantage of the former and to the advantage of the latter. That is how we come to the phrasing of the term "alienated from" as somehow opposite to "integrated with." This mystic faith in organic union invariably found its way into the work of Hegel and Feuerbach, the mystic organic union being for Hegel man as idea and for Feuerbach idea as man. But to the degree that alienation was seen as a negative concept, to the same degree was the philosophical approach considered abstract, and unreliable in terms of psychological and sociological facts.

(1:6) The really important break therefore which began with Marx is that in the modern usage of the concept of alienation, there is a distinctive concern for distinguishing therapy from description, and separating recommendations from analysis. There is in the dialectical approach a common belief that alienation is no better and no worse than integration, that either concept might serve positive social ends. Alienation is a driveshaft of revolution; and integration is a transitional equilibrium generating new forms of separation from the mainstream, i.e., new forms of alienation.

(2:0) Let us now examine three fundamental categories of the concept alienation.

(2:1) In the first place, let us take the psychological meanings of alienation. Perhaps the classic definition is that given by Fromm: "By alienation is meant a mode of experience in which the person experiences himself as alien. He has become, one might say, estranged from himself."[2] It is important to take note of the fact that Fromm severely modifies the Marxian concept. He gives a definition which converts a "mode of production" into a "mode of experience," while the Marxian proletarian laborer is neatly converted back into the Hegelian abstract person. It is evident in the work of Fromm that he is not just concerned with providing a psychological approach to alienation, but he is also giving renewed vigor to the older German romantic categorizations.

(2:1:1) Alienation is often used as psychological surrogate in the literature. Instead of being employed as a phenomenon of separation, it is used as a phenomenon of negation, or even of "lessness"—a suffix prefaced by "power-lessness," "norm-lessness," or "meaning-lessness." In this kind of approach, alienation becomes either part of a major body of literature on anomie, or in turn swallows up anomie. The difficulty is that this definition of alienation as negation does not connect up various forms of negation. Further, alienation as anomie tends to describe the social system in terms of an assumed rationality: that which has the power, norms, and meanings which is contrasted with the personality system or that which is not a condition of rationality.[3]

(2:1:2) At its most elevated form, the psychological definition of "alienation" is linked to the notion of ideology. This in turn is fused with the notion of how intellectuals view their roles in a social world. "A great deal of contemporary thought finds a state of alienation precisely in those ideologies which profess to predict with high confidence the outcome of people's behavior. Intellectuals especially find themselves alienated in a world of social determinism; they wish for a world in which the degree of social predictability would be low."[4] In Feuer's concept of alienation, the notion turns out to be much more positive in its potential effects than in almost any other theory. With Feuer it is almost as if one has to overcome integration to arrive at scientific truth rather than overcoming alienation. Integration is held to yield precisely

the kind of normlessness which is characteristic of an identification with rootlessness and machinelike behavior in general.
Feuer thus offers a prototype of what in the literary tradition of
Zamyatin, Huxley, and Orwell is the alienated man as an anti-
utopian—a social realist.

(2:1:3) The main contribution of the psychological school
of alienation has been to demonstrate the universality of the
concept, its connection to the personality structure as well as
the social structure, and therefore its existence in socialist
societies no less than in capitalist societies.[5] The psychological
school holds that the foundation, the reservoir of nonpartici-
pation in the social system (or even refusal to participate in
that system) may be constructive as well as destructive. In this
sense alienation is more akin to defiance than it is to disorganization. It is not a synonym for neurosis or psychosis so much
as it is a notion of marginality, which is consciously or unconsciously held. The problem of alienation stems more from
a lack of accurate perception of the norms than an active
defiance of these norms.

(2:2:1) The sociological tradition is perhaps a consequence
of this distinction between psychic disorganization and social
disorganization. A whole new set of variables is called into
force. In this Marx himself set the tone, since alienation was
viewed as the particular response of the working man to the
externality of the product he produced. It was, in effect, a
class phenomenon.

What, then, constitutes the alienation of labor? First, the fact
that labor is *external* to the worker, i.e., it does not belong to
his essential being; that in his work, therefore, he does not affirm
himself but denies himself, does not feel content but unhappy,
does not develop freely his physical and mental energy but
mortifies his body and ruins his mind. The worker therefore only
feels himself outside his work, and in his work feels outside
himself. He is at home when he is not working, and when he is
working he is not at home. His labor is therefore not voluntary,
but coerced; it is *forced labor*. It is therefore not the satisfaction
of a need; it is merely a *means* to satisfy needs external to it. Its
alien character emerges clearly in the fact that as soon as no
physical or other compulsion exists, labor is shunned like the
plague. External labor, labor in which man alienates himself, is a
labor of self-sacrifice, of mortification. The external character of
labor for the worker appears in the fact that it is not his own, but
someone else's that it does not belong to him, that in it he belongs,
not to himself, but to another. Just as in religion the spontaneous

activity of the human imagination, of the human brain and the
human heart, operates independently of the individual—that is,
operates on him as an alien, divine or diabolical activity—in the same
way the worker's activity is not his spontaneous activity. It belongs
to another. It is the loss of his self.[6]

(2:2:2) Once Marx opened this Pandora's box of the social
and cross-cultural locale of alienation, it was just a matter of
time before others would see alienation of different social
sectors from those Marx had dealt with. Thus, for example, in
a modern view of bourgeois society, that held by C. Wright
Mills, alienation comes to be understood as a lower middle-
class phenomenon, something which debases salesgirls, technicians, and even intellectuals in a similar way. In this, Mills
provided not only a bridge from one class to another, but
even more importantly, a way of viewing alienation as a problem
for all nonruling classes, and not only the factory-anchored
urban proletariat. "In the normal course of her work, because
her personality becomes the instrument of an alien purpose,
the salesgirl becomes self-alienated. Men are estranged from
one another as each secretly tries to make an instrument of
the other, and in time a full circle is made: One makes an instrument of himself and is estranged from it also."[7]

(2:2:3) Most recently we have had the example of alienation
as a specific artistic problem, as a problem connected to the
marketing of ideas rather than to the production of goods. In
this sense alienation is seen to have different functional prerequisites. The new work by Moravia contains a clear delineation
of the alienation of the worker from the alienation of the artist.
He offers a clearly defined expression of qualitatively different
notions of alienation that are involved in different social sectors.
In this approach there is an attempt to link alienation to specific
types of work done, and hence to a fragmentation of the notion
of alienation rather than fragmentation of the notion of
stratification.

(2:2:4) The standard sociological perspective is to see alienation
as a phenomenon of a unitary type, with differences being attributed
to the stratification system. In Moravia, quite to the contrary, we
have the unique case of a stratification system giving rise to
different forms of alienation. In this we have a more advanced
sociological notion of alienation than any thus far given. "There
is no relationship between the alienation of the worker and
the alienation of the artist. The worker is alienated because,

in the economy of the market, he is a piece of goods like any other and as such he is defrauded of his surplus value, or of what represents his value as a man, whereas the artist creates an object that has no market (or, if it has, it is not that of necessities that always have a market) and no real price in money or kind. The artist receives the price of his work of art in creating it. In other words, when he hands his book over to the publisher, his music to the conductor, or his painting to the art dealer, the artist has already been paid and whatever he receives after that is a bonus. Hence the alienation of the artist consists in the total or partial prevention of his expression, or of his true relationship with society."[8]

(2:3:1) The third general variety of alienation theory is based on considering it as part of a general cultural milieu. Within this framework, we find ideology spoken of in national terms, that is, the American ideology, the Soviet ideology, etc.; whereas Marx, in dealing with the German ideology, dealt with that ideology as it was a reflection of the ruling class diffused throughout the general society of the times. The newer cultural pluralistic approach emphasizes the mass cultural approach. Boorstin offers a particularly interesting variety of this approach.

We expect anything and everything. We expect the contradicting and the impossible. We expect compact cars which are spacious; luxurious cars which are economical. We expect to be rich and charitable, powerful and merciful, active and reflective, kind and competitive. We expect to be inspired by mediocre appeals for "excellence," to be made literate by illiterate appeals for literacy. We expect to eat and stay thin, to be constantly on the move and ever more neighborly, to go to a "church of our choice" and yet feel its guiding power over us, to revere God and to be God. Never have people been more the masters of their environment. Yet never have a people felt more deceived and disappointed. For never has a people expected so much more than the world could offer.[9]

(2:3:2) The culturalist approach is no less critical of alienation as a status than any of the other approaches. Even from the quotation just read one can see their criticism is severe. What is new and particularly interesting is the assumption of the national character from which the concept of alienation flows. The mass cultural school at its peak, with men like Dwight Macdonald and David Riesman, represents an interesting fusion of the psychological and sociological approaches. Alienation comes to be seen as a discrepancy, a measurable discrepancy, of achievements and expectations. At the general sociocultural level, it is a discrepancy between national demands or national purposes and individual demands for an extension of autonomy and pluralism.[10]

(2:3:3) One final expression of this cultural style is the tradition of alienation as a religious phenomenon, specifically, alienation as characteristic of marginal religious groupings. This view of alienation held by men like Karl Barth, Paul Tillich, and Martin Buber has strong ties to Feuerbach. Commentary on the current status of Jews in America is illustrative. As Isaac Rosenfeld once said, "Jews are specialists in alienation." They are alienated from a Diaspora, alienated from a redemptive God, and alienated from nationalism as such.[11] Of course, alienation as an authentic religious expression has become a major theme for all Western religions.

(2:3:4) This view of alienation as marginal has a great deal in common with the psychological view, just as the mass cultural view has a great deal in common with the sociological view. One can begin to detect a synthesis taking place in present-day expectations of alienation: a systematic linkage of psychological states, sociological classes, and cultural forms.

(3:1) The location of the problem has now decisively shifted. The problem is no longer a fusion of psychological or sociological cultural techniques. The study of alienation is now confronted with a distinction between two modalities of analyses, one formal and the other descriptive. The formal system tends to emphasize the root categories, such as those provided by Seeman in his work, or operationalized definitions capable of survey designs such as those provided by Nettler.[12] Descriptive analysis tends to emphasize the weaknesses in the psychological approach by pointing out that the formal modes of analysis are invariably ad hoc. They provide little indication, however, of how the types of alienation or the models built are related to each other or why they should be restricted to three, four, or five in number. Descriptive approaches tend to see alienation in a problem-solving context. It has a big problem in settling upon the relation of alienation to deviance, marginality, creativitiy, etc. But it does have the value of linking itself to empirical, rather than logical modalities.[13]

(3:2) It might well be that this is simply a social scientific reflex of the ongoing debate concerning the analytical and synthetic modes of argument. Whatever the case may be, it is clear that the literature on alienation has tapped into something extremely meaningful in the emergence of modern social science. Once the various meanings and levels at which the term alienation is employed can be properly understood, then social scientists will be better able to employ alienation as a central variable in discussing other features of social structure and process. The task of philosophy in this area might be a clarifying one, to show how various usages of alienation are either synonymous, overlapping, or entirely different from one another. The philosopher might develop some kind of logical or periodic table of alienation. I am given to understand that this is what modern philosophy of science is all about.

NOTES

1. For example, the following representative collections carry no information on alienation: Bernard Berelson and Gary A. Stelner, *Human Behavior: An Inventory of Scientific Findings* (New York: Harcourt, Brace & World, 1964); Solomon E. Asch, *Social Psychology* (Englewood Cliffs, N. J.: Prentice-Hall, 1952); and Robert K. Merton, Leonard Broom, Leonard S. Cottrell, Jr., *Sociology Today: Problems and Prospects* (New York: Basic Books, 1959).

2. Erich Fromm, *The Sane Society* (New York: Rinehart, 1955), pp. 120-121.

3. Melvin Seeman, "On the Meaning of Alienation," *Sociological Theory,* ed. L. A. Coser and B. Rosenberg (New York: Macmillan Co., 1964), 2nd ed., pp. 525-538.

4. Lewis Feuer, "What Is Alienation? The Career of a Concept," *Sociology on Trial,* eds. M. Stein and A. Vidich (Englewood Cliffs, N. J.: Prentice-Hall, 1963), pp. 127-147.

5. Adam Schaff, *A Philosophy of Man* (New York: Monthly Review Press, 1963).

6. Karl Marx, *Economic and Philosophic Manuscripts of 1844* (London: Lawrence and Wishart, 1959), pp. 67-84.

7. C. Wright Mills, *White Collar* (New York: Oxford University Press, 1951, 1956-1957), pp. 182-188.

8. Alberto Moravia, *Man as an End* (New York: Farrar, Straus, and Giroux, 1965-1966).

9. Daniel Boorstin, *The Image* (New York: Atheneum Publishers, 1961), pp. 3-6.

10. See in particular the recent collection of papers by David Riesman, *Abundance for What? And Other Essays* (Garden City: Doubleday, 1964).

11. Irving Malin, *Jews and Americans* (Carbondale, Ill.: Southern Illinois University Press, 1965). For an earlier consideration of Jewish alienation, see Simon Dubnow, *Nationalism and History* (Cleveland, New York: Meridian Books, 1961).

12. Gwynn Nettler, "A Measure of Alienation, *American Sociological Review* 22 (1957); and see his earlier paper, "A Test for the Sociology of Knowledge," *American Sociological Review* 10 (1945).

13. Marvin B. Scott, "The Social Sources of Alienation," *The New Sociology*, ed. Irving L. Horowitz (New York and London: Oxford University Press, 1964), pp. 239-252.

Part VIII

MARXISM AND EXISTENTIALISM

Chapter 26

Marxist Humanism and Existential Philosophy

JOHN WILD

The late John Wild was professor of philosophy at the University of Florida and earlier taught at Harvard, Yale, and Northwestern universities. He was a Guggenheim Fellow, a Powell Lecturer, and president of the American Philosophical Association. His books include *Plato's Modern Enemies and the Theory of Natural Law, The Challenge of Existentialism, Human Freedom and Social Order, Existence and the World of Freedom* (1963), and *The Radical Empiricism of William James* (1969).

If we look at the intellectual life of the world at the present time, I believe it is fair to say that there are two living philosophies which are actively growing and attempting to grapple with the concrete problems of living men. The analytic and linguistic philosophy which is still dominant in the Anglo-Saxon world, and which is absorbing much of our attention at this meeting,[1] cannot be so characterized. It is preoccupied with abstract problems which, no doubt, have their place, but which are remote from the vital concerns of living men. One indication of this is its indifference to the issues of social and political philosophy. I do not believe that this separation of critical reflection from the issues of lived existence is a healthy condition, for as it widens and deepens, professional thinking becomes a mere academic game, and the thinking of living men becomes provincial and fanatical. So I am glad to note that this divorce is a relatively local phenomenon.

The situation is different in other parts of the world, where the two styles of philosophizing I have mentioned are actively concerned with the questions of living men. These are phenomenology and existential philosophy in France and other countries of the Western world, and Marxism in Eastern Europe and the East. It is important to notice, I think, that these two movements of thought originated with two negative criticisms of the great speculative system of Hegel, that of Marx on the one hand, and that of Kierkegaard on the other. As discerning critics have now pointed out, there is a basic similarity in these two reactions to Hegel's philosophy. Both find it to be abstract and remote from the hard realities of actual life. Thus according to Marx, man is not an abstract consciousness concerned with ideal objects of thought. As he says: "the fact that man is *embodied,* living, real, sentient, objective being with natural powers, means that he has *real, sensuous objects* as the objects of his being. . . ."[2]   And in his *Postcript,* Kierkegaard asks of the abstract philosopher, "Is he a human being or is he speculative philosophy in the abstract?"[3] Both are trying to make philosophy more self-conscious, to see itself as it is, as belonging to human existence. But here a major point of difference emerges.

Human alienation is the central concept of the early writings of Marx. Man is dehumanized and forced to deal with himself as a thing by a system of production and exchange that is out of control. Human labor has lost its intrinsic value, and is bought and sold on the market as a commodity. This is an antisocial social system which separates each abstract individual from his fellows by a destructive competition in which success is judged by the amount of money, or things, possessed by him as against the others. As Marx says: "the division of labor and exchange are the two phenomena which lead the economist to vaunt the social character of his science, while in the same breath he unconsciously expresses the contradictory nature of his science—the establishment of society through unsocial particular interests."[4]

This is a disease of our social existence which can be corrected on a large scale only by a revolution that will regain control over the system of production and exchange by force. These primarily social and economic interests are evident in Marx's early writings, and become more pronounced as his thought matured. Hence it is not surprising that Marxism has brought forth revolutionary social action involving masses of men, and a mode of thought, joined to such action, that focuses on social and economic patterns and laws in an objective and scientific way, with little attention to individual existence as it is lived from within.

Kierkegaard *was* concerned with the individual human person and his self-alienation in the industrial society of the early nineteenth century. One symptom of this dehumanizing of the individual person is the way in which his fragile, ever-unfinished, contingent existence is ignored and apparently assimilated into the great conceptual system of Hegel. In his prophetic work *The Present Age,* Kierkegaard describes the many ways in which everything that is unique and personally authentic gets leveled down and streamlined into those de-personalized modes of thinking and acting which rule our alienated public life.[5] In the press, even when an author signs his individual name, he does not think or speak for himself. He sees the sort of thing that one sees, and says what one says in the given situation. But one evades choice, never repents, and postpones the thought of death. According to the Danish thinker, choice is the greatest thing that has been given to the individual. Kierkegaard devoted all his great imaginative powers to describing this individual existence as it is lived through in its major modes—the aesthetic, the ethical, and the religious—and to appealing indirectly for authentic existence in the ethico-religious mode which was his primary concern. For seventy-five years or so, his books gathered dust on the library shelves until, in the 1920s, they were read by thinkers like Jaspers, Heidegger, Sartre, and others in France. Through them, he has inaugurated a new style of existential thinking which now, in union with phenomenology, has become one of the two living philosophies of our time. It has not expressed itself in the form of large-scale social revolutions, for it is basically concerned with human freedom, and it does not agree with Rousseau that individuals can be forced to be free. Some of the difficulties may be removed by social organization. But in the last analysis, freedom and responsibility can only be elicited by what Kierkegaard called *indirect discourse,* and by what we call an *appeal.* As William James pointed out, freedom

cannot be proved to anyone by an objective demonstration.
If he is to become free, he must first believe in it, and then
decide to act freely on his own.

Existential philosophy already has had a marked effect on
literature and the arts, on psychiatry, and on some of the
human sciences, including sociology.[6] Its influence on individual existence as it is lived in our contemporary societies cannot be
measured. It has already created a literature intelligible to
the general reader, which reveals more clearly many patterns
of lived existence and which is capable of eliciting better
informed and more authentic choices for this individual.

But these two living philosophies of our time, in spite of
their common origin in similar reactions to the system of Hegel,
now seem to have become radically separated from each other.
In the East, we have a socially oriented Marxist style of
thought focused on social and political problems, but until
very recently paying little disciplined attention to the forms
of individual alienation with which Kierkegaard was concerned.
On the other hand, in the West, we find a personally oriented
style of thought focused on problems of individual existence
but paying little or no disciplined attention to the forms of
social and political alienation with which Marx was concerned.
But can we believe that these two types of alienation are
totally disconnected?

We may grant that there is a distinction between the large-
scale patterns of objective, social existence (*objectiver Geist,*
as Hegel called it) and the patterns of subjective individual
existence (*subjectiver Geist*). These social patterns must be
internalized and lived through by individuals who exist with
others. The subjective existence of the individual cannot be
separated from the objective existence of the group, and we
cannot hope to gain an adequate understanding of the one
apart from the other. Hence both traditional Marxism and
traditional existentialism seem to be partial and incomplete.
Each may perhaps learn something from the other, and a
further synthesis of some sort is required.

It is now interesting to note that this has been recognized
in the East. For the last thirty years, the early writings of
Marx have been widely read and have elicited a humanistic
style of thought that is increasingly influential in the so-called
satellite countries. Thus an orthodox Marxist, like the Polish
philosopher Adam Schaff, rejects many of Sartre's existential

concepts as anti-Marxist. "But," he says, "if it is a matter of Marxism undertaking, on the basis of the Marxist method, a more thorough investigation of the problems of the individual, which it has tended to neglect and which have been monopolized by Existentialism, then we have here an important proposal."[7] A similar concern for the problems of the individual has been expressed in recent Russian literature, and in dialogue with similar Marxist writings from the West, more intensively humanist versions of Marxist thought have recently come from the European communist countries.

These Marxist humanists agree with Sartre that man inhabits a human world that is constantly constructed and maintained on a natural foundation by human thought and labor. They agree that man is alienated by the capitalist system of production and to some degree, at least, by public ownership, and the "crude communism," as Marx once called it, which still prevails in the East. They criticize the rigid dogmas of orthodox Marxism and the tyranny of the Stalinist era. They accept historical materialism in a qualified form, and reject scientific determinism. Many of them share a deep respect for the freedom of the individual person (Petrović) and an urge for the establishment of a free society, though they are skeptical of traditional conceptions of freedom. They recognize the need for understanding social injustices and social processes as they are lived through by existing individuals. They agree that a basis for these views and attitudes can be found in Marx's early writings of 1842-1844. Most of them use the terms "democracy" and "democratizing" in a good sense, and many of them speak of democratic socialism. In this they also agree with another existential side of Sartre who sometimes writes of an active "constituting dialectic" in which the members of a group maintain a real control over its fixed structures, and, as he puts it, "intero-condition" themselves from the inside in what we would call a democratic manner.

As we have noted, existential philosophy and phenomenology in the West have been concentrated almost exclusively on individual existence with no serious attention being paid to the structures of social life. This is certainly true of Heidegger's major work, *Sein und Zeit,* in spite of his remarks about *Mitsein* and the depersonalized mode of being he calls *das Man.*[8] But in the text, *Mitsein* remains a blank heading that is never filled in with any careful description and analysis. Certain

sympathetic commentators have held that Heidegger's social
philosophy is included in his discussions of history in the later
parts of *Sein und Zeit*. But these discussions are very general
and abstract, and they say nothing about what an authentic
mode of political existence might be, if indeed there is any,
not about the relation of the individual to the group, nor about
any of the basic social and political issues of our time. This
neglect of careful analysis of social structures is probably
responsible for Heidegger's commitment to Nazism. But while
this was no accident, it was grounded on certain peculiar
features of his thinking, and not on principles in any way
essential either to existential philosophy or to phenomenology,
as is quite clear from later developments in France.

Here we find existential thinkers of the first rank, thoroughly
familiar with the early as well as the later writings of Marx,
attempting to explore the social and political implications of
existential philosophy in a disciplined manner. Thus Merleau-
Ponty in the editorials we know that he wrote for *Les Temps
Modernes* and in many other published works, was engaging
in a constant dialogue with Marxist concepts and attitudes.
But the most detailed and systematic attempt to arrive at a
humanist synthesis of existential and Marxist thinking is to
be found in the work of Sartre, *Critique de la raison dialectique*.[9]

In comment, let me only say that this humanistic revision
of orthodox Marxism has been strongly influenced by ideas
coming from existential philosophy and phenomenology. It
certainly opens up possibilities for a fruitful dialectic with
Western thinkers moved by the ideals of individual freedom
and democracy, but not in the rigid form of what we may call
Western liberalism and atomic individualism. Are there any
signs in our time of a loosening of these Western dogmas
similar to the revisionist Marxist humanism in the East? I
believe that there has been such a development in France of
a revisionist theory of democracy strongly influenced by
Marxist conceptions.

Sartre himself believes that his critique is basically Marxist.
In this, I think he is mistaken. We should read *Critique de la
raison dialectique* rather as a study of social and political
phenomena that is basically existential. I believe that we should
understand it as his friend Merleau-Ponty would have understood it were he now alive, as the expression of an existential
humanism strongly influenced by Marxism, and, with certain

corrections, capable of leading us to a new conception of democracy in the West. Sartre describes at great length and with great accuracy the ways in which group structures freeze and petrify. He speaks of the great need, especially in the socialist world, for "debureaucratization, decentralization and democratization."[10] But his antidemocratic feelings, derived from traditional Marxism, prevent him from dwelling on the ways by which this need might be satisfied. Let me now try to suggest a democratic philosophy of existential humanism which might provide us with some ways and some hope for the control of this blind drift which certainly takes place, and which Western liberalism has never clearly brought into focus.

First a critical point against Sartre with which, I think, most Marxists will agree. The loosely ordered seriality of individuals is not the first source from which all forms of group existence originate. This is an individualistic interpretation which resembles certain constructions of Western Liberalism, such as the social-contract theory, but has no real foundation in the facts of history. These show that the free individual person is a late-comer on the stage of history, and that even when he does appear, his existence (and that of the serialities Sartre describes) always depends on highly organized social structures that are already established. Thus to take Sartre's example of the individuals at an intersection, waiting for a bus, presupposes the organization of the bus company and the complex social structures of the town or city, that is maintaining traffic lights and order on the streets.

Sartre's concern for the individual has prevented him from ever clearly bringing into focus the kind of unity and integrity that belongs to human groups, and makes group action possible. Hegel called this *objectiver Geist.* But in spite of his knowledge of Hegel, Sartre has never succeeded in sharply articulating it, for it is neither pure consciousness *(pour soi)* nor physical nature *(en soi),* and thus escapes from the oversimple dualistic ontology of *Being and Nothingness.*[11] A modern factory, for example, occupies a region of space. This region gives places to physical tools and instruments of many kinds. Yet this complex array is not to be confused with a set of physical objects, for each of these bears a meaning, and is ordered toward a human purpose. These meanings are understood and worked out by the conscious habits and attitudes of the workers and managers. This is an *intermonde* (Merleau-Ponty) of embodied meanings, inseparable from the physical tools and processes with which they are concerned. Sartre is right in rejecting the mythical theory of a factory substance, independent of the individual operators and managers. But in and through them, it has a certain unity and integrity. This complex of ordered instruments, and the conscious attitudes supporting them, can be referred to in the singular as the operations of *this* factory which has produced certain goods at a certain rate from one time to another, and *it* will probably produce certain others in the future.

Not in any sense *apart from* the individuals, but *in them* and their instruments, *this single* factory has a unity and wholeness of its own which enables us to refer to *its* past record, *its* present status, and *its* prospects for the future. It is constantly training new individuals to replace others in carrying on *its* operations, so that *they* are taken up into its system to become workers, managers, and owners. But though this bipolar (social *and* individual) aspect of what is commonly referred to as "the training process" has not been sufficiently studied, it also works in another direction. In order to be taken up by this system of purposively ordered machines and habits, the individual worker, and even more the manager, must also take it up into his own world, and gain some understanding of it for himself.

Hegel called this *subjectiver Geist,* and Sartre uses two words for it, sometimes *internalizing,* and sometimes the Marxist term *totalizing.* Thus the individual worker must know what he is doing in carrying out the particular operations of his lathe. He must also have an understanding of what these operations contribute to the final product, and of its place into the total economy. This gives the worker a certain essential flexibility in doing his work, so that he can meet unforeseen contingencies by new responses of his own.

Sartre rightly sees these creative responses of the individual worker, or member of any organized group, as the first source of social freedom and responsibility. But he fails to distinguish clearly between two levels at which this individual freedom may be exercised, and two very different forms of social order which result from them. Can this creative, totalizing power of the individual be kept under the control of drifting group patterns as they are already crystallized, or can it become responsible and take over this drift of frozen habit and apparatus,

which is always present, to control it for meaningful ends?
Because of his negative attitude toward "democracy," Sartre
does not take this possibility seriously. But this is a question
we need to focus and bear in mind.

At the first and lowest level, the creative flexibility of
individual thought and action is used solely for the maintenance
of the status quo. The individual is allowed a certain degree of
flexibility in performing his function, or in certain areas of
what is called *his private life*. Within these limits, some freedom,
identified with disorder, is permitted. But the methods of
extero-conditioning, described by Sartre, and mass propaganda
of many kinds, are used to keep these individuals satisfied with
the accepted social frame, to keep them separate from each
other in what Sartre calls a seriality, like the passive listeners
to a television broadcast, and to prevent them from questioning
the established order as a whole, from coming together to
discuss possible answers to these questions, and, above all, from
joining together in responsible groups which might take over
the blind drift of this crystallized objective existence, or OE
as we shall call it.

This leads to a collectivist society in which there are strong
pressures for social conformity, though some flexibility is
tolerated among separated individuals in the private sphere.
In such a society, the basic social patterns are taken for granted.
The individual feels responsible for his functions and for what
he does in the private sphere, not for the social order as a whole.
The leaders are responsible for maintaining the dynamics
of the status quo, not to the people but to the congealed order
itself, the nation, or the state. In such groups, neither the
individual members nor the leaders are really responsible. They
are governed by the blind drift of the established social patterns,
the OE, which is often supposed to be determined by inflexible
natural laws. But as modern revolutions have shown, this is a
misconception. It is determined rather by lethargy and blind
drift.

At the higher level of totalizing, on the other hand, the
individual gains a distance from his situation, and, as Sartre
sometimes suggests, internalizes it as a whole, so that he is
able to make critical judgments on his own. Then, emerging
from his serial isolation, he is able to communicate with other
free men, to join with them in movements of protest against
injustice, and finally in concerted, responsible action to take

over the drift of social power and to infuse it with new meaning
from day to day. This, I think, is what Sartre denies and what
we basically have in mind when we use the term *democracy.*
In such a democratic group, whether it be small or large, the
individual feels responsible not merely for his functions and
for what he does in private, but for the social order governing
his acts and works, and for what his leaders or representatives
do. These leaders, on the other hand, to whom we may refer
as a *democratic elite,* are responsible not only to the status
quo, but also to the people, for engaging in that meaningful
action *(praxis)* which emerges from free criticism and debate.
Such control over the blind drift of social apparatus and power
has sometimes been achieved by small localized groups. In
large-scale nation-states, it has never been more than remotely
approximated. But it is only in so far as this sort of control
has been achieved that a society of any kind becomes not only
free in a negative sense, but also really free in an affirmative
sense and, therefore, also responsible.

Since Kierkegaard, existential philosophy has recognized the
individual as the source of human freedom, and has denied
that he can be forced to be free, as Rousseau held. I believe,
therefore, that existential humanism can bring forth a new
type of democratic theory not inconsistent with Marxist
humanism. Some of its features have been suggested by Sartre,[12]
but he has never carefully worked them out. This is a highly
important task for the future. If it is ever written, it will refuse
to follow contemporary political theory in identifying democracy with voting procedures of a certain kind, or with
majority rule. Striving for a more basic understanding, it will
identify it rather with a respect for the weak and fragile
individual as a latecomer in human history, and for his capacity
to work out freely, with other free men, patterns of meaning
to guide responsibly that social apparatus and power without
which human existence is impossible.

This philosophy will see stable structures in this complex,
like mass education, an individual autonomy that is presupposed,
free communication, and the possibility of protest, without
which there can be no real democracy. It will, therefore, also
reject the ideological relativism which is so prominent in recent
formulations of democratic theory. Voting procedures are not
fundamental. They are derived from a respect for the autonomous
individual who can totalize a world of his own, and who cannot,

therefore, be justly reduced to the level of a thing or an object in some other world. This is why each individual vote should count for one, and why the largest number, the so-called majority, should prevail on a given issue. But as is well known, the term *majority*, when applied to current practice, must be seriously qualified. What it really means is a majority of those who care enough to vote, so that in a highly important presidential election, for example, in this country, a minority, 33 percent of the eligible voters, will win. If these are the facts, and if democracy is rooted rather in the social responsibility of the autonomous individual than in voting procedures and in majority rule, taken in a literal sense, then we should widen our conception of democratic government, especially in underdeveloped countries.

These countries are making the crucial transition from a primitive to an industrialized economic and social organization. There is certainly nothing undemocratic in this, for, as the Marxists have shown us by now, the individual cannot become autonomous without sufficient food, education, and leisure. Such transitions require centralized power and rapid decisions. And we must remember that in similar crises, "democratic" nations have been able to grant exceptional powers to executive leaders and agencies, and to abrogate voting procedures without falling into autocracy. Hence, we should envisage the possibility that, in spite of the temporary absence of opposition parties and what we call free elections, the government of an underdeveloped country may still be democratic in the more basic sense we are suggesting. In making such a judgment, we need to get below the surface. Is an autocratic elite using its power for the sake of external forces or special class interests, or is it a democratic elite concerned for the welfare and autonomy of the people, taken distributively, one by one? Are these leaders supported by an active minority of the educated and well informed? Is mass education strongly supported? Are individuals encouraged to participate actively in the management of smaller groups? Can new groups be readily formed? These are the questions we should have in mind in making judgments of this kind.

The human individual is weak and fragile and transient. But he alone is conscious and free. The cooperation of many individuals in group formations always brings forth established patterns of power that long outlast individual acts. But these

patterns lack freedom and consciousness, and are constantly
falling into the sluggish drift described exhaustively by Sartre,
which may terminate in blind eruptions of force. The ideal of
democracy is to control this drift of power by the free
consciousness that resides only in the puny individual, that is,
any individual, *all* individuals potentially.

Is there any means by which real grievances may be pro-
tested by a minimal use of force to avoid destructive chain
reactions? The usual answer by traditional defenders of
democracy is free discussion and assembly. But in the mass
societies of our time, grave questions may be raised as to
whether this is sufficient to attract public attention and to
show the need for basic change. Is there any way, in short,
by which the critical dynamism required for responsible
government may be brought within the democratic process?
I believe that the methods of social protest recently developed
in the West, and perhaps those of nonviolent resistance
developed in India, only casually mentioned by Sartre, are
techniques of this kind which are worthy of more serious
consideration. These include demonstrations by groups of
individuals, sit-ins, picketing, strikes, and boycotts of
various kinds.

In these protests, armed weapons are not required, and
personal violence need not be used by the protesters, so
chain reactions of vengeance are avoided. And yet they are
sufficient to show the seriousness of the charges and to
attract public attention to the injustices involved. Thus
restaurants have been forced to close by sit-ins, chain stores
put out of business by boycotts, and whole industries and
institutions paralyzed by strikes without any positive use of
force. It is interesting to note the trend toward legal acceptance
of these protests in the past fifty or sixty years. If certain
procedures are followed, many demonstrations, sit-ins,
picketings, and boycotts are now within the federal law, though
not accepted in the past.

And similarly many types of strike, once illegal, are now
accepted as within the law. This is a significant and imaginative
development in recent times of what we may call the right
of protest which is essential to democracy. The techniques
of nonpayment of taxes and filling the jails have not been
used anywhere on a large scale, though they were suggested
and put into practice on a one-man basis by Thoreau in

Concord, Massachusetts, in 1848. So they belong to our tradition, and may be developed as a means of individual protest against unjust laws. Indeed, I believe it is fair to say that the survival of democracy in mass cultures of the future will depend on such developments. This sketch of an existential political philosophy draws heavily from the later thought of Sartre, though it is closer to Merleau-Ponty and William James, who is now beginning to be recognized as an existential thinker in a broad sense of this phrase. Now, in conclusion, let us ask: to what extent could such a philosophy be accepted by a Marxist humanist of our time?

First of all, there are certain similarities that must be recognized, and which make the question worth discussing. Both positions agree that the individual exists in a matrix of economic and cultural patterns which condition his choices at any given time. Both agree that in spite of this, he possesses a certain limited freedom of choice. Both recognize the need for controlling the blind drift of social power, and for correcting the inequalities and class war to which this drift must lead. They agree that both individual ownership of capital and public ownership administered by the *new owning class,* so clearly described by Djilas, are now examples of drift that need to be subjected to more adequate forms of control.

In spite of the difficulties, both positions envisage the possibility of establishing such control by a socialist or democratic elite. This may be able to move us toward a free and democratic society in which many traditional forms of alienation may be removed. There is considerable agreement concerning the nature of the humanized world that is the end. But differences arise in connections with the ways of achieving it which, in turn, lead to different conceptions of the goal. Here, then, is a list of six basic differences between the democratic philosophy of an existential humanism and that of a humanism which can still call itself Marxist.

1. In his understanding of the complex relations of interdependence between the individual and the group which have been carefully described by Sartre, the Marxist humanist will more clearly focus the conditioning of the individual by group patterns already established. He will grant to this individual a certain limited freedom of choice, but always as the member of a class or group. The existential humanist, on the other hand, will see, following Sartre, that these group structures are sustained

by the internalized thoughts and attitudes of the individual members who can always transcend them to form new groups. In Hegelian terms, we may say that the Marxist humanist will see in this bipolar dialectic the priority of an *objectiver Geist* that is internalizing itself subjectively in its members, while the existential humanist will see in it rather the priority of an existential *subjectiver Geist* that is constantly externalizing and objectifying itself.

2. Marxist humanist writers may wish to qualify certain orthodox formulations of "historical materialism," but I do not see how they can abandon it without ceasing to be Marxist except in name. For them, therefore, human history is basically determined by the laws of economic and social change which operate with a certain natural necessity, apart from human consciousness and desire, and the revolution is inevitable, though its coming may be hastened or delayed by human intervention. The existential humanist, on the other hand, will interpret this reign of unconscious law as a blind drift of social power which is not necessary but rather always open to purposive control by conscious individuals. This means that the deterministic theory of the inevitability of the revolution, which has attracted so many to Marxism, will have to be abandoned. Human freedom has to be taken more seriously. The events of history are contingent (as Merleau-Ponty recognized).

3. His faith in the large-scale forces, which seem to him to dominate the course of history, will lead the Marxist to disparage individual consciousness as weak and subjective, and to place his trust rather in some powerful nation or class, like the working class of the nineteenth century whose interests are on the side of history. The existential humanist, on the other hand, will see in these fixed interests and forces only a blind drift which *can be* constantly transformed by the invention of new meanings and new formations, brought forth ultimately by individual initiative. To illustrate this, he will point to the radical decline of working class solidarity in advanced industrial countries, and the coming of managerial groups, neither capitalist owners nor proletarians, and not foreseen by Marx.

4. In line with his trust in the "necessary" developments of world history, the Marxist humanist can consistently follow Sartre in tolerating the use of force for what he regards as the "correction" of tyranny and injustice. The existential humanist, on the other hand, and against the practice of so-called

"democratic" nations at the present time, cannot consistently do this. He will see the resort to mass violence as an abandonment of conscious control for a blind drift which is against the very *ethos* of democracy. Hence he will have to side with Camus against Sartre, and in spite of their relative contingency and weakness, put his faith in rebellion and protest rather than in forceful revolution.

5. The Marxist humanist thinks of free action in terms of its culminating phases as a common life or *praxis* in which individuals are already united together under responsible leadership for the achievement of a meaningful aim. He will therefore stress the need for sound guidance on the part of the leaders, and the need for obedience from below. The existential humanist, on the other hand, thinks of free action in terms of its *incipient* phases when autonomous individuals are thinking for themselves and working out meaningful patterns of action with representative leaders responsible to them. He will, therefore, stress the need for constant criticism and protest from below, and for the protection of this individual freedom by a bill of rights, never emphasized by Marxist tradition nor even by recent Marxist theory.

There is, no doubt, some truth as well as some partiality on both sides. Thus in its present form, Marxism is open to the charge of ignoring the dangers of drift and tyranny, while existential humanism can be attacked as a mere revival of an atomistic liberalism which confuses democracy with chaos, and never gets anything done. These issues might be settled by responsible argument which would correct the partialities on both sides.

6. Finally, I believe that two different conceptions of freedom are at issue here. Thus Marxist humanism tends to identify freedom with something external to man, like the absence of external restraints, or with something external that has been internalized, as in the Hegelian formulation "freedom is the knowledge of necessity," or internalized and exploited in some way as in the modern formulation that "freedom is power over nature and power over oneself based on the knowledge of the external and internal necessity." All of these theories are reconcilable with an ultimate determinism. I know, however, that the Yugoslav writer Petrović, whom I know personally, has rejected all of these views in his interesting article "Man and Freedom" in the volume *Socialist Humanism,*

edited by Fromm in 1965. In place of these, he defends
another view according to which "freedom is something
'internal' becoming also 'eternal,' namely, the self-determining
creative activity, the creative deed of enlarging and enriching
humaneness," and which he traces back to the early Marx.[13]
But I can no longer clearly distinguish this supposedly Marxist
view from that of the existential humanist with which I would
substantially agree.

There is now sufficient agreement to make discussion
possible. I have tried to clarify the two positions, and thus to
take the debate one step beyond Sartre who has often confused
them. I believe that these are the chief issues on which Marxist
humanists are now divided from existential humanists. Can
they be overcome? I do not know. But I believe that the issues
are important, and worthy of further comment and consideration.
The dialectic should be carried on.

NOTES

1. The annual meeting of the Eastern Division of the American
Philosophical Association held in Philadelphia, December 27-29,
1966.

2. "Critique of Hegel's Dialectic and General Philosophy," in
Karl Marx: Early Writings, trans. and ed. T. B. Bottomore (New
York: McGraw-Hill, 1964), p. 207.

3. S. Kierkegaard, *Concluding Unscientific Postscript*, trans. David
F. Swenson and Walter Lowrie (Princeton: Princeton University
Press, 1941), p. 109.

4. "Needs, Production, and Division of Labor," in *Karl Marx: Early
Writings*, p. 187.

5. S. Kierkegaard, *The Present Age*, trans. Alexander Dru (New
York: Harper and Row, 1962).

6. Cf. Edward A. Tiryakian, "Existential Phenomenology and
the Sociological Tradition," *American Sociological Review* 30
(October 1965), pp. 674-688.

7. Adam Schaff, *A Philosophy of Man* (New York: Monthly
Review Press, 1963), p. 31.

8. Martin Heidegger, *Sein und Zeit*, 9th ed. (Tübingen: Max Niemeyer
Verlag, 1960), sections 26-27, pp. 117-130.

9. Jean-Paul Sartre, *Critique de la raison dialectique* (Paris: Gallimard, 1960).

10. Ibid., p. 629.

11. Sartre, *Being and Nothingness,* trans. Hazel E. Barnes (New York: Philosophical Library, 1956).

12. Sartre, *Search for a Method,* trans. Hazel E. Barnes (New York: Alfred A. Knopf, 1963), pp. 95-96.

13. Erich Fromm, ed., *Socialist Humanism* (Garden City: Doubleday, 1965), p. 254.

Chapter 27

Marxism and Existentialism

BARROWS DUNHAM

During 1970-1971 Barrows Dunham was Kenneth L. M. Prey Visiting Professor, School of Social Work, the University of Pennsylvania. From 1937 to 1953, he was professor of philosophy and chairman of the department at Temple University in Philadelphia, and he has been lecturer in Philosophy at Montgomery County Community College, Pennsylvania. He is the author of *Man Against Myth* (1947, 1962), *Giant in Chains* (1953, 1964), *The Artist in Society* (1960), *Heroes and Heretics* (1964, 1968), and *Ethics Dead and Alive.*

I'm sure you know that when the noun "Marxism" is joined in a title with another noun, this second noun is likely to be swallowed up, along with all it signifies. The canary meets the cat, the minnow the whale, and nothing remains to be described but digestion.

Yet even if we suppose, as comfortable Marxists do, that the whale has swallowed all those minnows, the minnows have a way of reappearing in the tissue of the whale. M. Sartre acknowledges that he has gone through this process, that he is now somewhere within the whale, possibly near the spout. Other existentialists may be in other portions. They don't report clearly where they are, just as, before, they didn't report clearly where they were.

We can get round the difficulty. It happens that all philosophies have second versions of themselves, namely, what people think the philosophers have said. It may be hard to know what existentialists say, but it isn't hard to know what people think the existentialists say. People have made their notions of it quite plain—in their speech, their behavior, their dress, and even their hair.

I once met a Danish physician, who told me that his suite of offices contained the room in which Kierkegaard died. Every summer, he said, a certain number of Americans come into that room to sit and meditate. It is people such as these who have established a sort of social convention as to what existentialism means, and it is this socially established meaning that competes with Marxism.

The Marxism thus in competition has itself suffered similar changes. It is no longer, historically, the Marxism of the founders, but it is the Marxism that contemporary Marxists (especially those who govern) believe Marxism to be. Here an odd thing has happened. The existentialist philosophers were diverse of view, but social convention has composed their views into unity. Marxism began as a system—flexible, to be sure, as dialectics requires, but a system nevertheless. It is now as various as the Marxists themselves. Dialectics has proved, it may be thought, uncomfortably dialectical.

Now, it happens that Marxism and existentialism speak different languages, whatever the national speech may be. Marxism regards itself as a science, and its language refers, or is intended to refer, directly to the real world. The language of existentialism, however, is almost entirely poetical: it treats metaphors as statements of fact. You must read the existentialists, not as they ask to be read, but as the poets they do not know they are. Perhaps, not knowing they are poets, they are not the poets they might be. If they had known, they might have shrunk their volumes into a single couplet from Keats, and have said, retiring before a master, that the sedge is withered from the lake, and no birds sing.

"The sedge has wither'd from the lake." Keats got this line, with exquisite discipline, from a source that has no discipline at all—the dim and mighty stirrings beneath consciousness. Existentialism comes thence also, with the same message but without the discipline. The world has proved disappointing. One is angered; one feels guilt for the anger; one fears punishment for the guilt.

We have all had such feelings, and if we turned them into a metaphysic, we would be existentialists. There cannot be an

older idea than that life is brief and distressful, with an end even
more abrupt than its beginning. The interval, to be sure, is lit
with many glories—with laughter and love and the splendors
of art. Existentialism seems unaware of these, but very much
aware of the brevity and distress.

This, at any rate, is how I understand the doctrine that
existence is prior to essence, and the further doctrine that
being lies always on the edge of nothingness. In the existentialist
view, the existence that is prior to essence appears to be human
existence; the being that is next to nothingness appears to be
that of human persons. "Prior" appears to mean "more
important." Thus, if I read these poets aright, they are saying
that the most important thing is for people to survive.

In their view also, as I judge, the next most important thing
is that the individual human person be not threatened, not
nudged continually toward the dread abyss. Governments and
other social institutions do this all the time, by diminishing our
personal power of decision. The existentialist complaint is here
the old anarchist complaint, even the nihilist. It was for some
such reason that Nietzsche wanted to "transvaluate" values, and
Sartre asks us not merely to understand a certain convict and
homosexual but to regard him as a saint. Perhaps it was this
mood that made Heidegger a Nazi, for national socialism had
some rebellion in it. Yet the mood, however rebellious, is
gloom-struck, a black raven of the night. I marvelled to find,
some years ago, how prophetically Pope had described it in the
Dunciad (I, 289-90):

. . . a monster of a fowl,
Something betwixt a heideggre and an owl.

And then those tombstone-nouns: dread, alienation, nothingness. They suggest, as nouns and tombstones do, that the state
of affairs is permanent. There will be some thrashing-about by
the unhappy self next the abyss; there will be much crying
aloud. But remedy there is none.

By contrast, all the Marxists, however quarrelling among
themselves, believe that there is remedy, amounting indeed to
salvation. Let mankind but come out of "pre-history," out of
commercial rivalries and wars, out of the absurd economy that
suffers crisis whenever it gives abundance—and then we shall have
the chance to lift all burdens and adorn all lives. There can even

be an approach to physical immortality. For if we give to
medicine the wealth we give to war, we may all survive (possibly
beyond our wish) to populate the planets and chase the expanding
universe.

Such things may be, but we are now in no such paradise. Quite
to the contrary, we live even more dangerously than existentialists
have supposed. They seem to have meant, simply, that anyone
may die at any time.

Death rides on every passing breeze,
He lurks in every flower;
Each season has its own disease,
Its peril every hour.

But present fact is rather worse: the entire human race may
destroy itself, may become extinct. Such a result would be
nothingness indeed. It would also be absurdity beyond anything
the existentialists have called absurd. For then it would be the
case that human beings, or some of them, had used such means
as would defeat, not this or that end, but all ends whatsoever.
Lunacy itself cannot do so much. The ultimate catastrophe
takes brains.

Now, Marx observed, in the eighth paragraph of the *Manifesto*,
that class struggles had sometimes ended in "the common ruin
of the contending classes." He would hardly fail to see that danger
now and to let it modify strategy. He would say, of course,
that the follies of capitalism can end only when capitalism ends.
But he would perhaps think that the mode of ending now demands
a more exquisite care, a calmer wisdom, than the less risky struggles
of the nineteenth century required.

Moreover, Marx cared rather more about people as people
than existentialists care about society as society. According to
the popular idea at any rate, existentialists regard society as
something to be "alienated" from. But Marx, though he thought
social causes decisive for history, rose into his true Jeremiads
whenever he described (as in volume I of *Kapital*) the effect of
capitalism upon people. He was, after all, an offspring of the
Enlightenment, and his favorite author, as he said, was Diderot.

Thus there is in Marx a hopeful humanism that complements,
and may cure, the despairing humanism of the existentialists.
In just the same way, Marx's idea that the members of society
can establish common control over the conduct of society

forecasts a time when alienation will be needless and perhaps impossible. Both the philosophies say that people are what is most important. Given this much unity of opposites, perhaps we may think that Marx's vigor can make existentialists less passive, while at the same time a little existentialist anxiety disciplines the more flamboyant Marxists. For if it is silly to do nothing about danger, it is also silly to do things that will make danger worse.

Having said so much, I think I cannot say more without departing from the *ipsissima verba* (the very words) of all these masters. Yet Marx himself requires that I say more: with him, things thought are always joined with things to be done. As the eighth of the *Theses on Feuerbach* tells us, all mystifications of theory "find their rational solution in human practice and in the comprehension of this practice."

Now, theories may be old, but practice is always new. We are therefore fated—doomed, if you like—to be original. In the mire of circumstance we may hear the masters' voices telling us, instructively, to move on; but it is we, and only we, who can discover how to lift our legs in that particular mire. Accordingly, it won't be easy for us to observe Engels' warning about people who "think they have fully understood a theory and can apply it without more ado from the moment they have mastered its main principles." To which remark he added, "I cannot exempt many of the more recent 'Marxists' from this reproach, for the most wonderful nonsense has been produced from this quarter too." (Letter to Joseph Bloch, 21 September 1890).

Well, we shall have to risk producing rubbish, because without that risk there is no way to get a comprehension of practice, thus to solve mysteries and to tell theorists what they really mean. Practice requires that we put a practical question. Let the question be, What is the most important thing for us to do during these present years?

The existentialist answer, I suppose, is, Keep making decisions at least, whether or not you can do anything about them. The Marxist answer is—well, who knows? For this is just the question that Marxists, or people who so style themselves, are debating. But I have an answer, I know not of what school. It seems an answer rational beyond the needs of reason, and it is this:

Our chief task will be to keep the human race in existence, to keep people alive. Unless this is done, nothing else can be done. It is more than humane, it is necessary. Does one prefer capitalism?—there'll be no capitalism after universal death. Does one prefer socialism?—there'll be no socialism after universal death. Is one loyal to this or that nation, race, tribe?—there'll be no nations, races, tribes, after universal death. Wisdom and folly, love and hatred, loyalty and indifference will alike perish in that final flame.

The peculiarity of our age is that, for the time being at least, means are a more important problem than ends. Some years ago, the Earl Russell remarked, quite truly, that the conflict between capitalism and communism is more dangerous to mankind than either system could be. Similarly, we may add, the conflict between Soviet Marxism and Chinese Marxism is more dangerous to Marxism than either of the versions. I think that Marxists in order to save Marxism, and all of us in order to save the world, must set firm limits upon intensity of conflict. Whatever social virtues we possess we have acquired not so much from love of them as from a certain impossibility of avoiding them. It may therefore happen that, retreating from catastrophe, we move backward into brotherhood.

I began, you remember, with a minnow and a whale, but I have not allowed any swallowing. The temptation was, to be sure, extreme. But no man, by himself, can cause one theory to swallow another; only history can do that. Moreover, I have lost whatever love I had for mere triumphs of the intellect. It seems much more useful to find and report agreement among doctrines, for when you do this, you unify people. We shall need all the unity we can get, in order to preserve our race and some measure of happiness for it in a woeful world.

If that achievement comes, I may want to call it Marxism. But, in truth, it will be as sweet with any other name.

Chapter 28

Remarks on the Papers of Professor Wild and Dr. Dunham

CHAIM PERELMAN

Chaim Perelman is professor of philosophy at the University of
Brussels and has been visiting professor at Pennsylvania State
University, the State University of New York at Buffalo and at
Stony Brook, and McGill University. He has received honorary
degrees from the University of Florence and the University of
Jerusalem. He is the author of several books, among them *The
New Rhetoric, The Idea of Justice and the Problem of Agreement*
(1963), *An Historical Introduction for Philosophical Thinking*
(1967), and *Justice* (1967).

I have accepted the invitation of your president, Professor
Somerville, to present some remarks in the discussion between
Marxism and existentialism, because, while no one considers
me an orthodox Marxist or a convinced existentialist, I
sympathize with their concern with respect to the problems
of action, the relations of the individual, society, and history,
the significant aspect of human existence.

Is the dialogue between Marxists and existentialists possible?
It would be difficult in any event to envisage a dialogue between
Marx and Kierkegaard. For if it is true, as underlined by Professor
Wild, that these two thinkers are opposed to the system of Hegel
because it is too abstract and remote from concrete reality, they

are searching for that concrete reality, the determinant reality, in fields so far apart that they would be able to display toward one another only an extreme lack of understanding. What is more idealistic, for a Marxist, than the vision of Kierkegaard for whom the fundamental relation for the individual is his relation with God? What for Kierkegaard could be more remote from the privacy of the person than the vision of Marx according to which the social relations which are established in the process of production constitute the fundamental alienation of the proletariat and the primary source of every other form of alienation? Likewise, it seems that a dialogue between Marxism and the existentialism of Heidegger and of Jaspers or of Gabriel Marcel would be futile. The only known dialogue with Marxism is that of the French existentialists Jean-Paul Sartre, Simone de Beauvoir, and Maurice Merleau-Ponty, at first in the columns of the review *Les Temps Modernes* and then in the works of Merleau-Ponty (*Les aventures de la dialectique*), and of Sartre (*Critique de la raison dialectique*).

We notice first of all that in the years immediately after the last world war, the communists, as if obeying a watchword, responded unanimously by a rejection, an unqualified condemnation which is apparent as much in the articles of the official press as in the works of men as different as Henri Lefèbvre[1] and Georg Lukács.[2] For them, as for all the spokesmen of communism at the time, "the existentialism [of Sartre] is only a class phenomenon which serves reaction"[3]; an "up to date form" of idealism, which "reflects the spiritual and moral chaos of bourgeois intelligence in the final period of imperialism" (Lukács). At that time, no communist even considered the possibility of a dialogue with existentialism (even left-wing existentialism); no communist wondered whether there was a possibility of learning something from the opponent.

But the situation was to change with political developments. At first there were the Yugoslav Marxists who, after 1948, found some interest in a dialogue with the Sartreans, who were deeply interested in the Yugoslav experience.

Then, beginning in October 1956, after the psychological storm caused by Khrushchev's speech revealing the misdeeds of the cult of personality, a reaction occurred in communist countries, but it found public manifestation in the circles of Polish Marxism, where increased attention had been devoted to personal problems, to moral problems of responsibility and of individual liberty. Encouraged by the attitude of Adam Schaff, the official spokesman for Polish communism, the Marxist theoreticians attached a growing importance to the writings of the young Marx,[4] as well as to the Sartrean existentialism which induced them to elaborate a Marxist-inspired anthropology.[5] In the latter work, the author does not criticize any existentialist thesis, but recognizes the importance of problems which the existentialists have raised and which up till then the Marxists had entirely neglected.

The two lecturers we have just heard are very different in the style they adopt for the confrontation between existentialism and Marxism. Whereas Professor Wild takes his subject very seriously, Dr. Barrows Dunham is content to treat existentialism with scorn.

In a text of undeniable literary excellence, Dr. Dunham presents the existentialists as unwitting poets, who "treat metaphors as statements of facts."

If this is a fault for a philosopher, we are bound to conclude that Dr. Dunham makes himself guilty of it as early as the first sentence of this lecture, when he says "I'm sure you know that when the noun 'Marxism' is joined in a title with another noun, this second noun is likely to be swallowed up, along with all it signifies. The canary meets the cat, the minnow the whale, and nothing remains to be described but digestion."

As this metaphor suffices for him to get rid of existentialism, it suffices for him to speak of the impact that the latter has had on the public at large. But he does not hesitate to acknowledge that Marxism has equally undergone a change, since, for the great public, it is identified with what the official Marxists, those who hold power, insist that it is.

Unfortunately, official Marxism is not as foreign to scientific Marxism as the young people with long hair and checked blouses are to the existentialism of Heidegger and Sartre. In fact, the very possibility of an official Marxism is incompatible with the scientific pretensions of Marxism. Indeed, to the extent that Marxism is not ideology but science, its thesis ought to be, like every other scientific thesis, capable of amendment, of correction, without the consequence that those who offer this improvement be immediately accused of revisionism, of deviationism, that is, of heresy. We know the fate reserved by the Polish communist party for the philosopher Leszek Kolakowski,

who, in his book *The Man Without Alternatives* (1961), opposed
institutional Marxism to scientific Marxism; he was in revolt
against the undeniable fact that some official authorities of the
party decided that which all Marxists, and more particularly
intellectuals, must acknowledge as Marxist orthodoxy, these
decisions varying with the political, economic, and social context.
There is thus nothing astonishing in the fact that Marxism, having
become an official ideology, should have become a little too
dialectical, even for the taste of Dr. Dunham, for it is normal
that its conception should vary with the social and political
conditions that it ought to reflect. But if so, which is the Marxism
which is to be compared to the cat or whale—is it either a variant
of institutional Marxism, or one of the diverse variants of
scientific Marxism, which can, however, hardly be separated from
the other?

This problem brings us back to what seems to oppose Marxism
more pointedly to existentialism—that is, the different relations
that they lay down between the individual and the power groups
to which he belongs, such as the Party or the State.

For Professor Wild, the opposition between the primacy of
the objective Spirit and that of the subjective Spirit would be
characteristic of the opposition between Marxism and existentialism, but this opposition seems to me to characterize better that
which exists between Hegel and Kierkegaard than that between
Kierkegaard and Marx. For with the latter, far from the Spirit,
whether objective or subjective, being the determinant factor,
it is rather the material and social conditions as they exhibit
themselves objectively which play that part. In fact, if there is
a conflict between existentialism and Marxism, it finally comes
down to the predominant role accorded by the first to the
initiative and responsibility of the individual, whereas the
second insists on the primacy of history, of its objectivity and
even its determinism, at least in the long run. A fertile dialogue
between Marxism and existentialism would have to deal first
with the respective role of the individual and of the material
conditions of his action in the determination of historical
phenomena.

And this leads us to the final question which I would like to
raise, and which is a question of method. How can a dialogue
between two different philosophical systems be initiated?
Do some criteria exist, other than internal ones, which allow
us to make a decision in a debate between some philosophical
positions that are incompatible?

Both Professor Wild and Dr. Dunham attempt to supply the beginning of an answer to this question. Professor Wild suggests that a substantial agreement obtains between Marxism and existentialism with regard to ends, but that there is no agreement on means. Unfortunately, he immediately corrects himself by pointing out that this disagreement cannot fail to affect the conception we have concerning the ends themselves. Dr. Dunham concludes that all reasonable men are perhaps in agreement not on what there is to investigate, but certainly on what must, at all costs, be prevented, namely the destruction of humanity. Any philosophy that would enable us to avoid the final catastrophe seems to him welcome.

One may wonder to what extent the prevention of an atomic war depends on philosophical discussions. But what is certain is that the very idea of a fruitful philosophical dialogue requires the existence of criteria, whether they concern facts or values, which transcend each of the philosophical positions in question. We should apply ourselves to the investigation of dialectical tools which would make a philosophical dialogue possible and fruitful.

NOTES

1. Henry Lefèbvre, *L'existentialisme* (Paris, 1946).

2. Georg Lukács, *Existentialisme ou marxisme* (Hungarian ed., 1947; French ed., Paris, 1948).

3. Roger Vailland, *Pour et contre l'existentialisme* (Paris, 1948).

4. See Marek Fritzhand, *Cztowiek, humanism, moralnošc* [*Man, Humanism,* and *Morality*] (Warsaw, 1961).

5. Cf. Adam Schaff, *A Philosophy of Man* (New York: Monthly Review Press, 1963).

Part IX

SARTRE AND MARXISM

Chapter 29

The Significance of Jean-Paul Sartre

WILFRID DESAN

Wilfrid Desan is professor of philosophy at Georgetown University, Washington, D.C. He has taught at Kenyon College and, as a Carnegie Fellow, at Harvard University. He is the author of *The Tragic Finale: Essay on the Philosophy of Jean-Paul Sartre* (1954, 1960), *The Planetary Man*, Vol. I (1961), and *The Marxism of Jean-Paul Sartre* (1965).

When I entitle this paper "The Significance of Sartre," it sounds both ambitious and vague. It sounds ambitious because, to draw even in outline what we consider to be the importance or the failure of a philosopher before he has terminated his career, is presumptuous, not only because he himself may still introduce essential changes in his philosophy but also because we ourselves are too close to him in order to judge with objectivity that which is commendable or not in his philosophy. I should add that the title is vague, purposely vague, because I realize that the topic is too vast. To present a paper which describes the total impact of Sartre in such diverse domains as philosophy, literature, and politics cannot be done in present circumstances. There is, therefore, in this evaluation—and that is precisely what this paper is—out of necessity a certain modesty built in. To evaluate implies a readiness to reevaluate.

Behind every philosophical vision there stands a man. Philosophy itself I consider to be a collective enterprise and although it

sometimes has been called *philosophia perennis*, it should be clear
by now after centuries of research, that as *total* and *global* answer
it is available to nobody. Philosophical visions then, privately
owned and limited in their expansion, fulfill a function. They
correct one another. If we want to grasp what eventually might
be considered Sartre's corrective or complementary function
in a Marxistic world view, let us briefly observe the main tenets
of his doctrine.

"Every man has his natural place," wrote Sartre in his brilliant
autobiography *The Words*.

> Its altitude is determined by neither pride nor value: childhood
> decides. Mine is the sixth floor in Paris with a view overlooking
> the roofs. For a long time I suffocated in the valleys; the plains
> overwhelmed me: I crawled along the planet Mars, the heaviness
> crushed me. I had only to climb a molehill for joy to come rushing
> back: I would return to my symbolic sixth floor; there I would once
> again breathe the rarefied air of belles-lettres; the Universe would
> rise in tiers at my feet and all things would humbly beg for a name;
> to name the thing was both to create and take it.[1]

This already is the Sartre of later years. ". . . to name the thing
was both to create and to take it." *Being and Nothingness* is
the forceful illustration of a thought where man is presented
as organized by a world where he is made not to be ruled but
to rule. Man is meaning-giving center: without man nature
would be deaf-mute.[2] Sartre would agree with Heidegger in
claiming that "knowledge is the world,"[3] not in creating the
world in the strict sense of the word but in making it "to
appear." Nobody like Sartre has emptied consciousness—it
is "néant," yet paradoxically this consciousness which has
nothing to be has everything to do. It makes that "there is"
being, it makes that there is *this* being, it makes *time* and
juxtaposing *this* thing to *that* thing, it makes *space*. All the
so-called categories, unity-multiplicity, whole-part, more and
less, outside of . . . are ideal manipulations of things which
leave reality itself completely intact. They are different ways
in which the For-itself or individual consciousness "attacks"
and organizes the "apathetic indifference" of things.[4]
Meyerson was wrong when he accused reality of a "scandalous
diversity." It is man who is responsible, who stands at the
center of reality and constitutes the diverse. "I would return to
my symbolic sixth floor . . . and all things would humbly beg

for a name; to name the thing was both to create and to take it."

> . . . Children played in the Luxembourg Gardens. I would draw
> near them. They would brush against me without seeing me. I
> would watch them with the eyes of a beggar. How strong and
> quick they were! How good-looking! In the presence of those
> flesh-and-blood heroes, I would lose my prodigious intelligence,
> my universal knowledge, my athletic physique, my blustering
> shrewdness. I would lean against a tree, waiting . . . to save me
> from despair, [my mother] would feign impatience: "What are you
> waiting for, you big silly? Ask them whether they want to play with
> you." I would shake my head. I would have accepted the lowliest
> jobs, but it was a matter of pride not to ask for them. She would
> point to the ladies sitting in iron chairs and knitting: "Do you want
> me to speak to their mothers?" I would beg her to do nothing of
> the kind. She would take my hand, we would leave, we would go
> from tree to tree and from group to group, always entreating, always
> excluded. At twilight, I would be back on my perch, on the heights
> where the spirit blew, where my dreams dwelt.[5]

At that moment the famous play *No Exit* was born. "L'enfer,
c'est l'autre!" Sartre's theory of the *Look* grounds the theory
of the Other: the Other who looks at me, annihilates me as a
subject and reduces me to the rank of object. No rational
demonstration proves it, but feelings like shame, envy, resent-
ment, etc., make it manifest. The presence of the Other is
hostile: in some ways he limits my own consciousness. When
Spinoza says that thought is only limited by thought, Sartre
would claim that awareness. But—and this is important—this
limitation is active: it encloses me, it surrounds me and yet I
never reach it. For Sartre, the Other no less than I myself is
center, his whole life is a continual disposition of the world
around *himself*. The other is an "absence-presence," a mysterious
being which ought to be handled with care. "I want him to
stay object and I hate him to see Subject again. Yet he makes
it again and again. Only the dead stay object."

It is banal by now to stress the element *freedom* in the global
view of Sartre's philosophy. Let us merely mention that it is part
of his concept of nought. What is *not*, is free; what is *not*, is not
and cannot be caught within the laws of a mechanistic world like
any other being other than consciousness. In being *not*, individual
consciousness knows that which is, and at the same time escapes
determinism. "Man is the future of man." This implies that
there is no weight of the past on him and that man with no

support or aid is condemned at every moment to invent man.
"Consequently there is no action from things on the Subject,
there is only a centrifugal signification (in the active sense of
the word, i.e., the Subject himself gives sense and value to the
external thing)."[6] This attitude of total freedom and of
incessant departure is also Sartrean. It is a pleasant feeling of
course, but like other pleasant feelings, it may be illusory.
". . . At the age of ten, I had the impression that my prow was
cleaving the present and yanking me out of it; since then, I
have been running, I am still running. For me speed is measured
not so much by the distance covered in a given time as by the
power of uprooting."[7]

Sartre went to the Lycée and to the university, where, as is
well known, René Descartes dominates the philosophical scene.
Sartre, like anybody else who went to school in France in those
days, was a Cartesian and, at his best, a Bergsonian. No less
than any other Frenchman but with far more talent than most,
Sartre has carried on a lifelong struggle to protect what the
French have so aptly called *la lucidité*, which is of course
Descartes' old *Cogito*, the privilege that mind alone has of not
being earth, or any kind of matter. In the depths of his doubt,
Descartes discovered one certainty, namely that he thinks, and
therefore is a spiritual being. *Lucidité* is that unique light that,
containing a world of sense data, itself stands outside and
above the world. This is Descartes' defense against a world that
is myth—*mundus est fabula*—and Sartre, as a descendant of the
Cartesian tradition, introduces it into his own life and doctrine
as the negation of matter. Mind alone is supreme and free. In
the Cartesian view, thought contains the complex activity of
perceiving, knowing, willing, and desiring. Yet knowing is
not exactly desiring, since the latter has no limits. Only because
you know as a *man*, can you desire as a *god*. This Sartre has
inherited, but he has eliminated God from his inheritance and
replaced him by man, who now has absolute freedom. The
conclusion of Sartre is obvious: man must take over the
freedom of God.[8]

So there we have Sartre. The child and the philosopher.
Subjectivism, conflict with the other, and all-out freedom.
The method no less than the content stresses the superiority
of the Self. The method is phenomenological no less and by
this must be understood that one attempts a description of
the world and oneself in the world "as they appear." Sartre

has a method but a method which does only emphasize his Cartesian seclusion.

Where is the Marxist in all this? There is none except in desire. No doubt, as a young intellectual Sartre nurtured a strong opposition to the bourgeoisie. While a teacher at the Lycée, he refused to wear a tie, as if he could shed his class with his tie and thus come closer to the worker. For this he deserves no blame. Like the petit-bourgeois intellectual that he is, he uses more words than the workers, words with which he can analyze their status and revel in their name. His concern for the worker is the reverse side of his contempt for the strength of the bourgeois, his concern with man is the fight against anything that humiliates man, and his rebellion the reaction against all power. . . . The freedom and the power and esteem of the subject that are so deep in Sartre revolt against the suffering itself, whether that suffering results from the egoism of the continental bourgeoisie or from oppression preached in the name of Marx and Lenin. Sartre virtually grew up writing and attempting to publish his writing, for he was devoted to literature, not as art for art's sake but as a means whereby man justifies himself and at the same time fills a need for others.[9]

Sartre now stands at high noon: we are in the 1950s, our author has reached world fame as a philosopher, as a playwright and a novelist, but he has not declared himself in the domain of social studies and ethics. He will do so in another *magnum opus, Critique de la raison dialectique,* 755 pages of small print which came from the press in 1960, unbelievably difficult and chaotic with one central message: Marxism is the answer, Existentialism is merely a correction. Sartre himself is a Marxist.

Keeping in mind what we know already about his speculative philosophy, we shall at present attempt a brief answer to the following three questions:

1. What does Sartre favor in Marxism?

2. What does he repudiate in the same?

3. Can Sartre be called a Marxist, and, if not, can he be considered a correction of Marx?

1. *What Sartre favors in Marx.* In the *Critique*, the concept
of *need* is presented as essential, and human reality is called
a *being of need, un être de besoin,* a being that is, which in
order to live must have an object capable of assuaging its hunger.
This of course is Marx: "Hunger is a natural need: it requires
therefore a nature outside itself, an object outside itself in order
to be satisfied and stilled."[10] Hunger is only *one* need. Man
also seeks clothing, sex, habitation, etc. All these needs are
inseparable from material production. We can assert therefore,
that material production lies at the beginning of History. On
all this Sartre agrees. He does add though that it is precisely in
a world of scarcity, *dans un monde de la rareté*, that *need*
originates: because there is not enough of certain things, need
originates. This correction may seem merely redundant. It is
not. It is on the contrary, *important,* for once more, it is
because there is not enough of certain things, that the other
is transformed into a menace. The other for Sartre more than
for Marx is the *opponent* who threatens me in my very survival.

Need thus lies at the beginning of the dialectic between
man and matter, man and man. The dialectic continues and
transforms individual man into the common man (member
of the group), into the organization man and the institutionalized
man. Proceeding along that road his freedom has dwindled yet
his power is a hundredfold. When the moment shall come when
all will share alike in the abundance of things, freedom itself
will again triumph in all its sovereignty. That is the dream of
tomorrow. As for today—and on this Sartre seems to agree with
Marx—the need to unite has clipped the wings of freedom.

2. *What Sartre repudiates in Marx.* Before answering this
question, it should be understood that the opposition of the
French existentialist is directed not so much against Marx as it
is against a modern interpretation of Marx by certain present-
day communists, who, in his opinion, have distorted the pristine
Marxist view.

Sartre is dead set against what he calls the Marxist rigidity
which so often in the past has forced the ways of living of a
country or of an individual into a prearranged scheme without
regard for their peculiarity or uniqueness. He calls this the
sclerosis of modern Marxism. Examples are, among others,
the repression of the Budapest revolt in 1956 and the interpretation of cultural achievements like the ones of Paul Valéry or
Gustave Flaubert. It is a naiveté to call their achievement merely
an expression of bourgeois idealism or a result of economic

factors. Such generalities explain everything and nothing. Although our author has no wish to deny the relation between culture and economics, he wants to deepen the meaning of that relationship in trying to show that both are "mediated" through the individual. In Sartre's opinion, the modern Marxist has forgotten that a case is something unique, that it is not just money which shapes man but the way in which it is directed in and by the individual, in and by his parents. Childhood and growth play a role and they may in one way or other alter the impact of economic factors.

This commutation of the economic situation by the "mediating" individual must be understood in light of some of the views developed in *L'être et le Neant*, where man is seen above all as capable of "going beyond" a given situation through his "project" which is precisely his attitude towards the multiple possibles open to him. "To say what a man is implies to say what he can," and conversely "to say what a man can is to say what he is."[11] Man surpasses the given and in this sense surpasses the merely mechanical.[12] Through his "project" he surpasses the given and looks towards the future as that which needs to be fulfilled.

Even the worker's rebellion implies in depth that attitude, for it presumes a "going beyond" towards the possibility of change in his situation. Because the worker is not a "mere" thing, his act of rebellion plans and fulfills a new set of possibles.[13] If one would object that the material conditions of his existence determine the number of possibilities which are open to man, Sartre would agree. Yet although limited, there *is* a choice of possibles from which he can positively realize one. The Subjective in man can surpass one objectivity and reach unto another and in doing so, define himself. Man is very much defined in his project.

It is paramount therefore to discover this (fundamental) project which will then reveal the uniqueness of the self. In order to do so, Sartre suggests to return (regressively) unto the beginnings, and from there then with the erudition obtained, climb back unto the deed itself, where the project is fulfilled in a work or a book or some other accomplishment. Man must be studied as an entity which is in tension towards a future as towards an end to be fulfilled.

If we apply this method to *Madame Bovary*, the masterpiece of Flaubert, we shall discover that it is much more than the product of an epoch. Descending into the genesis of the work, we shall discover who the author was and how his "project" was fulfilled and how in order to escape from himself and from his inner contradictions, he had to tell a story. Flaubert then will go through this instrument and tell a story, but what a story it will be: "L'ouvrage monstrueux et splendide. . . . *Madame Bovary.*"

Such then is in brief the function which Sartre sees fit to attribute to the individual. When one reads this, one may at first gather the impression that the individual is merely getting his due. Unfortunately Sartre does not limit himself to emphasizing the role of the individual and to imparting to him the power of creation. The examination of this aspect leads us to point three.

3. *Whether Sartre is a Marxist.* The obsession of the *Critique*, not always overt yet always there, at least subterraneously, is that the *individual* is *center* and that the other in one way or other is a menace. In the analysis of the sociological development, Sartre makes it abundantly clear that the group is born through me as individual and for my protection. When the Other is no longer a help, he becomes in the world of scarcity a menace. In a world as ours, where there is not enough for all, he appears a menace, scandal, contre-homme, perpetual opponent.[14] Since there is no *we*, but only *I* in this age of decadent Cartesianism, we find in Sartre's writing neither charity nor benevolence. Above all, we do not find the oneness and organic unity of the collective as we should. Having erected an impressive defense of the subject, Sartre has exploded the concept of the intersubjective. The foremost French existentialist has no philosophy of the group as an ontological totality and his constant insistence upon the Self as the prime mover of all activity has resulted in a speculative egotism. Sartre still is *not* a Marxist, although in these later publications much more than previously he is attempting to be one. Yet in my opinion, as long as he installs the *individual* as sovereign and refuses to accept the group as ontological entity the existence and the accomplishment of which surpasses the being and the activity of the individual self, one must conclude, I believe, that Sartre has not really and in depth given us the speculative basis to build a philosophy of the collective.

Where then lies Sartre's merit? Sartre's merit is precisely the glorification of his sin: namely, of the Self. Sartre more than his predecessors has drawn attention to the individual, his freedom, and his creation. This Marxism had not sufficiently seen (and in stating this, I merely repeat Adam Schaff). At present the power of the Subject comes to the fore. Besides the indubitable impact of the economic factors and of matter, there is also in individual man that ineffable something, which escapes quantification, so it seems, which is irrepressible, starts anew, affects and mutates a surrounding world and in this very deed creates. In this Sartre corrects Marx. But to correct does not mean to become. *Obviously one is not what one corrects.*

NOTES

1. Jean-Paul Sartre, *The Words*, trans. Bernard Frechtman (New York: Braziller, 1964), p. 60.

2. Wilfrid Desan, *The Marxism of Jean-Paul Sartre* (New York: Doubleday, 1965), p. 41.

3. Wilfrid Desan, *The Tragic Finale* (New York: Harper, 1960), p. 49.

4. Ibid., p. 55.

5. Sartre, *The Words*, p. 134.

6. Maurice Merleau-Ponty, *La phénoménologie de la perception* (Paris: Gallimard, 1945), p. 498.

7. Sartre, *The Words*, p. 232.

8. Desan, *Marxism of Sartre*, p. 262.

9. Ibid., p. 3.

10. Karl Marx, *Economic and Philosophical Manuscripts of 1844*, in Erich Fromm, *Marx's Concept of Man*, trans. T. B. Bottomore (New York: Frederick Ungar, 1961), p. 182.

11. Sartre, *Critique de la raison dialectique*, p. 64.

12. Desan, *Marxism of Sartre*, pp. 56 ff.

13. Ibid., p. 57.

14. Ibid., p. 265.

Chapter 30

Sartre's Dialectical Reasoning on Individual Freedom

WALTER ODAJNYK

Walter Odajnyk is assistant professor of philosophy at Columbia
University, with a special interest in political philosophy. He has
held a Kent Fellowship and a Columbia University President's
Fellowship. He is the author of *Marxism and Existentialism* (1965).

The philosophical question of freedom has always served to
separate Sartre from Marxism. This separation remains in
Sartre's latest philosophical work, *Critique de la raison
dialectique,* where he undertakes a serious attempt to unite
existentialism and Marxism. The task is unenviable, for these
two systems of thought are based on almost diametrically
opposed views of human nature and human consciousness. And
in the *Critique,* Sartre would still like to maintain that man
and his *praxis* are "free," i.e., capable of transcending the given
conditions of the moment, and giving rise to radically different
and new conditions. The object of this essay, however, is to
demonstrate that, despite Sartre's desires, the logic of his own
argumentation in the *Critique* leads to the conclusion that man
indeed is bound and limited by his given conditions and for
all *practical* purposes unable to transcend or overcome them.

It is Sartre's treatment of individual freedom in the *Critique*
that is central in his attempt to unite Marxism and existentialism.

It is exactly individual freedom that Sartre wishes to incorporate into the socially oriented Marxist theory. This was to be his existentialist contribution to and correction of Marxism. As Wilfrid Desan notes in the preface to *The Marxism of Jean-Paul Sartre:* "whatever may be its limitations, the *Critique* is an impressive performance and undoubtedly makes an eloquent plea for freedom."[1]

But in fact, the individual freedom that Sartre describes in the *Critique* is meaningless. It may have a certain abstract or theoretical validity, but it is an empty concept when dealing with the individual's concrete activity in the world. And since Sartre, both as an existentialist and a potential Marxist, readily admits the necessity of a union of theory and practice, if individual freedom is void in practice it is void altogether. For in the notion of the unity of theory and practice, the emphasis falls on the practice.

The *Critique* describes, with numerous illustrations and details, two forms of dialectical movement. The first, which may be called the *material dialectic,* deals with man's existence and activity in nature; the second, the *social dialectic,* develops man's activities and relationships within society.[2]

The following sections will briefly describe and examine each of these forms of the dialectic, and attempt to demonstrate that in both the material and the social activity of man, the freedom of the individual is lost in a dialectical determinism.[3]

MATERIAL DIALECTIC

For Sartre, broadly speaking, the *dialectic* means "that man is 'mediated' by things to the extent that things are mediated by man":[4] man acts upon and forms the world and the world in turn reacts back upon and forms man. Or stated in more technical terms, man encounters objectivity, and because of the nature of his being, engages in a dialectical interrelationship with the objectivity during which the processes of transcendence, negation, and synthesis occur. The chief characteristic of man is that only he can transcend the objectivity that he encounters. However, once it is transcended and synthesized by him, a new objectivity is formed requiring a new transcendence and synthesis; in this manner, the objectivity also takes part in directing the form and the manner of the transcendence and synthesis. This is especially true if the possibilities of the given conditions are not unlimited, which is the case for Sartre in the *Critique*, in contrast to his views in *Being and Nothingness*. In other words, the dialectical method provides the appearance of freedom, choice, and mobility, but upon closer analysis it is equally as limiting as the causal method; in reality it is merely a more sophisticated description of causality.

For Sartre, the basic fact of man's existence in the *Critique* is that man is defined by needs while the world is defined by scarcity. To fulfill his needs and to overcome scarcity man labors, i.e., he establishes a purposeful *project*. In every case it is the individual who first feels a need, defines scarcity, and establishes a project. He is the motive force behind the dialectic and the creator of history.

However, in the process of overcoming his needs, man "objectifies" himself in matter and then estranges himself from his own products, for "what the *praxis* of man has produced and unified hits back at him; man is indeed produced by his own product."[5] In addition, Sartre describes another manner in which man relates to the world in his argument that man inevitably signifies or "totalizes" the reality around him. The reality so "totalized," either by an individual or a group, is defined as a *practico-inert*. It is possible, and indeed often the case, that men may in certain instances posit themselves as *practico-inerts,* as inert matter, and this may be done consciously or unconsciously, willingly or unwillingly; at times, the activity of a typist or of an assembly-line mechanic, or the conception of the function of the working class is often of this type. But these are forms of "pseudo-inertia," for man is chiefly defined by the possibility of "free *praxis*" and not by his ability to become a *practico-inert*.

In his presentation, Sartre assumes that man is basically free in positing the ends and the means of his *praxis* and his "totalizations," of his activity and his signification. But in fact, how free is he? His own needs and the scarcity in the world are given. By definition he is limited in the needs that he will strive to satisfy; and he is further limited in the manner by which he will make this attempt in the world. For the material world also has its *given*—its particular existence, its scarcity, and its own laws. Furthermore, what is it that causes man to signify and to transcend the material world and himself in the manner that he does? Obviously these are not completely arbitrary processes. There is a *structure* in matter, in society, and in the mind that shapes the mode of the signification and the transcendence. What is the nature of these structures? Supposedly the *Critique* addresses itself to these matters, but in fact it leaves these fundamental onto-logical and epistemological questions unanswered. Here is the *nothingness* that allows for the transcendence and the "free *praxis*" that Sartre describes. Had he persisted in his ontological and epistemological analyses he might have again reverted to his former existentialist views of reality and consciousness, or what is more likely at this point, to some form of determinism. By refusing to force these questions to their logical conclusions, he can afford the luxury of arguing for both necessity and freedom.

Thus, for example, Sartre will argue that at the beginning of an activity man is free to choose the means he will employ to achieve a specific end, but once he has chosen his means, he is driven in a determined manner; for example, if one desires to visit Chicago, the means of transportation may be freely chosen—one flies, rides, or walks, with all that each of these involves, although the delays, the crowds, the tension, or the fatigue were not part of the desired means or ends. Con-sequently, Desan observes, "it seems as if one chooses the means toward some particular end, but once one's act is perpetrated, it escapes and in its objectification leads to ends other than the perpetrator had intended or desired."[6]

Adopting the Marxist formulation of alienation, Sartre notes further that regardless of how man acts to satisfy his needs. once he commences to work on the material world surrounding him he estranges himself and even becomes the victim of his own products. Thus man is not able to control the ends for which he strives, for every *finality*—a result in accordance with the purpose of the act—carries with it elements of *counter-finality*—indirect and unforeseen results joined to the *finality* (e.g., industrialization of a city—a desired finality—producing air-pollution—an undesired *counter-finality*). Although the *counter-finality* is an unforeseen and often undesired end, it is still man alone who is responsible for it: either it may be unavoidably associated with his desired end, or man may not have acted positively in order to circumvent it.[7] Sartre's argu-ment, at this point, appears to be that since man freely chose the ends he also consented to the means. But even if the choice were truly free, which it is not, this would be a non sequitur.

Thus, man may choose *some* means, but all the ends escape him. And the paradox is that the necessity involved appears more stringent when an act is performed with complete knowledge of the results.[8] The awareness of necessity, for Sartre, does not bring with it greater freedom; it merely leads to a more conscious acceptance of inevitability. Nevertheless Sartre continues to assert that freedom and responsibility remain even under these conditions because man can always "re-interiorize" or transcend the *counter-finality* through another free project, through additional free *praxis*. Here again, this would be a viable argument if the possibilities and the results of man's *praxis* were limitless or in fact controllable, But such is not the case; man and the world have limits, and certain unforeseen results of *praxis*—certain *counter-finalities*—have lasting effects that can hardly be "re-interiorized" and changed. Besides in the attempt to counter the *counter-finality* new forms of *counter-finality* may be encountered and the matter might get completely out of hand: a high-powered nuclear explosion setting off a chain reaction is a frightening possibility and a case in point; similar uncontrollable chain reactions can be conceived in man's social activities.

Therefore at the very outset of his activity the individual's freedom is greatly circumscribed by his existential conditions. He is limited by his own needs, by the mode of his totalization, by the world's structure and scarcity, and by the laws of nature. Once he begins to act, both the ends and the means of his activity escape him. His *project* is not freely chosen—it is determined by the above factors. Often the results of his *praxis* turn against him, and unavoidably he gives rise to phenomena which he is unable to control and which he did not desire to appear. Awareness of these facts does not liberate him from their deterministic force; it merely confirms it, and places the entire responsibility upon his own shoulders.[9] Whatever freedom there is, appears to consist in the conscious recognition of necessity, of the absence of freedom.

Further, Sartre notes that historically it is evident that every attempt by man to overcome scarcity has only resulted in the numerical increase of what he defines as the "subhuman" element—the slave, the serf, the worker.[10] And once history begins to develop man is always trapped between what Desan calls a "double materiality": the products of his past activity determine the present style of his work and at the same time dictate the direction of his future activity.[11] The machine, for example, has its own potentialites and ends, and, once set into motion, man can only follow its inherent laws and development.

And lastly, it is the "matter" which surrounds man, with which he works, that defines him—for himself and for others— that places him in a social class. It is the job that makes the worker what he is; or conversely, the *essence* of the large majority of men may be defined by the work that they do. And in most cases, the individual does not even choose his work or his class—he is born into them. He merely possesses a degree of personal latitude within the bonds that define him. He makes himself what he is, but he does so within a predetermined, circumscribed area.[12]

If one recalls the discussions concerning the concept of freedom in *Being and Nothingness,* the contrast at this point is jarring. Sartre, however, does make an attempt to retain some elements of transcendence and revolt. He stresses that the individual may always rebel and go against the practico-inert that surrounds him: "for however strong may be the inertia which holds him down, for man there is always the possibility of going beyond."[13] At every stage of the dialectical process, man is free to decide whether to submit or to rebel. And Sartre claims that "even the worker freely engages himself although he knows that the machine will be his prison and his alienation."[14] But by now it is commonplace to point out that this so-called "free choice" of the worker to engage himself is a theoretical, ideologically biased argument. If there is any freedom here, it is either the freedom to starve, or, at times, to choose the manner of one's bondage. In either case, this is a perverted use of the concept of freedom, and it is curious that a philosopher with proletarian convictions should rely upon a classic capitalistic definition of the workers' "freedom." And yet, even though the argument may not be cogent, the observation is realistic. At least it is an advance on the radical and unrealistic definition of freedom in *Being and Nothingness.* But the fact remains, that the *Critique* clearly fails to retain the individual's freedom in his dialectical activity within the material world.

SOCIAL DIALECTIC

A similar absence of "concrete" freedom is evident in the individual's relationships within the social sphere.

In Sartre's description, society at its basis is made up of *series*—unconscious groupings of individuals. Some of the series are of a fairly permanent nature: place of residence, socioeconomic status, race, religion. Others are more elusive and transitory: a group waiting for a bus, flying in a plane, listening to a lecture. Characteristically, the series is passive, inert, inorganic, and unstructured, and every individual in it is solitary —he is an Other among Others. In some cases, he may not be conscious of the series to which he belongs. And it is an accidental object that unites the series—the bus, the place of residence, etc.

The series may be inert and unorganized, but it can also be powerful: for example, sales prices are largely determined by the unstructured series composing the free market. And because the series is made up of atomized, isolated individuals, these individuals are powerless to oppose it. In their collective isolation they constitute the series, give it power, and then become its victims. Man has once more succumbed to alienation; he has again forged his own chains.

And when Sartre proceeds to a detailed examination of the seriality of classes, the inescapable historical and sociological facts lead him to an admission of "the presence of a strong trend of 'necessity' and [he] appears to be quite fatalistic in his views. Clearly, he has nowhere been confronted with such a power of inertia and such deeply ingrained resistance of the seriality."[15]

At the start of his dialectical activity in nature the individual was trapped by the material conditions of his existence; here, he is engulfed by the fundamental social conditions of his existence. Also, it is necessary to remember that these social conditions were originally structured by the material conditions. The enslavement, therefore, is circular and double.

In order to escape the inert, but enveloping, seriality, man forms a purposive *group*. This is a social imitation of the individual who first began to labor purposively on the inert matter surrounding him. It appears that at least the *group in fusion* (a group in the process of formation before it becomes

rigidly structured) is a result of the free consent of every individual involved. Instead of being the inert, passive Other,
the individual now becomes the *third man*—a freely "acting
subject who himself totalizes."[16] But in fact, the formation
of the group is triggered by an outside threat. And often the
choice is one of "unite or perish": that is, some segment of
the seriality is threatened by an already formed group. Therefore, "although it can be said in all truth that the individual
freely joins the group, it is no less certain that if he wants to
survive, he *must* join, for salvation lies where the group is."[17]
To live, man must labor, and now he must also unite. But in
both cases, once he begins to act he is engulfed by dialectical
processes which he is unable to control and which frustrate
his original purpose. Sartre refers variously to this phenomenon
as the *anti-dialectic,* the *anti-man,* or the *anti-praxis.* The
individual's so-called "free choice" is immediately transformed
into a self-imposed limitation. In the social dialectic this becomes evident when the spontaneous *group in fusion* unavoidably
evolves into a stable organization in order to escape returning
into the atomized, powerless, and inert seriality.

First the *oath* and later *terror* are relied upon as devices for
counteracting the danger of atomization and disunity within
the group. The oath, in Sartre's vocabulary, is "the affirmation
by the third man, of the permanence of the group as a negation
of its exterior negation"[18] (i.e., of the external threat that
forced the individuals to unite). The oath, whether explicit
or implicit, is an act whereby the individual's freedom used
in the formation of the group becomes a permanent property
of the group. In other words, the individual agrees to limit
his freedom for the sake of the continued and united existence
of the group. In this manner, the group creates a degree of its
own inertia, without which it would easily dissolve into the
seriality that it is attempting to conquer. Still, it is paradoxical
that in order to conquer its former inertia the group must
similarly become at least partially inert.

Up to this point, however, there may be little objection to
Sartre's new definition of individual freedom; although it is
limited in some respects, it gains in scope and possibility as
a result of the permanent existence of the group. But it
appears that the oath is merely a prelude to the inevitable
imposition of terror. The oath must be given in common, and
freedom must be enjoyed in common, and if an individual

breaks the oath he has become a traitor. For the individual
is not free to leave the group that he created; neither can he
be dismissed—he must be eliminated.[19] And what is more,
"the violence inflicted upon the traitor implies a bond of love
among the executers."[20] Here, curiously, Sartre fails to
stress the principle that at every stage the individual is free
to break away from the dialectical scheme that he has set
into motion. It appears that at least in this instance he is
clearly contradicting himself.

As the group continues to evolve, it becomes a structured
organization. The organization is characterized by a specific
distribution of functions aiming toward the common purpose
of the group. And now the function becomes essential and
the individual unessential. It is possible to become a better
functionary than someone else, but that is the extent of one's
private initiative and freedom. For the individual's freedom is
irrelevant and his activity is judged on the basis of his performance as a functionary. Since functions and their interactions
are objective, abstract entities, Sartre concludes that it should
be possible to describe an entire society in mathematical
terms. Since at this stage the individual is expendable, even if
he leaves the organization the function and the structure will
remain intact. And yet, although the individual did not directly
create the series of organizations making up the social structure—
often he is merely born into them—Sartre still insists that its
continued existence is proof of the fact that most men have
bestowed their consent upon it. And the consent, as with John
Locke, may be either explicit or tacit.

With the organization comes the *institution,* defined by its
aversion to change and the appearance of authority. The
institution is more stable and therefore more rigid and inert.
And now, if the individual merely proposes a change in the
institutional structure he is immediately suspect, for he thereby
reveals his freedom, and individual freedom is a threat to the
organizational structure of the institution.

And lastly, in order to maintain discipline and unity of
purpose, the institution must develop a *bureaucracy*—a hier-
archical order in which only the highest level is relatively free
of the inertia that it necessarily imposes upon all lower levels.

Sartre concludes this section of the *Critique* by emphasizing
that the increasing institutionalization of the group is an
inevitable phenomenon. And it is obvious that in the process

not only the individual but the group as well has lost all freedom and initiative. For "the true efficiency of the group lies in its immersion in the matter, but where this happens completely, where *praxis* becomes *processus* and action becomes inert and passive, the common ends are no longer controllable. Without ceasing to be the common ends of the group, they become destinies."[21]

From an unstructured, inert seriality, the individual has passed into a structured, inert seriality. In both cases his life is threatened, but at least in the unstructured seriality he was free to defend himself, whereas in the structured seriality even a minor demonstration of his freedom makes him suspect, and the full use of it is punished by death. Ironically, it was the original use of his freedom that caused this later tyrannical situation. Inevitably the individual's freedom turns against him and enslaves him.

SARTRE'S LOSS OF FREEDOM

From the above discussion, it is evident that Sartre has taken on an enormous task. He has made an attempt to describe in detail man's entire material and social reality. In order to accomplish his task, he has drawn freely and haphazardly from the disciplines of philosophy, economy, political theory, sociology, history, and psychology. The enormity and the complexity of the task have often led him to contradictions, illogical conclusions, and numerous poorly developed hypotheses.

In reviewing the arguments centered on the question of individual freedom, it is difficult to concur with Professor Desan's conclusion that the *Critique* with all its limitations "undoubtedly makes an eloquent plea for freedom."[22] More correctly, it would appear that the *Critique* is a description of man's futile attempts to escape an all-encompassing determinism. For from his birth man and his condition are largely fixed. His activity, whether solitary or within a group, always rebounds against him; and he is unable to control either his means or his ends. It seems as if the universe were deliberately attempting to thwart all his endeavors to be creative, to be free.

Yet man is able to understand that it is often his own activity that is the cause of this inevitably frustrating condition. Sartre

cannot fully accept the optimistic Marxist faith that awareness
or knowledge of the laws of reality, of the operations of the
dialectic, will somehow increase man's freedom. There is history,
there is movement, but there does not appear to be any progress
toward greater freedom—whether individual or social. On the
contrary, the tendency seems to be that the more complex man's
activity, the more "progress" he makes, the greater the limitations
upon his freedom. The contradictions of Sartre notwithstanding,
even if it were true that each man freely consents to his condition,
and that at every stage he is free to rebel and to withdraw, what
would be the result of such a rebellion? Man must eat, and to
eat he must labor even if his activity is responsible for various
forms of alienation. Man must live in a society: if he rebels he
will be punished, and if he withdraws he will perish. And when
he is able to exercise a degree of freedom in his initial choice
and activity, he knows that with the dialectical development
of events he will lose his freedom once again. How often will
an intelligent man rebel when he knows the unpromising and
unchanging results of his rebellion? Sartre himself acknowledges
that the greater awareness of reality—of the dialectical processes—
the greater acquiescence to reality. Philosophically, *consciousness* of freedom and of slavery may be freedom, but *practically,*
if this is how freedom is defined, it is abstract and meaningless.
Clearly the "free *praxis*," the free totalization," the "re-
interiorization" of *counter-finality,* and the existentialist
rebellion that Sartre invokes from time to time in the *Critique*
are this type of abstract, unrealistic concepts, and Sartre implies
as much at every crucial stage of his argument. For in its more
empirical analyses the *Critique* is basically a eulogy to necessity
and determinism.

Therefore, instead of incorporating a degree of existentialism
into an already deterministic Marxism, Sartre has buried his
former existentialism in a Marxism of his own making. He has
passed from one extreme to another and created a Marxist
dialectic more deterministic than that of Marx himself. Other
differences also appear: unlike the Marxist dialectic, Sartre's
dialectic is dependent upon man's conscious activity; also, it
is the individual, for Sartre, who is the motive force behind
all dialectical movement. Sartre may have thought that by
placing the individual at the center of all human activity and
history he would somehow ensure the continued creative and
free movement of the individual. But apparently as he began

to develop his ideas, this original intention was foiled by the logic of the argument itself, and consequently he also failed to accomplish his stated purpose—the union of Marxism and existentialism.[23]

NOTES

1. Wilfred Desan, *The Marxism of Jean-Paul Sartre* (New York: Doubleday, 1965), pp. vii-viii. The book is a faithful and excellent outline of Sartre's *Critique de la raison dialectique.*

2. Unlike the Hegelian and Marxist dialectic, Sartre's dialectic is not even partially independent of man; it is directly initiated by man's activity: "outside man and without man, the dialectic is mere hypothesis." Ibid., pp. 77-78.

3. For an opposed view, see Howard R. Burkle, "Jean-Paul Sartre: Social Freedom in *Critique de la raison dialectique,*" *Review of Metaphysics* 19, no. 4 (June 1969): 742-757.

4. Desan, *The Marxism of Jean-Paul Sartre,* p. 82.

5. Ibid., p. 100.

6. Ibid., p. 105.

7. Ibid., pp. 101-102.

8. Ibid., p. 106.

9. This description of man, his activity, and his existence in the world is reminiscent of Sartre's somewhat contradictory contention in *Being and Nothingness* that man does not create the world, and he does not control it, but nevertheless, he alone defines it, shapes it, and therefore is totally responsible for it.

10. Desan, *Marxism of Sartre,* pp. 96-97.

11. Ibid., p. 101.

12. Ibid., pp. 106-107.

13. Ibid., p. 107.

14. Ibid., p. 120.

15. Ibid., p. 119.

16. Ibid., p. 130.

17. Ibid., p. 135.

18. Ibid., p. 139.

19. Ibid., p. 141.

20. Ibid.

21. Ibid., p. 194.

22. Ibid., pp. vii-viii.

23. A more detailed examination of this problem may be found in Walter Odajnyk, *Marxism and Existentialism* (New York: Doubleday Anchor Books, 1965).

Part X

DIALOGUE AND HISTORY

Chapter 31

Dialogue Between American and Soviet Philosophers

JOHN SOMERVILLE and DALE RIEPE

Dale Riepe is professor of philosophy at the State University of New York at Buffalo. He has received Fulbright awards to study in India and Japan, a grant from the Carnegie Foundation, and a Fellowship from the American Institute of Indian Studies. He is a co-editor of *The Structure of Philosophy* (1966) and is the author of *The Naturalistic Tradition in Indian Thought* (1961) and *The Influence of Indian Thought on American Philosophy* (1970).

Described by the *Excelsior* of Mexico City in a banner headline on the front page as *Conclusiones de los Filosofos de Rusia y E. U., en Junta Secreta; Lucha con las Ideas, Nunca con las Armas,* an unprogrammed conference of American and Soviet philosophers took place during the XIII International Congress of Philosophy. While in a sense private, since it was confined to members from the two countries, and while its form was agreed to only after the start of the congress, it was in no sense secret. The initiative in organizing and sponsoring the session, which lasted about two-and-a-half hours, came from the Society for the Philosophical Study of Dialectical Material-ism, a specialized group open to all members of the American

For biographical information about John Somerville, see page 43.

Philosophical Association. Co-chairmen of the meeting were
the present president of the society, Professor John Somerville
of Hunter College, and its first president (1962-63), Professor
Howard Parsons of Coe College.

In form, the meeting was a sort of panel session, in which
the Soviet philosophers had agreed to discuss any aspect of
their congress papers, including philosophic aspects of the
problem of peaceful coexistence, in relation to which questions
might be raised. In fact, the questions ranged over the whole
extent of Soviet philosophy, were seldom directed to any
specific individual, and were answered mainly by the three
leading members of the Soviet delegation who were seated at
the dais: Professor P. N. Fedoseev, vice-president of the U.S.S.R.
Academy of Sciences, Professor M. B. Mitin, member of the
U.S.S.R. Academy of Sciences and editor-in-chief of *Problems
of Philosophy*, and Professor F. V. Konstantinov, director of
the Institute of Philosophy of the U.S.S.R. Academy of
Sciences. Other Soviet philosophers sat among the fifty or
more American philosophers around the conference chamber.
Each participant spoke in his own language. Everything said
in English was translated into Russian by Professor V. Semenov
of the Soviet delegation, assisted by a colleague. Everything
presented in Russian was translated into English by Professor
Somerville.

The present report cannot claim to be a verbatim record, or
even a complete summary of all that was said. In some cases,
the present writers were not sure of the identity of the
questioner; and some of the questions and answers, or parts
of them, may have eluded our notes and recollection. But we
hope that all the main lines of discussion are fairly accurately
reflected in what follows.

The first question was put by Professor Parsons: in the view
of Soviet philosophers, what are the chief problems of the
contemporary world which were not foreseen and dealt with
by Marx and Engels?

In replying, Professor Fedoseev pointed out that this was,
of course, an extremely broad question, touching matters of
very great importance, and covering a very wide area. Some
of the main divisions into which the subject matter might
be broken down are: the evolution of productive forces; the
evolution of scientific knowledge; the concrete conditions of
transition from capitalism to socialism and from socialism to

communism; the types of conflict, both internal and external, involved in such transitions. It should be kept in mind in this connection that Marx and Engels proceeded on the basis of an explicit theory of social evolution and social progress, so that they had already envisaged certain broad lines of development, which, in fact, have come about, and which they may be said to have predicted. The distinction Fedoseev seemed to be drawing was one between basic structure and fundamental direction of movement on the one side, and concrete content and concrete problems on the other side, the unforeseen and undealt with (by Marx and Engels) being on the latter side. What was in point here he termed the dialectical contradictions of our epoch, suggesting that these could be traced at different levels—the level of large-scale events, such as the transition from socialism to communism, the level of the "dialectics and the logic" of scientific knowledge, including the whole area of epistemology, methods of research, and so on. Dwelling especially on this aspect of the matter, the speaker emphasized the significance of new and unforeseen developments in science, such as nuclear physics, cybernetics, recent studies of the higher nervous system, advances in our knowledge of the cosmos, and in special fields like crystallography, and the progress made in our understanding of the processes of development from the inorganic to the organic.

Fedoseev developed the thought that the concrete problems of the present day not dealt with by Marx and Engels, to which contemporary philosophers must address themselves, included also the whole range of the social sciences (a field of work historically relatively new), as well as traditional disciplines, such as the history of philosophy, the philosophy of art, and ethics. The implication appeared to be that there are new possibilities of content in these traditional disciplines which no one could have foreseen a century ago. In this connection, Fedoseev concluded with the remark that today special importance attaches to problems centering on the person, on the development and interrelationships of individuals as individuals.

Professor Mitin added a comment in relation to this question, pointing out that the charactor of Marxist philosophy must be taken into account. It does not aim at solutions which will stand as frozen positions. "It is not to be approached as a dogma but as a guide to action." In other words, one must not presuppose that its claim is in some sense to foresee everything and answer all questions in advance. It does not consider that the emergence of new conditions and problems constitutes a defeat for itself. On the contrary, it points out that there will continue to be new problems and new conditions; its basic methodology takes precisely that into account. Mitin applied this thought to the present epoch by way of emphasizing that the problem of paramount importance today is international peace. While in its general features this problem was foreseen by Marx and Engels, not even Engels (who was something of a specialist in the technology of warfare) could have foreseen the character of present-day weapons, in all their unimaginable destructiveness. Several times the speaker returned to the point that Marxism from its beginnings had put forth as an over-all social slogan, "peace and labor."

Looking at the original question from its positive side, Mitin made the point that "foreseeing" raised the issue of scientific prediction, in this case as applied to society and the evolution of society. In that sense, he said, the basic predictions made by Marx in relation to the course which human history would take could truly be said to represent "the most important" ever made in that field. New details, of course, have entered and will continue to enter into these phenomena; new contra- dictions emerge; new complexities develop. The "dialectics of the transition from socialism to communism" was indicated as affording abundant illustration of this truth.

Professor Brand Blanshard, Emeritus of Yale University, asked: What is the explanation of the surprising degree of uniformity which apparently exists among Soviet philosophers? In the American tradition, philosophers have many different points of vew. They by no means agree on their positions or in their allegiances. This, however, does not seem to be the case among Soviet philosophers. The formulation of the question carried the implication that, whereas American thought is pluralistic, Soviet thought is monolithic. Illustrating with generally appreciated humor the point of this question, Professor Blanshard remarked that he would like to read sometime that a Soviet philosopher had promulgated a new proof for the existence of God.

In replying, Professor Fedoseev posed a counterquestion: why is it necessarily better that there should be a number of different viewpoints in regard to a given problem? What is at issue in the context of philosophic discussion is the truth about something, which truth, if it is sought in a rational sense, is by definition one and not many. The implication was that a major reason for greater agreement among Soviet than among other philosophers was that the viewpoint of the former was more scientific. Just as there is one mathematics and one physics which we seek, so there is one philosophy. Having once discussed our differences, we Soviet scholars then tend to form a group to defend a common general position (though not a permanently frozen one) because we are convinced that it is the best. There is, moreover, a kind of specious pluralism about American bourgeois thought. The suggestion was that it only seems like a wild assortment of tropical flowers, but should fool no one who recognizes the daisy in each position. The differences which exist are largely differences within idealist and anticommunist groups. In a sense, it is a scene of many tendencies, but one world-view. It should also be pointed out that the so-called divergences of Western views reflect idealistic and unscientific pretensions. Questions of dialectics and interpretation are hotly disputed in the Soviet Union, but in the end some kind of scientific agreement may be reached because the conclusions are based upon objectively verifiable reality. One need not list the number of bourgeois philosophies which are not only not scientific, but to all intents and purposes antiscientific. In this sense, Soviet philosophy cannot take seriously the supposed many-viewed approaches of bourgeois philosophy.

Professor Konstantinov also commented on this question, emphasizing that there is much more freedom of intellectual discussion in the Soviet Union than is usually realized. American philosophers, it was pointed out, could convince themselves on this score by coming to the Soviet Union, observing these discussions and taking part in them, as a number of American philosophers had already done. Professor Fedoseev remarked parenthetically that they would not encounter the kind of difficulty about entrance visas which had on several occasions prevented Soviet philosophers from accepting invitations to take part in philosophical discussions in the United States. A recent series of publications in the U.S.S.R. centering on philosophical questions concerned with research in the field of higher nervous activity was cited as an example of sharp and sustained debate in the field of philosophy of science.

A question was raised by Professor Richard Hocking, requesting
clarification of the concept of dialectics in point of its range
of applicability. If contradiction, as a concept going even
further than opposition or conflict, be taken as the essence
of dialectics, must not this concept, strictly speaking, be
limited to the level of consciousness? Is not the attempt to
apply it to inorganic phenomena open to the charge of imputing
to these phenomena conditions which could only be found at
more complex levels?

The reply to this question, given by Fedoseev and Mitin, was
that the principles of dialectics may be seen in operation at all
levels of phenomena, although each level is also characterized by
laws unique to that level. The principles or laws of dialectics
represent the basic patterns of relationship found common to
all levels. They are thus the most general laws. Certain observed
patterns of change, development, and evolution are common to
the behavior of phenomena as widely separated as the most
distant clusters of the largest stars and the smallest atomic
particles within chemical elements. These patterns are found
both in what happens inside crystals and inside a higher nervous
system. Recent films have shown in a remarkable way what
goes on inside crystals previously thought to be impenetrable.
The dialectical aspect is seen in those conflicting relations of
form and content which can only be adequately expressed
by terms like "contradiction." Such a term is necessary in view
of the actual outcomes of the processes or dynamics which
these relationships represent.

Several interrelated questions were raised concerning the
Soviet interpretation of aspects of the transition to communism,
the role of classes, class struggles, and the state. The answers
were given by Professors Fedoseev, Mitin, and Konstantinov, with
occasional interjections from Professors Melvil, Kopnin, and
other Soviet philosophers.

The first point which was emphasized in answering these
questions was that such social transitions as those from capitalism
to socialism and socialism to communism become necessary
because a system other than the prevailing one is better adapted
to manage the problems which have arisen. The old joke to the
effect that the post office was the first socialist institution has
a serious point. The system of private ownership and individual
control simply cannot manage to solve the sort of problems
which we face today, in terms of the ever growing technological

complexities of production. An efficient and satisfactory solution of these problems is unthinkable except on a basis of social planning and widespread social organization of production.

As to the kind of opposition, conflict, and contradiction at the conscious and the social level which would be present even under socialism and communism, it was pointed out that this would not take the form of struggles between classes, but would be basically struggles of man against inimical or limiting forces of nature and of his environment. It is true, as Marx long ago maintained, that class struggles were the chief dynamic of human history in all those epochs characterized by the existence of antagonistic classes—groups having such differing relationships to the means of production as to bring them into constant conflict with one another—but, as Marx of course also maintained, the price of class struggle as a social dynamic is too high. Antagonistic classes in the economic sense must be eliminated as soon as possible, and are eliminated under socialism and communism.

The role of the state, it was emphasized, must always be seen in relation to classes and class antagonisms. Marxism has always located the essence of the state not in social organization or administration as such—that is quite possible without a state— but in the permanently organized apparatus of physical enforcement based on law. The necessity for that came about with the rise of deep-seated economic conflicts within a society. Thus one could say that a world without antagonistic classes could do without the state; the state would "wither away." But the state could not be expected to wither away in a single society from which antagonistic classes had been eliminated if that society existed within a world where antagonistic classes were elsewhere to be found. It was again stressed that it would be incorrect to conclude that a world without the state would be a world without planning and organization. On the contrary, future stages of society would probably be such as to call for very far-reaching planning and organizing. It should also be emphasized that the disappearance of antagonistic classes does not involve any lessening of individual differences among persons, any decrease of individuality at the psychological or cultural level. It involves in fact an increase in the forms of growth, and thus in the needs and demands, of the human person. What follows is an enrichment of individuality, and the rise of new challenges.

An inquiry was made as to what the Soviet answer would be to criticisms advanced by Plekhanov and Rosa Luxembourg in the initial period of the Bolshevik regime charging that regime with betraying basic principles of Marxism. However, as the question did not specify the content of the criticism nor the evidence on which the charge was founded, Professor Fedoseev replied that it was too vague to be answered concretely. Also, the context was necessarily restricted, as Plekhanov had died as early as 1918, and Luxembourg in 1919.

A question concerning the doctrine of dialectics was posed to this effect: if the dialectical movement is discernible every-where, as presumably it is for Soviet philosophers, then in what form does it appear in chess games, in paintings, or in musical scores? How does dialectics manifest itself in things not immediately connected with economics and politics? For instance, do you find dialectics in some relation between the white keys and the black keys on a piano? This question was posed at considerable length, with a number of hypothetical examples of the *reductio ad absurdum* variety, intended to show that various ways of construing dialectics would be ridiculous. Professor Fedoseev preferred not to take this question seriously. The answer could be worked out, though probably not to the satisfaction of the questioner. Fedoseev's attitude seemed to be that since the problem was posed only in a facetious or "needling" spirit a serious solution need not be suggested.

At this point Fedoseev took the floor to make a statement relative to the meeting. He said he was greatly surprised at the content and nature of questions now taking up valuable time. Many of us have traveled thousands of miles to come together in these philosophical meetings. This would hardly be worth the effort unless we are going to keep to questions more important than the dialectics of chess. In fact, one cannot help wondering, as one thinks of the course of our discussion so far, what has happened to so important a problem as peaceful coexistence. Put more concretely, what is the explanation of the fact that among a group of American philosophers so little interest and attention seem to be given to the philosophic aspects of such a tremendously grave question as that of peace-ful coexistence?

Professor Parsons, as chairman, inquired if any present had questions which they would wish to raise concerning problems of peaceful coexistence. He recognized Professor George Kline of Bryn Mawr, who presented an inquiry along the following lines: if there can be peaceful coexistence in

relation to the problem of international warfare in the military
sense, why cannot there be peaceful coexistence in the realm
of ideology?

In reply, Professor Fedoseev pointed out that what is usually
meant by peaceful coexistence in the realm of ideology is
cessation of the conflict of ideologies; but this conflict is a
contest of ideas, and there is nothing wrong with that. There is
no reason to stop a contest of ideas, since, from such a contest,
an improvement of ideas may result. The conflict one seeks to
prevent is the contest of force, since such a conflict may destroy
the world. It is very important to remember that the ideological
conflict, the contest of ideas, should not be identified with the
cold war, as if they were of necessity one and the same thing.
What one objects to in the cold war is not any competition of
ideas, but such phenomena as refusal of normal diplomatic
relations, naval blockade, illegal interference in the internal
affairs of other countries. Such happenings are very far from
being a contest of ideas. If persisted in, they become a preliminary
to hot war.

What must be recognized as basic in the situation, continued
Professor Fedoseev, is the fact that there are in the world today
powerful states which, like ours and yours, represent different
ideological viewpoints. Now it is, of course, absurd to entertain
the notion, for example, of making any kind of treaty that you
must think as we do, or that we must think as you do. That is
nonsense, and is impossible in any case. But we can agree not
to use weapons, or the threat of weapons, to settle the ideological
differences between us. That is the root meaning of peaceful
coexistence. We feel that all philosophers should oppose the cold
war; but that does not mean that they should oppose a contest
or competition of ideas.

Professor Dale Riepe of the State University of New York at
Buffalo, presenting the next question, said that when he traveled
in Asia the Asian philosophers claimed that American philosophy
was too materialistic; and now the Soviet philosophers claimed
that it was too idealistic. What is the truth of this matter? Is there
any hope, from the Soviet point of view, for American philosophy?
Professor Fedoseev replied that there certainly were indications
of positive elements in American philosophy. He did not enter
into any specific critique, but pointed out that a number of works
of American philosophers had been translated into Russian, and
were favorably evaluated by Soviet critics. In Soviet philosophical

literature one could find a great deal of reference to American philosophy of the past and present, reference by no means always negative in its import.

A question was specifically directed to Professor T. I. Oizerman of Moscow University, relating to the paper, "Man and His Alienation," which he had presented at the congress. The point raised was whether Professor Oizerman considered alienation to be essentially an economic phenomenon. Could it be dealt with adequately if so considered? Professor Oizerman stated in reply that he quite agreed that alienation was a many-sided phenomenon, which must be treated at many levels beside the economic—the political, the ideological, the psychological level, and so on—just as the overcoming of alienation was a many-sided process, which must also work itself out at the different levels. The specific thesis which he had tried to demonstrate in his paper, Oizerman pointed out, was that alienation had deep economic roots, and that these must be properly dealt with if the problem is to be solved. In other words, alienation has an objective, as well as a subjective, side. It must also be borne in mind that conflict is not necessarily alienation. There are many forms of conflict and difference which lie outside the sphere of alienation.

Professor Paul Weiss of Yale University, having been recognized for a question, said he would like to use his time to express a sense of gratitude and appreciation to the guests and participants in the conference, and to those who had organized it. He voiced the strong feeling that this kind of philosophic dialogue was one of the most important in which contemporary scholars could engage. His comment was met with marked approbation by the gathering.

In the estimation of the present writers, the confrontation of these two groups of philosophers had the following significance:

1. It was the first large-scale meeting of American and Soviet philosophers since the founding of the U.S.S.R. From an intellectual or cultural point of view, this was long overdue.

2. The mere fact that the conference gave an opportunity to American and Soviet philosophers to look at and listen to one another in the flesh, and in the give and take of philosophic discussion, was significant in a psychological and moral sense, in addition to the philosophic value represented by the communication of ideas.

3. The experience of organizing this conference warrants the belief that conferences between American and Soviet scholars, in the interests of greater mutual understanding, could be brought to pass in almost any intellectual area, if approached with a presumption of mutual good faith and on a basis of equal rights.

Chapter 32

Necessary Polarities in Western Reflection Upon History

RICHARD BOYLE O'REILLY HOCKING

From 1949 to 1971 Richard Boyle O'Reilly Hocking was professor of philosophy at Emory University in Atlanta, Georgia. He has held teaching positions at the University of Chicago, the University of California at Los Angeles, and Williams College, and was exchange professor at the University of Frankfort in 1949. He has contributed "Process and Analysis in the Philosophy of Royce" to *Josiah Royce's Seminar, 1913-1914;* "Existenz and Objectivity" to *Process and Divinity: The Hartshorne Festschrift;* and "Other Persons, Other Things" to *The Problem of Self.*

"It is reflection which constitutes truth the final result, and yet at the same time does away with the contrast between result and the process of arriving at it." (Hegel, *Phenomenology of Spirit*, Preface).

Given the theme of this symposium, I wish to approach it in terms of the heightened consciousness of history which characterizes the thought of at least the past century and a half in the Occident. The technical term "dialectical" has come to be associated intimately with this heightened consciousness of history. Indeed, since the time of Hegel, "dialectic" is counted a principle in the constructive reflection upon human history. Even in its classical use, "dialectic" carried the meaning of an intellectual journey with a goal and, in that sense, a sort of history. The direction of the journey was intentionally, though tentatively, toward the grasp and clarification of first principles. In modern thought, the new emphasis may be expressed without distortion in terms of the conviction that reflection upon history and the history of reflection are identical in principle, since philosophical work takes the order of human living as its point of departure and also is itself human living in one preeminent form.

In the context of this modern heightening of historical consciousness, the time-honored imperative that philosophers meet in dialogue receives a like intensification. We grow readier to see that the life of reflection is no exception to the rule that all human effort is concretely history-bound for better or worse. In each new situation we learn anew, as philosophers, how to escape the drift into monologue, how to sustain dialogue.

(Parenthetically, our symposium, as both a little bit of history and a little bit of reflection, is a case in point. In this double light, it should mirror itself in responsible autonomy.)

A SHARED LEGACY

We join in this symposium ("dialogue" is a better term) as philosophers coming from two different traditions *within* the Occident. At the outset, let us identify three of our shared inheritances (moving from the broader to the more special) as preliminary to detecting the shape of three philosophical issues upon which we might join forces in our future intellectual work.

(*a*) In a general way we may think of Russia and America as two daughters of Mother Europe. I personally have found this metaphor helpful and often moving. We should claim "The West" as our shared family name, in order to remind ourselves that the Mediterranean legacies, both Greek and Biblical, both Byzantine and Latin, interpenetrate variously in contributing to the modern characters of these two daughter civilizations.

We inherit, for example, an intellectual and institutional familiarity with certain contrasts which are much more generally Western traits than they are non-European (India, China, and Japan). Take the contrasts between science and faith, state and church, nature and history. To be sure, these have been

perennial storm centers of debate in Western history. They
have repeatedly been themes requiring clarification. My point
is that they are shared orientations, "Western commonplaces,"
so to speak, within which we as philosophers know how to
declare our positions and oppositions. They sustain dialogue.
Despite the record of disagreements associated with such
contrasts, they represent a pattern of "aporetic" agreement.

Russia and America are relatively young as far as distinctive
intellectual traditions are concerned. Both reach back some
three hundred and fifty years, to the close of the fifteenth
century.

It is recorded that there arose in Moscow, in the late
fifteenth century, for reasons both political and ecclesiastical,
an emphasis on the expansive thought of Moscow as "the
Third Rome." Constantinople had been long enough the
Second Rome. Coupled with this idea was the addendum,
pronounced with a note of finality, that "there will not be
a Fourth Rome." In many ways this thought has found
embodiment over the intervening generations. We of the Atlantic
shores forget too often the great momentum of the transmigra-
tion eastward of the Roman idea. We are conversant enough
with the fifteenth-century effort to bring the Roman and
Orthodox churches together. We are, on occasion, as philosophers, proud to remember the role of that great dialectical
thinker, Nicholas of Cusa, in preparing for this effort. We
confess that the Russian perspective on this turn of events
usually escapes our historical imaginations.

For Americans, both Latin and Northern, the parallel
expansive thought over the same three and a half centuries
is that of "The New World," first for the Latin explorers and
then for the Northern Europeans. America is still the New
World in our imaginations and in much of our thinking about
our historical relationships to Mother Europe.

I recall these guiding thoughts because they are rich suggestions of the *telos* of the two daughter traditions, this, rather
than because of conceptual precision.

(b) Whether in "the Third Rome" or in "the New World,"
it was long before one could speak of a philosophical tradition
in a strictly academic sense. The coming of age in terms of this
sort of philosophical work may be related to the radiant
influence of Immanuel Kant and the constellation of philosophers who closely followed him during and after the French

Revolution. One advantage which is shared by the philosophical
traditions of Russia and America, and which is the consequence
of our relative youth as daughter civilizations, is the clarity
of this illumination upon the thought of our philosophers.
There is here a shared inheritance which strengthens the
promise of present dialogue.

The Kantian time was one of the axial times of our intellectual history (if I may be allowed this use of Jaspers' term).
The swing upon the axis was away from metaphysics as an
abstract Cartesian deductive discipline toward a renewed and
critical metaphysics as a concrete, inductive, and markedly
dialectical discipline. The Cartesian association between metaphysics and the mathematical sciences was modified, and for
a while even displaced, by a new association between metaphysics and the evolutionary disciplines then coming forward:
geological, biological, and social. The important point to
remark is that this turn has influenced both Russian and
American academic philosophy in comparable degrees.

The traits of the Kantian philosophy which are telling in
view of the subsequent rise of dialectical philosophies of
history are simple to recall. There are two, especially, which
disclose the raison d'être of the whole critical program. There
is the centering on the autonomous moral individual, the
unit in time of self-legislative rational freedom. Also there is
the teleological character of the whole categorial scheme, its
whole-istic or rationally organic character. Even Kant's careful safeguarding of Newtonian nonteleological science is to
be viewed as an effort to provide a teleological context for
the non-teleological. Quite dialectically, Kant regards the
purposelessness, the moral opacity, of the physical world as
a divine and intended withholding of a part of the world's
rationale for the sake of human moral autonomy.

(c) I come now to the third and special shared inheritance
which has to do with a dialectic of history. Kant was tentative in his disposition to bring the dialectic of reason to bear
upon human history. Poor old Kant's effort to emerge from
the Age of Reason was not a success in his own person, but
was explicitly worked out among his followers. To be sure,
there are such remarks as those in the essay "On Perpetual
Peace" about "Nature's" devices for maneuvering mankind.
through the instrumentality of war itself, into a situation of
reasonable peace. But he remained half-hearted about this

sort of theme. He was downright alarmed by the proposal of
his contemporary, Herder, that the logic and language of
reason itself has a history.

But among the immediate followers of Kant, we find the
idea of a dialectical logic of the process of human history
emerging as a completion of Kant's own reflections on freedom
and the moral law, on time and teleology. I have in mind Fichte,
Schelling, and Hegel—particularly Hegel. At their hands, the
doctrines of concrete freedom and of historical evil as a
function of concrete freedom and of historical destiny in
terms of a fully harmonious community take shape.

Hegel, sensitive historian of the Western philosophic dialogue
that he was, saw in the Kantian revival of dialectic the reappear-
ance of the Socratic theme which runs through our shared
tradition. He writes (Shorter Logic,No. 81): "In modern times
it was, more than any other, Kant who resuscitated the name of
Dialectic, and restored it to its post of honour." Enlarging
on this insight, Hegel characterizes dialectic as a judgmental
power in the cosmos which unsettles every attempt, human
and other, to pretend that some part of truth is the whole. He
writes: "All things, we say,—that is, the finite world as such,—
are doomed; and in saying so, we have a vision of Dialectic as
the universal and irresistible power before which nothing can
stay, however secure and stable it may deem itself." This is
manifestly a teleological conception the principle of which may
be formulated: the intention to present a part of truth as the
whole will encounter the neglected other part of truth sooner
or later in the course of experience.

We remind ourselves that Hegel is at his best in exhibiting
this dialectic where the various moments, or dimensions, of
freedom are concerned. For example, the (individual) moral
imperative is not the whole story; if insisted upon exclusively,
the freedom of economic achievement will sooner or later
confront it. *Per contra,* freedom through the making of
commodities is not the whole story; if insisted upon exclusively, conscience will sooner or later rise up to confront it. To
paraphrase this polarity in the words of our own day, freedom
of moral inwardness is not the whole of freedom, freedom of
economic outwardness is not the whole of freedom; "fetishism"
of either will undergo dialectical judgment sooner or later.

If I have appeared to go far afield to disclose these three
factors of shared inheritance as capable of sustaining dialogue

between Russian and American philosophers, it seems to me that the complaint is really a judgment upon the ahistorical movements of thought current in the English-speaking world, such as positivism and analysis, Aristotelian scholasticism and the New Ontology (of N. Hartmann and others). So far, these movements of thought have not been adequate to sustain such a dialogue because they have not yet succeeded in generating a constructive philosophy of history.

THE SHAPE OF ISSUES

Now, in the context of a shared legacy, let us identify three issues of a philosophical nature which I take to be familiar and before us for clarification.

As we look back across a century and a half of Western thought, being aware of our present concern with constructive philosophies of history, we are probably more sensitive today to the two anti-Hegelian polemics associated with the names of Marx and Kierkegaard than any intervening generation has been. We can see the present unfoldings of their protests all about us in the philosophical work of our day. The name of Marx we associate with the emergence of a new materialism which is not classical but historical. Likewise the name of Kierkegaard we associate with the emergence of a new theism which is not classical either, but also historical. It was the vastness, and to some extent the arrogance of the claims of the Hegelian encyclopedia (all philosophical encyclopediae are liable to arrogance), which provoked these reactions; but curiously enough both remained recognizably and essentially Hegelian in dialectical character. In Hegel and the two Hegelian anti-Hegelians, Marx and Kierkegaard, taken as a trio, we have three philosophical thinkers as influential as any group of three to be found in the past one hundred and fifty years. In the light of the present interpenetration of influences of these three, it is somewhat surprising that the two younger men probably knew nothing of each other's work although they were con- temporaries of note and products of a more or less Lutheran middle-class culture.

(a) One issue touches the contrast between a dialectic of "Either-Or," made famous by Kierkegaard, and the dialectic of "Both-And" exemplified by Hegel. Is this contrast such as to prevent dialogue between representatives of the viewpoints involved?

The Kierkegaardian "Either-Or" states, for instance, that the life of moral autonomy and the life of the community of faith are incompatible. The Marxian "Either-Or" states, for instance, that an economy of exploitation and the classless community are incompatible. There is an anti-Hegelian thrust in each of these positions. Each of these dialectical criticisms of Hegel seems to play havoc with the harmonizing dialectic for which economy, morality, and faith require each other in due order. Yet all three viewpoints are much alike in being dialectically historical. And if one compares, for instance, what the three thinkers are emphatically against with regard to human community, we need only recall Hegel's rejection of the "contract policy," Marx's rejection of the "laissez-faire" economy, and Kierkegaard's rejection of the elite of aesthetes to see all three protests as being alike opposed to a kind of abstractness, nonhistoricalness, and mechanical conception of the relations between fellow humans.

I propose that there is philosophical promise in taking the two "Either-Or" protests as correctives upon the Hegelian categorial program. Hegel's categorial scheme is liable to correction cries out for it, in fact, in a number of regards. The Marxian corrective, in terms of the Europe of a hundred years ago, discloses the ironies of economic alienation in the antique world of laissez-faire (no longer extant); the ways in which human individuals perforce lost their very selves in the process of becoming commodities rather than creators of commodities. The Kierkegaardian corrective, in terms of the same Europe, discloses the ironies of aesthete and proud moralist; the ways in which human individuals lose their very selves in the midst of the individualistic venture after coterie pleasures or egalitarian duties. Suppose both lines of correction be accepted, the Hegelian categorial scheme may still claim to offer a greater philosophical harmony and comprehensiveness than the "Either-Or" points of view taken separately. Neither correction claims to be based on a balanced grasp of the Hegelian encyclopaedic "System"; both of the intense and special correctives as correctives are justified and enduring.

(b) A second issue arises with the question whether one or another of the three philosophies before us is transitory, merely the reflection of the conditions of a passing epoch. If this were so, much of the inducement to dialogue would fade away. The philosophical situation seems, however, to be otherwise. All three thinkers are engaged in the clarification of categories. The differences between them touch categorial order, and for this reason the philosophical positions cannot be regarded as transitory. Rather, it becomes our task to work out the terms of compatibility so that we may earn our claim to be called philosophers. We are in particular debt to Hegel for disclosing categories of man the citizen, to Marx for disclosing categories of man the maker of commodities, to Kierkegaard for disclosing categories of man the religious pilgrim. Necessities are involved here which are both rational and ontological, the coherence of which will sooner or later be brought home to us in experience and reflection. (Necessities are not foreign to a dialectically inductive metaphysics.)

(c) If the Hegelian, Marxian, and Kierkegaardian contributions to the constructive philosophy of history are to interact within a dialogue, a third issue calls for clarification which has to do with terms liable to one-sided use. The term "ideology" is such a term. We, as philosophers, have often experienced the strain upon a dialogue when one of the viewpoints represented is called "ideological" while another is not, but is adjudged "scientific" instead. The trouble arises from taking ideology to mean the use of ideas as tools of strategy, with or without concealment of motive, and then imputing this use to one side of the dialogue only. The term "freedom" is similarly liable to one-sided use. But in a dialogue it may not be appropriated by one side and denied to the other. So also of the term "matter," in view of the wide recognition of "the principle of concreteness" in the development of metaphysics since Kant's time, especially in the context of constructive philosophy of history.

Mark that it is not my intention to say that these terms be banished; rather, that their use is to be granted to all sides. In particular, there is a Marxian materiality, an Hegelian materiality, and a Kierkegaardian or existential materiality, all historical in character. There is a Marxian, and Hegelian, and a Kierkegaardian conception of concrete freedom. There are possible ideological deflections of any of these three positions, although in philosophical dialogue the overriding commitment is to "science" (in the French sense of *science* or the German sense of *Wissenschaft*), not to ideology.

The rule here might be worded: keep reciprocity in categorial use.

NECESSARY POLARITIES

Granting that this sketch of a shared legacy and of the shape of certain issues needing clarification has some warrant, our task as I see it is to work toward a mutual polarity of the positions involved. We tend to focus, often, nowadays, on the two positions of Marxism and existentialism, taking for granted some modified form of the Hegelian background. Could we come to see that each of these two positions in principle requires the other in its intensity and in its contrast? This would not be an inclusion of one position within the other by reduction or by overlooking the categorial conditions which guarantee the contrast. It would be a kind of complementarity.

If we proceeded to apply a principle of "closure" similar to that of Whitehead (recall his conception of nature's "closure" to mind), we could make good the claim that the domain of man's freedom as commodity maker, with its characteristic dialectic, does not lose its autonomy through being recognized as necessarily polar to the domain of man's freedom as existing in inwardness in the community of faith, with another characteristic dialectic. And the reciprocal claim could be made in the reverse direction. To do justice to the spirit of "Either-Or" which animates both the dialectical materialism of the Marxian sort and the dialectical theism of the Kierkegaardian sort, such a principle of "closure" seems to be required. Each freedom is essential to the other while being "closed" to it in something like the Whiteheadean sense. The necessity of this polarity would be for the sake of unfolding the fullest dialectic of human freedom. Either domain cut off from its polar opposite, or denied its proper autonomy, can be shown by experience sooner or later to have denatured itself.

I have read that efforts along this line are being made, taking economic categories in a more or less Marxian way as a starting point and moving in the direction of existentially theistic categories without forfeiting the autonomy of the two domains. It would be most rewarding to learn more about this development.

Meanwhile there is much evidence of taking existential categories as a starting point and approaching the dialectic of economic institutions from this perspective. I refer particularly to suggestions of the more Socratic existentialists like Marcel, and to the contributions of Jaspers, Reinhold Niebuhr, and

Paul Tillich. It becomes increasingly clear that the individualism and subjectivity stressed in the Existenz philosophy (and often misrepresented as anarchic) is always to be achieved in the context of community, always "with others." It becomes clear also that a form of radical materiality is expressed in the identity of person and body in a sort of epiphany doctrine of selfhood, the individual as self-manifesting within the matter of the shared world. There appears to be no barrier in principle to acknowledging and exploring the dialectic of alienated and communal labor so long as the categorial necessities of the dialectic of guilt and authenticity are observed in their full clarity.

I suggest in closing a philosophical experiment, continuing along these lines. Let theistic existentialists try to do full justice to the essentials of historical materialism while holding to their own standpoint. Let dialectical materialists try to do full justice to the essentials of theistic existentialism while holding to their own standpoint. Then see whether a non-transitory polarity of these two constructive philosophies of history emerges.

My solicitude in this paper has been mainly for dialogue and the categorial setting of dialogue. The mood is Socratic.

Index